Getting the Expert Edge from SAP

 Whether you are just beginning to work in R/3 System management, or you would like to improve your grasp of the subject, you will benefit from the first-hand, practical experience and information in these books.

Gerhard Oswald
Member of the Executive Board, SAP AG

Dr. Uwe Hommel
Executive Vice-President, SAP AG
R/3 Technical Core Competence

SAP R/3 Change and Transport Management:

The Official SAP Guide

SAP™ R/3® Change and Transport Management:
The Official SAP™ Guide

Sue McFarland Metzger
Susanne Roehrs

SYBEX®

San Francisco • Paris • Düsseldorf • Soest • London

Associate Publisher: Harry Helms

Contracts and Licensing Manager: Kristine O'Callaghan

Acquisitions & Developmental Editor: Melanie Spiller

Editor: Ronn Jost

Project Editor: Jill Schlessinger

Book Designer: Kris Warrenburg

Graphic Illustrators: epic, Tony Jonick, Jerry Williams!

Electronic Publishing Specialist: Adrian Woolhouse

Project Team Leader: Leslie Higbee

Proofreader: Jennifer Campbell

Indexer: Matthew Spence

Companion CD: Keith McNeil

Cover Designer: Calyx Design

Cover Photographer: Courtesy of West Stock

Library of Congress Card Number: 99-67590

ISBN: 0-7821-2564-6

Manufactured in the United States of America

10 9 8 7 6 5 4 3 2 1

Software License Agreement: Terms and Conditions

The media and/or any online materials accompanying this book that are available now or in the future contain programs and/or text files (the "Software") to be used in connection with the book. SYBEX hereby grants to you a license to use the Software, subject to the terms that follow. Your purchase, acceptance, or use of the Software will constitute your acceptance of such terms.

The Software compilation is the property of SYBEX unless otherwise indicated and is protected by copyright to SYBEX or other copyright owner(s) as indicated in the media files (the "Owner(s)"). You are hereby granted a single-user license to use the Software for your personal, noncommercial use only. You may not reproduce, sell, distribute, publish, circulate, or commercially exploit the Software, or any portion thereof, without the written consent of SYBEX and the specific copyright owner(s) of any component software included on this media.

In the event that the Software or components include specific license requirements or end-user agreements, statements of condition, disclaimers, limitations or warranties ("End-User License"), those End-User Licenses supersede the terms and conditions herein as to that particular Software component. Your purchase, acceptance, or use of the Software will constitute your acceptance of such End-User Licenses.

By purchase, use or acceptance of the Software you further agree to comply with all export laws and regulations of the United States as such laws and regulations may exist from time to time.

Software Support

Components of the supplemental Software and any offers associated with them may be supported by the specific Owner(s) of that material but they are not supported by SYBEX. Information regarding any available support may be obtained from the Owner(s) using the information provided in the appropriate read.me files or listed elsewhere on the media.

Should the manufacturer(s) or other Owner(s) cease to offer support or decline to honor any offer, SYBEX bears no responsibility. This notice concerning support for the Software is provided for your information only. SYBEX is not the agent or principal of the Owner(s), and SYBEX is in no way responsible for providing any support for the Software, nor is it liable or responsible for any support provided, or not provided, by the Owner(s).

Warranty

SYBEX warrants the enclosed media to be free of physical defects for a period of ninety (90) days after purchase. The Software is not available from SYBEX in any other form or media than that enclosed herein or posted to *www.sybex.com*. If you discover a defect in the media during this warranty period, you may obtain a replacement of identical format at no charge by sending the defective media, postage prepaid, with proof of purchase to:

SYBEX Inc.
Customer Service Department
1151 Marina Village Parkway
Alameda, CA 94501

(510) 523-8233

Fax: (510) 523-2373

e-mail: info@sybex.com

WEB: HTTP://WWW.SYBEX.COM

After the 90-day period, you can obtain replacement media of identical format by sending us the defective disk, proof of purchase, and a check or money order for $10, payable to SYBEX.

Disclaimer

SYBEX makes no warranty or representation, either expressed or implied, with respect to the Software or its contents, quality, performance, merchantability, or fitness for a particular purpose. In no event will SYBEX, its distributors, or dealers be liable to you or any other party for direct, indirect, special, incidental, consequential, or other damages arising out of the use of or inability to use the Software or its contents even if advised of the possibility of such damage. In the event that the Software includes an online update feature, SYBEX further disclaims any obligation to provide this feature for any specific duration other than the initial posting.

The exclusion of implied warranties is not permitted by some states. Therefore, the above exclusion may not apply to you. This warranty provides you with specific legal rights; there may be other rights that you may have that vary from state to state. The pricing of the book with the Software by SYBEX reflects the allocation of risk and limitations on liability contained in this agreement of Terms and Conditions.

Shareware Distribution

This Software may contain various programs that are distributed as shareware. Copyright laws apply to both shareware and ordinary commercial software, and the copyright Owner(s) retains all rights. If you try a shareware program and continue using it, you are expected to register it. Individual programs differ on details of trial periods, registration, and payment. Please observe the requirements stated in appropriate files.

Copy Protection

The Software in whole or in part may or may not be copy-protected or encrypted. However, in all cases, reselling or redistributing these files without authorization is expressly forbidden except as specifically provided for by the Owner(s) therein.

FOREWORD TO THE SAP EXPERT KNOWLEDGE BOOK SERIES

Enabling you to operate your R/3 System at a minimum cost is of the utmost importance to SAP. You can attain this *lowest cost of ownership* both by implementing R/3 efficiently and quickly with *AcceleratedSAP*, and through optimized and secure production operation. *TeamSAP* brings together the most important resources: *people, processes,* and *products.* SAP acts as the central contact in this team and shares its knowledge with partners and customers.

To keep your knowledge up to date, TeamSAP conceived this book series, which offers you a detailed overview of the technical issues and concepts of R/3 System management. The books cover subjects ranging from the technical implementation project to R/3 System and database operation.

Whether you are just beginning to work in R/3 System management or you would like to improve your grasp of the subject, you will benefit from the first-hand, practical experience and information in these books. This book series also supports you in your efforts to prepare for a Certified Technical Consultant exam for R/3 Release 4.0. However, this book series cannot, and makes no claim to, be a substitute for your own experience in working with the R/3 System. The authors provide recommendations for your daily work with R/3.

With the increase in R/3 installations, there is an increased need for qualified technical consultants. Through certification, SAP has been setting high standards for many years now. Certification not only confirms whether you are familiar with the R/3 System administration for a particular R/3 release, it also establishes whether you can administer one of the database systems and the extent to which you are familiar with one of the supported operating system platforms.

Upgrades to the R/3 System regularly introduce new challenges and solutions for R/3 System management. A certification can therefore only be valid for specific R/3 Releases and must be renewed with every major revision.

Gerhard Oswald
Member of the Executive Board, SAP AG

Dr. Uwe Hommel
Executive Vice-President, SAP AG
R/3 Technical Core Competence

Walldorf, July 1998

ACKNOWLEDGMENTS

This book has been an undertaking that neither one of us knew would involve so many people and so much effort. Thankfully, we have completed a book we know will be advantageous to many people involved in an R/3 implementation. We also know that this book would not be in print if not for the efforts of Andre von Rekowski, who worked through our words to provide you with something cohesive. We also want to thank the editing efforts of Melanie Freeman and Pamela Tabbert.

We relied on the support of SAP developers to ensure the technical accuracy of this book. Those people who deserve special thanks for their time spent providing us insight into new functionality and design objectives, and reviewing every chapter, include Thomas Brodkorb, Dr. Meinolf Block, Dr. Ulrich Frenzel, Anja Gerstmair, Dr. Hans-Jürgen Hennrich, Dr. Matthias Melich, Stefan Rossmanith, Herbert Stegmüller, Dr. Carsten Thiel, and Dr. Wulf Krümpelmann.

We would also like to thank all the people in the R/3 Technical Core Competence (TCC) department at SAP. Providing R/3 implementation solutions is beyond the scope of any one individual and requires the expertise and experience of others. TCC provides a rich wealth of knowledge from which this book has been leveraged. Those people who were particularly valuable in supporting us throughout this book include Carmen Fuhlbrügge, Roland Hamm, Manfred Kester, Dr. Wilhelm Nüsser, Marc Thier, and Liane Will.

Finally, we must thank those of you around us in the office and those involved in our lives for listening to our countless number of deliberations regarding the production of this book. We know the efforts have paid off, and we thank you for your understanding. Susanne would especially like to credit Rosemarie & Henning Roehrs and Jochen Speicher for their patience during this endeavor.

—Sue McFarland Metzger

—Susanne Roehrs

CONTENTS AT A GLANCE

TABLE OF CONTENTS

INTRODUCTION

R/3 is a software package that provides wide-ranging functionality to meet the needs of organizations and industries of all sizes. Although this functionality is built into the software, R/3 must be configured during its implementation to meet the specific needs of an organization. This process, known as *Customizing*, uses special R/3 adaptation tools. A customer's R/3 adaptation may also require *development* work; that is, the customer must program new or modified functionality using R/3's ABAP programming language.

In general, R/3 resembles most other business software installations in that its implementation requires:

- Configuration and/or development work
- A carefully planned realization of business needs
- The realization of an appropriate technical infrastructure in the system landscape
- Project management that controls the scope of what is to be implemented and defines the roles and responsibilities of the people on the implementation team
- Thorough testing and validation of the changes achieved through Customizing or development
- Training for end users
- Future expansion of the software's initially implemented functionality and usage

To provide an infrastructure that fulfills these implementation needs, SAP recommends implementing R/3 with three strictly separate environments:

- An environment for Customizing and development work

- A quality assurance environment for testing business functionality using representative test data

- A production environment for normal business operations, which is secure from changes made in other environments until those changes have been verified and are ready for transfer into the production environment

These three environments are realized through R/3 Systems and *clients*, which are logical divisions within an R/3 System. The collection of clients and systems required for an R/3 implementation forms the *system landscape*.

Figure I.1 depicts the standard three-system landscape used to support R/3 and recommended by SAP. The development system is an R/3 System for Customizing and development efforts. The quality assurance system is then used to test and verify Customizing and development work. Once Customizing and development changes have been validated and approved, they are delivered to the production system.

FIGURE I.1:

The SAP standard three-system landscape

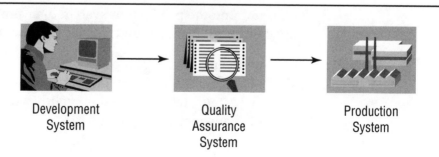

Development System   Quality Assurance System   Production System

To manage changes created during Customizing and development, and to ensure that applications remain consistent across multiple R/3 Systems, changes are recorded and organized in *change requests* and are *transported* to different clients and R/3 Systems within the system landscape. The process of transporting requires the *releasing* and *exporting* of the change requests from the development system and then *importing* them into another R/3 System. The techniques for change and transport management are also known as *software logistics*—the process of moving or transporting changes made to the R/3 software.

Implementing change and transport management includes the following tasks:

- Setting up a system landscape

- Regulating the systems and clients in which Customizing and development changes are made

- Recording Customizing and development changes to change requests during the initial implementation of R/3 *and* during any subsequent improvement of the production environment

- Managing the transport of changes to all clients and R/3 Systems within the system landscape

- Testing, validating, and approving changes using the quality assurance system

- Maintaining the production system over time by applying SAP Support Packages and upgrades of the R/3 product

Although the main goal of a particular R/3 implementation is to fulfill your business requirements, this can be realized only if you ensure system stability and data validity through correct change and transport management.

Many aspects of change and transport management are technical in nature, but the procedures you define to implement it will affect all staff members. The business knowledge required to perform Customizing and test R/3 is possessed mainly by the staff in the corresponding functional departments, and it is they who perform Customizing and testing. Therefore, not just technical staff, but all people involved in an R/3 implementation need to understand change and transport management and the structure of the system landscape. Those who actually make the changes to the R/3 System need additional expert knowledge of the relevant tools and procedures.

How This Book Is Organized

The information in this book is organized into three parts, each aimed at people involved in this procedure at different levels. Part 1, "The Big Picture," provides a basic explanation of how changes are made and distributed. It enables those managing the R/3 implementation to develop a valid change and transport management strategy.

Part 2, "Technical Tasks," is essential reading for technicians coordinating the setup of the technical infrastructure or performing, for example, system administration tasks.

Part 3, "Tools," is the how-to section, providing detailed information on the tools described in Part 1. This part is also a reference section for those requiring in-depth knowledge. The first three chapters of Part 3 will be of particular use to anyone performing Customizing or development work during an R/3 implementation.

The information in this book is valid for R/3 Release 4.0 or Release 4.5. However, explanation is given of the functionality and benefits of Release 4.6. Unless otherwise stated, all references to R/3 screens correspond to R/3 Release 4.5.

SAP's New Dimension products, including the Business Warehouse (BW) and the Advanced Planner & Optimizer (APO), are built on techniques and functionality similar to that found in R/3. However, the change and transport management considerations for these products vary somewhat from those described in this book. For example, different menu paths and transport requirements are used in some areas. If you are using New Dimension products, this book will enable you to understand the basic concepts and tools for change and transport management, but you should also refer to the specific product documentation.

About the CD-ROM

The CD-ROM is a timed test engine containing practice questions and answers from each chapter of the book. The questions are designed to review the concepts presented in each chapter. The test engine simulates the SAP exam and allows you to determine which chapters you may need to review in more detail.

For details on how to install the test engine, see the inside cover of this book, or take a look at the readme file included on the CD-ROM.

PART ONE

THE BIG PICTURE

During customer activities in the R/3 System such as development and Customizing, changes are made to the R/3 software. Change and transport management consists of special procedures for distributing these changes across your system landscape. The need for logistics or coordination of changes arises the need to ensure data consistency in all R/3 Systems. It requires that you:

- Set up change management

- Implement a transport strategy

- Build a system landscape that allows you to make and test all the required changes while preventing inconsistencies and protecting the integrity of your production system

In Part 1, this procedure is explained in more detail, and you are encouraged to use SAP-recommended standards. The specific topics covered in Part 1 include:

- An introduction to the components of the system landscape.

- An introduction to the realization of business requirements through Customizing and development efforts.

- An explanation of R/3 clients and client roles used in an implementation.

- Guidelines for setting up and maintaining a system landscape.

- An introduction to the relevant R/3 tools. These tools receive more extensive coverage in Part 2 and Part 3.

CHAPTER
ONE

R/3 Architecture and Data Components

R/3 architecture is shaped by its use of client/server technology—that is, the way it distributes the software services needed by users over multiple servers. R/3 System administration and performance optimization require a detailed understanding of this client/server technology. In contrast, change and transport management, which is implemented by configuring the R/3 System appropriately, focuses mainly on a specific element within the architecture, namely the database. Change and transport is concerned with:

- The role the database plays in the R/3 architecture
- The architecture of the database itself, in terms of the R/3 data components and R/3 clients

The R/3 database stores the R/3 software. An important part of this software is the *R/3 Repository*, which provides the runtime environment for the various R/3 business applications. The database also contains the various R/3 data components, such as the business data that is required for or generated by day-to-day business transactions.

Data can be isolated by assigning it to one of several separate "containers" in the R/3 Repository. These containers are called *R/3 clients*. When a user logs on, they log on to a particular client and can display or change only the data corresponding to that client. Data that can be displayed or changed from only one client is called *client-dependent data*. Data that can be accessed from all clients is called *client-independent data* or *cross-client data*.

To ensure the success of your change and transport management strategy, the people performing Customizing or development during R/3 System implementation need to understand:

- The different data components in the R/3 database
- Which data is client-dependent and which is client-independent

After a brief look at client/server architecture, this chapter describes the R/3 database, clients, and the various data components, and explains which data is client-dependent and which data can be accessed by all clients.

For information on how to create and maintain the various R/3 data components, see Chapter 2.

Client/Server Architecture in Brief

SAP recognized early on that to provide a scalable and global business software package to meet a wide range of customer needs, the way to go was client/server technology. Client/server technology distributes different applications and system services across multiple hardware servers. Servers may contain a combination of services, and run on different hardware platforms. SAP's use of multilayer client/server computing maximizes performance and provides flexibility in management and hardware options.

The client/server architecture of R/3 consists of three types of services:

- A database service for storing and retrieving business data
- An application service for running business processes
- A presentation service for the graphical user interface (GUI)

From a hardware perspective, these three layers—the database, application, and presentation layers—can run separately on different servers or all together on the same server. A typical installation supporting numerous R/3 users uses multiple presentation servers. To increase system performance, the application layer can be distributed over multiple servers. This is depicted in Figure 1.1, where a database server and multiple application and presentation servers support an R/3 System.

FIGURE 1.1:

The three-layer architecture of R/3

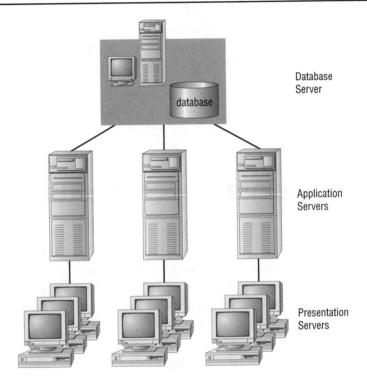

Database Server

Application Servers

Presentation Servers

Regardless of the number of application and presentation servers, each R/3 System has only one database. It is the number of databases (one for each R/3 System) in which changes originate or to which changes must be transported that is of central importance for change and transport management.

Example: R/3 Client/Server Technology in Practice

A medium-sized distribution firm purchases a Hewlett-Packard server for running the Windows NT operating system. An Oracle database is chosen because the company is already using Oracle for other applications. Both the Oracle database and the R/3 applications run on the Hewlett-Packard server. The presentation servers are PCs using SAP's graphical user interface (SAPGUI) to connect to R/3's database and application processes.

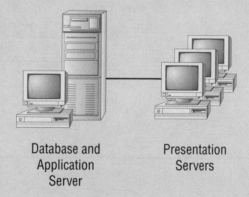

Database and   Presentation
Application   Servers
Server

After some time, significant growth in the data volume and the number of users reduces system performance. Therefore, two additional Hewlett-Packard servers are purchased and added to the R/3 System as application servers. The only service running on the original server is the Oracle database.

Continued on next page

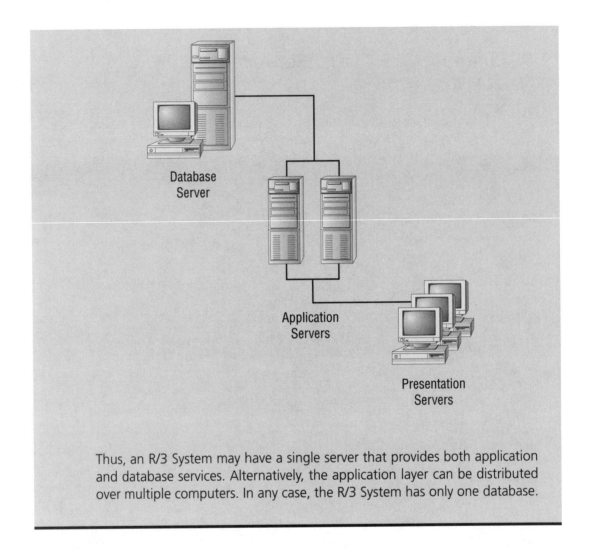

Thus, an R/3 System may have a single server that provides both application and database services. Alternatively, the application layer can be distributed over multiple computers. In any case, the R/3 System has only one database.

The R/3 Database

In many software packages, the actual software is considered to be separate from the data that is entered or created using the software. The term *software package* is synonymous with *program* or *executable*, and the data is stored external to this software in a file.

When you print a spreadsheet, for example, you require both a software executable and a spreadsheet file.

Unlike other software packages, R/3 software is not separate from its data. Both application functionality and business data are stored together in the R/3 database, along with R/3 documentation and performance statistics. The R/3 database contains almost everything the users can see: transaction data, program source code, text, menu options, screens, and even printer and fax definitions. In other words, the R/3 database contains virtually all R/3-related components. Only a few R/3-related files reside outside the R/3 database—for example, the R/3 kernel.

The R/3 database can be divided into two logical components: the R/3 Repository and *customer data*.

The R/3 Repository

The R/3 Repository provides the data structures and programs you need to maintain data in the R/3 System.

The central part of the R/3 Repository is the *ABAP Dictionary*, which contains descriptions of the structure and the relationships of all data. These descriptions are used by R/3 to interpret and generate the application objects of the runtime environment—for example, programs or screens. Such objects are referred to as *Repository objects*.

During R/3 implementation, you may wish to perform development work in R/3 to adapt the R/3 Repository to meet specific requirements. Using the tools in the *ABAP Workbench,* you can create or modify R/3 Repository objects, thus adding or changing table structures or programs. The result of such development work is one or both of the following:

- New customer Repository objects are added to the R/3 Repository.

- Standard SAP objects in the R/3 Repository are modified.

WARNING SAP recommends that you do not modify standard SAP objects in the R/3 Repository. See Chapter 2.

Customer Data

In addition to the R/3 Repository, the other logical component of the R/3 database is customer data. This customer data consists of any kind of data entered into R/3 by the customer—the organization or company that purchased and uses the R/3 software—either during R/3 implementation or during day-to-day business processing. Customer data includes:

- Customizing data
- Application data
- User master data

Customizing data is generated when R/3 is configured to meet the particular needs of the customer through Customizing. *Application data*, also known as *business data*, is the data required for or generated by day-to-day business processing in R/3. *User master data* is the records of R/3 users' passwords and authorizations.

To return to the analogy of the spreadsheet application, the data in the spreadsheet file is the equivalent of the customer data. Of this data, the application data is the data entered to fill the cells of the spreadsheet. The Customizing data is the formatting data— for example, the data specifying bold characters or colored cells in the spreadsheet. The equivalent of the R/3 Repository objects is the spreadsheet application itself, with its menu options, macros, and screens.

Technical Implementation

R/3 requires a database that has a *relational database management system (RDBMS)* such as Oracle, Informix, MS SQL Server, ADABAS D, and DB2 databases. The chosen database system is R/3-neutral until it is populated with the R/3 Repository during the R/3 installation process.

The name of the relational database and the name of the R/3 System are frequently the same and consist of three uppercase alphanumeric characters. Examples of R/3 System names include DEV, P11, or ST0. Some names, such as the system identifier *SAP*, are reserved by SAP and may not be used as system names. (See Chapter 7.)

NOTE   The abbreviation SID, for system identification, is often used as a placeholder for any R/3 System name.

R/3 Clients

An R/3 System has only one R/3 Repository, which provides the runtime environment where you create and maintain customer data. Within this single Repository, you can set up subdivisions called *clients* that help separate customer data into different groups.

When you log on to R/3, you must log on to a specific client and can read or change only the data of that particular client. This data is client-dependent. Each client has its own data, but accesses the same R/3 Repository objects.

Most customer data is client-dependent. More precisely, application data is entirely client-dependent, while some Customizing data is shared by all clients and thus is client-independent. Figure 1.2 shows an R/3 database with multiple clients containing client-dependent data, and sharing all client-independent Customizing data and all R/3 Repository objects. These R/3 Repository objects provide the runtime environment.

FIGURE 1.2:

An R/3 database contains separate R/3 clients that share client-independent Customizing data and Repository objects.

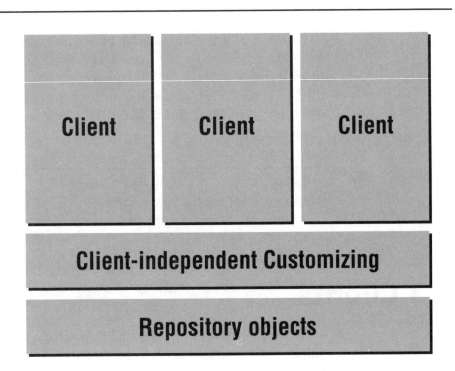

Technical Implementation

To protect customer data created in different clients, when you log on to an R/3 System, you must log on to a specific client within that system. The client-dependent data you can access from this client is restricted to the data assigned exclusively to that client. Once you are in that client, the client-dependent data of all other clients in the R/3 System is inaccessible. You can still access all client-independent Customizing data and R/3 Repository objects.

Clients are technically identified by a three-digit number, the client ID. R/3 uses the client ID as a key field in all tables that contain client-specific data. The data in these tables can be displayed or changed only if you log on to a specific client.

Example: Client-Dependent Data

The clients of an R/3 System are simply logical constructs within the database of that R/3 System. Tables for client-dependent data have the client ID as the first key column. This column is always called MANDT, from the German word *Mandant*, meaning "client."

An example of a client-dependent R/3 table is VBAP, which contains detailed line-item information for all sales documents created in the R/3 System. This table contains over 200 columns, of which the first 3 columns are unique for each row, thus enabling the database to uniquely identify the relevant sales document item.

In the table VBAP, the first three columns are MANDT (client ID), VBELN (sales document number), and POSNR (sales document item number). All other columns, for example MATNR (material number), are used to specify the details of the sales document item.

Here is an example of the kind of data stored in the table VBAP:

MANDT	VBELN	POSNR	MATNR
400	0000006398	000010	C-1100
400	0000006401	000010	CCS-99
400	0000006401	000020	CCS-80

Continued on next page

MANDT	VBELN	POSNR	MATNR
400	0000006403	000010	C900
520	0000000844	000010	C-1100
520	0000000844	000020	C-2000

Although the table VBAP stores data from both client 400 and client 520, you cannot access the sales document data associated with client 520 when you are logged on in client 400. This is because table VBAP contains the column MANDT as its first key column, making the table's data client-dependent. To display or change any data in table VBAP, you must log on in the R/3 client indicated in the column MANDT.

Data Components

The data components of an R/3 client are the types of data that a user can access after logging on to a particular R/3 client (see Figure 1.3). As mentioned above, these include:

Customizing data: This is the configuration data that results from Customizing and is a mandatory task during R/3 implementation. Most Customizing data is client-dependent; some is client-independent.

Application data: This is the sum of business data including *transaction data*, which is generated by individual sales or other transactions, and *master data*, which is a prerequisite for entering day-to-day transactions. Application data is the main source of database growth and eventually occupies the most space in the database. All application data is client-dependent.

User master data: This is data specifying which users can work in R/3 and which transactions they are authorized to use. All user master data is client-dependent.

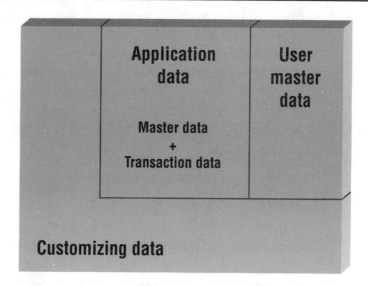

Customizing Data

Customizing data is generated when the customer configures the required parameters and settings during Customizing, thus enabling R/3 to meet the customer's specific business requirements. Customizing data defines what kind of application data can be generated and how this data will look. Examples of Customizing data include:

- Organizational units such as companies, plants, and sales organizations
- A specific purchase order process flow
- Distribution requirements for production planning
- Multiple-language text for reports

Most Customizing is client-dependent. Some Customizing, however, is client-independent. This includes adjustments to global settings that affect all clients and the creation of or changes to R/3 Repository objects. A global setting may be technical in nature, such as the setting defining a printer, or more business-related, such as the setting specifying a company's factory calendar. More complicated customizing efforts may require the creation of a table to house data and configuration settings. Such a table structure is client-independent because it is a Repository object. For example, to configure your pricing strategy for a given product, you are required to create a table that specifies discounting criteria and amounts. This Customizing change, unlike the definition of the sales organization, is a client-independent change.

Application Data

Application data is the sum of all R/3 business data, and comprises both master data and transaction data. Application data is affected by Customizing settings, which determine what kind of application data can be generated and how this data will look. Application data is client-dependent.

Master data is the prerequisite for processing day-to-day transactions, and includes lists of approved vendors, supplier addresses, materials used in production, and purchaser data.

Transaction data is generated by day-to-day business operations, and includes customer orders, production orders, debits and credits, and payroll transactions. Transaction data is frequently accessed and is the fastest growing data in the R/3 System.

While application data is logically a construct of both master data and transaction data within R/3, there is no formal distinction between the two. In other words, it is not possible to separate master data and transaction data.

User Master Data

R/3's user and authorization concept is an essential part of R/3 security. Information about R/3 users, known as user master data, is recorded in the system to authenticate users at logon and check their authorization for particular transactions.

When the user logs on to an R/3 client, the R/3 System authenticates whether there is a user ID in the user master data that matches the entered password. As the user triggers each new transaction they wish to use in R/3, the R/3 System checks whether one of the authorization profiles assigned to that user in their user master data contains the necessary authorization for that transaction.

User IDs and authorization profiles are client-dependent, and therefore are valid only in the client in which the corresponding user master data records were created. User master records contain, for example, the user's logon name, assigned authorizations, and other attributes such as address and user type.

Standard R/3 Clients

SAP delivers R/3 with three standard clients:

- Client 000
- Client 001
- Client 066

Client 000 is reserved by SAP to enable the maintenance of the standard R/3 Repository objects and the baseline Customizing settings in the system. For example, during R/3 upgrades, new functions are supplied to this client and subsequently transported to the other clients in the R/3 System. Client 000 contains the basic Customizing settings with organizational structures and business parameter settings that are legally required for German organizations in regard to, for example, payment and tax structures. Even if you are not implementing R/3 in Germany, these settings provide helpful examples for your own Customizing. Due to its special role in the R/3 System, client 000 may not be modified or deleted by the customer. It contains no application data.

Client 001 is simply a copy of client 000, including the sample organizational structure and configuration, except that customers can modify Client 001. There is no application data in client 001.

Client 066 is reserved for SAP accesses to its customers' system to perform remote services such as EarlyWatch® and GoingLive™ Check. Almost no data exists in this client; it simply serves as a mechanism to allow remote access for the purpose of system monitoring without compromising the security of your system. This client should not be modified or deleted.

To create new clients in R/3, you can use the technique known as *client copy*, which creates a copy of an existing client (see Chapter 9). To perform Customizing and development in R/3, you should use client 001 or create a new client with a client copy. Normally, a copy is made of client 000. This copy is then used to realize company-specific business processes.

Review Questions

1. Which of the following components indicate that R/3 is a client/server system?

    A. Multiple databases

    B. A database server

    C. Three separate hardware servers—a database server, an application server, and a presentation server

    D. A database service, an application service, and a presentation service

2. Which of the following is *not* contained in the R/3 database?

    A. The R/3 Repository

    B. The R/3 kernel

    C. Customer data

    D. Transaction data

    E. Customizing data

    F. The ABAP Dictionary

3. Which of the following statements is correct in regard to R/3 clients?

    A. An R/3 client has its own customer data and programs, which are not accessible to other clients within the same R/3 System.

    B. An R/3 client shares all R/3 Repository objects and client-independent Customizing with all other clients in the same R/3 System.

    C. An R/3 client shares Customizing and application data with other clients in the same R/3 System.

    D. An R/3 client enables you to separate application data from Customizing data.

4. Which of the following statements is correct in regard to SAP's client concept?

    A. All Customizing settings are client-independent.

    B. A client has a unique set of application data.

    C. A client has its own Repository objects.

    D. All Customizing settings are client-dependent.

CHAPTER
TWO

Realizing Business Processes in R/3

The software SAP delivers to its customers is referred to as the *SAP standard*. It contains over 1,000 business process chains and their associated functions. Before working with R/3, you not only have to install the software, you must also *implement* it. To meet the specific requirements of your company, you need to make decisions about *which* business processes and associated functions and settings you require, and possibly even create new programs or functions. To effect the implementation of these decisions, R/3 offers two main techniques:

- Customizing

- Development

Customizing involves using the *Implementation Guide* (IMG), and development is performed using the *ABAP Workbench*. Development is further divided into three methods:

- Creation of new Repository objects

- Enhancements

- Modifications

Figure 2.1 shows the R/3 software resulting from the implementation process. The software, represented by the horizontal bar, consists of the R/3 business applications and customer programs. The techniques used to add to, configure, and change the SAP standard are shown as arrows.

Customizing

Customizing is a mandatory activity during an R/3 implementation. When performing Customizing, you use the IMG (Transaction SPRO) to select the R/3 business processes your company requires, and to adjust all associated settings, such as those used

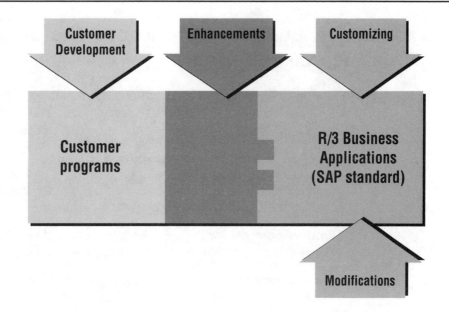

FIGURE 2.1:

Methods of adding to
and changing the SAP
standard

to specify units of measurement and relevant business concepts. Customizing alterations adapt the SAP-standard solution for different branches of industry and company types, as well as for multiple languages and country-specific characteristics.

The Customizing procedure basically adds customer-specific data to the tables corresponding to SAP-standard objects. Therefore, Customizing is often thought of as table maintenance. These tables are later read by the programs that comprise the different business workflows.

Example: Business Transactions That Are Set Up through Customizing

An international company manufacturing bicycles begins installing its new R/3 System. To meet the company's specific needs, the following business processes and features are selected and set up during Customizing:

Sales organizations and distribution channels: To enable wholesale customers to place orders for bicycles, R/3 is customized to recognize the sales organization responsible for the order and the distribution channel used in getting the order to the customer.

Production planning: The R/3 application module Production Planning is customized to enable orders to be filled on time.

Materials management: The R/3 application module Materials Management is customized so that all required materials, such as tires and chains, are recognized and can be made available during the manufacture of all types of bicycles.

Billing and cost-allocation processes: Customizing in this area sets up invoicing by defining pricing structures and applicable taxes.

As this simple example shows, Customizing covers numerous features of business processes. The people performing Customizing, whether they are company employees or external consultants, require a detailed understanding of the company's business processes.

R/3 Reference Model

In addition to the IMG (discussed in the next section), another R/3 tool that is helpful for Customizing is the *R/3 Reference Model* accessed in the *Business Navigator* (Transaction SB09). The Reference Model is a collection of modeling tools that provides configuration recommendations by offering different business scenarios to help you map out your company's business requirements.

The Reference Model enables you to model all essential elements of a company, such as organizational units, business processes, business objects, and the applications that use these business objects.

Subsections of the R/3 Reference Model include:

- R/3 process model
- Data model and object model
- Organization model
- Distribution model

The R/3 Reference Model and its various graphical tools act as a bridge between a company's everyday business needs and the actual implementation of its R/3 System (see Figure 2.2). Using the R/3 Reference Model to determine and model the scope of the R/3 implementation makes it easier to perform Customizing activities using the IMG.

Implementation Guide (IMG)

To simplify Customizing, the IMG (Transaction SPRO) guides you through the various Customizing stages and procedures. In addition, the *project management* function within the IMG enables you to set up and manage Customizing projects, complete with planned and actual deadlines, resources, and activity completion status.

To start Customizing in the IMG, access the *SAP Reference IMG* (from the initial screen of Transaction SPRO, choose *Implement projects* ➤ *SAP Reference IMG*). The SAP Reference IMG is a tree structure in which you drill down to specific Customizing activities (see Figure 2.3). The nodes of the tree structure that you see first are organized to reflect the different R/3 application modules such as Financial Accounting, Sales and Distribution, Materials Management, and Plant Maintenance. Drilling down within

FIGURE 2.2:

Modeling business
needs to facilitate
Customizing

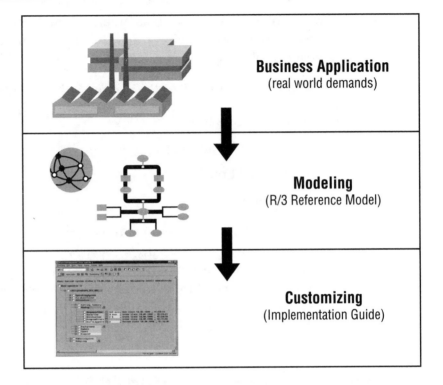

(or expanding each branch of) the tree structure ultimately reveals lists of Customizing activities that are arranged in the order these activities should be performed.

Figure 2.3 shows some sample Customizing activities in the typical IMG tree structure. Clicking the icons beside each Customizing activity name enables you to access:

- The screen where you perform the Customizing activity

- Relevant R/3 documentation

- The screen where you can document why and how you perform this Customizing activity

- The relevant project management data (assuming you have chosen to set up the project management functionality)

FIGURE 2.3:

A sample IMG tree structure

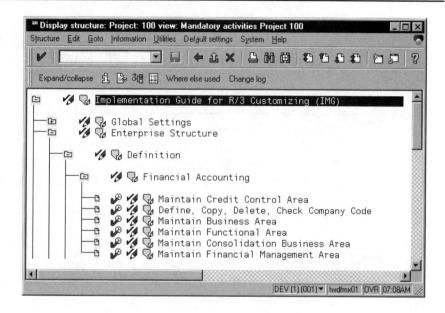

The preliminary task for Customizing is to filter out the parts of the SAP Reference IMG that your company does not require, and save the remainder as your *Enterprise IMG*. You can then divide your Enterprise IMG into various subdivisions called *Project IMGs*, representing groups of related Customizing activities. These various IMGs are explained in more detail below.

Enterprise IMG

The SAP Reference IMG contains the Customizing activities for all R/3 application modules and functions. However, many R/3 implementations do not need all of the available application components; in fact, they may require only specific modules implemented for particular countries. For example, a company may initially wish to implement the Human Resources (HR) module to support only North American countries. To simplify Customizing, you generate an Enterprise IMG that contains only those parts of the SAP Reference IMG that are relevant to your implementation.

To generate an Enterprise IMG, from the initial screen of Transaction SPRO, choose *Basic functions* ➤ *Enterprise IMG* ➤ *Generate*. Select the relevant countries and deselect all application components except the components you require. Save your work to generate the Enterprise IMG. (See Chapter 11.)

TIP   One Enterprise IMG can be generated for each R/3 System. If you subsequently need to implement additional countries or more business application components, you can regenerate the Enterprise IMG. Regeneration does not affect the existing documentation or project management information.

NOTE   Beginning with R/3 Release 4.6, the Enterprise IMG will no longer be used. SAP will deliver the SAP Reference IMG, and from this IMG, you will create Project IMGs only.

Project IMGs

Customizing requires expertise from different areas of business. In addition, most implementations are rolled out in phases; that is, new functionality is added over time by different user groups. Therefore, while it is possible to perform Customizing from either the SAP Reference IMG or the Enterprise IMG, a useful alternative is to divide the Enterprise IMG into subsets. These subsets, called Project IMGs, reflect the various business areas and implementation stages, and make it possible to organize Customizing activities according to the different types of business expertise and project teams.

Example: Project Teams for an R/3 Implementation

Before beginning R/3 implementation at a bicycle company, the responsible manager decides to set up several teams to handle different aspects of the implementation project. Initially, two project teams are formed: one for Finance and another for Logistics. These teams are again subdivided into different areas of expertise. The Finance team splits into one group for Controlling and one for Accounting. Similarly, the Logistics team divides into two teams: one for Production Planning and another for Materials Management. Thus, a total of four project teams emerge. After creating an Enterprise IMG tailored to the company's needs, four Project IMGs are created. Each team can begin Customizing in the respective Project IMG.

One year later, the management decides to extend its use of R/3 to include Human Resources. A new implementation phase is created. The Human Resources team is divided into two sections, one for Payroll and one for Personnel Management. The Enterprise IMG is regenerated and two additional Project IMGs are created, and Customizing for Human Resources is started.

TIP   To coordinate the efforts of the various implementation teams, SAP recommends that you perform all Customizing activities from within a Project IMG.

Note that the settings assigned in a specific Customizing activity may affect one or more application components. Therefore, cross-application activities may appear in a Project IMG, even though the second application was not selected when the Project IMG was generated. For example, a Project IMG for Production Planning contains activities relating to Production Planning and Controlling.

Project IMGs provide project management functions to enable you to:

- Maintain status and resource information
- Maintain project documentation in SAP Office folders using either a standard text editor or Microsoft Word
- Transfer data between a Project IMG and Microsoft Project

> **NOTE** The Enterprise IMG and Project IMGs are cross-client. In other words, the Enterprise IMG and Project IMGs, and their documentation and project data, are all accessible from any client within the R/3 System.

Prioritizing with Project IMG Views To organize your Customizing activities more effectively, Project IMGs can be filtered into views based on priority (see Figure 2.4). This helps you decide which Customizing activities are critical or mandatory and should be tackled first, and which activities can wait until a later time. You can create the following views when generating a Project IMG:

- Critical activities
- Mandatory activities
- Non-critical activities
- Optional activities

Development

The R/3 System creates the runtime environment by drawing on the R/3 Repository, which contains object definitions, user interfaces, and business transactions. These R/3 Repository objects are configured through Customizing, which normally satisfies all

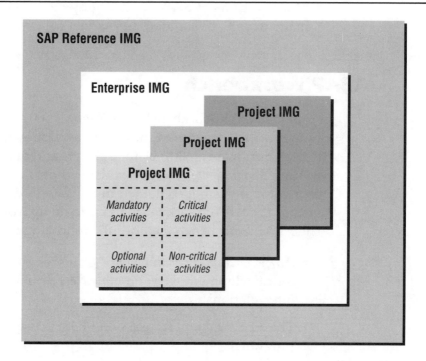

FIGURE 2.4:

The different views of
Customizing activities

business requirements. When this is not the case, you can use the
ABAP Workbench to develop new R/3 Repository objects or modify existing ones. Development can take the following forms:

Creation of new Repository objects: The customer devel-
ops new R/3 Repository objects, such as new reports,
screens, and tables.

Enhancements: These are customer-developed objects that
are anticipated in the standard R/3 software; that is, they are
referenced by SAP-standard objects. Such development does
not really change the SAP standard; it only "enhances" the
software. For example, certain SAP tables are constructed so
that you can append fields to them without modifying them,
and some SAP programs contain built-in "branches" to possible customer programs.

Modifications of SAP-standard objects: These are changes made to an SAP-standard object in a customer system.

ABAP Workbench

From the ABAP Workbench (Transaction S001), you can access all the R/3 tools required for ABAP development work. You can create your own R/3 Repository objects and enhance or modify existing SAP objects. Thus, if a business process that is vital for your company is not contained in the standard R/3 System, you can use the ABAP Workbench to build an appropriate solution. The ABAP Workbench includes the following tools:

- *ABAP Dictionary Maintenance* (Transaction SE11) is used for development work on table descriptions and their interrelationships.

- The *ABAP Editor* (Transaction SE38) is used to modify ABAP programs.

- The *Function Builder* (Transaction SE37) is used to develop, maintain, test, and document function modules, and contains a function library, which serves as a central storage facility for all function modules.

- The *Menu Painter* (Transaction SE41) is the tool for creating the user interface of an ABAP program. You can use it to create or modify screen titles, menu bars, the standard toolbar, the application toolbar, and function keys.

- The *Screen Painter* (Transaction SE51) is the tool for creating dialog boxes and the underlying flow logic. The Screen Painter can be run in either a graphical or an alphanumeric mode.

> **NOTE** ABAP stands for Advanced Business Application Programming and is SAP's proprietary programming language. It is designed to support the development of data processing applications in distributed systems, and handles multiple currency and multilingual issues. ABAP also contains a special set of commands for database operations called *Open SQL*, which allows R/3 to be programmed independently of the database system and operating system.

SSCR for Developers

SAP Software Change Registration (SSCR) is a procedure that registers all developers of R/3 Repository objects. Before creating or modifying Repository objects using the ABAP Workbench, developers must register and obtain an access key from SAPNet, SAP's online service system. The SSCR access key for a developer needs to be entered into the R/3 System only once; that is, during the developer's subsequent attempts to create or change Repository objects, the R/3 System will not request the SSCR access key.

Customer-Developed R/3 Repository Objects

Customer-developed R/3 Repository objects include programs, screens, menus, function modules, and data structures. These objects are created by an R/3 customer using the ABAP Workbench to satisfy business needs beyond the scope of the SAP standard.

Example: A Possible Customer Development

The head of Sales at a bicycle company wishes to obtain some sales order statistics based on a nonstandard type of user input, and to simplify the screens where the orders are entered by the end users. The order-entry screen in the SAP standard is replaced with a new screen, created by the company's developer using the R/3 Screen Painter. Using the ABAP Editor, this developer then attaches the new screen to an ABAP program that reacts to user input and performs the required statistical analysis. Finally, a further program is created, which displays the results in multiple currencies.

Not all customer-developed objects are completely unique. The new objects may have SAP-standard objects incorporated in their design. A customer-developed ABAP program may include, for example, SAP-standard function modules, such as user input validation routines.

Customer-developed R/3 Repository objects are not completely isolated from the existing SAP-standard objects, and like the SAP standard, are contained in the R/3 Repository. Therefore, to distinguish SAP-standard Repository objects from customer-developed objects, SAP requires you to heed the following precautions:

- All customer-developed Repository objects must be assigned to a customer *development class*. Development classes are used to group similar business objects, and every Repository object is assigned to a development class. SAP-standard Repository objects are all assigned to SAP development classes.

- New Repository objects must be given a unique name that falls within the *customer name range*. In R/3, the name range of customer-developed objects typically begins with Y or Z.

- In larger, decentralized R/3 implementations, Repository objects may also be assigned to a *namespace*. A namespace is a name field that provides an integrated validation that checks for allowed object names. Namespaces provide a method by which objects for specific development can be created without the risk of creating objects with the same names.

Enhancements

SAP-standard programs that have been designed to allow enhancements can call customer-developed R/3 Repository objects. Enhancements also exist for ABAP Dictionary objects. To be enhanced, SAP objects must have one of the following:

User exits: Points in an SAP program from which a customer's own program can be called

Program exits (also known as function module exits): Predefined function module calls in the standard system for accessing customer-developed function modules

Menu exits: Predefined placeholders in the graphical user interface for customer-developed menu options

Screen exits: Predefined places in R/3 screens where customers can insert a dialog box they have created

Table appends: Placeholders in ABAP Dictionary tables or structures for customer-defined fields external to the table or structure

Field exits: Fields on screens that trigger processing of the field contents by customer-developed function modules

Text enhancements: Enhancements in SAP data elements that allow customers to replace SAP-specified text with customer-defined keywords or documentation

User exits, program exits, menu exits, field exits, and screen exits enable customers to extend R/3 applications by adding their own processing logic at predefined points. These types of customer exits are inactive when delivered. For the exit to call an enhancement developed by the customer using the ABAP Workbench, the exit must be activated. Customer exits provide you with a predefined interface between SAP programs and customer-developed programs.

Enhancements to tables and structures in the ABAP Dictionary are realized using append structures and text enhancements.

Appends are placeholders in R/3 standard tables that refer to an append structure external to the table. By adding fields to the append structure, you are adding fields to the table without changing the table itself. Once the new fields have been added and the table has been activated, these fields can be referred to in ABAP programs just as normal table fields.

The merit and purpose of SAP enhancements are to enable you to add functionality to SAP-standard objects by creating new objects rather than modifying the SAP-standard objects. Customers who avoid modifying SAP-standard objects enjoy three benefits:

- They can receive customer support from SAP more easily.

- They have fewer problems applying SAP's periodic corrections to its software in the form of *Support Packages*.

- They can perform R/3 Release upgrades more quickly.

SAP guarantees that when you use enhancement techniques, you will not lose the functionality provided by your enhancement at the time of an R/3 Release upgrade or when applying a Support Package. SAP encourages the use of enhancement techniques as they reduce the periodic effort required to update your R/3 System—a reduction that is particularly significant in the long term.

User exits do in fact change an SAP-standard object—specifically, an INCLUDE module (see example in the next section). However, SAP guarantees that functionality provided by user exits will not be lost as long as the customer performs a modification adjustment for the INCLUDE module during R/3 upgrades.

Modifications

The benefit of enhancement technologies, such as program exits and append structures, is that they do not require the customer to modify SAP-standard objects. SAP does not recommend making modifications to SAP-standard objects other than the user exit modifications described above. In general, modifications are not guaranteed to work after an R/3 Release upgrade or the application of Support Packages. This means more support is required for updates to modified R/3 Systems.

WARNING   SAP recommends avoiding modifications to the standard code because this may have unwanted effects or cause errors in other parts of an application. SAP cannot ensure error-free R/3 operation after customers make modifications.

Apart from activating user exits, customers usually perform modifications to their R/3 Systems for one of two reasons:

- To adjust R/3 functionality to meet a business need that SAP does not provide or provides differently

- To manually apply a correction to fix a known programming error as described by SAP in an *R/3 Note*

Instead of modifying SAP objects, SAP recommends using Customizing, customer developments, or enhancements. If modifications are unavoidable, consult SAP.

Example: A Common Modification: The User Exit

The Sales and Distribution application has a wide variety of user exits that can be used to enhance existing functionality. You can implement a user exit by changing the INCLUDE module MV75AFZ1 to define a more complex sort procedure for contracts. This module is an SAP-standard object, and, prior to the customer's changes, looks like this:

Include MV75AFZ1

```
1
2  form user_sort using u_rcode.
3   clear u_rcode.
4  * Sort rules
5  * u_rcode = 4.
6  endform.
7
```

This INCLUDE module is called by another SAP-standard program, SAPMV75A, which lists contracts:

Program SAPMV75A

```
1   *_____
2   * Central Report to Display Contracts
3   *_____
...   ...   ...   ...   ...   ...   ...   ...   ...
...   ...   ...   ...   ...   ...   ...   ...   ...
222  * customer modifications
223  include mv75afz1.
224  include mv75afz2.
```

Continued on next page

```
225  include mv75afz3.

226
```

Inserting sort criteria to MV75AFZ1 is a customer modification. SAP guarantees that it will continue to support the use of this module and its call from program SAPMV75A in future R/3 Releases. Therefore, while the program SAPMV75A may change from one R/3 Release to another, the customer version of MV75AFZ1 will remain effective after the modification adjustment process.

NOTE   During an R/3 upgrade, you are given the opportunity to check whether you still require previously created user exits, and to allow those exits no longer needed to be overwritten.

Modification Adjustments

An important reason for not making modifications is to avoid *modification adjustments* during R/3 Release upgrades or when applying Support Packages, also known as *patches*, from SAPNet, SAP's online support services formerly known as SAP's Online Service System (OSS). Modification adjustments are adjustments to SAP objects that ensure previous modifications remain implemented in the system after upgrade. Depending on the number and scope of modifications, the adjustment process may make an R/3 Release upgrade or application of Support Packages a complex and time-consuming process, requiring developers to have extensive application knowledge.

As of R/3 Release 4.5, the *Modification Assistant* tool guides you when making modifications and when subsequently performing modification adjustments. The Modification Assistant structures the way changes are made to SAP standard objects and logs all changes, providing you with a detailed overview that is easy to read and that drastically reduces the amount of effort needed to upgrade your system.

Even with the advent of the Modification Assistant, you should keep the number of modifications you make to an absolute minimum. Extensive background knowledge of application structure and process flow is indispensable for deciding whether modifications are avoidable, and if not, what kind of modifications should be made and how they should be designed.

NOTE   See Appendix C of Hartwig Brand's *SAP R/3 Implementation with ASAP* (from Sybex) for more information on access to SAPNet and SAP's Online Service System (OSS).

Modifications Recommended in R/3 Notes

The R/3 Notes in SAPNet provide you with a database of task- or problem-oriented recommendations regarding SAP software and the applicable hardware. These recommendations sometimes provide solutions that require the customer to perform modifications to SAP objects—for example, manual programming corrections for R/3 Repository objects.

To eliminate the need for manually keying in such corrections, SAP offers Support Packages, or patches, to replace the objects affected by the error with improved versions. Support Packages are not customer modifications because the objects modified by Support Packages are overwritten during an R/3 Release upgrade, and there is no need to make modification adjustments.

If there is no Support Package available for solving your problem, you may have to make a manual change to the SAP-standard object based on R/3 Notes. Before starting work, however, you need to confirm that the R/3 Note is applicable to your R/3 Release, and that the symptoms it describes actually match those in your R/3 System. If you are not sure, contact the SAP Hotline.

TIP Because modifications can subsequently entail modification adjustments during R/3 Release upgrades or when applying Support Packages, you should fully document the modification to accelerate modification adjustment. In your documentation, include the R/3 Note number and the R/3 Release dependencies.

SSCR for Modifications

Before making a modification, you must be registered as a developer in the SAP Software Change Registration (SSCR) in SAPNet. In addition, you must register each SAP-standard object you intend to modify. After registering an SAP-standard object, you receive an SSCR access key that must be applied to that object. Once the SSCR access key has been applied, it remains stored in the database so that subsequent changes to that object at the current R/3 Release level do not require additional SSCR registration.

By requiring this type of registration, SAP is made aware of the frequency of changes to the different Repository objects, and can respond by creating more enhancement technologies. Knowing which objects a customer has modified also makes it easier for SAP to provide quality customer support.

Review Questions

1. Which of the following strategies enables R/3 customers to avoid making modifications to SAP-standard objects?

   A. Using enhancement technologies such as program exits and menu exits

   B. Modifying SAP-delivered programs

    C. Changing SAP-standard functionality using the Implementation Guide (IMG)

    D. Performing Customizing to provide the required functionality

2. Which of the following statements are correct in regard to the Implementation Guide (IMG)?

    A. The IMG consists of a series of Customizing activities for defining a company's business processes.

    B. The IMG is an online resource providing the necessary information and steps to help you implement R/3 application modules.

    C. The IMG is client-independent.

    D. All of the above.

3. Which of the following strategies enables an enterprise to meet its business needs by changing or enhancing R/3 functionality?

    A. Maintaining application data using the various R/3 business transactions in the SAP standard

    B. Using the ABAP Workbench to create the required R/3 Repository objects

    C. Using Customizing to modify R/3 programs after obtaining an access key from SAP's Online Support Services (OSS)

    D. Using customer exits to enhance the functionality of existing SAP-standard objects

4. Which of the following statements are correct in regard to modifications?

    A. A modification is a change to an SAP-standard object.

    B. A modification must be registered through SAP Software Change Registration (SSCR).

C. SAP recommends modifications only if the customer's business needs cannot be met by Customizing, enhancement technologies, or customer development.

D. All of the above.

5. Which of the following statements is correct in regard to Customizing?

A. Customizing enables R/3 application processes to be set to reflect a company's business needs.

B. Customizing can be performed only from within a Project IMG.

C. Customizing is necessary because R/3 is delivered without business processes.

D. None of the above.

6. Which of the following statements are correct in regard to R/3 Repository objects?

A. Customers can develop new Repository objects using the tools in the ABAP Workbench.

B. Customer-developed Repository objects reside in the R/3 Repository alongside SAP-standard objects.

C. Customers can create and assign new Repository objects to a development class.

D. All of the above.

CHAPTER

THREE

The R/3 System Landscape

Your system landscape consists of the R/3 Systems and clients required to take you from the first stages of an R/3 installation, through realization of your business needs within the software, to the start of R/3 production activities. Once in production, your system landscape will need to support continuous changes to the software—due to corporate demands for additional business functionality as well as updates to R/3 in the form of R/3 Release upgrades or SAP Support Packages. So, the objective of a system landscape is to provide an implementation environment where:

- You can perform Customizing and make development changes without affecting the production environment.

- You can validate business processes before using them in the production environment.

- You can simulate and test R/3 Release upgrades and the application of Support Packages before they impact the production environment.

- You can work on Customizing and development to meet future business requirements without influencing the current production environment.

To meet the needs of your software implementation and to ensure smooth production operation, your system landscape must contain multiple R/3 clients and multiple R/3 Systems. R/3 clients provide isolated environments in which changes can be developed, tested, and then rolled into production. At least one client is needed for each step in this process; that is, every R/3 implementation requires at least three R/3 clients. In addition, due to the immediate impact of client-independent changes on all clients within the same R/3 System, SAP recommends that an R/3 implementation also have more than one R/3 System. Although every implementation will have a unique system landscape, SAP provides some recommended system landscapes and methods for setting up and maintaining landscapes. This chapter will present the different system landscapes and explain their advantages and disadvantages.

R/3 Client Roles

Access to R/3 is always in the context of a specific client number. In other words, when you log on to an R/3 System, you log in to a specific client within that R/3 System. Because different clients have different roles, your R/3 implementation needs several clients. For example, one client is required for Customizing and development, another for quality assurance testing, and yet another for end users to record business transactions and build production data.

Often, R/3 implementations acquire clients over time that no longer have a purpose or value for the implementation. Each client uses database space, which equates to hardware resources. Even more costly are the organizational efforts necessary to keep and maintain the client over time. Such maintenance efforts include managing user access and ensuring that the client receives the latest Customizing and development changes. To ensure optimal performance, your R/3 implementation should have only enough clients to fulfill your specific needs.

Critical Client Roles

To begin R/3 implementation efforts, one client is required. However, as the implementation progresses, this single client will no longer suffice. Other separate clients will be necessary, each devoted to a particular task. To function properly, an R/3 implementation requires a minimum of three R/3 clients. The critical client roles needed to fulfill the basic requirements of your R/3 implementation include the following:

- Customizing and development

- Quality assurance

- Production

NOTE   R/3 clients are technically represented in the R/3 System with three digits. For example, the three standard clients delivered by SAP and explained in Chapter 1 are client 000, client 001, and client 066. However, to promote consistency and ease of reading, three abbreviations will be used throughout this book to represent the three standard R/3 client roles: CUST for the Customizing-and-development client, QTST for the quality assurance client, and PROD for the production client.

The Role of CUST

In the Customizing-and-development client (CUST), you adapt R/3 to meet your specific needs. In other words, this is where you perform Customizing and development work with the ABAP Workbench. All changes performed in this client are documented and recorded in *change requests*, so they can be promoted to all other clients in the system landscape. A change request is an important mechanism for recording, documenting, and transporting changes throughout the system landscape (see Chapter 4).

While it is technically possible to perform Customizing in different clients and then merge these Customizing efforts in a third client using change requests, SAP does not recommend this procedure. The end result is neither predictable nor retractable. If functionality that works in the original client does not work in the merged client, you will have problems tracking down the conflict responsible for the disrupted functionality. It is much more efficient for the people customizing your R/3 System to work together in one central location, the CUST client.

TIP   To meet your implementation needs, Customizing R/3 should be performed in and distributed from a single R/3 client.

The Roles of QTST and PROD

The quality assurance client (QTST) provides the environment for testing and verifying new as well as existing Customizing settings and business application functionality. Application data can be added and manipulated for quality assurance testing. The production client (PROD) is needed for all production activities; in other words, this is where your company's business is carried out. This client harbors the production data.

It is important to remember that the effects of Customizing changes on application behavior are similar to those involved in changing a program; that is, the effect is immediate and, if incorrect, may negatively impact existing data. As a result, changes should first be performed in a Customizing-and-development client. It is only after Customizing and development are carefully tested in the QTST client that the changes are promoted to the PROD client. This ensures disruption-free production operation and the availability of valid functionality.

TIP   SAP recommends avoiding Customizing and development work in the QTST and PROD clients.

The roles the required clients play during R/3 implementation are comparable to the operation of an assembly line (see Figure 3.1). Assembly lines require a well-defined procedure with different mandatory steps performed at different yet linear stages to arrive at a final deliverable result. Similarly, each change made to your R/3 System starts at the beginning of the implementation process (CUST), moves on to testing (QTST), and, once the change is verified, makes its way into production (PROD). Making all changes originate from a single client ensures all of the following:

- The changes all follow the same testing procedures.

- The associated documentation is centralized, and is therefore easier to manage.

- Customizing settings and Repository objects in your system landscape remain consistent.

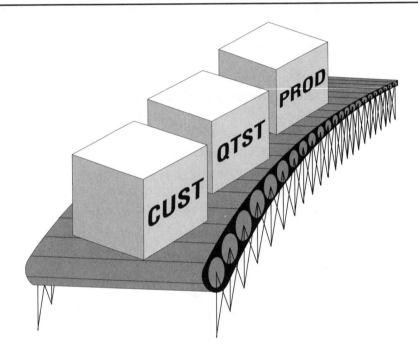

Additional Client Roles

To function properly, your R/3 implementation requires the three standard clients mentioned above. However, you may find it necessary to define additional clients to fulfill certain needs. These alternative client roles can include any of the following:

- Unit test client

- Specialized development client

- Sandbox client

- End-user training client

Unit Test Clients

Before you promote Customizing and developments to the quality assurance client, SAP recommends that you perform *unit testing*. Unit testing is the lowest level of testing, where the program or transaction is tested and evaluated for faults. It is normally a part of the development phase and focuses on the inner functions of the program rather than on integration. For example, after configuring a new sales document type, you should test it and see whether you can create a sales order using that document type. Or perhaps you have written a report to analyze plant utilization. You should run this report several times to verify the results and achieve the desired layout. This requires a cyclical combination of Customizing and development and then testing to get the desired results.

Unit testing of R/3 functionality requires application data— more specifically, transaction data and master data. For example, to create a sales document, you need to have a customer number and materials (both master data). The result of the test is a new sales order, which is transaction data. To be able to provide results, most reports require some set of transaction data. Therefore, to unit test your Customizing and developments, you require sample application data and the ability to create new application data.

You can perform unit testing in the client CUST. However, SAP recommends setting up a unit test client to keep CUST free of application data. There are two reasons for this:

- Over time, unit testing causes a client to be cluttered with "bad" data—that is, data that is no longer suitable for unit tests. Inappropriate data does not allow for predictable test results.

- Application data is tightly coupled to Customizing settings. A Customizing change may not be possible because application data is already associated with the present Customizing settings. In fact, some settings, such as the configuration of your organization structure, cannot be changed once application data is associated with it. To enable such a change, you would have to delete all application data associated with the original setting. This is a very tedious task.

Example: Application Data Associated with Customizing

When Customizing the application Sales and Distribution, a project team creates the required sales organizations within their company. In addition, the team configures all possible distribution channels that are used by the different sales organizations. For example, the Canadian sales organizations distribute only to retail centers, whereas the American sales organizations distribute to retail centers and wholesalers, and by mail order.

The team assigns the sales organizations to the appropriate distribution channels and verifies the combinations through testing with different types of sales orders. During the first round of user acceptance testing, it becomes obvious that the mail order business is not really valid for the American sales organizations. Because mail order sales already exist for the American sales organizations, the team cannot simply delete this Customizing assignment. Before eliminating it, they must first delete all related sales orders—that is, the application data.

To avoid such complications, you can create another client that contains the necessary application data for unit testing. This *unit test client* provides an environment for maintaining a variety of application data separate from the Customizing environment. It is here that people performing Customizing can test transactions and developers can test reports and programs. (See also Chapter 6.)

NOTE For the sake of consistency and ease of reading, the abbreviation TEST will represent the unit test client throughout this book.

If your developers have diverse testing requirements for special programs, such as data conversion routines or interfaces to other computer systems, you may wish to provide them with their own unit test client. This allows for a unique set of business data that can be manipulated by the developers without impacting Customizing tests. In more complex R/3 implementations, you may need a *development unit test client* to test reports, screens, and other new functionality.

NOTE CUST is the client in which all Customizing, both client-dependent and client-independent, and developments are performed. TEST enables people performing Customizing to test the contents of their tasks and change requests. It also provides an environment for maintaining application data separate from the Customizing environment.

Specialized Development Client

SAP recommends that both Customizing and development be performed in the same R/3 client. It is more efficient to have changes and documentation supporting an R/3 implementation originate from a single source.

However, developers often demand a separate client in which they can develop their programs in isolation from the Customizing environment. They want a more stable client where the Customizing does not change every hour. Because each additional client in your system landscape requires you to make more administrative efforts to ensure that all clients are updated regularly with the latest Customizing efforts, other alternatives should be tried first. First, you should try a single CUST client. If that does not suffice, try using a combination of two TEST clients, one for Customizing and one for development. Only when these alternatives do not provide your developers with satisfactory results should you consider creating a unique *development client*.

Other Common Client Roles

In addition to clients for Customizing and development (CUST), unit testing (TEST), quality assurance testing (QTST), and production (PROD), two clients commonly found within a system landscape include the following:

Sandbox client: This client is a playground for people who are Customizing R/3 and want to test their efforts before actually impacting the Customizing-and-development client.

End-user training client: This is an environment for training end users who will be using R/3 to supply and access production data.

NOTE   For the sake of consistency and ease of reading, the following abbreviations will be used throughout this book when representing the additional R/3 clients: SAND for a sandbox or playground client, and TRNG for the end-user training client.

Defining an R/3 Client

An R/3 client is defined by its unique client settings. When you first create a client—for example, using *client maintenance* (Transaction SCC4)—you provide a client ID number and a short description. In addition, you make selections for all of the following parameters:

- The client's default currency
- The client role, such as Production, Test, or Customizing
- The client-dependent change option
- The client-independent change option
- The client protection and restrictions—for example, protecting the client against overwrites and upgrades

The last four settings allow only approved activities to take place in that particular client. It is your responsibility to see that the correct role, restrictions, and change options have been chosen for each client in your system landscape. These settings are established when the client is created, but you can change the settings for a client at any time. For more details on creating a client and selecting the appropriate settings, see Chapter 9.

The critical client settings are the client-dependent change option and the client-independent change option. They will be explained in more detail below.

Client-Dependent Change Options

The most critical client setting used to define a client is its client-dependent change option. This option determines whether changes are permitted in a client and whether the changes are going to be recorded automatically to change requests (see Figure 3.2). The client change options for client-dependent attributes include:

Changes without automatic recording: This setting allows changes to client-dependent Customizing, but does not automatically record or include the changes in change requests. Customizing changes can be manually included in change requests for promotion to other clients and systems at any time. However, because it is difficult to keep track of changes and then manually record them, SAP does not recommend this option for any client in your system landscape. This setting will be useful only if you need a client from which certain selective changes will be promoted.

Automatic recording of changes: This setting allows changes to client-dependent Customizing settings and automatically includes them in a change request. This enables their promotion and distribution to all other clients within your system landscape. This option should be assigned to your Customizing-and-development client (CUST).

No changes allowed: This setting prevents all users from making client-dependent Customizing changes from within the client. This option is useful for those clients in which Customizing changes do not take place—that is, clients that are used for testing and training purposes as well as production activities. Most clients in your system landscape, including TEST, QTST, TRNG, and PROD, should have this option.

No transports allowed: This setting allows client-dependent Customizing changes that will not be promoted either manually or automatically to other clients. This option can be used to isolate a sandbox client (SAND), where Customizing settings are sampled, but do not need to be moved to any other client.

FIGURE 3.2:

The path for determining the appropriate client-dependent change option

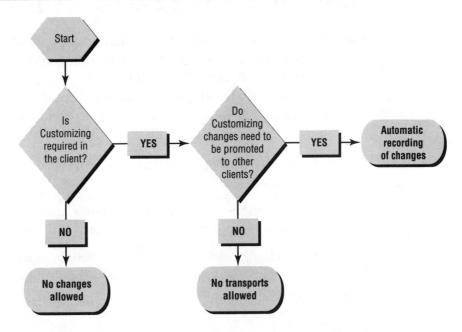

As mentioned above, SAP recommends setting the *No changes allowed* option for your PROD client. An alternative option for the PROD client is *No transport allowed*. This option is required for the production client if you also use the *Current settings* function. When special Customizing changes, known as *data-only Customizing changes*, need to be carried out in a production client without being saved to change requests, the *No changes allowed* setting is no longer valid. An example of data involved in such change is currency exchange rates, which may require frequent adjustment in R/3. To avoid having to use change requests for these changes, SAP has introduced the *Current settings* function (see Chapter 11).

Client-Independent Change Options

The client change options for client-independent attributes protect both client-independent Customizing and R/3 Repository objects (see Figure 3.3). R/3 Repository objects and cross-client Customizing are categorized separately and can therefore be protected against changes either together or individually. The client-independent change options are as follows:

- Changes to Repository and client-independent Customizing allowed

- No changes to client-independent Customizing objects (Changes to Repository objects are still allowed.)

- No changes to Repository objects (Changes to client-independent Customizing are still possible.)

- No changes to Repository and client-independent Customizing objects

All clients in your system landscape—except for the Customizing-and-development client (CUST)—should be assigned the last client-independent change option, *No changes to Repository and client-independent Customizing objects*. The CUST client needs the setting *Changes to Repository and client-independent Customizing allowed*.

Technically, the client-dependent and client-independent change options are two different settings. Logically, the two settings are linked with regard to Customizing changes. Customizing changes rely and build upon other Customizing changes regardless of whether they are client-dependent or client-independent. For this reason, all Customizing activities should take place in a single R/3 client, the CUST client. Although a second client such as the sandbox client (SAND) may allow for client-dependent Customizing changes, client-independent Customizing should not be performed in this client.

FIGURE 3.3:   The path for determining the appropriate client-independent change option

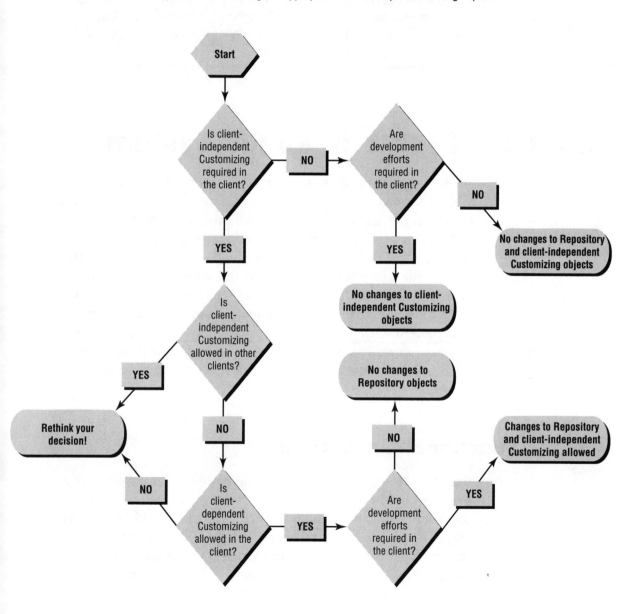

TIP   If client-independent Customizing takes place in a client, that client should also be used for client-dependent Customizing. Only one client within an R/3 System should allow for both client-dependent and client-independent Customizing.

Multiple Clients in an R/3 System

An R/3 client is used to keep the application data of one client isolated and completely independent from another client. Because development, quality assurance, and production tasks each require different sets of application data, each area is provided with a different R/3 client. Based on the uniqueness of application data in each client, one might assume that any number of independent clients could operate in the same R/3 System. With regard to hardware costs and required system maintenance, such a setup (one R/3 System with all required clients) makes financial and organizational sense. The multiple-client concept for the R/3 System does have certain limitations that are both functional and technical in nature.

Functional Limitations

Standard functions of the R/3 System are implemented as programs in the R/3 Repository. The client independence of the entire Repository—with all its program objects and Dictionary objects—is a fundamental characteristic of the R/3 System. Customizing provides the finishing touches to the standard R/3 functionality that supplies you with an operational client.

The R/3 System provides full multiple-client capability at the application data level; that is, all data created in a client is visible for only that one client and cannot be changed or even displayed by other clients. The vast majority of Customizing settings are also client-dependent. These *client-specific* Customizing settings are valid for only that one client. However, some IMG Customizing activities are client-independent; they create globally valid settings (such as decimal places for currencies) or result in the generation of programs and Dictionary elements. Because client-independent Customizing and all Repository objects are always accessible from every client, they provide a potential source of conflict. Customizing and Repository changes in one client could accidentally change, overwrite, or conflict with the needs of another client. An even worse scenario involves clients that do not detect changes to client-independent settings and objects that affect them.

To deal with these functional limitations, SAP recommends that you have only one client in an R/3 System where changes to client-independent Customizing and Repository objects are allowed. This helps ensure the integrity of each client in a multiple-client system. Using the appropriate client-change options ensures that client-independent changes are made only in a single client within the R/3 System.

SAP also recommends that only "like" clients reside in the same R/3 System. For example, test or training clients can be in the same R/3 System. This does not cause problems because these clients are generated as a copy of an existing Customizing-and-development client. The similar clients are based on the same Customizing and the same developments. Thus, such clients are not self-sufficient Customizing environments, but simply derivatives of the Customizing client that require the same client-independent objects and settings.

Technical Limitations

At a technical level, a client ID is the primary key field in the Customizing and application tables of the R/3 database. An R/3 database can house as many clients as you wish—up to a total of 1,000 clients. The required database resources and hardware performance are largely derived from the number of active users and not from the number of clients used.

You need to consider the influence of the number of clients in a system with regard to performance under the following technical concepts of the R/3 System:

- More clients require additional main memory for the R/3 buffers. As a general rule, an additional 10MB is required for each client under R/3 Release 4.0B.

- Because each client occupies entries in database tables, more clients in a system may lead to higher database access times. This is especially true when accessing tables with a full table scan.

- The runtime of an R/3 Release upgrade depends on the number of clients. The more clients that have been defined in a system, the greater the import effort will be, as new entries have to be distributed to all clients within the R/3 System. Although the runtimes of an upgrade will always increase with each additional client, note that a major portion of the upgrade time is spent delivering new Repository objects and not client-dependent data. Therefore, the increased effort in upgrading a system with more clients is not directly proportional. For example, the upgrade of a four-client system will not take twice as long as the upgrade of a two-client system.

- Only limited technical maintenance is possible due to increased availability requirements. Multiple clients within an R/3 System will have different roles and therefore different end-user demands. Technical maintenance, such as reorganizing the database or making an offline backup, requires the R/3 System to be down and unavailable. Scheduling of system unavailability is more difficult if the end-user audience has varying demands.

NOTE   For more information on the database requirements of a standard R/3 client, see R/3 Note 118823 in SAPNet.

Protective Measures for Multiple-Client Operations

SAP provides you with the following protective measures to prevent inadvertent changes from being made from a client within a multiple-client R/3 System and to ensure the successful coexistence of multiple clients in the same physical system:

Client-change options: Changes to client-independent Customizing and Repository objects can be restricted to a specific client using the appropriate client-change options.

User authorizations: Special user authorizations must be assigned for client-independent maintenance.

Special popups: Whenever you perform client-independent Customizing activities or maintain a client-independent table, a warning message informs the user that the changes made will affect all clients throughout the R/3 System.

NOTE   For more information on the limitations of multiple clients in a single R/3 System, see R/3 Note 31557 in SAPNet.

The SAP Three-System Landscape

R/3 clients provide an environment where application data can be isolated while sharing a common Repository and client-independent Customizing. Because of the functional and technical limitations of multiple clients in a single R/3 System including the sharing of a common R/3 Repository, SAP recommends you distribute the critical R/3 clients among several R/3 Systems. The three standard systems in this distribution are as follows:

- Development system
- Quality assurance system (sometimes referred to as the *test* or *consolidation* system)
- Production system

Standard R/3 Systems

Customizing and development take place in the *development system*. All changes made in the development system are recorded to change requests and then promoted to quality assurance for validation. This system contains the CUST client.

In the *quality assurance system*, the R/3 functionality is tested without affecting the production environment. A quality assurance system enables you to integrate Customizing and developments and to check the validity and consistency of transported changes before moving the changes into the production environment. This system contains the QTST client.

All changes imported into the quality assurance system are then delivered to the *production system*. In this system, your business data will be collected and accessed. The system contains the PROD client.

NOTE For the sake of consistency and ease of reading, the following abbreviations will be used throughout this book to represent the different R/3 Systems: DEV for the Customizing-and-development system, QAS for the quality assurance system, and PRD for the production system. Each system needs a unique three-character alphanumeric system ID. For all purposes, the above-mentioned abbreviations can be considered the system IDs.

Distribution of Client Roles

As explained above, each required R/3 client is housed in its own R/3 System. Additional client roles should then be distributed accordingly within the system landscape:

- The sandbox client (SAND), where sampling of client-dependent Customizing takes place, should be in the development environment. After testing Customizing settings in the sandbox client, the person performing the Customizing can go into the CUST client and implement the changes.

- The unit test client (TEST) must be in the same R/3 System as the CUST client. Customizing changes and development changes are tested in the unit test client. Once unit tested, changes can then be promoted to the QTST client.

- Since the quality assurance system is more stable than the development system, the end-user training client (TRNG) is often found in the quality assurance system, where it will not impact the production system.

To meet the needs of your software implementation and to ensure smooth production operation, your system landscape should therefore contain at least three R/3 Systems, the required clients, and any additional clients that are necessary and advantageous for your implementation. Figure 3.4 shows the standard system landscape and the distribution of required and other commonly used client roles.

FIGURE 3.4:

The SAP standard three-system landscape with its client distribution

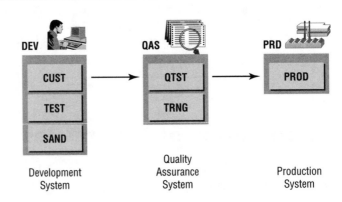

The three distinct R/3 Systems and the clients recommended by SAP benefit your implementation in the following ways:

- For reasons of testing, security, and system performance, all Customizing and developments are separate from production activities.

- A quality assurance system enables you to integrate Customizing and development and to check the validity and consistency of transported changes before they are delivered to the production system.

- Upgrades and application of SAP Support Packages can be simulated and tested before applying them to the production system.

Example: Derivation of SAP's Recommended Three-System Landscape

A large chemical firm decided to implement R/3 to alleviate its Y2K issues. Its objective was to move all manufacturing and distribution processes from an existing, antiquated system to R/3. This also required migrating historical data from the legacy system to R/3 at the start of production activities.

Initially, the company began its implementation using the three-system landscape SAP recommends with the following clients:

- CUST client 100, TEST client 200, and SAND client 400 in the development system (DDV)

- QTST client 100 and TRNG client 300 in the quality assurance system (DQA)

- PROD client 100 in the production system (DPR)

It immediately became obvious that testing data conversion routines with the legacy system was interfering with the testing of Customizing changes. To alleviate this problem, two new clients were created—client 210 in DDV for the unit testing of data conversion routines and client 210 in the quality assurance system (DQA) to support stress testing of conversion routines.

Also, because training sessions for end users occurred on a weekly basis, a master training client 310 was created in DQA. From this master client, the training client 300 in DQA was generated each week. This ensured a base level of application data and default user accounts for the support of each training session.

Continued on next page

The company's system landscape looked like this:

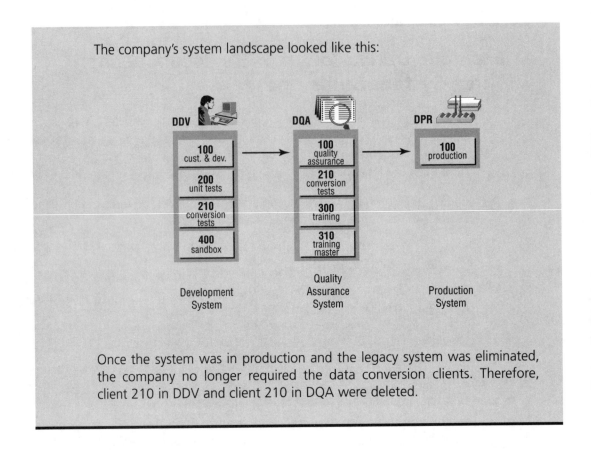

Once the system was in production and the legacy system was eliminated, the company no longer required the data conversion clients. Therefore, client 210 in DDV and client 210 in DQA were deleted.

Alternative System Landscapes

SAP's recommended three-system landscape is simply a template from which you can build your system landscape. However, many customers have specific or temporary client needs that are added to the system landscape. Other customers see the need for additional R/3 Systems—for example, a system that may be used solely for end-user training. Some customers may have constraints that require them to implement a one-system or two-system landscape. Or, a customer may begin with the three-system implementation recommended by SAP, but over time require more R/3

Systems due to the need to introduce more functionality while still providing support changes to the production system.

Regardless of your environment, it is important to note that more clients and also additional R/3 Systems pose certain costs to your implementation:

- More hardware resources are needed.
- Managing the distribution of Customizing and development changes becomes more difficult.
- Support for R/3 Release upgrades and the application of Support Packages has additional complications.
- The administrative responsibilities with regard to user access and authorization increase.

When designing your system landscape, you need to compare these costs with the necessity for providing environments in which Customizing and development can take place without impacting other implementation efforts, such as quality assurance testing and production activities. You should carefully weigh the limitations and disadvantages against the advantages the different system landscapes can provide to meet your specific needs.

One-System Landscape

A one-system landscape consists of a single R/3 System used for Customizing and development as well as for quality assurance testing and production activities. A single R/3 System for implementation requires that all clients share the same hardware, the R/3 Repository, and client-independent Customizing. Sharing these resources results in the following limitations for a one-system landscape:

- Changes to Repository objects are client-independent and immediately affect the runtime environment; therefore, changes are tested in the runtime environment of your production system, and there is a danger of production data loss as a result of inconsistencies or incorrect changes.

- The Customizing-and-development client as well as the quality assurance client can affect production performance.

- System availability is required for production activities at all times, not allowing opportunities for unique development and quality assurance demands.

- Production data security is compromised. For example, developers can create reports that access production data from another client.

- The system administrator cannot perform upgrades on a nonproduction system before upgrading the production system.

As a consequence of these limitations, no further development is possible after production work has started. Changes to Repository objects can be made only when production operations are stopped for development and testing. For these reasons, SAP does not recommend using a one-system landscape.

Two-System Landscape

A small, uncomplicated R/3 implementation may need only two R/3 Systems. This two-system landscape is able to support an R/3 implementation with standard business functionality and limited customer development needs.

A two-system landscape allows development and production to be performed in two separate environments. However, this landscape has its weaknesses. Because development and quality assurance testing both occur in the development system, the stability of central resources during actual quality assurance testing may be jeopardized. Therefore, changes to Repository objects or client-independent Customizing cannot be made while quality assurance testing is in progress.

Change management also presents a problem for the two-system landscape. Complex development projects often involve transporting partial functionality, sometimes without taking dependencies into account. Change requests and the functionality in the change requests are not fully tested until after the changes have been imported. In addition, a change request upon import may result in an error due to dependencies on other change requests or problems within the change request itself. Therefore, in a two-system landscape, the transport of a change request cannot be fully tested before it is imported into production. This can cause inconsistencies and affect the production system.

Figure 3.5 depicts a two-system landscape. In this landscape, the development system has four different clients. Customizing and development activities occur in client CUST. Unit testing takes place in client TEST before being delivered to the quality assurance client (QTST). End-user training also takes place in this system in the client TRNG. The production system is reserved solely for production activities in the client PROD.

FIGURE 3.5:

A two-system
landscape

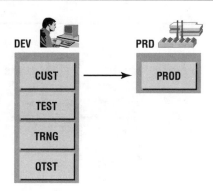

A three-system landscape provides a unique environment dedicated to quality assurance testing and, just as importantly, allows for the testing of transported change requests. The two-system landscape, in contrast, does not offer this option. This means the two-system landscape is viable only for environments where very few complex Customizing and development changes have to be promoted to production after the start of production activities.

Four-System Landscape

The SAP-recommended system landscape requires three R/3 Systems. These three systems house the critical roles for the R/3 implementation. However, customers frequently include more systems in their landscape to support a variety of testing demands or training needs. Noncritical clients, such as the sandbox client, the training client, or an additional testing client, are then isolated on their own R/3 System, extending the landscape to a four-system landscape. Such a system landscape is valid as long as the additional system provides long-term value for the R/3 implementation plan. It will require the latest copy of Customizing and development changes. An example of such a system is a training environment that is isolated from quality assurance activities (see Figure 3.6).

FIGURE 3.6:

A four-system land-scape with a special training environment

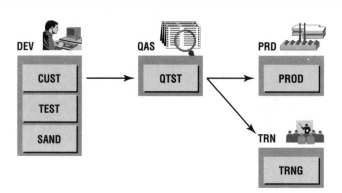

Complex System Landscapes

Some customers require implementations that go beyond the SAP-recommended system landscape—for example, a large, multinational implementation. Such customers may need a *complex system landscape*—that is, an environment that extends beyond the standard three-system landscape. More specifically, you can think of a complex system landscape as a system landscape that includes more than one client playing any one of the critical client roles. For example, a system landscape that has two different production clients or two different Customizing-and-development clients is considered complex.

Because of its complexity, this type of system landscape requires strong management efforts and centralized coordination that still allows for localizing particular implementation tasks. It may also require the use of special R/3 tools for the support of Customizing and development as well as the distribution and/or sharing of application data.

There are several kinds of complex system landscapes. To reflect the most common customer issues, this book will focus on the following three types:

- A *multiple production system landscape* has a single development system that supports many production systems.

- A *phased system landscape* is used to support the introduction of new business functionality to an existing production system. Customizing and development changes are made in two different clients, but all changes ultimately support the same production system.

- A *global system landscape* has multiple production and development systems sharing some common Customizing and developments.

Multiple Production System Landscape

A multiple production system landscape has multiple production data clients with similar Customizing and development needs. Such a landscape is shown in Figure 3.7. Since the multiple production systems stem from just one Customizing and development system, you may find yourself asking the following questions:

- If the data and business needs of the production environments are similar enough to share the same Customizing and developments, why isn't a single production system enough?

- Once in production, what happens if the different production systems have different Customizing and development demands that can no longer be served by a single development system?

- Different production systems require multiple production data environments. How do these different production systems share business data, such as master and transaction data?

FIGURE 3.7:

A system landscape with multiple production systems

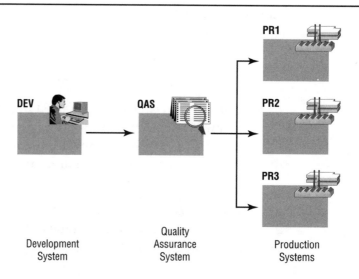

PR1

DEV   QAS   PR2

PR3

Development   Quality   Production
System   Assurance   Systems
                System

The first two questions regarding the need for and support of multiple production systems are addressed in this chapter. A discussion regarding the management of business data across multiple R/3 Systems is highlighted in Chapter 4.

Company Codes versus Multiple Production System Landscapes

Some organizations divide their R/3 implementation and production data among different subsidiaries. In such an organization, one subsidiary may demand that its production data be in a separate R/3 System (or even a separate R/3 client) from the production data of the other. The subsidiary could be accommodated by implementing a multiple production system landscape. However, this would impair the parent organization's ability to view all its subsidiaries' business data from within a single R/3 client.

A more fitting alternative for sharing business functionality and business data between different organizations can be provided by using *company codes*. Company codes in R/3 define the smallest organizational element for which a complete, self-contained set of accounts can be drawn up for external reporting. Company codes are either separate legal entities, as in the case of a second company, or part of the same legal entity, as in the case of two subsidiaries that report to a parent organization. One client in an R/3 System can support several company codes. The standard clients 000 and 001 delivered by SAP already have a company code 0001, which is set up for Germany. This company code can be adapted or copied during Customizing.

Using company codes in conjunction with user authorizations, you can integrate several companies or subsidiaries in a single R/3 client. The SAP authorization concept enables the parent company to access all subsidiaries for report purposes, while subsidiary-specific data is protected against access from other subsidiaries through company code definition.

TIP To meet the needs of different companies within a parent organization, SAP recommends that customers first consider using company codes within a single production client rather than using multiple production clients.

Specific Scenarios for Multiple Production Systems

When the use of company codes and user authorizations does not provide a large organization with the production requirements it demands, a multiple production system landscape is necessary. This type of system landscape would then satisfy the following requirements:

Unique language demands: R/3 supports more than 24 languages. However, due to the technical requirements of specific character sets such as Japanese, Chinese, and Russian, there are limitations to the combinations of languages that may be supported by a single R/3 System. With the introduction of Unicode technology, SAP will be able to support all languages of the Western and Eastern industrial world. If you are not in a position to implement Unicode technology, you will need multiple production systems to support complicated language combinations.

Performance concerns: R/3's client/server technology and newer hardware technologies allow for the distribution of many active users across multiple application servers. This distribution of resources typically meets the needs of even our largest customers. However, some customers have performance needs, networking concerns, and varying end-user demands that go beyond what one production system can provide. These customers require the multiple production system landscape.

Example: A Multiple Production System Landscape to Meet Specific Language Requirements

A multinational distribution company has facilities spanning the globe, from its headquarters in North America to distribution centers in Eastern Europe and its subsidiaries in Korea and China. The organization uses R/3 to manage corporate sales and financial data. However, due to the inherent cultural differences and autonomy of many of the Asian subsidiaries, the Board decides that all business data must be maintained in its local language. In other words, not only is the R/3 presentation interface for the end-user community in the local language, data is also entered in the respective languages. At present, SAP's language support for Korean and Chinese is not possible in a single R/3 System. The company therefore requires multiple R/3 Systems to support the needed languages.

The respective end-user communities use production systems with the following system IDs:

- PNA supports North America by providing English.

- PEE supports Eastern Europe by providing Czech, English, Polish, and German.

- PCH supports China by providing Simplified Chinese and English.

- PKO supports Korea by providing Korean and English.

Customizing and Development in Multiple Production Systems

A multiple production system landscape depends on the fact that all production systems have the same Customizing settings and Repository objects. After the initial start of production activities, Customizing and development activities continue in the development system to support production activities, enhance existing functionality, and introduce new business processes. Although many of these changes are created to satisfy a specific need of one production system, the changes still have to be distributed to all clients and systems to ensure consistent Customizing and development.

However, once in production, there is more reluctance to introduce changes into a production system, especially if there is no apparent benefit for the production activities. Therefore, over time, as the multiple production systems in a multiple system landscape become more autonomous, such landscape-wide Customizing and development transports become a hindrance. In this case, the multiple production system landscape may need to expand to become more like a global system landscape, which is explained in more detail later in this chapter.

NOTE   Support for a multiple production system landscape requires centralized Customizing and development that are rolled out to all production systems.

Phased System Landscape

Customers often implement R/3 in different phases to meet varying business objectives within a specific time frame and to deal with management constraints and resource limitations. The first phase might be used to start up certain production plants or to install a particular application module such as Financial Accounting. The next phase then adds either additional plants or even a new module, such as Human Resources. A further phase could be an upgrade to the latest R/3 Release. (See also Chapter 6.) To support a multiple-phased implementation and to provide an environment in which new business processes can be introduced while current production activities are supported, SAP recommends using a *phased system landscape*.

Note that the word "phase" is used to represent a customer's need for implementing new functionality in its production system. This functionality may or may not be an R/3 Release upgrade. The implementation phase is often the introduction of new business processes through additional R/3 configuration. For example, Phases 1 through 3 may be the rollout of all company codes, plants, and financials. Phase 4 may be an upgrade of the R/3 software, and Phase 5 may be the introduction of Internet functionality. The phased system landscape is designed to support both the rollout of new Customizing to address business needs and SAP R/3 Release upgrades.

Requirements of a Phased System Landscape

A phased system landscape requires resources to support production while at the same time providing an environment for new Customizing and development. To realize these goals, the following environments need to be added to the SAP-recommended three-system landscape:

Production support system: This is a Customizing and development environment that closely resembles the production system; that is, its Customizing data and Repository objects are identical to those in the production system. This client is used for making changes or corrections demanded by production while the next phase of the implementation is being planned and tested in the DEV and QAS systems.

Final quality assurance system: This is a quality assurance environment that closely resembles the production system and includes sample or complete production data. This client is used for testing and verifying any changes demanded by production—that is, those changes made in the production support system. This testing, also known as *regression testing*, is necessary so that the changes will not have an adverse affect on production data after import; that is, the new functionality will not negatively impact existing business functionality.

Realizing a Phased Implementation

With the addition of these two new systems, the phased system landscape recommended by SAP should have five R/3 Systems. As in the case of the three-system landscape, each critical environment required for the implementation has its own R/3 System.

Figure 3.8 depicts the standard client roles and R/3 Systems for a phased system landscape. The notation *Phase N* represents the phase currently in production. *Phase N+1* represents the next phase of the implementation to be brought into production at a later date and time. Phase N+1 is the introduction of a new module or an R/3 Release upgrade.

FIGURE 3.8:

The SAP-recommended phased system landscape

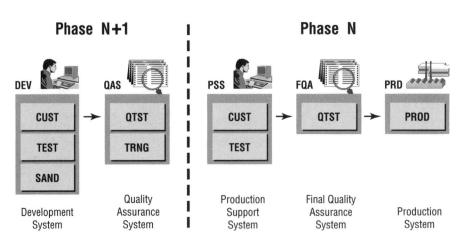

In a phased system landscape, Phase N changes are only those changes required to immediately support production. These take place in the production support system (in Figure 3.8, the R/3

System PSS). All other Customizing and developments are part of the next phase and take place in the original development system. Phase N+1 functionality is unit tested in the development system (DEV) and then promoted to the quality assurance system (QAS) for validation.

Figure 3.9 shows the next step, the promotion of Phase N+1 functionality into production. SAP recommends first applying the changes to the final quality assurance system (in Figure 3.9, the R/3 System FQA). This provides an opportunity to perform business integration testing on a system most like a production system. During this final quality assurance testing, if any changes are required for the new phase, they must originate from the development system (DEV). The production support system (PSS) then remains consistent with production and can provide any needed production support in the meantime.

FIGURE 3.9:   The procedure for promoting changes in a phased system landscape

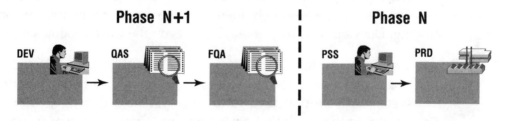

After validation of Phase N+1 on the final quality assurance system (FQA), all of these changes are applied to the production system (PRD) and eventually to the production support system (PSS). All R/3 Systems, including the production system, are then at Phase N+1. At this point in time, *Phase N+2* changes can be promoted from the development system to the quality assurance system to start preparing for the testing of the next phase to be rolled into production at a later date.

If Phase N+1 is a new R/3 Release, an upgrade of the R/3 Systems to the newest release is a prerequisite for the promotion of change requests. This is because change requests are R/3 Release–dependent. The development and quality assurance systems are first upgraded to the new R/3 Release. Changes required for the support of this R/3 Release are then made in development and verified in quality assurance. Prior to promoting the changes to the final quality assurance system, that system must also be upgraded to the new R/3 Release. Likewise, the production system will first need the upgrade before the change requests from Release N+1 can be applied and the production can be moved from Release N to Release N+1.

Multiple Customizing-and-Development Clients   An initial rule with regard to client and system strategies is that Customizing and development originate from a single R/3 client. Customizing is the configuring of the R/3 software and requires changes that are both client-dependent and client-independent. Customizing changes also build upon one another, creating dependencies that cannot be separated and are often hidden from those performing the Customizing. Development work then depends on the Customizing settings.

A phased system landscape requires that this rule be discounted, and Customizing and development take place in two different systems. To support the production system in Phase N, you need a client with identical client-dependent Customizing and central resources such as client-independent Customizing and Repository. In other words, if a problem with the setup of a plant needs to be corrected in production, the production support environment cannot have undergone any changes to that plant or changes that may impact that plant.

Likewise, if a report is not working properly in production, a developer needs to modify the same version of the report in the production support environment—not a newer version of the report. Therefore, Customizing and development support for Phase N requires a constant environment, not one in which new business processes are being added. Accordingly, Phase N production support and configuration of Phase N+1 functionality must be in separate R/3 environments.

Any changes made to support Phase N production activities need to be part of the Phase N+1 rollout, and must be realized in the Phase N+1 development system, as shown in Figure 3.10. For example, if a Production Planning scheme is adjusted to support production needs, the required change must also be made in the development system. SAP recommends that these changes be manually applied to avoid conflicts with the current configuration in the Phase N+1 environment.

FIGURE 3.10:

Ensuring consistency between DEV and PSS

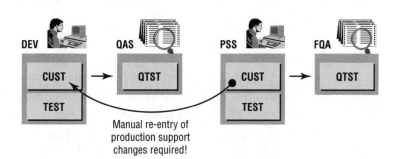

DEV   QAS   PSS   FQA

CUST → QTST   CUST → QTST

TEST   TEST

Manual re-entry of production support changes required!

SAP provides several tools that help manage Customizing and development changes in multiple clients. These tools are explained in more detail below in the section "Global System Landscape."

Alternative Phased System Landscape   Often, phased implementations that are small and uncomplicated do not require five R/3 Systems to maintain a stable production environment while also introducing new functionality. Based on the stability of your production system, the extent of customer developments, and the aggressiveness of your phased implementation, you may find that a four-system landscape suffices for a phased implementation. However, this option does have its limitations.

This four-system landscape functions without the final quality assurance system (FQA). The quality assurance system (QAS) is used in its place. First and foremost, the quality assurance system serves Phase N by providing immediate support for production. This is depicted in Figure 3.11.

FIGURE 3.11: The role of QAS in a four-system phased landscape prior to testing Phase N+1

When the time comes to begin thorough testing of Phase N+1, the quality assurance system supports Phase N+1 as shown in Figure 3.12. At this time, any changes required for the support of production are made in the production support system, unit tested there, and then transported into production without true quality assurance validation. As pointed out in the section about two-landscape systems, when the transport of changes cannot be fully tested before import into production, inconsistencies may arise and affect production.

FIGURE 3.12: The role of QAS in a four-system phased landscape while testing Phase N+1

Global System Landscape

Many enterprises today are implementing R/3 on a worldwide scale and coordinating their efforts centrally. The demands of many subsidiaries and different legal and financial marketplaces require unique implementations. To maximize the benefits of a company's global business, such a global R/3 implementation has to provide all of the following:

- Core business processes on a global basis while coping with local and legal regulations

- Universal user access using different types of interfaces and supplying interfaces in local languages

- Global data consistency

While a global organization may wish to implement R/3 globally from a centralized production system or perhaps using a multiple production system landscape, local requirements may not be addressed with such approaches. Therefore, many organizations centrally define their R/3 organizational standards and default business processes, and then implement unique systems worldwide. To do so, a central corporate office supplies multiple subsidiaries with a set of Customizing and developments, which the subsidiaries use as a baseline when configuring R/3 to meet their local requirements. This procedure is often referred to as a *rollout strategy*. The resulting environment is considered a *global system landscape*.

Realizing a Global System Landscape

Figure 3.13 shows a global system landscape where different subsidiaries accept Customizing and developments from their corporate headquarters. This Customizing and development package, referred to as the *global template*, is created in the corporate development system and tested in its quality assurance system. The global template is then passed on to the individual subsidiaries, which continue to customize and develop R/3 to meet their specific needs. This procedure takes place in each subsidiary's unique system landscape, which can be a standard three-system landscape or any of the alternatives mentioned above. Ultimately, all subsidiaries are in production with similar settings and functionality, while unique requirements are fulfilled. This forms a system landscape with decentralized yet loosely coupled production systems.

FIGURE 3.13: A global system landscape

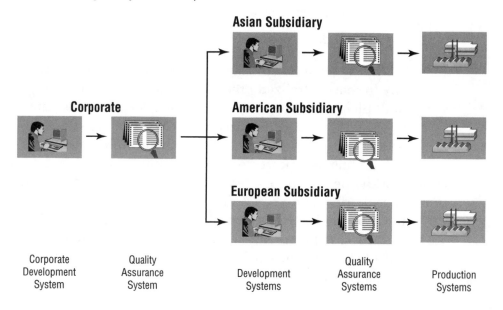

Managing a Global Template

The difficulties in managing a global rollout strategy, as depicted in Figure 3.13 (in the previous section), involve the need for a global template. The use of a global template is not a one-time effort. As R/3 expands throughout the organization and more and more business functionality is demanded, new global templates will have to be distributed on a regular basis. This sparks many concerns, particularly within the subsidiaries, and the following questions need to be addressed:

- What is considered global business functionality and what is considered localized? Can Customizing be easily divided into global and local terms?

- What assurance do subsidiaries have that new changes delivered from the corporate development system will not negatively impact local Customizing and developments? With Customizing dependencies and the coupling of R/3 function modules causing possible complications, how can global templates be introduced into a subsidiary over time?

SAP's first response to these questions is that a strong, centrally managed implementation with representative resources from all subsidiaries is needed. From a technical rather than an organizational perspective, change management in a global system landscapes requires that centrally created Customizing and development objects not be changed locally. Likewise, a global template should not change the Customizing settings or development objects of a subsidiary.

Repository objects have a sense of "ownership." An attribute for every Repository object is the R/3 System from which it originated. Therefore, development objects in a global system landscape can easily be managed and protected as follows:

- Every R/3 System has a *system change option* (Transaction SE06; *Goto* ➤ *System Change Option*). Within this option, you can simply disallow modifications to different namespaces. This determines which Repository objects in the R/3 System can be changed. If a global implementation requires a lot of central development, one namespace can be created for all global objects. This global namespace can then be protected in all local development systems, disallowing any changes to such objects.

- You can use development classes and naming conventions to prevent the creation of an object with the same name within two different R/3 Systems.

For more information regarding the use of system change options, namespaces, and development classes for the protection of customer developments, see Chapter 10.

Customizing is more difficult to manage in a global system landscape. Unlike for Repository objects, there is no concept of ownership for Customizing settings, nor are there standard methods by which subsets of Customizing can be "locked" or protected against change. To manage a global template from a Customizing perspective, corporate standards must define which Customizing settings are part of the global template and which can be maintained locally. Such a strategy requires detailed definitions, and the procedure must be managed not from within R/3, but as project efforts. This well-defined strategy for protecting both global and local Customizing settings can be realized using one or a combination of the following methods:

- Corporate headquarters determines and documents all global Customizing settings. These global settings are then reentered manually in the local development systems. This ensures successful merging with local settings. However, in addition to the duplication of Customizing efforts, manual reentry of global settings leaves a margin for error. Changes may not be realized in the local development system, or worse, they may be realized incorrectly.

- By assigning specific user authorizations, you can prevent the person performing local Customizing from accessing Customizing activities and tables that are "owned" by the corporate system. This requires added effort to not only single out these activities, but also to develop the proper user profiles to ensure that those performing local Customizing can perform only the appropriate activities.

- *Cross-System Tools*, such as the *Customizing Cross-System Viewer* and the *Transfer Assistant*, allow you to compare clients in different R/3 Systems. Using the Cross-System Viewer (Transaction SCU0), you can find the global template settings that conflict with a subsidiary's local settings before you apply the global template to that subsidiary's local development system. The Transfer Assistant (Transaction SADJ) then uses change request functionality to transfer differences between clients. (See Chapter 11.)

- *Business Configuration Sets* (Transaction SCPR2) allow a local subsidiary to preserve its current Customizing settings and compare local and global settings after applying a global template. This tool provides a mechanism for determining conflicts between global templates and local Customizing.

For more information regarding the use of the Customizing Cross-System Viewer, the Transfer Assistant, and Business Configuration Sets as a means to support a global system landscape, see Chapter 11.

Management of a global system landscape is difficult, more from a business application perspective than from a change management perspective. Using a variety of the tools mentioned, you can provide a template of global Customizing and development settings while still maintaining local needs. However, you will need to invest a lot of energy in both testing global functionality at each of the local levels as well as regression testing the existing local functionality. Performing valid tests for all local implementations is the ideal method of confirming any functionality—regardless of the advance efforts you make in protecting changes to Customizing and developments.

Review Questions

1. Which of the following statements is correct in regard to critical client roles as recommended by SAP?

   A. Customizing changes can be made in any client.

   B. All Customizing and development changes should be made in a single R/3 client.

   C. Repository objects should be created and changed in the quality assurance client.

   D. Unit testing should take place in the Customizing-and-development client.

2. Which of the following activities should *not* be performed within a system landscape?

   A. Customizing and development changes are promoted to a quality assurance client before being delivered to production.

   B. The R/3 System is upgraded to new R/3 Releases.

   C. Development changes are made directly in the production client.

   D. Clients are assigned a specific role.

3. Which of the following benefits does the three-system landscape recommended by SAP have?

   A. Customizing and development, testing, and production activities take place in separate database environments and do not affect one another.

   B. Changes are tested in the quality assurance system and imported into the production system only after verification.

    C. Client-independent changes can be made in the development system without immediately affecting the production client.

    D. All of the above.

4. Which of the following statements is correct in regard to multiple R/3 clients?

    A. All clients in the same R/3 System share the same R/3 Repository and client-independent Customizing settings.

    B. No more than one client in the same R/3 System should allow changes to client-independent Customizing objects.

    C. If a client allows for changes to client-dependent Customizing, the client should also allow for changes to client-independent Customizing objects.

    D. All of the above.

5. Which of the following statements is correct in regard to the setup of a three-system landscape?

    A. There is only one R/3 database for the system landscape.

    B. One client should allow for the automatic recording of client-dependent Customizing and client-independent changes.

    C. All R/3 Systems have the same system ID.

    D. All clients must have unique client numbers.

6. Which of the following statements is correct in regard to the CUST client?

    A. It should allow changes to client-independent Customizing, but not Repository objects.

    B. It should automatically record all changes to Customizing settings.

    C. It should not allow changes to client-dependent and client-independent Customizing settings.

    D. It should allow for all changes, but not require recording of changes to change requests.

7. Which of the following statements is correct in regard to a two-system landscape?

    A. It is not optimal because there is limited opportunity to test the transport of changes from the development system to the production system.

    B. It allows for changes to Customizing in the production system.

    C. It is recommended by SAP because Customizing and development do not impact quality assurance testing.

    D. All of the above.

8. Which of the following statements are correct in regard to a phased implementation?

    A. All Customizing changes made in the production support system must also be made in the development system.

    B. The system landscape requires five R/3 Systems.

    C. Changes in the production support system do not have to be made in the development environment.

    D. The system landscape needs an environment that supports the production system with any required changes.

9. Which of the following statements is *not* valid in regard to a global system landscape?

   A. A global template can be used for the rollout of corporate Customizing settings and development efforts.

   B. Management of different Repository objects (those developed by the corporate office versus those developed locally) can be managed using namespaces and name ranges for the Repository objects.

   C. Merging the Customizing settings delivered by the corporate office with local Customizing efforts can easily be done using change requests.

   D. SAP provides different tools to aid in the rollout of a global template.

CHAPTER

FOUR

4

Managing Changes and Data in an R/3 System Landscape

Within the R/3 System landscape, you need to be able to transfer both Customizing or development changes and business data from one client or R/3 System to another. This chapter explains the tools and strategies for transferring these changes and data. The first half of the chapter concerns managing and distributing changes using the tools in the *Change and Transport System* (CTS). The second half of the chapter concerns the techniques used to transfer business data—master data, transaction data, and user master data—into R/3 or from one R/3 System or client to another.

Transporting Customizing and Development Changes

The implementation of R/3 requires, at the bare minimum, that you customize the R/3 System using the IMG. Customizing is performed in a client in the development system; transferred to a client in the quality assurance system for testing; and, finally, made available to a client in the production system. Similarly, changes due to development in the ABAP Workbench require organized techniques of distribution from the development system to the quality assurance system and the production system.

Although it is possible to manually reenter the changes in successive systems, this is not a desirable option due to the quantity and complexity of the changes required. Therefore, R/3 enables you to record changes to change requests, which can then be distributed to other clients in the same R/3 System or in another R/3 System.

> **NOTE**   The word "change" is used loosely. It refers to the creation or modification of an R/3 Repository object; a change in the attributes associated with Repository objects; or the addition or modification of entries in tables (as often occurs during Customizing).

Change Requests and Tasks

In R/3, *change requests* and their constituent *tasks* provide the mechanism with which you can record the objects you have changed. When changes to either Customizing objects or Repository objects are made, the changed objects are recorded to a task. A single R/3 user owns each task, which is simply a list of objects changed by that user. Tasks are grouped together into change requests corresponding to specific project objectives.

In addition to listing changed objects, in each task those who customize and develop record their documentation of the change and its purpose. Change requests and tasks provide a complete history of all changes made during R/3 implementation.

Types of Change Requests

Since the software changes created during R/3 implementation are the result of either Customizing or development, there are two types of change requests:

- Customizing change requests
- Workbench change requests

Customizing change requests are used to record only client-specific changes. Since most Customizing activities in the IMG are client-specific changes, they are recorded to Customizing change requests. All client-independent (cross-client) changes are recorded to Workbench change requests. Workbench change requests are used for:

- Client-independent (cross-client) Customizing objects
- All Repository objects created and maintained through the ABAP Workbench

Keep in mind that changes in application and user master data are not recorded to change requests, as depicted in Figure 4.1.

Recording changes to
change requests

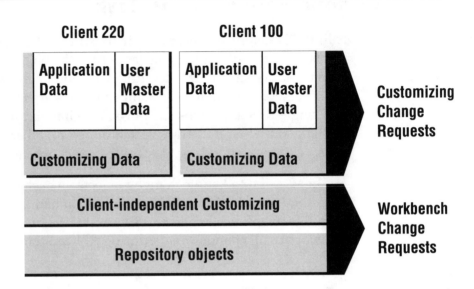

Customizing Changes   Customizing activities in the IMG
must be performed in a client that permits Customizing changes.
To determine whether Customizing changes are permitted in a
particular client, and whether these Customizing changes are automatically recorded to a change request, set the client-dependent
change option (Transaction SCC4) appropriately. (See Chapter 3.)

TIP   To ensure that changes are recorded and can be distributed, SAP recommends that you set the client change option for the Customizing-
and-development client so that Customizing changes are
automatically recorded to change requests.

The IMG guides you through the configuration of business
processes, the recording of changes, and the saving of changes to
change requests. In the *Customizing Organizer* (Transaction SE10),
you can display, create, change, document, and release change

requests. The Customizing Organizer enables you to see which Customizing objects have been changed, and whether they have been released. (See Chapter 11.)

Development Changes   The *Workbench Organizer* (Transaction SE09) enables you to display, create, change, document, and release Workbench change requests. When you make a client-independent change, the change is recorded to a Workbench change request for release and transport to the quality assurance system and eventually the production system. As with Customizing change requests, the actual contents of a change request are recorded in a task corresponding to a specific user. Unlike Customizing changes, development changes can be made only in conjunction with a change request. All client-independent changes must be saved to a change request. Therefore, you do not need to specify *Automatic recording of changes* in the client-dependent change option to have development changes automatically recorded to a change request.

You can permit or disallow the creation or modification of R/3 Repository objects on two levels:

- To permit or disallow changes from any client in the R/3 System, use the system change option (Transaction SE06; *Goto* ➢ *System Change Option*). (See also Chapter 7.)

- To permit or disallow changes from within a specific client, set the appropriate client-independent change option (Transaction SCC4).

Technical Representation of Change Requests and Tasks

The ID number for change requests or tasks begins with the three-character system ID—for example, DEV, followed by K9 and a sequential five-digit number. Thus, DEVK900105 is the 105th change request or task to be created on the R/3 System DEV. The next task or change request created will be DEVK900106.

A project leader who creates change request DEVK900116 assigns two users to the change request. These users are assigned by creating the tasks DEVK900117 and DEVK900118. If, after other change requests are created, the project leader wishes to add another user as a task to this change request, the corresponding task will receive the next available ID number—for example, DEVK900129. Figure 4.2 depicts these examples as they would appear in the Customizing Organizer.

FIGURE 4.2:

The Customizing Organizer displays Customizing change requests and tasks.

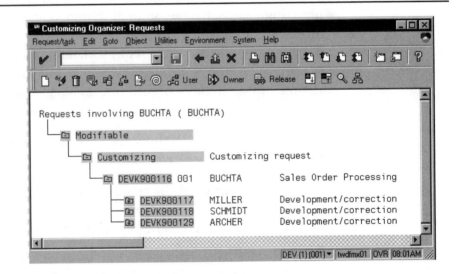

The ID numbers of change requests or tasks reveal only the R/3 System in which each change request or task was created, and the temporal order of creation. Therefore, it is important to maintain the associated title and documentation for later reference.

Promoting Changes

Change requests are simply a collection of tasks that list the different objects in the R/3 database that have changed. This information enables you to update any other client within the system landscape with a new copy of the changed objects. To do this, you use the technical procedure for transport, which consists of two steps: promotion and import. Promoting changes involves releasing changes and then exporting them out of their R/3 System and onto the operating system level; in a further step, they are imported into another R/3 System.

The value of SAP's techniques for promoting and importing changes is the way they enable a system landscape to be kept tidy and orderly. It is only in an orderly landscape that you can know exactly which changes are operative in each system and client, and whether particular clients and R/3 Systems are functionally identical, or in which functions they differ.

When testing new functionality in the quality assurance system, for example, you need to be sure that the quality assurance system differs from the production system only with regard to the new functionality being tested. This ensures that such testing is meaningful. There is no value in testing new functionality in a system whose Customizing settings and programs differ dramatically or to an indeterminate extent from those in the production system. Functionally identical systems are known as *synchronized* systems.

Defining Transport Routes

Before promotion and import can occur, you must define strict *transport routes* between the different R/3 Systems in the system landscape. To define the routes change requests will follow, use the *Transport Management System* (TMS), which is called with Transaction STMS. The TMS is essentially the "traffic cop" of change requests: it centrally monitors the export process to ensure that changes are delivered in the correct order, and notifies you of errors during import.

During R/3 implementation, all clients and systems must be synchronized by defining appropriate and fixed transport routes. Typically, you test and verify changes from the development system in the quality assurance system before importing them to the production system. The appropriate transport routes include a transport route from the development system to the quality assurance system, and a subsequent transport route from the quality assurance system to the production system (see Figure 4.3).

FIGURE 4.3:

Transport routes defined in the TMS for a standard system landscape

Prior to R/3 Release 4.5, the transport routes defined in the TMS could move change requests only from one R/3 System to another R/3 System as depicted in Figure 4.3. As of R/3 Release 4.5, however, a transport route can also be defined from one client to another client by activating *extended transport control*. In the example depicted in Figure 4.4, a change request that is released in the Customizing-and-development client is added to the import queue of both the sandbox client and the quality assurance client. After import to the quality assurance client, the change request is automatically added to the import queues of the training client and the production client.

Client-specific transport routes provided by *extended transport control* in R/3 Release 4.5 allow more control over the delivery of changes, ensuring that changes not only reach all the R/3 Systems but also all clients.

FIGURE 4.4:

Client-specific transport routes within R/3 Release 4.5

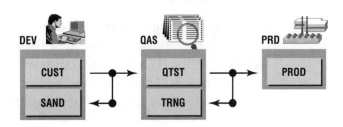

Regardless of whether you transfer your change requests along transport routes defined in terms of clients or in terms of R/3 Systems, the important issue is maintaining consistency. The clients and the R/3 Systems in your system landscape will be synchronized only if all changes are promoted in an orderly way and the import of changes is verified. The TMS provides the necessary tools, but they need to be set up and used properly.

Releasing Changes

Promotion of a collection of changes begins with the release of the change request. To release a change request, each separate task in the change request must be documented and released.

Before you release the objects recorded in a change request, the objects must be tested for internal coherency and effectiveness. This is known as *unit testing* and can be performed in the current client or another client (see also Chapter 3). To perform unit testing in another client, you can use the tool *client copy according to a transp. request* (Transaction SCC1) to copy the contents of a change request (released or not released) to another client within the same R/3 System (see also Chapter 6).

The owner of a task should release the task as soon as it has been completed and unit tested.

Exporting Changes

Releasing a change request initiates the export process. This process is the physical copying of the recorded objects from the database of the R/3 System to files at the operating system level (see Figure 4.5). These files are located in the *transport directory*, which is a file system associated with the R/3 System that can be shared by all R/3 Systems in the system landscape (see also Chapter 7).

A change request is promoted to ensure that its objects reach other clients and systems along the transport route. When the objects in the change request are exported, the change request ID number is automatically added to the *import queue* of the next target client or system, according to the transport route set up in the TMS (see Figure 4.5). The import queue is a list of change requests that have been released and exported and are awaiting import.

FIGURE 4.5:

Exporting a change request

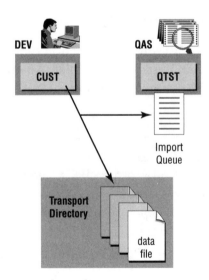

Importing Changes

Importing is the process by which copies of the changed objects listed in a released change request are brought from the transport directory into the database of the target system. The import queue of the target system will have been notified during the export process that a request is ready for import. However, no automatic mechanism imports a change request into the target immediately after export. To trigger and monitor imports into R/3 Systems, use the import queue in the TMS.

The Import Queue

The TMS import queue enables you to determine which change requests have been exported and to ensure that change requests are imported in the same order as they were exported. To access the import queue of a given R/3 System, from the TMS initial screen (Transaction STMS), choose *Overview* ➤ *Imports*. This TMS screen shows all relevant R/3 Systems. To access the import queue of a particular R/3 System, double-click the system name. The import queue is displayed, listing any change requests that are awaiting import.

During an import, files in the transport directory corresponding to each change request are read and copied into the database of the target system. In Figure 4.6, the target system of the development system is the quality assurance system. To examine the various log files generated during the import process, from the import queue screen, choose *Goto* ➤ *TP system log* (for example). The logs will show whether any errors occurred during the import. (See Chapter 13.)

After change requests have been imported successfully, they are deleted from the import queue, and are automatically added to the import queues of the next target clients and systems as defined by the transport route specified in the TMS. Typically, the target

R/3 System after an import to the quality assurance system is the production system.

FIGURE 4.6:

Import to the quality assurance system and delivery to the production system

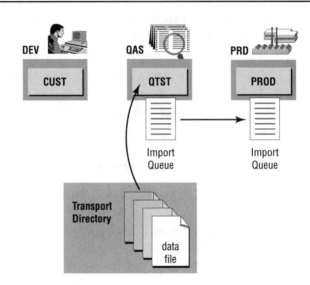

Subsequent imports into R/3 Systems such as the production system are similarly monitored and triggered in the TMS. During these imports, the files corresponding to the change requests in the transport directory are again copied to the database of the target system. By using the same files that were originally exported from the development system and tested in the quality assurance system, the TMS ensures that the same changes are delivered to both R/3 Systems (see Figure 4.7).

FIGURE 4.7:

Importing the same files into the production system

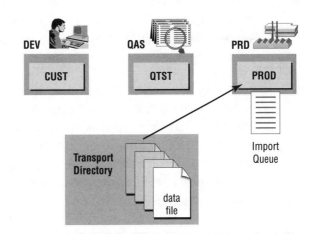

Sequence in Import Queues

Change requests are only lists of changed R/3 objects that need to be promoted and imported to other clients and R/3 Systems. The export of a change request is the process that copies the changed objects in their current state to a file at the operating system level, and simultaneously adds the change request to the relevant import queue as defined by the TMS transport route. The sequence of change requests in the import queue of the respective R/3 System is strictly chronological. The order of change requests in the import queues is always the order in which they were exported.

This sequencing is important. For example, if successive change requests are created to change the same object, when they are released, they will each deposit new versions of the object at the operating system level. Since the change requests in the import queue are processed sequentially, the last import of the object will represent the most recent version.

The import process then ensures that defined delivery systems, such as the production system, receive the change requests in the same order in which they were imported into the quality assurance system.

The significance of the import queues is that they control the order in which changes are imported into an R/3 System. By ensuring that this order is consistent, import queues enable the various R/3 Systems to be functionally synchronized. Import queues track the order in which changes are imported and ensure that changes are not imported into the production system in the wrong sequence.

Example: Sequencing Change Requests in an Import Queue

Two developers at a multinational company receive the assignment to write data conversion programs in the development system—programs that will be used to convert legacy data to match R/3 data requirements.

One developer named Miller creates a program called ZLEGACY_DATA. The new Repository object is recorded in change request DEVK900834. Miller releases the change request. At the same time, other people are releasing change requests containing Customizing settings.

The second developer, whose name is Schmidt, adds additional functionality to the program ZLEGACY_DATA and saves his change to change request DEVK900876. Schmidt then releases the change request.

When it is time to import the changes into the quality assurance system, the import queue of the quality assurance system contains the following change requests (in the order in which they were released):

Change Request	Owner	Description
DEVK900834	MILLER	Conversion routine

Continued on next page

Change Request	Owner	Description
DEVK900912	HAMM	Customizing for Materials Management
DEVK900820	THOMAS	Organizational data
DEVK900876	SCHMIDT	Conversion routine with validation loop

Two change requests, DEVK900834 and DEVK900876, recorded changes to the program ZLEGACY_DATA. Therefore, the transport directory contains two different versions of the program. If change request DEVK900876 is imported before the import of DEVK900834, the program ZLEGACY_DATA in the quality assurance system will not have the additional functionality provided by Schmidt. The program in the quality assurance system would then differ from that in the development system, and the two systems would be inconsistent.

By having the imports occur in the order indicated in the import queue, the developers ensure that DEVK900834 is imported first, since it was released before DEVK900876. Program ZLEGACY_DATA is imported twice, but the final import, which overwrites its predecessor, is the current version. This helps to ensure consistency between the different R/3 Systems.

Manipulating Import Queues

Within the TMS, users are able to manipulate import queues to add or delete change requests, or to change the order in which they appear in the queue. However, SAP does not recommend such activities, since they may create inconsistencies between the source system and the target system.

Users often wish to delete a change request because it contains incorrect information. However, deleting a change request may delete more than the incorrect data, since change requests typically contain more than one change. In addition, deleting a change request may make the objects in another change request fail, due to a dependency on the objects in the deleted change request. For example, if you delete a change request containing a new data element, all other transported objects containing tables that refer to that data element will fail.

To avoid these inconsistencies, you are strongly advised against manipulating import queues. It is more prudent to make the necessary corrections in the development system and release a new request.

TIP   SAP recommends that you do not manipulate an import queue. For example, you should not delete change requests or alter the sequence in the queue.

Technical Aspects of the Transport Process

The program *tp* resides on the operating system level and controls both the export and import process. It is responsible for reading the change requests in the import queues and making adjustments to the import queues after completion of successful imports. The TMS import functionality is the user-friendly interface that communicates from within R/3 with the transport control program *tp*.

Another relevant program is *R3trans*. To accomplish an export, *tp* triggers another tool on the operating system level called *R3trans*. *R3trans* creates the operating system data file for the export. During import, *R3trans* reuses this data file. *R3trans* is used to communicate with the R/3 database to read or insert data.

Change and Transport System (CTS)

SAP refers collectively to the tools that support change management as the Change and Transport System (CTS). These tools include:

- The Change and Transport Organizer (CTO)

  The CTO consists of the Customizing Organizer, the Workbench Organizer, and the *Transport Organizer*. The most frequently used component is the Customizing Organizer. The Customizing Organizer enables the creation, documentation, and release of change requests generated during Customizing. It enables the people implementing R/3 to track their changes to change requests, and then view the change requests for which they are responsible and make the changes available to other systems by releasing the change requests. The Workbench Organizer provides similar functionality for developers using the ABAP Workbench. The Transport Organizer then provides support for the transports that do not fall within the realm of the Customizing Organizer and the Workbench Organizer.

- The Transport Management System (TMS)

  You use the TMS (Transaction STMS) to organize, monitor, and perform imports for all R/3 Systems within a system landscape. For example, you use the TMS to import change requests into the quality assurance system for testing and verification. In addition, you use the TMS to centrally manage the setup of your transport environment by adding R/3 Systems and defining transport routes.

- The programs *tp* and *R3trans*

  These are executables on the operating system level used to communicate with the R/3 System, the database, and the files in the transport directory necessary for the export and import processes. For example, when you import the objects in a change request into the quality assurance system, *R3trans* copies the data to the database of that system.

The CTS comprises all the tools required to support R/3 change and transport management (see Figure 4.8).

FIGURE 4.8:

The components of the CTS

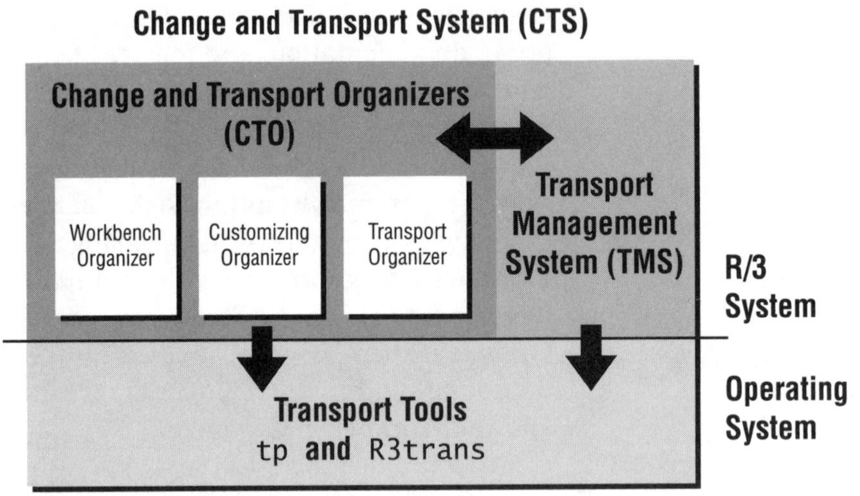

Change and Transport System (CTS)

Change and Transport Organizers (CTO)

| Workbench Organizer | Customizing Organizer | Transport Organizer |

Transport Management System (TMS)

R/3 System

Transport Tools
tp **and** R3trans

Operating System

Transferring Data

Change requests do not transport application data such as master data, transaction data, and user master data. That you would have to distribute this type of data may surprise you. After all, this data is required for production activities, and there is only one production client in most system landscapes. However, you may need to distribute business data to perform:

- Functionality testing and end-user training

  Master data is required for both unit testing in the unit test client in the development system and testing in the quality assurance system. For example, when you test the creation of sales orders, the database needs to contain at least one specified material that a customer can purchase. Ideally, the entire material master list should be available. This is especially the case for quality assurance testing and end-user training.

- R/3 report testing

  To test most reports (for example, month-end closing reports) data from multiple business transactions is required—that is, data from various business processing scenarios.

- Authorization assignment testing

  Quality assurance testing includes testing authorization assignment for certain users and also for randomly selected users. The test system therefore requires user master data. To avoid having to manually re-create users in the quality assurance system, you may wish to transfer existing user master data from the production system.

- Production data replication

  Complex system landscapes, such as those found in companies with international subsidiaries, often contain more than one production R/3 System. To ensure the consistency of application data across such a landscape, you may need to ensure that the various production systems are synchronized as to master data records such as customer master data, or transaction data such as financial transaction data.

During the initial and subsequent implementation phases, you may need to transfer application data for unit testing, quality assurance testing, and training. After going live—that is, after work begins in the production system—you may need to transfer application data to synchronize multiple production environments or to share application data with other computer systems.

Transferring business data to different clients is not as straightforward as transferring changes that can be recorded to change requests. The methods used vary according to whether you wish to:

- Transfer application data
- Share application data with other R/3 Systems, R/2 Systems, or non-SAP computer systems

Whether you need to distribute and the methods for distribution of application data should be determined early in the R/3 implementation process.

Master Data

Master data is a type of application data that changes infrequently, but is required for the completion of most business transactions. Examples of master data include lists of customers, vendors, and materials, and even the company's chart of accounts. Master data usually exists in an organization prior to the introduction of R/3. Before implementing R/3, you need to determine how to import the data into R/3. Ideally, the method used for the initial migration can also be used to subsequently transfer the data between R/3 clients.

Since master data changes over time, you must also consider how to provide for data transfer across all your clients to maintain the consistency of master data within the landscape.

Importing Master Data into R/3

Master data can be imported into R/3 from non-R/3 Systems using the following techniques:

- Manually entering each data item
- Loading the data from sequential data files outside R/3
- Communicating with other SAP or non-SAP systems through various interface technologies

To save time and ensure consistency, you should import master data either through data loads from external data files or through interface technology. These techniques enable you to supply copies or subsets of the master data to multiple clients. Manual data entry may be more cost-effective for some implementations, since data loading and interface technology can be handled only by someone with programming knowledge or R/3 interface experience. However, manual entry is not an efficient way of distributing data to multiple clients.

NOTE   When importing data by loading it from files outside R/3, SAP provides the Data Transfer Workbench and the Legacy System Migration Workbench to help you plan and develop programs to perform your data transfer. For more information on these tools, refer to R/3 online documentation.

Transferring Master Data between R/3 Systems

Although master data is relatively static, it will change over time. You need to determine whether changes to master data in the production system will be distributed to all clients in your system landscape. You also need to determine how frequently this synchronization process is required—that is, whether a large delay is acceptable. Master data can be transferred by:

- Manually entering each data item

- Using change requests (only possible for some types of master data)

- Using interface technologies

Manual data entry may be an adequate method for transferring master data to R/3 clients other than the R/3 client in the production system. It isn't necessary, for example, to make known a customer's change of address to the quality assurance client, since a change in the details of an address will not affect general business processing. However, if new customers are added to the production system, they can be manually entered into the quality assurance system to ensure their inclusion in testing.

Some master data is transferred using change requests in conjunction with special IMG activities. Examples of this type of master data include the chart of accounts, material groups, and cost accounting areas.

SAP also provides extensive interface technologies that support the transfer of master data. One such technology is *Application Link Enabling* (ALE), which enables you to exchange data between R/3 Systems or between R/3 Systems and R/2 Systems or non-SAP programs. ALE is the technology that is most frequently used to support master data in an environment with multiple production clients, or where master data is required to be identical in more than one client. When you use ALE, master data can be either:

- Managed centrally and distributed to other clients when necessary (as is the case in Figure 4.9, where master data is distributed from the R/3 System PR1 to clients in system QAS and PR2)

- Managed in different clients and then transferred to a central client and distributed from there to all other clients

---

FIGURE 4.9:

An example of ALE data exchange between different R/3 Systems

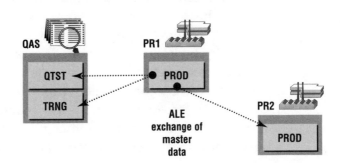

To help you implement ALE, SAP provides preconfigured master data templates known as *ALE scenarios*, which you can adapt to meet your specific master data needs. Examples of ALE scenarios for master data include scenarios for materials, vendors, customers, profit centers, chart of accounts, bill of materials, and cost centers. ALE is not limited to master data—it can also be used to distribute transaction data.

In principle, you can use ALE to distribute master data freely between all R/3 Systems. However, a certain degree of common Customizing is required in the target systems. R/3's *ALE Customizing Distribution* enables you to ensure that the Customizing settings related to ALE scenarios are identical on the different R/3 Systems in the system landscape.

NOTE   For more information on ALE Customizing Distribution, refer to the R/3 online documentation. For more information on ALE, see Chapter 13 in Liane Will's *SAP R/3 System Administration* (from Sybex).

Transaction Data

Transaction data is shared across different computer systems—for example, for testing, training, or multiple production environments. These systems can be other R/3 Systems, R/2 Systems, or non-SAP systems. Transferring the data requires a communication link using interface technology. Transaction data distribution is complex because of transaction data's high volume, its dependency on the Customizing environment, and its need for master data. These factors mean transaction data cannot simply be transferred from one client to another, nor is there a way to extract a subset of transaction data from one client and distribute it to another.

You must carefully consider how sample transaction data will be made available in different clients for testing and training. Since transaction data is altered during testing and training, you may need to delete and replace all transaction data for each successive test or training course.

Creating Sample Transaction Data

Sample transaction data will be required in the quality assurance and training clients in your system landscape. Users can manually create this data during testing or training. However, manual data creation is tedious if testers require many completed transactions—for example, when testing month-end financial reports. SAP recommends that you develop scripts to generate standard sets of transaction data. These scripts can evolve over time to generate data reflecting new functionalities, and can also be used to test existing business processes in *regression testing*. (See Chapter 6.)

A general example of a script is one that creates 20 production orders for a specific plant. If necessary, this script can be copied and altered for all other plants. The data produced by the script is used for testing new versions of the production-planning functionality. During every rollout cycle for this functionality, the script and its data can be altered and used for testing the way in which the new functionality will impact production operations.

SAP's *Computer Aided Test Tool* (CATT) provides scripting tools. CATT allows you to combine and automate business processes as repeatable test procedures and use them to generate sample data. CATT can also simulate transaction results, analyze the results of database updates, and monitor the impact of changes in Customizing settings.

> **NOTE** In addition to CATT, other scripting and testing tools can be obtained from manufacturers certified in SAP's Complementary Software Program.

Interfaces for Transaction Data

SAP's open interface provides several methods and tools for communication between different types of computer systems (see Figure 4.10). In regard to transaction data, you can create interfaces to:

- Distribute transaction data from one R/3 client to another
- Import existing transaction data from a non-R/3 System into the R/3 System
- Distribute transaction data to non-SAP systems

FIGURE 4.10:

Possible interfaces for sharing application data

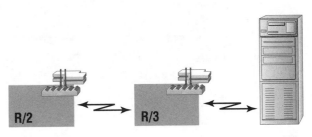

non-SAP

To help you plan and realize your interfaces, SAP provides the *R/3 Interface Advisor Knowledge Product* on CD-ROM. The Interface Advisor introduces different scenarios that help you decide which interfaces you require for business processing, which interface technology you should use, and how each interface should be designed.

NOTE   To get a copy of the *Interface Advisor Knowledge Product* CD-ROM, access the Internet site `http://sapnet.sap.com/int-adviser`. For more information on planning and implementing interface technologies, see Chapter 13 of Hartwig Brand's *SAP R/3 Implementation with ASAP* (from Sybex). For more information on the support and management of data distribution between different SAP Systems and non-SAP Systems, see Chapter 13 of Liane Will's *SAP R/3 System Administration* (also from Sybex).

Example: Using ALE with Multiple Production Systems

Large organizations often require centralization of financial data. Producing millions of sales orders every day conflicts with the management's need for timely reports and with the needs of the finance department. A large computer component supplier decides that while the Customizing and development of the different function modules is possible in a single development system, multiple production systems are required. The production system SAL is used for all sales order entry and processing. A second production system, FIN, is used for financial and accounting data.

To configure R/3 for multiple production systems, the company must determine which master data must be shared among the different systems, and how this master data will be shared. The company decides to set up an enterprise reference data "library" to centrally manage all master data. This

Continued on next page

requires yet another production R/3 System, MDR, for the sole purpose of managing master data. ALE is used to transfer master data changes to FIN and SAL.

ALE is also used to share other data between the different production systems. For example, when a sales order is entered in SAL, ALE is used to make the customer's credit information from FIN available to SAL. To ensure that management reports are up to date, ALE enables sales information to be transferred from SAL to FIN, and accounting information to be transferred from FIN to SAL.

All the production environments receive changes originating in the same Customizing and development system, DEV. The company's system landscape and ALE strategy can be represented as follows:

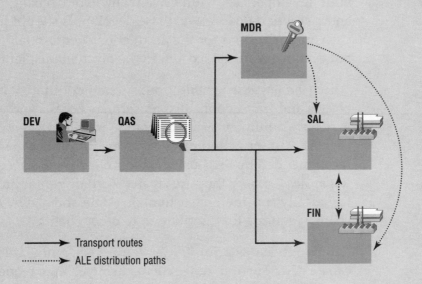

User Master Data

User master data includes the data used by the R/3 System to validate a user's ID at logon and assign user access rights based on passwords and authorization profiles. User master data also includes the user's name, phone number, and default printers, and the default screen the user will see after completing logon.

User master data is a type of master data—much like material master data and vendor master data. User master data is client-specific data. SAP separates user master data from other types of application data because user master data must be different in different clients, even if master data is the same. For example, in the development client, you must give extensive authorizations to your developers so that they can view tables, change programs, and test reports. However, these developers should not receive such authorizations for the production client. In fact, they may not even need a user account in the production client.

Each *authorization profile* groups together different business objects and transactions that a user may access, and each user may have a number of authorization profiles assigned to their user ID. Authorization profiles are created either manually or, as recommended by SAP, using a tool called the *Profile Generator*. Regardless of how they are created, authorization profiles are technically considered Customizing data and can be recorded to change requests for distribution to other clients.

In R/3 Releases prior to R/3 Release 4.5, authorization profiles can be distributed to other clients using change requests, while user master data—including the authorization profiles assigned to the user ID—cannot be transported using change requests. The definition of authorizations is managed in a central location such as the Customizing-and-development client. The user master data is separately maintained in each client to ensure that users have different authorizations in each client and that specific clients are reserved for specific activities.

In R/3 Releases prior to R/3 Release 4.5, if you need to have the same user master data and the same authorization profiles in two clients, you must perform a client copy that copies only user data. This procedure copies the user master data and authorization profiles from one client to another. However, this requires that all users be distributed to another client, rather than just some of the users.

As of R/3 Release 4.5, you can manage user data and authorization profiles in your system landscape centrally using *Central User Administration*. This allows you to maintain all R/3 users in a single client and assign the user IDs to other R/3 clients in the system landscape with the same or different authorizations. Authorizations can be assigned either centrally or locally in each client, as required. Central User Administration simplifies user management and system security by allowing you to globally change a user's data.

NOTE   For more information on how to set up and use Central User Administration, refer to the R/3 online documentation for R/3 Release 4.5.

Copying R/3 Systems and Clients

Repeatedly, the following question is asked: "Why must I record all my changes to change requests—can't I just periodically copy the development system or the Customizing-and-development client?"

The answer to this question is that, technically, you can always copy an R/3 System or even a client. However, the result may create extra work or even cause chaos in your system landscape. While copies of R/3 Systems and clients have their advantages, they should be used only to set up or create a system or client. A copy of a system or a client does not help you maintain your existing system landscape because it completely overwrites the target system or client, and eliminates all application data.

SAP recommends using change requests to record Customizing and development changes, so that these changes can be distributed to all systems and clients without deleting existing application data.

System Copy

A copy of an R/3 System is called a *system copy* and is used to create an identical copy of an existing R/3 System. A system copy is sometimes referred to as a database copy, because you are copying the database of one R/3 System to another R/3 System. A system copy copies everything from the source database, including all clients, all Repository objects, and all data such as transaction data.

SAP does not recommend using system copies to set up critical systems, such as the quality assurance system or the production system (see Chapter 5). However, a system copy is useful when you need an exact copy of an R/3 System for a limited scope and a limited time frame, or when you need to establish another non-critical R/3 System in your system landscape. For example, to set up an R/3 System for training purposes, you may wish to use a copy of the quality assurance system. Alternatively, you may wish to make a copy of the production system to use as a temporary system for simulating data archiving routines.

Often, customers make a copy of the production system to set up a quality assurance system with good production data. They believe that a copy of production data is the easiest way to provide for a true quality assurance environment, or even to rebuild a development system. While this may be technically true, remember that since the size of the production system grows dramatically as more and more transaction data is collected, the cost of hardware required to support a copy of the production system may render such a copy unfeasible. For large production systems, consider the alternative methods of transferring business data previously discussed in this chapter.

Avoid using a copy of the production system to create the development system, as you will lose all data stored in the development system. This includes your Enterprise IMG, Project IMGs, and associated project documentation with your change history in the form of change requests and version histories of Repository objects.

NOTE For technical details on how to perform a system copy, see the White Paper "R/3 Homogenous System Copy" available at the Internet address **www.sapnet.com** from the Support Service's *Installation/ Upgrade Guides* page.

Client Copy

SAP's client copy tools enable you to copy one client to another client in the same or a different R/3 System. Whenever you use client copy (except when copying user master data or a single change request), the target client is deleted prior to copying the source client.

Like a system copy, a client copy is useful for creating a client, but generally cannot be used to maintain a client. Because the target client is deleted prior to copying data from the source client, client copy does not provide a way of merging the source client with the target client. Client copy enables you to copy application data that cannot be transferred using change requests. (See also Chapters 5 and 9.)

Review Questions

1. Which of the following statements is correct in regard to Customizing and development changes?

    A. All changes are recorded to tasks in Customizing change requests.

    B. The changes should be recorded to tasks in change requests for transport to other clients and systems.

    C. The changes must be manually performed in every R/3 System.

    D. The changes can easily be made simultaneously in multiple clients.

2. Which of the following statements in regard to change requests is FALSE?

    A. The Customizing Organizer and the Workbench Organizer are tools used to view, create, and manage change requests.

    B. A change request is a collection of tasks where developers and people performing Customizing record the changes they make.

    C. All changes made as a result of IMG activities are recorded to Customizing change requests.

    D. SAP recommends setting your R/3 System so that Customizing changes made in the Customizing-and-development client are automatically recorded to change requests.

3. For which of the following activities is the TMS (Transaction STMS) *not* designed?

    A. Releasing change requests

    B. Viewing import queues

    C. Viewing log files generated by both the export process and the import process

    D. Initiating the import process

4. Which of the following statements is correct after you have successfully imported change requests into the quality assurance system?

    A. The change requests must be released again to be exported to the production system.

    B. The data files containing the changed objects are deleted from the transport directory.

    C. The change requests need to be manually added to the import queue of the production system.

    D. The change requests are automatically added to the import queue of the production system.

5. Which of the following statements is correct in regard to the change requests in an import queue?

    A. They are sequenced according to their change request number.

    B. They are sequenced in the order in which they were exported from the development system.

    C. They are sequenced according to the name of the user who released the requests.

    D. They are not sequenced by default, but arranged in a variety of ways using the TMS.

6. Which of the following techniques can be used to transfer application data between two production systems?

    A. Recording transaction data to change requests

    B. Using ALE to transfer application data

    C. Using the client copy tool

    D. All of the above

7. Which of the following types of data transfer are possible with an appropriate use of interface technologies?

    A. Transferring legacy data to an R/3 System

    B. Transferring data between R/3 clients

    C. Transferring data to non-SAP systems

    D. Transporting change requests to multiple R/3 Systems

8. Which of the following statements is correct in regard to user master data?

    A. User master data can be transported in a change request.

    B. User master data is unique to each R/3 System, but is shared across clients in the same R/3 System.

    C. A specific client copy option enables you to distribute user master data together with authorization profile data.

    D. User master data includes all user logon information, including the definition of authorizations and profiles.

Setting Up a System Landscape

The strategy you use to set up your system landscape determines how all the R/3 Systems in your system landscape will be created and how they will receive Customizing settings and development changes. This chapter outlines the various setup steps—taking you from the initial installation of the development system, through the setup of the quality assurance system, and finally to the production system. The focus will be on how Customizing and development changes are properly transferred throughout the landscape.

Ideally, you should set up your system landscape using change requests. However, since change requests cannot always be used to support the setup of your critical clients, the client copy strategy is a viable alternative. In rare cases, using a system copy may prove an appropriate method for creating your quality assurance system and possibly the production system. The advantages and disadvantages of these different strategies are outlined in this chapter.

Setting Up the Development System

Every R/3 implementation begins with the installation of one initial R/3 System. Since those individuals in charge of Customizing and development will be anxious to begin configuring R/3 to meet your company's different business needs, this first R/3 System is typically your development system. This is the system where all changes to the R/3 software—both Customizing and development—originate.

Before you make changes to the software, you must ensure that the environment has been properly prepared and is ready for changes to take place. Once you begin making changes to the R/3 software, you must record them to change requests to allow for their transport.

Post-Installation Processing

After the installation process is complete, you may need to perform any or all of the following activities collectively known as *post-installation processing*:

Languages: The R/3 System delivered by SAP supports two languages, English and German. If your implementation requires additional languages, you need to install them at this time. A language import inserts language-specific text into the standard client 000. For example, if you import the languages French and Spanish after installation, these languages will be available in client 000. To add these additional languages to your other clients, use the Language Transport Utility (Transaction SMLT).

Industry solutions: To fulfill the unique needs of different industries or business solutions and to help accelerate the Customizing process, R/3's product line includes different industry solutions, such as SAP Automotive, SAP Banking, and SAP Oil & Gas. These types of solutions provide customers with additional R/3 functionality by adding special Repository objects to the R/3 System.

Support Packages: SAP provides Support Packages, also known as patches, to remedy any possible programming errors. Support Packages are bundles of corrections in the Repository of the R/3 software. Before you start Customizing and development activities, SAP recommends applying all available and relevant Support Packages to your development system.

You should document all of these post-installation activities. You want to use the same setup procedure for the quality assurance and production systems. The documentation will assist you when establishing these critical R/3 Systems or any other system within the landscape.

Setting Up the Transport Management System (TMS)

The Transport Management System, as its name implies, enables you to manage the transport process for all R/3 Systems within your system landscape. The TMS ensures that all R/3 Systems share the same transport configuration. This uniformity allows changes to be promoted and delivered to the right clients and systems in the correct order. Without the TMS, you will not be able to save changes to change requests for transport to other R/3 Systems.

After installing an R/3 System, your next task is to set up its TMS (Transaction STMS). This allows you to define the role of the system in your landscape. Since the development system is typically the first R/3 System installed, it is also used to define the system landscape and the other R/3 Systems that will eventually be supported with the same changes and transport process.

Most importantly, you use the TMS to indicate which system is the target for changes promoted from your development system. For example, if you have a three-system landscape, changes from the development system are transferred to the quality assurance system. The TMS helps you create the transport route between the development and quality assurance systems. In a two-system landscape, the transport route leads directly from the development system to the production system.

In many implementations, the quality assurance system is not installed or does not even physically exist until much later in the process. However, you still need to establish a transport route to connect it with the development system. Without this transport route, you cannot create change requests for later release to the quality assurance system. You need a placeholder for the quality assurance system. This *virtual system* is created using the TMS. This procedure requires that you provide a three-character alphanumeric system ID for the virtual system. You should also create a virtual system to represent your production system. For more details on setting up the TMS, including information on creating virtual systems and defining transport routes, see Chapter 8.

Although it is possible to later change the name of the development and quality assurance systems (or the production system), SAP recommends that you maintain the same system IDs throughout your R/3 implementation. It is important to keep the relationship between the development and quality assurance systems consistent and the transport route invariant for the following reasons:

- Change requests for Customizing by default cannot export data from the development system without an established target system. The standard transport route defined for the development system determines the target system.

- Customer development objects can be created only for a particular development class. Each development class is associated with a transport layer. The transport layer in turn depends on a transport route to identify the location of the change request after release and export.

Changes are moved from one R/3 System to another according to the relationships established by the transport route. Changing an R/3 system name and/or transport route will therefore impact existing and future change requests.

Creating Clients

Once you have set up the TMS, you can begin creating clients in the development system. After installation, an R/3 System contains the SAP-standard clients 000, 001, and 066. SAP reserves clients 000 and 066 for maintenance and support, leaving client 001 for your implementation process. Client 001 can function as your Customizing-and-development client, known as CUST.

However, client 001 may not contain the settings established during post-installation processing, such as imported languages. You must integrate all additional settings into this client using tools provided by SAP. Alternatively, you can copy client 000 to create a new client that contains all of the post-installation settings. This copy will ensure consistent settings throughout the system, and allows you to preserve client 001 as it was delivered by SAP. Retaining clients 000 and 001 provides you with a reference for comparing your changes in subsequently created clients with the SAP standard.

TIP   SAP recommends that you create a new client as a copy of client 000 for Customizing and development efforts.

Procedure

To create a client within R/3, follow these steps:

1. Access *client maintenance* (Transaction SCC4).

2. Define the client with a three-digit client number and text description.

3. Select the client's role, restrictions, and client change options. Once this new client has been defined, you can log on to it with the special R/3 user SAP*.

Your brand-new client does not contain the data necessary for performing Customizing. This data consists of basic Customizing settings and language data. Neither does the new client have the SAP-standard user authorizations needed to create additional users: SAP-standard authorizations and profiles. After using client maintenance to define the new client, you need to perform a *client copy* to copy the contents of client 000 into the new client. A client copy transfers the user data and Customizing data that currently exist in client 000 to the new client.

NOTE For more details on how to use client maintenance and client copy, see Chapter 9.

SAP recommends including a unit test client (TEST) in your system landscape so that you can evaluate new Customizing settings and developments using sample application data. You may also consider creating a sandbox client (SAND) to allow the people performing Customizing to experiment with settings. Use client copies of client 000 to create both the unit test and the sandbox clients (see Figure 5.1).

FIGURE 5.1:

Creating new clients in the development system

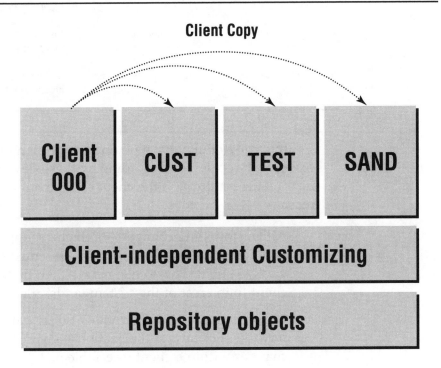

Client Copy

Client 000   CUST   TEST   SAND

Client-independent Customizing

Repository objects

Setting the Client Change Options

Before starting Customizing and development, you must set the client change options for the different clients that you have created. For the development system, SAP recommends setting the client change options in Transaction SCC4 as indicated in Table 5.1.

TABLE 5.1: Recommended Client Change Settings

Client	Client-Dependent Change Option	Client-Independent Change Option
Customizing and development (CUST)	Automatic recording of changes	Changes to Repository and client-independent Customizing allowed
Unit test (TEST)	No changes allowed	No changes to Repository and client-independent objects allowed
Sandbox (SAND)	No transports allowed	No changes to Repository and client-independent objects allowed

Although you may have planned your own unique system landscape, SAP recommends abiding by these development system restrictions set through the client change options for the following reasons:

- All Customizing changes—both client-dependent and client-independent Customizing changes—must originate in a single R/3 client. These changes are then distributed from this client to the rest of the system landscape.

- Client change options provide a solid wall of protection—regardless of user authorizations—by restricting the possible changes within a client (see Table 5.1). You should limit the number of people with the authority to alter client settings.

Recording Changes Automatically

SAP recommends that you use automatic recording of all changes to change requests for your CUST client. Occasionally, customers question the importance of this procedure, thinking that it is tedious and slows down their Customizing work. Nonetheless, changes should be recorded to change requests consistently from the beginning of your R/3 implementation. This provides the following benefits:

- A documented history of the changes to different Customizing settings, including who made them and when they were made.

- A mechanism that copies changes to other clients in the same R/3 System prior to the release of the change request. The contents of a change request can be unit tested, modified if necessary, and verified before the actual release of the change request. (See Chapter 12.)

- A method ensuring that all changes originate in one client and are systematically transported to other clients in the system landscape.

- Project management through the allocation of change requests to teams for the completion of different parts of the Customizing project.

You can track Customizing changes by activating *table logging*. Table logging records the changes made to many tables and Customizing settings. (See Chapter 9.) Table logging does not, however, provide a method to document and distribute changes. You can also successfully set up clients and systems without automatically saving all changes to change requests. However, you *cannot* maintain clients within a system landscape over time without change requests. There is no other alternative for supplying existing clients with the most recent Customizing changes.

Since all people performing Customizing will eventually need to save changes to change requests to maintain existing clients and systems, you should train them to use change requests early in the implementation process. Changing procedures and providing training in the middle of an implementation is awkward. At such a time, concerns will involve testing and completing business functionality and not learning to work with change requests.

TIP   To obtain a complete history of all changes made and to simplify your implementation process and future client maintenance, SAP recommends recording all changes to change requests from the very beginning of your R/3 implementation.

Setting Up the Quality Assurance and Production Systems

Eventually, you will reach a point when you are ready to test the entire R/3 System equipped with your Customizing and development changes. To run this *integration* testing, you will need to set up the quality assurance system. Keep in mind that you also need to start planning for the production system. The quality assurance system acts as your proving ground for production activities. Setting up and testing the quality assurance system ensures that, subsequently, the production system as well as the procedure for setting it up will function properly.

There are different methods for setting up—transferring Customizing and development changes to—the quality assurance and production systems. SAP recommends using change requests to move Customizing and development changes from the development system to the quality assurance system. Another alternative, the client copy strategy, is also available. Each method has certain advantages and disadvantages.

TIP   SAP recommends that you use the same techniques to set up both your quality assurance and production systems. This is a safeguard for the production system and ensures consistency between the two environments.

After Installing the New R/3 System

Before using the change request or client copy techniques to distribute Customizing and development changes, you need to install the R/3 System that is to become your quality assurance system or production system. Both systems require the same post-installation support that was necessary for the development system. You need to provide the systems with the necessary Support Packages, industry solutions, and languages. After completing the post-installation processing, you can begin setting up the TMS and creating the required clients.

Setting Up the TMS

Regardless of how you will subsequently set up the quality assurance system and production systems, after they are installed, you first need to set up the Transport Management System. The TMS allows you to import change requests into the quality assurance system and ensures that these change requests are also delivered to the production system.

Ideally, your quality assurance and production systems, though not physically present until this point in time, have already been represented in the TMS by placeholders. In other words, virtual systems have been used to define the two systems. Since these virtual systems do not contain any technical details, they need to be deleted before you can continue with the TMS setup on your installed quality assurance or production systems. The TMS includes the new R/3 Systems and their technical settings in the system landscape. (See Chapter 8.)

TIP

Before importing the first change request into the quality assurance system, you must represent the production system in the TMS, either as a virtual system or, if it exists, as the installed system. A transport route from the quality assurance to production system must be active.

As changes are imported into the quality assurance system, the import queue of the production system also receives notice of the changes. The objective is to ensure that those steps used to create the quality assurance system are recorded and then replicated to create the production system—this includes the import of all change requests in the exact order in which they were applied.

Creating Required Clients

The quality assurance system requires at least one client, the quality assurance test client (QTST). The production system, in turn, needs the production client (PROD). To import changes or clients from the development system into these clients, you must first create the QTST and PROD clients in their respective systems.

The procedure for creating the QTST and PROD clients is the same as the procedure used for creating the Customizing-and-development client. Using client maintenance, you define the client by providing it with a client number and description as well as selecting its role, restrictions, and client change options. The quality assurance and production clients should both be protected against changes by setting the client change options to *No changes allowed* and *No changes to Repository objects and client-independent Customizing*. For additional protection or to use

Current settings (see Chapter 11), you can assign the production client the client role *Production*.

Before you can supply the newly created client with the latest Customizing settings and developments using change requests, you must use a client copy tool to copy the contents of an existing client into the new one. To ensure consistency, the QTST and PROD clients are created in the same manner as you created the CUST client—that is, by making a copy of client 000.

Change Request Strategy

SAP recommends using change requests to set up your quality assurance system and ultimately your production system. In this way, you can ensure that only those changes promoted or released from the development system are imported into the quality assurance and production systems. Change requests also provide you with a methodical process for adding business functionality to an R/3 System after realizing that functionality in a development environment.

Requirements

To set up your quality assurance system using change requests, you must have saved all Customizing changes made in the development system to change requests. This is the single requirement for using this setup strategy. If you follow SAP's recommendations regarding the client-dependent change options when setting up your CUST client, your changes are automatically recorded to change requests from the beginning of your implementation. An incomplete recording of Customizing change requests results in only partial functionality in the quality assurance system. There is no easy method for transporting changes that were not recorded; instead, the changes have to be manually assigned to change requests through the respective IMG Customizing activity.

TIP	If a large number of changes made in your Customizing-and-development client were not recorded to change requests, do not use the change request strategy to set up your quality assurance and production systems. Use a client copy.

Procedure

Before and during the installation of your quality assurance system, you record changes to change requests and unit test functionality in the development system. By releasing and exporting the change requests, you cause the changes to be copied to files at the operating system level. There, they are added to the import queue of the quality assurance system. Once you have copied the contents of client 000 into the quality assurance client and selected the appropriate client change options, the changes in the import queue of the quality assurance system can be imported into the system itself.

After the change requests are successfully imported into the quality assurance system, they continue along any other defined transport routes. The next transport route typically leads from the quality assurance system to the production system. After the changes are imported into the quality assurance system, they are also delivered to the import queue of the production system. Eventually, you will import the same changes into the production system, in the same order as they were imported into the quality assurance system.

Figure 5.2 shows the steps involved in setting up a system landscape using the change request strategy. This setup strategy is actually the same method you will use later to maintain the system landscape: Changes are released and exported from the development system, imported into the quality assurance system for verification, and then imported into the production system.

FIGURE 5.2:

Setting up a system landscape using change requests

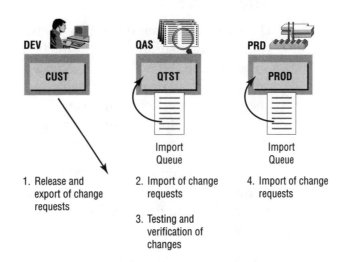

1. Release and export of change requests

2. Import of change requests

3. Testing and verification of changes

4. Import of change requests

At this stage in the implementation procedure, your quality assurance client (and perhaps your production client) contains the latest Customizing settings and developments transported from the development. However, the client contains no application data or user data. Unless you specifically transport user data or manually create users in the client itself, only the default SAP user is defined in this client. Your next step is to verify user accounts and authorizations. Also, since the client has no application data, it also has no master data. Master data will be needed in quality assurance for validation to take place. Ultimately, master data will be needed in the production client prior to the start of production activities.

NOTE   For solutions on how to manage master data within a system landscape, see Chapter 4.

Advantages

The most significant advantage of using change requests to set up your quality assurance and production systems is that this strategy is identical to the maintenance strategy. No additional training or procedures will be required before or after the start of production. The procedures defined during project preparation and system setup are valid for the entire implementation cycle, future upgrades, and the addition of any new business functionality.

The other main advantage of using change requests is that this strategy provides project control and management. It allows the project leader to improve the efficiency of the implementation project by:

- Assigning different tasks or activities to individuals

- Bundling a collection of tasks into one or several change requests

- Ensuring that Customizing and development work has been unit tested before it is released

These steps provide the project leader with an up-to-date overview of the configuration and ensure that only completed Customizing units are transported for quality assurance testing.

Client Copy Strategy

Although SAP recommends that you use change requests to set up your system landscape, the change request strategy can be used only when most (ideally *all*) changes made in the source client have been saved to change requests. If you are unsure whether this has been done in your implementation, SAP recommends an alternative for the setup of your quality assurance client and eventually your production client—the client copy strategy.

Requirements

Before beginning the client copy procedure, you must have installed the quality assurance or production system, completed all post-installation processing, and defined the required quality assurance or production clients. There is no need to copy the contents of client 000 into the new clients. Instead, you will transmit data into the new client using a client copy of the Customizing-and-development client, CUST.

Procedure

The setup procedure using the client copy strategy consists of the following steps:

1. Import change requests that have already been released.

2. Begin a *client transport* by exporting data in the source client CUST from the database of the development system to files at the operating system level.

3. Import the files at the operating system level into the target client, providing it with a copy of the data found in the original client.

4. Perform post-import activities with Transaction SCC7. (See Chapter 9.)

Any change requests with new developments must be imported into the new client before commencing with the client transport. A *client transport* (Transaction SCC8) is a special type of client copy used to set up your critical R/3 Systems. The client transport corresponds to steps 2 through 4 above. It makes use of standard transport functionality; that is, data is exported to files at the operating system level and then imported into the target client.

Several client copy tools are available, including a client transport or a *remote client copy* (Transaction SCC9). A remote client copy employs *Remote Function Calls* (RFCs) to transfer a client from one R/3 System to another. A client copy using remote functionality does not provide a method to "freeze" the client; that is, the stream of data that is transferred is not stored at the operating system level (see Chapter 9). Therefore, you do not have a physical copy of the client that can be used later to set up the production system. Since your setup strategy should aim at creating the production system in the same manner as the quality assurance system was created—using the same recorded changes and clients—SAP recommends using a client transport rather than a remote client copy.

TIP   When you cannot use the change request strategy, SAP recommends using a client transport—not a remote client copy—to set up your quality assurance and production systems.

Importing Existing Change Requests   Before and during the installation of your quality assurance system, you may have released change requests with unit-tested changes and functionality from your development system. These change requests appear in the import queue of the quality assurance system. Although they may seem irrelevant for the client copy setup of the quality assurance system, they need special attention.

Some of these change requests contain development changes to Repository objects such as programs. Since the client copy procedure duplicates only client-dependent data and the related client-independent Customizing changes, the client-independent development changes affecting Repository objects will not be transported into the quality assurance system. For this reason, SAP recommends that all change requests promoted before the start of the client transport—that is, those change requests already released and exported—should be imported into the quality assurance client.

TIP　A client copy does not copy changes to Repository objects made in the ABAP Workbench. Such changes are automatically recorded to change requests and can be imported into a new client from the import queue before performing the client copy.

As the existing change requests are imported into the quality assurance system, they are also placed in the import queue of the production system. When the production system is created, the same change requests are imported into the production system in their correct order.

Exporting the Client　When you export a client from an R/3 System with Transaction SCC8, you can specify the type of data you wish to copy from the source client. Possible selections include:

- Client-dependent Customizing data

- Client-independent Customizing data

- Application data

- User data

Although you can select different data combinations, SAP recommends that you copy only the two types of Customizing data to create the quality assurance and production clients. Avoid copying application data, since typically the transaction and master data in the CUST client is either nonexistent or simply test data that should not be duplicated.

User data may be included in the copy, but this is potentially problematic. Current users and their authorizations will be distributed from the development system into your production client. For example, your developers will have the same user authorization in the production system that they needed for the development system. This could lead to a possible security problem in the production system.

If you do copy application and/or user data, you will have to "clean up" the new client to remove unnecessary data and users. This clean-up process is complicated and time consuming. It also requires extensive knowledge of the data model to ensure that dependent data is eliminated in the correct sequence. Perhaps the biggest disadvantage is that you will have to repeat the clean-up procedure for the production client.

Importing the Client Export   The import of change requests released prior to the client transport ensures that all development changes promoted from the development system exist in the quality assurance system. After you have imported these change requests, you import the exported client into the quality assurance client. This import process (using TMS) has the following steps:

1. The existing quality assurance client, QTST, and any client-dependent data in this client, including Customizing imported in change requests, are deleted.

2. The exported copy of the CUST client is imported into the new QTST client, thereby placing all Customizing data that existed in the development system in the client. This ensures consistency with the CUST client.

Example: Import Sequence for the Client Copy Strategy

Assume that your development system has been installed for three months and that you have just recently installed your quality assurance system. Although you recorded all ABAP Workbench changes to change requests, you did not start recording all Customizing changes until the second month

Continued on next page

of the implementation procedure. Therefore, to set up your quality assurance system, you need to perform a client export of the CUST client from the development system.

After you export the CUST client with all of its Customizing settings, the import queue for the quality assurance system looks like this:

Order	Change Request	Description
1	DEVK900034	Conversion routines
2	DEVK900012	Customizing for Materials Management
3	DEVK900020	Organizational data
4	DEVK900076	Sales Reports and New Routines
...	...	...
158	DEVK900410	Production Reports
159	DEVK000005	Client export (client-independent Customizing)
160	DEVKT00005	Client export (client-dependent Customizing)
161	DEVKX00005	Client export (texts)

The import queue contains 158 change requests released prior to the client export and 3 change requests containing the client copy data. Some of the 158 change requests contain reports and programs that you will need but that are not part of the client export. You must first import the 158 change requests into the quality assurance system.

When you import the client export files, both the client-dependent and client-independent Customizing imported from the 158 change requests are overwritten. This is of no consequence since the client export contains all current Customizing settings from your CUST client.

If you discarded the 158 change requests and just imported the client export, your quality assurance system would not contain the new sales reports or conversion routines. If you imported the client export before

Continued on next page

importing the other 158 change requests, some relevant Customizing settings would have been overwritten by older versions. For example, the change request DEVK900012 is second on the list in the import queue. After that change request was released, you may have modified the Materials Management settings in the CUST client. If you then imported DEVK900012 after the client export, the settings would revert back to an older and incorrect version. The correct procedure is to import the 158 change requests prior to the client export.

To provide a consistent environment and ensure that the production system is the same as the tested and verified quality assurance system, you must set up the production system in the same way you set up the quality assurance system. The procedure is as follows:

1. All change requests in the import queue of the production system—that is, those change requests released *before* the client export—are imported into the production system.

2. The exported CUST client is imported into the system.

3. Any change requests that appear in the import queue after the client export are imported into the system.

Disadvantage

The major disadvantage of the client copy method concerns the type of Customizing settings copied. A client copy copies *all* Customizing settings, even those that provide only partial functionality. There is no way to filter out these incomplete settings. In other words, those Customizing changes that are incomplete or perhaps even unnecessary for the start of production activities will be transferred to the quality assurance client and eventually the production system.

System Copy Strategy

Many customers mistakenly think that a system copy is a viable method for establishing any kind of additional R/3 System within a system landscape. A *system copy*, also known as a *database copy*, can be useful for creating optional systems, such as a training system or a copy of the production environment for upgrade tests. However, SAP does not recommend using a system copy to set up a critical system. This means you should not use a system copy of the development system to set up a quality assurance or production system.

SAP has several reasons for advising against the use of a system copy and alternatively recommending either the change request or the client copy strategy:

- A system copy transfers all Customizing settings and developments, even those that are incomplete. The task of removing unwanted Repository objects and Customizing entries to ensure that only complete business transactions exist in the R/3 System is a difficult one.

- A system copy transfers application data. While SAP does provide some production start and reset routines to eliminate existing application data, these routines do not exist for all application data.

- A system copy provides you with no true documentation on the creation of the environment. The system copy procedure in conjunction with the manual elimination of data eliminates the audit history and documentation provided by change requests.

System Copy of Quality Assurance

SAP strongly advises against using a system copy of the development system to set up your quality assurance system and ultimately your production system. However, on occasion, customers still choose to make a system copy of the quality assurance system to set up their production system. They do this for any of the following reasons:

- They believe that too much time and effort is required to apply the necessary Support Packages, languages, and change requests to the production system.

- They have made manual changes on the quality assurance system that either cannot be transported using change requests or were not performed nor recorded in the development system.

- They have no record of the sequence in which change requests and/or a client copy were applied to the quality assurance system. In other words, the import queue of the production system does not match the list of change requests imported into the quality assurance system.

- They no longer have the data files required by the change requests. The change requests used to build the quality assurance system are no longer in the transport directory, nor can they be located on backup devices.

The three latter reasons are typically the result of poor planning and incorrect procedures. Changes in the quality assurance system should never take place, but if they do, the changes must always be re-created on the development system. Such manual changes should also be performed on the production system. Although it is possible to re-create an import buffer using information currently stored in the quality assurance system, missing data files cannot easily be re-created. By properly planning and structuring your implementation, you can avoid having to make a system copy for any of these reasons.

The time factor, however, may still be compelling. The initial setup of the quality assurance system is straightforward. It requires post-installation processing, possibly a client copy, and some change requests. However, over time, more and more change requests are imported into the quality assurance system. When you begin to install the production system, the list of change requests may number well over a thousand. To complicate matters, during the quality assurance testing, you may have applied additional Support Packages. (See Chapter 15.) Setting up the production system suddenly seems an insurmountable task. A system copy may appear to be the only solution. Keep in mind that this is not a solution recommended by SAP.

WARNING   SAP does not recommend using a system copy to set up your quality assurance or production systems.

Cleaning Up after a System Copy

If you do use a system copy of the quality assurance system to set up your production system, you will encounter several complications before the start of production. You must ensure that all application data is eliminated and that the new production environment is thoroughly tested.

Initial Activities   After performing the database copy and prior to eliminating application data, you must complete the following activities:

- Reinitialize the Change and Transport Organizers (Transaction SE06) to close any open change requests that originated in the source system. (See Chapter 7.)

- Verify that the TMS configuration is correct and active so that change requests can be delivered to the new R/3 System.

- Assign the clients in the new system unique logical system names to avoid conflicts with the logical system names of other clients. (See Chapter 9.)

- Use authorization techniques to manage user access to the R/3 System.

Eliminating Application Data One of the reasons SAP advises against using a system copy is that production start programs to remove transaction data exist only for certain functional areas. To remove the data not covered by such a program, you could use a combination of archiving, running your own deletion routines, and removing data manually—overall, a very tedious and time-consuming process.

A more practical method of removing the test data copied from the quality assurance system is to use a client copy to generate a client without application data. For example, after the system copy of the quality assurance system, you can make a client copy of what was once the quality assurance client to create the production client. When you make this client copy, you allow only Customizing data to be transferred. This ensures that no application data will be in the production client at the start of production activities. Figure 5.3 illustrates this procedure.

FIGURE 5.3:

Setting up a production client using a system copy

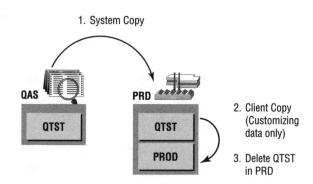

Validating the Production Environment SAP advises customers setting up a system landscape to always employ the same method when establishing the critical R/3 Systems. In the system copy procedure, however, the production system—more specifically, the production client—is created in a manner different from that used to create the quality assurance system and client. This means you must verify the new production system before starting production. You should make a system copy of the new production system and use it for testing purposes. These validation tests need to be thorough and comprehensive. Remember that, as in any other step of the implementation procedure, a system copy is only as good as the tests that are performed to verify it.

Example: Using a System Copy to Set Up a Production System

An implementation team that lacked the necessary technical expertise early in the project plan hires a woman who is an experienced technical consultant. Her first objective is to determine the best strategy for setting up the production system. Although the quality assurance system has been in place for the past two months, she is unable to determine which change requests have been successfully imported. She discovers that several Support Packages were applied at various times. Also problematic are the client change settings, which may have allowed additional Customizing changes in the quality assurance client.

The consultant recommends setting up the production system with a system copy. She proceeds as follows:

1. To support a system copy and hopefully provide an opportunity for verifying the production system setup, she creates an additional client in the quality assurance system, client 200. This is a client copy of client 100, the quality assurance test client, and contains only Customizing settings. After creating this client, she makes a system copy of the quality assurance system.

2. The consultant then checks and confirms that no Customizing changes can be made in the quality assurance system. All changes imported into the quality assurance system are added to the import queue of the production system. She also works with the testing teams to migrate all business validation to client 200. While this involves establishing

Continued on next page

new application data in client 200, it helps ensure that the environment most resembles the soon-to-be production client.

3. When the production system arrives, the consultant installs R/3 with the system copy from the quality assurance system. She deletes client 100 from the system and sets up client 200 as the production client with the appropriate settings. Any changes applied to the quality assurance system after the system copy are also applied to the production system.

R/3 Release Considerations

When choosing a method to set up your system landscape, you must also consider R/3 Release levels. Ideally, the R/3 Release installed within the system landscape should be the same for all systems. However, implementations frequently begin at one R/3 Release and are upgraded as soon as newer releases become available.

When considering an upgrade within your implementation process, you must keep an important factor in mind: Change requests and the client transport are R/3 Release–dependent. This means you should not transport changes from one R/3 Release to another. The change requests used to create a system must originate in a system at the same R/3 Release level.

TIP Change requests and the client copy tools, such as a client transport, are R/3 Release–dependent.

An upgrade delivered by SAP may contain Repository objects that differ from those in the original release. The table structures that house the Customizing data also vary in the different releases. If the data recorded in a change request originates from a system at a higher level of release, you may not be able to import the data into a system at the lower release level. For the same reason, a client transport can be imported only to an R/3 System at the same level of R/3 Release.

If you need to upgrade your development system prior to the installation of the quality assurance system, first check whether any change requests have been released. If there are no released change requests, you can upgrade the development system and install the quality assurance system at the new R/3 Release level. However, if change requests have been released, to ensure that these released changes are distributed to the quality assurance and production systems, you need to employ one of the following methods:

- Install the quality assurance and production systems at the initial R/3 Release level. After the released changes are imported, upgrade the systems to the latest R/3 Release.

- Upgrade the development system to the new R/3 Release. The released change requests are re-recorded to a new change request at the new release level. This *bundling* of several requests *includes* the contents of the old, released change requests in a new change request (see Chapter 10). You install the quality assurance and production systems at the newer R/3 Release level and then promote this single bundled change request.

- Instead of using change requests for the initial setup of the quality assurance and production systems, upgrade the development system and use the client copy strategy. All change requests released prior to the upgrade are discarded. After the upgrade, you release a change request from the development system for all modified Repository objects. This is accomplished using the Transport Organizer (Transaction SE01) to create a transport of copies (see Chapter 10). This ensures that all Repository changes are transported to the quality assurance and production systems, both of which are installed at the newer R/3 Release level.

Example: An R/3 Release Upgrade during Implementation

Based on needs for the latest R/3 functionality, a company decides that its development system should be upgraded from R/3 Release 4.0B to R/3 Release 4.5B in the middle of the implementation process. The company's system administrator, a man named Frank, is concerned that the upgrade will significantly delay his plans for setting up the quality assurance system.

After a little thought, Frank decides to upgrade the development system to R/3 Release 4.5B and install the quality assurance system at the new R/3 Release level. Then Frank discovers that change requests were released from the development system. Because the change requests now at the operating system level originated in Release 4.0B, Frank realizes they cannot be imported into an R/3 System at the Release 4.5B level.

Frank's alternative plan has the following steps:

1. Install the quality assurance system at the R/3 Release 4.0B level.

2. Apply the R/3 Release 4.0B change requests to the quality assurance system.

3. Upgrade the quality assurance system to the new release.

4. Import any change requests released from the R/3 Release 4.5B development system into the quality assurance system.

Frank's manager, Barbara, is not in favor of his plan. She feels it would take too long to install and then later upgrade the quality assurance system. As an alternative, she suggests the following procedure:

1. Upgrade the development system and install the quality assurance system at the Release 4.5B level.

2. Include all the released 4.0B change requests into a single change request in the upgraded development system; this single bundled change request is then at the R/3 Release 4.5B level.

Continued on next page

3. Import the bundled change request into the quality assurance system, thereby providing the system with a copy of all Customizing and development changes released earlier.

Frank follows her suggestions. When he installs the production system at the Release 4.5B level, he imports all change requests that were imported into the quality assurance system, including the bundled change request.

Review Questions

1. Which of the following clients should you copy to create new clients and ensure that all data from post-installation processing is also copied?

    A. Client 001

    B. Client 000

    C. Client 066

2. Which of the following is *not* an SAP-recommended strategy for setting up a system landscape?

    A. Using a client copy from the development system to set up your quality assurance and production systems when the change request strategy is not an option

    B. Creating the production system as a combination of a client copy from the quality assurance system and change requests from the development system

    C. Using the same setup strategy to establish both the quality assurance and production systems

    D. Setting up the quality assurance and production systems by importing change requests promoted from the development system

3. Which of the following are correct in regard to the setup of the TMS?

    A. The TMS should be set up when the development system is installed.

    B. The TMS should include all R/3 Systems in the system landscape even if the R/3 Systems do not physically exist.

    C. The TMS is critical in establishing the transport route between the development and quality assurance systems.

    D. The TMS should be set up before change requests are created in the Customizing-and-development client.

4. Which of the following is correct in regard to the system copy strategy?

    A. SAP recommends the system copy strategy, because all Customizing and development objects are transferred.

    B. SAP does not recommend the system copy strategy, because there is no easy way to eliminate unwanted application data.

    C. A system copy is the easiest setup strategy recommended by SAP.

    D. A system copy eliminates the need for change requests for your entire R/3 implementation.

CHAPTER

SIX

Maintaining a System Landscape

In the early phases of your implementation, you require not only a setup strategy, but also a plan for maintaining your system landscape to enable the systematic implementation of changes in R/3 Systems. This maintenance includes:

- Managing implementation projects through change requests
- Setting up a transport process that ensures that approved changes are distributed to all clients in the system landscape
- Applying SAP Support Packages and performing R/3 Release upgrades

The responsibilities, roles, and procedures involved in recording and transporting changes must be clearly defined and documented. In addition, defined procedures are required to support the import of changes outside the standard transport process—for example, when implementing Support Packages.

This chapter focuses on these issues, and outlines the decisions you will have to make. It explains SAP's recommended system landscape maintenance strategy, as well as SAP's recommendations for testing and validating changes, which play an important role in all maintenance strategies. The maintenance strategy mapped out in this chapter is based on the standard three-system landscape recommended by SAP. The processes and procedures presented here can be adapted to cover system landscapes that differ from that standard.

Implementation Plan

A system landscape is in a continuous state of maintenance, and maintenance activities need to be coordinated. The overall maintenance process focuses on successive implementation phases—that is, phases in which new or changed R/3 software is to be implemented in the system landscape. To coordinate these implementation phases, you need to map them in an *implementation plan*, as shown in Figure 6.1.

The various implementation phases in the life of an R/3 System can be summarized as follows:

- An initial phase to configure the R/3 software to meet your business needs and start production

- A series of subsequent phases to introduce new or improved business processes and functionalities

All implementation phases presuppose that changes to be implemented have been created through Customizing and development activities in R/3, and require subsequent *production support*, which is the use of a special R/3 System or client to perform the Customizing and development needed to repair any errors associated with the changes already implemented in the production system.

Time and security concerns vary depending on the maintenance activity. Both factors are especially significant for production support. Creating new business processes is not as time-critical as production support, but results in a greater need for end-user training, business process validation, and new test scenarios. Before going live with new or modified business processes, stringent testing is required in the quality assurance system.

FIGURE 6.1:

Implementation cycles in the implementation plan

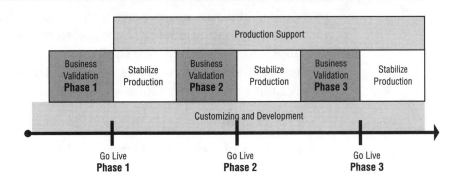

The implementation cycle is indicated as a horizontal bar at the center of the implementation plan in Figure 6.1. It is a repeating pattern consisting of a business validation period followed by a going-live date and a stabilize production period. Prior to the going-live date for each bundle of development or Customizing changes, the *business validation* period consists of:

- Extensive testing in the quality assurance system of R/3 business processes to verify that the changes will work smoothly in the production system

- Stress tests to validate the technical environment and ensure that the introduction of new changes will not reduce performance in the production system

After going live, the *stabilize production* period is a time that is set aside to allow the production system to stabilize. Any conflicts resulting from the introduction of changes in the production system should be resolved before the beginning of the business validation period of the following implementation phase.

In addition to the business validation and stabilization cycles, Figure 6.1 also shows the related, ongoing activities of production support, and Customizing and development. Customizing and development begins immediately after R/3 installation, while production support commences after the start of production.

Your implementation plan will consist of a schedule based on a diagram such as is shown in Figure 6.1, as well as documentation that defines the business processes that you intend to introduce in each implementation phase. The associated Customizing and development tasks are then assigned to particular individuals to prevent conflicts and procedure overlaps. The three main parties involved in an implementation are as follows:

- Project leaders

- Members of the project teams—that is, customizers and developers

- The system administrator responsible for transports

Their roles and responsibilities will be outlined below.

Managing Implementation Projects

To facilitate implementation, you should use the project management capabilities provided by change requests in R/3.

Throughout the implementation procedure, changes made in the Customizing-and-development client must be recorded to change requests. These change requests not only provide a change history and documentation, but also a method of organizing the efforts of the different people who are contributing to the implementation project. Most importantly, change requests provide a method for transporting different implementation projects—first, to the quality assurance system for testing, and then to the production system.

Implementation Phases

Most implementation projects introduce new R/3 functionality to the production system in successive phases. Initially, one new application component is introduced to the production system, and then, after a few months of production activity, another component is introduced. Although it is possible to Customize and develop for multiple projects and phases in the development system, you want to transport to the quality assurance system and the production system only those changes that are relevant to a specific phase of the implementation project. By using change requests, you can appropriately limit what you release and transport.

If you include all people working on the project as tasks in a single change request, you can then transport the project as a whole by simply releasing the change request. Or, for larger projects, the project needs to be divided into parts using multiple change requests. For transportation to the quality assurance system, you will need to transport together these change requests.

For example, a company may choose to start production activities with the Financials applications, and a few months later, implement the Logistics applications. To save time, Customizing and development for both application areas are done simultaneously. However, change requests related to Logistics will not be released from the development system until it is time to transport them to the quality assurance system, which is after production is stabilized for Financials.

Example: Change Requests for Implementing in Phases

When implementing R/3, a manufacturing firm decides to introduce the software in different phases. The implementation begins in May, when the firm's largest plant goes live with the Production Planning application. In July, the firm's other plants start using R/3. Finally, in October, the Financials applications are added.

To coordinate the procedure, different Project IMGs are created for each different phase of the project. The customizers and developers are careful to save changes to the correct change requests for each different phase. Likewise, project leaders release only those Customizing and development changes that are related to the business processes currently being tested in the quality assurance system. In other words, prior to the start of production in May, only change requests relevant to Production Planning are released.

After the start of production in May, only the changes required for the July implementation phase (implementing R/3 at the firm's other plants) are released from the development system for business validation in the quality

Continued on next page

assurance system. The change requests required for the testing of the Financials applications are released only after the new plants are in production.

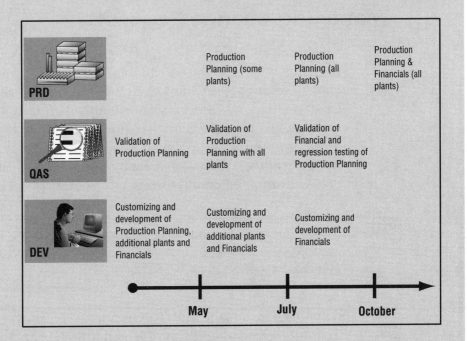

Having different change requests for the different implementation phases allows development and unit testing for all phases to occur at the same time in the development system. Only releasing and exporting change requests for a specific phase allow for complete business validation of each successive phase.

It is not always possible to separate Customizing activities and assign them to specific implementation phases. During quality assurance testing, missing Customizing may be discovered that is due to the dependencies between the different implementation phases. It may then be necessary to release the change requests of a subsequent implementation phase to supply the missing

Customizing. Such dependencies between changes in different phases may not become apparent until quality assurance testing.

Managing Change Requests

Ideally, all changes in the implementation process are recorded to change requests. You can do this by using the appropriate client-change settings (see Chapters 3 and 9). A user working in the Customizing-and-development client is then forced to save all changes to a task in a change request. Therefore, to save a change, a user must either be assigned to a task in a change request or have the authorization to create a change request and task. (For more information on authorizations, see Chapter 11.)

NOTE   User authorizations and the assignment of users to change requests provide you the ability to manage whether and when an R/3 user can make changes.

Every change made in R/3 does not need its own change request. To limit overhead and simplify validation, changes should be grouped in a logical manner by project objectives and collected in a single change request. This is the project leader's responsibility.

In Customizing, for example, a change request does not need to contain all changes made by an entire Customizing team over a three-month period. Ideally, a change request should be a testable unit of work. This means the objects in the change request correspond to a set of business processes that can be tested together, or to an executable program. A testable change request can more easily be unit tested prior to release, and can more easily be verified after being imported into the quality assurance system.

Responsibilities

Project leaders assign project responsibilities to their team members—the people performing Customizing and the developers. These responsibilities correspond to Customizing activities or development work in R/3. To manage the team, the project leader should create change requests and assign team members to them (see Figure 6.2). The project leader is responsible for the change request, and team members are responsible for their *task* within the change request. Team members, although they cannot create a change request or task, are able to save their changes to the task created by the project leader.

FIGURE 6.2:

Organizing a project team

The Customizing Organizer (Transaction SE10) and the Workbench Organizer (Transaction SE09) enable project leaders to view, create, and delete change requests. Team members can use these same tools to view any change requests in which they have a task, view the contents of any task in the change request, and record changes to their tasks.

An example of a project objective is to use Customizing to define the process chain for a sales order. After this objective has been agreed on, the project leader, using the Customizing Organizer, creates a change request and assigns each person working on the project to a separate task within the change request.

Documentation

All customizers and developers working on change requests are required to write documentation associated with a task. The documentation must be completed prior to the release of the task. The documentation should state the aims of the changes, the completion status of the task, and any special features that result from the changes. The objects in the task tell you which objects were changed, the time they were changed, and who made the changes. The documentation provides more details on the status and purpose of the changes.

Project IMGs

Ideally, you should be able to look at the change requests and determine to which Customizing project they belong. In R/3 Releases before 4.6, the IMG does not automatically set up change requests that recognizably belong to a specific Project IMG; nor can you, from the Customizing Organizer (Transaction SE10), easily determine which Customizing activity was used to modify an object. Therefore, before R/3 Release 4.6, make it your policy to:

• Include the project name in the title of a change request

- Indicate the relationship of the task to the relevant IMG activities in task-level documentation

As of Release 4.6, R/3 provides a direct link between change requests and IMG activities. By activating *CTS Project Management*, you can set up change requests specific to a Project IMG. Then, when you perform Customizing activities from within the Project IMG, changes are recorded to change requests of the corresponding project. The project management functionality also organizes the change requests in the import queues in groups according to project. This makes it easier to choose what to import. During import, the project management functionality also detects the sharing of objects between different projects and monitors such dependencies during import activities.

NOTE   For more information on the CTS Project Management functionality, see R/3 online documentation for R/3 Release 4.6.

Example: Managing Change Requests

An international travel services group plans to implement SAP's Human Resources applications over a four-month period. During the first month of configuration, a large number of R/3 users record changes to change requests, often saving a change to a new change request. At the end of the first month, over 600 change requests have been created.

Fearing that this number will only continue to grow, the system administrator realizes that a strategy for managing change requests is necessary and that the users have to be informed of new procedures. In conjunction with the project leaders, the system administrator defines a change request strategy that includes:

- Changing most user authorizations so that only project leaders can create change requests

Continued on next page

> • Educating project leaders about the procedure for creating and managing change requests and properly assigning users to change requests
>
> The development projects are made the responsibility of the developers themselves rather than the project leaders. The developers are then directly responsible for their change requests.
>
> At the end of the second month, only 120 change requests have been released and exported and are waiting for import—a much more manageable number than the 600 at the end of the first month.

Unit Testing

Before releasing the Customizing and development changes in a change request, you must unit test the changes. Since unit testing requires application data, SAP recommends conducting unit tests in a separate unit test client rather than in the Customizing-and-development client (see Chapter 3). Use the unit test client as follows:

- To copy the latest Customizing changes to the unit test client, use the function *client copy according to a transp. request* (Transaction SCC1; see Figure 6.3). After performing unit testing, return to the Customizing-and-development client to make any necessary corrections. Again, test the latest changes in the unit test client. This process continues until the task required for the project has been completed and is ready for promotion.

- Since Repository objects are client-independent, a developer does not need to copy development changes from one client to another in the same R/3 System. Developers developing in one client can immediately perform unit testing in another client that has sample application data. After developments are completed and unit tested, they can usually be promoted to the quality assurance client for integration testing. If the development consists of SAPscript and report variants, however, which are types of client-dependent data, copying the development to different clients within the same R/3 System for testing requires special attention (see Chapter 12).

Performing unit testing in a special unit test client enables you to ensure that the objects in your change request include all the changes that they should contain and that will be required for testing in the quality assurance system.

FIGURE 6.3:

For unit testing, use the function *client copy according to a transp. request* (in Transaction SCC1).

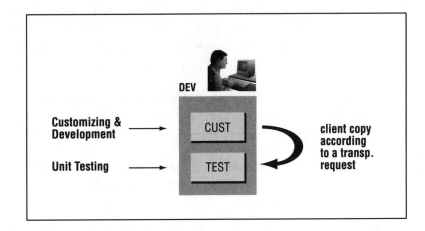

Responsibilities

Team members unit test the tasks for which they are responsible. After a team member has completed unit testing at the task level, the task is released.

Releasing a task to a change request indicates to the project leader that the task has been completed. However, it is not as final a step as releasing a change request. If a person performing Customizing or development realizes that additional changes are required after releasing a task, the project leader can create another task for that user.

The project leader unit tests the functionality of the objects listed in the change request before releasing the change request.

Releasing and Exporting Change Requests

Before transporting a change request from the development system to the quality assurance system, the project leader must release the change request. In general, releasing a change request automatically initiates the export process. (For details on the release and export processes and examples of change requests that are released but not exported, see Chapter 12.)

Releasing and exporting a change request is a significant step in the overall change management process, and achieves the following:

- It indicates that the changed objects recorded in the change request have been unit tested and are ready to be transported.

- It "freezes" the objects recorded in the change request by copying them in their current state to a file external to R/3.

- It places the change request in the import queue of the target system, which is typically the quality assurance system.

A change request only lists the changed objects—it does not contain the changed objects themselves. Releasing and exporting a change request causes the physical download of the changed objects and table entries—in their current state—to a file at the operating system level. The target system receives an entry in its import queue, indicating that the change request (and its collection of changes) is waiting to be imported. If a change request is not ready for promotion to the quality assurance system, it should not be released, because release and export initiates the transport process for that change request.

TIP	Perform release and export only for change requests that are ready to be validated in the quality assurance system.

Repository Object Checks

Before you release a change request, you can subject the Repository objects in the request to various checks. Unit testing the change request can reveal errors. In addition, the Workbench Organizer enables you to activate *object checks* for Repository objects contained in a change request (see Chapter 12). Object checks identify and display errors found in customer developments before the change request is released. These errors, such as program syntax errors, must be either corrected or verified by the developer before the change requests are actually released.

TIP	SAP recommends that developers activate object checks in the development system.

Responsibilities

The person who creates a change request—also known as the *owner* of the change request—initiates the release and export process. That person is normally the project leader. Prior to releasing the change request, the owner is responsible for ensuring that the request is ready to be transported. After releasing their change requests or tasks, neither the project leader nor team members play any further role in the transport process. Instead, the system administrator is responsible for importing and managing change requests in the import queue. However, the system administrator does not determine whether a change request is placed in the import queue. The project leader should act as a control point, and release and export only changes that are genuinely ready to be imported into the target system.

Transport Management

The task of transporting change requests is an important responsibility in any R/3 implementation. After the start of production, it becomes even more critical because you need to protect the production system from untested changes. Before beginning an R/3 implementation, ensure that your system landscape maintenance strategy covers transport management in detail.

Your transport process should be based on change requests as summarized in Figure 6.4 (see also Chapter 4). To establish a transport management plan for your system landscape, focus on the critical steps of the transport process, define how each step is managed, and assign the roles and responsibilities for each.

FIGURE 6.4:

Transporting change
requests

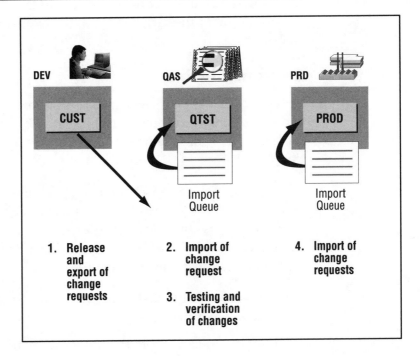

1. **Release
    and
    export of
    change
    requests**

2. **Import of
    change
    request**

3. **Testing and
    verification
    of changes**

4. **Import of
    change
    requests**

Exporting Change Requests

Releasing a change request in the development system normally automatically triggers the export process and is the first step in transporting the changed objects listed in the change request to the quality assurance system.

During the export process, the changed objects listed in the change request are copied from the database to a data file at the operating system level. The change request is automatically added to the import queue in the target system, the quality assurance system. If data from the source database cannot be exported, or if releasing the change request fails to add the change request to the import queue of the target system, the export will fail.

Responsibilities

Only responsible people such as project leaders should release and export change requests in the system landscape. To limit these activities, set the user authorizations appropriately. (See Chapter 11.)

The person who releases the change request must also verify the success of the export. The owner of a change request can determine the success or failure of an export from the Customizing Organizer and the Workbench Organizer (see Chapter 12). Examples of errors during export include:

- Lack of available disk space in the transport directory for the data and control files

- Inability to connect to the database of the quality assurance system

Sometimes, the failure of an export is due to a technical problem that a project leader cannot solve. Although the owner of the change request is responsible for verifying exports, a technical consultant or system administrator may need to assist in solving any reported problems.

Importing Change Requests

As change requests are released in the development system, they are automatically entered in the import queue of the quality assurance system. Your procedural documentation for performing imports using change requests should include:

- A policy of preventing users from manipulating the order of change requests in the import queue to ensure that target clients receive the released change requests in the correct sequence

- A time schedule for imports and a procedure for managing change requests that fall outside the schedule

- A duty roster assigning responsibility for performing imports and listing who has authorization

- Procedures for verifying imports and handling errors that occur during the import

Initiating Imports

An import queue displays change requests that are awaiting import. The change requests are listed in the order of their release. The import process, however, is not initiated automatically. To initiate and control imports into R/3 Systems, use the Transport Management System (Transaction STMS) as described in Chapter 4.

Prior to the introduction of the TMS in R/3 Release 3.1H, the only method for performing imports was to use transport commands at the operating system level. The TMS import functionality consists of a user-friendly interface in R/3 that communicates with the transport control program *tp* using Remote Function Calls (RFCs). Instead of using the TMS to communicate with *tp*, you can still use *tp* directly at the operating system level to perform imports. This requires the appropriate operating system commands. To automate the import process, you can also use *tp* commands in scripts at the operating system level (see Chapter 14).

TIP   SAP recommends that you use the TMS to perform imports. However, if the transport activities you wish to perform are not currently supported by the TMS, consider using the appropriate *tp* commands as part of your documented procedure.

Regardless of whether you use the TMS or the transport control program *tp*, when performing an import, you have the following options:

- Use an *import all* to import all change requests waiting to be imported. This option is accessed in R/3 with the menu option *start import*, and is accessed at the operating system level using the command *tp import all*.

- Use a *preliminary import* to import individual change requests. This option is accessed in R/3 with the menu option *Request ➢ Import*, and is accessed at the operating system level using the command *tp import <change request ID> u0*.

Import All   Since an *import all* imports all change requests waiting in the import queue, the import sequence plays an important role. By importing change requests in the chronological order in which they were exported—that is, the order in which they are listed in the import queue—you ensure that objects in earlier change requests are replaced by any corrections in later change requests during import.

TIP   SAP recommends that change requests be imported in the chronological order in which they were exported—that is, the order in which they are listed in the import queue.

To help you import only the change requests you require, you can add an *end mark* to the import queue after the set of change requests you wish to import. When you perform an *import all*, any change requests listed in the queue after the end mark will not be imported.

To add an end mark, in the import queue screen (Transaction STMS; *Overview ➢ Imports*), double-click the system ID and choose *Queue ➢ Close*. The end mark is indicated by the statement *End of import queue* that appears at the end of the import queue.

If required, you can move this statement further up the import queue to include fewer change requests in the next import. For example, you may wish to import only the first 15 change requests in an import queue. To do this, place the cursor on the 16th change request and choose *Edit* ➢ *Move end mark*. This places the end mark between the 15th and 16th change requests. You can now start the import.

Preliminary Import   A *preliminary import* allows you to rapidly transfer single requests through the defined transport routes. For example, you may have a production problem that needs immediate correction. The corresponding change request is released from the development system and needs to be tested immediately. Although there are other change requests waiting in the import queue of the quality assurance system, you want to import only the single change request at this time. Therefore, you import the individual change request using a *preliminary import*. If the contents of the change request successfully correct the problem, you can import the change request to production immediately using another *preliminary import*.

To minimize the risks associated with *preliminary import*s, the imported change request remains in the import queue after import and is reimported the next time the entire import queue is imported. This guarantees that export and import sequences are the same and ensures that the target system does not return to the way it was prior to the *preliminary import*.

To prevent inconsistencies that may result from object dependencies, SAP recommends avoiding *preliminary import* and using only *import all*. For example, if you import a change request with an ABAP report that refers to a table, and that table is contained in another change request that has not yet been imported, executing the report will only generate short dumps until the table is also imported.

Example: A Preliminary Import

A multinational company purchases a new facility and begins making adjustments to its R/3 System. After the rollout of the required accounting settings to support the new manufacturing facility, it is discovered during a month-end closing period that the real-estate accounting settings are incorrect, and due to the error, month-end closing cannot be completed. The error is immediately simulated in the quality assurance environment, the problem is pinpointed, and corrections are made in the development system. A change request with the required changes is released from the development system.

The import queue of the quality assurance system looks like this:

Change Request	Owner	Description
DEVK901832	MARY	Plant configuration
DEVK901910	SUE	Real-estate controlling
DEVK901830	ALEX	Rental accounting
DEVK901676	JON	Manufacturing
DEVK902015	BILL	FIX: month-end with new facility
DEVK901703	MARY	Plant maintenance

The import queue of the quality assurance system already included recently released changes that support manufacturing requirements for the new facility. However, these application settings are neither ready for validation nor required in production immediately.

Change request DEVK902015 contains the changes needed to complete month-end closing. This request needs to be imported immediately. Since the other requests are not ready for validation, an import of the entire import queue is not possible. The individual request itself is imported using a *preliminary import.*

Importing DEVK902015 to the quality assurance system enters this change request in the import queue of the production system. After the correction contained in this change request has been validated in the quality assurance

Continued on next page

system, DEVK902015 is imported into the production system with a further *preliminary import*.

During the next scheduled import into the quality assurance system, DEVK902015 is again imported, this time as part of the listed series of change requests. Because the change request is imported in sequence, changes made to solve the month-end closing problem are not overwritten by earlier requests such as DEVK901910 or DEVK901830, which may contain conflicting changes.

Import Considerations

Before importing a change request, consider:

- Importing to all clients in all R/3 Systems. This ensures consistency of all clients and systems in your system landscape.

- Scheduling imports into the quality assurance system at times that are known to the entire implementation team. This creates transparency for project management and for the business validation team.

Importing into Multiple Clients   Typically, a quality assurance system contains more clients than just the quality assurance client. One or two additional clients may be dedicated to end-user training, and another client may be reserved for data conversion tests. Regardless of the number of clients, your import procedure needs to ensure that all clients in the quality assurance system receive the change requests in the same order that they were exported from the development system.

To enable you to import to multiple clients, SAP introduced functionality known as *extended transport control* in R/3 Release 4.5, which allows client-specific transport routes. These transport routes allow you to assign imports to multiple clients in a single

R/3 System at the same time or at different times. Client-specific transport routes use client-specific entries in import queues. (See Figure 4.4 in Chapter 4.)

If you do not use extended transport control, you have to import the change requests several times, once for each client in the system. Ensure that all change requests are imported into all clients in the same sequence so that client-independent functionality is not overwritten by older versions of the functionality delivered in earlier change requests (see Chapter 13).

TIP   When you have multiple clients in the quality assurance system, SAP recommends that you use a documented strategy to ensure that all change requests are imported to all clients in the quality assurance system.

Additional Clients in the Development System   While development changes automatically impact all clients in the system, Customizing changes are typically specific to the Customizing-and-development client in which they originated. You need to take special steps to ensure that all clients in the development system are also supplied with all client-dependent changes.

Although unit testing copies the changes to the unit test client, importing released change requests into the unit test client provides a way of ensuring that all changes are entered into the unit test client. Similarly, a sandbox client updated with the latest changes ensures that the people working in that client are working in an up-to-date environment.

There are a number of ways to ensure that the clients in the development system contain the latest client-dependent changes:

- Using the client-specific transport routes of the *extended transport control*.

- Performing a *client copy according to a transp. request* (Transaction SCC1) for all change requests released from the development system.

- Importing released Customizing change requests. To do this, you need to give the development system its own import queue (through transport parameter *testsystems*). Released change requests are then transferred into the development import queue.

NOTE   Prior to using the import queue of the development system to import to other clients in the development system, you must eliminate change requests containing development work. This prevents these change requests from overwriting recent changes to client-independent objects in the development system.

- Performing periodic client copies of the Customizing-and-development client to other clients such as the sandbox client. Note that this will eliminate all data including application data in the target client.

Scheduling Imports   Imports into the quality assurance system can be automated to occur at specific, predefined intervals. However, SAP recommends such scheduling only when responsible people such as the project leaders control the release process—whatever is to be released has been checked and is needed in the quality assurance system. If you have established no such control, you must provide some other method by which users can inform a system administrator or technical consultant that released change requests should be imported. This can be a complicated process and may cause misunderstandings.

TIP   As a prerequisite for scheduling imports to the quality assurance system, import queues should contain only those requests that are ready for import. Therefore, only responsible people such as project leaders should be in charge of the release and export process.

Timed Intervals for Imports   You need to determine when imports should be scheduled. All imports introduce changes and thus invalidate previous test results, even test results for other areas of R/3. Thorough testing is required after all imports. Since thorough testing takes time, the timing of imports is governed by whether the business validation team is ready to perform the testing.

Early in an implementation phase, imports are usually scheduled at regular intervals—for example, once a day; every hour; or at 9:00 A.M., noon, and 4:00 P.M. As you get closer to the going-live date, business validation teams need more time for testing, and you may wish to limit the import process to once a week.

> **TIP**   Define an import schedule that allows sufficient time for the testing and correction of changes prior to the next import.

Tools for Scheduling Imports   As of R/3 Release 4.6, the TMS contains the *Import Scheduler*, which enables you to schedule change requests for immediate import, periodic import, or import at specific times. You can use the Import Scheduler to schedule TMS activities such as *import all*, *preliminary import*, and import to a specific client.

In releases prior to R/3 Release 4.6, you can perform imports at specific intervals either manually or using scheduling programs. To manually schedule imports, the system administrator performs an *import all* in the TMS. Alternatively, at the operating system level, scheduling programs can be used to issue the appropriate *tp* commands. For example, if UNIX is your operating system, you can schedule *tp* commands using the UNIX program *cron* (see Chapter 14).

> **TIP**   Even when your import process is automated, you must still monitor and verify the results of each import.

Responsibilities

Traditionally, when the import process was more technical and required access to the operating system level, the import process was the responsibility of the system administrator. With the introduction of the TMS, the import process is controlled from within the R/3 System. This means any R/3 user with the correct user authorization can initiate either an *import all* or a *preliminary import*.

TIP   To avoid errors, prevent unauthorized imports by carefully assigning and monitoring all relevant user authorizations.

Post-Import Issues

To complete the import procedure, you need to:

- Review the relevant logs
- Resolve any errors that occurred during import
- Notify the people who will perform testing and business validation

Responsibilities

The post-import issues are the responsibility of both the technical team and the project leaders (or owners of the change requests). Ensure that communication between the people involved is accomplished using a formal notification procedure.

Import Logs   Every import activity, such as an *import all* or a *preliminary import*, results in a *return code* in the TMS. These logs can be viewed in the Import Monitor in Transaction STMS as described in Chapter 13. If the return code indicates an error, it is initially the responsibility of the system administrator to evaluate the error.

During import, errors can be the result of a particular change request or a problem with the target R/3 System.

Transport Logs   To determine whether the import of individual change requests was successful, project leaders should check the logs specific to each change request, which are known as transport log files. Using either the Customizing Organizer (Transaction SE09) or the Workbench Organizer (Transaction SE10), you can access an overview of change requests that have been released, exported, and imported. Traffic-light icons on the right-hand side of the initial Organizer screens show the color red to indicate transport errors, yellow for warnings, and green for successful imports.

By activating the setting *display transport errors at logon* in the Workbench and Customizing Organizers, a user can obtain information at logon about the status of change requests that have been transported. After this setting is activated, whenever a user logs on and a change request import has failed since the user last logged on, a message box appears informing the user of the failure. The user can access the transport log files and determine which import errors have occurred. You can activate this setting either for an individual user or globally for all users. (See Chapter 12.)

TIP   SAP recommends having all users automatically informed of transport errors when they log on to both the development and quality assurance system.

Problem Resolution   The system administrator should review and evaluate the import log to check for errors after every import. Severe errors can cause the import process to stop, leaving change requests in the import queue and only partially imported into the quality assurance system. Such errors need the system administrator's immediate attention. Even when scheduling routines for import into the quality assurance system are used, a system administrator should always check the import log after each import.

Errors in the import log indicate either problems with the import process or problems with specific change requests. The change request owner, who is normally the project leader, must resolve problems affecting specific change requests. Correcting a problem may simply require releasing additional changes from the development system. In more difficult situations, the project leader may need to consult the system administrator to understand and resolve the problem.

Problems not with specific change requests but with the import process must be resolved by having the system administrator analyze the R/3 System and database (see Chapter 14 for troubleshooting tips).

Notification of Imports   After the import of change requests into the quality assurance system, the people responsible for the business validation must be notified so that they can begin testing. Notification may occur informally in the early stages of implementation. As the final, more general phase of testing approaches, the business validation team requires more formal notification. The project leaders should provide this notification, since they are responsible for the project at the going-live stage.

Importing into the Production System

When planning for import into the production system, your procedural documentation for performing imports using change requests should include:

- Procedures for signing off the change requests that contain approved functionality after testing in the quality assurance system

- A procedure and time schedule for imports of change requests required to support production problems

- Procedures for verifying imports and for the immediate handling of errors that occur during the import

- A duty roster assigning responsibility for performing the import

Imports into the production system are performed using the same tools used to import change requests in the quality assurance system (the TMS and the transport control program *tp*), but the import process itself must be more closely managed. The exact focus of this management differs depending upon whether the import is the going-live step in an implementation phase or is providing production support for current production activities. The support for introducing an implementation phase to production requires more testing and business validation testing. In contrast, imports for production support require more careful management of the import queue.

Going Live at the Conclusion of an Implementation Phase

Ideally, all change requests imported into the quality assurance system are also imported into the production system in the same order. This rule applies not only for the initial setup of the production system (as described in Chapter 5), but also for going live at the conclusion of an implementation phase.

Before going live at the conclusion of an implementation phase, a formal business validation of the entire quality assurance client is necessary to ensure that the collection of imported change requests provides the expected business processes. In addition, regression testing is required to ensure that the new business processes do not conflict with existing business functionality. The approved collection of change requests is introduced into the production system by importing the entire import queue.

Production Support

Even after the introduction of a new implementation phase and a period of time dedicated to stabilizing the production environment, further changes to the production environment may be required—for example, due to the emergence of errors or changed configuration requirements. These changes are the responsibility of production support, which should introduce only urgently required corrections, not new functionality. Every system landscape should include the system resources and transport processes required for production support. (See Chapter 3.)

Corrections made during production support must be tested in an R/3 client that is identical to the production client. This ensures that the testing is a true validation of business functionality and provides a simulation of the impact that the changes will have on the existing production data. Only when a change request has been tested and verified in the quality assurance system should it be imported into the production system.

The change requests required to support production may be the responsibility of different project initiatives, with different priorities. It will not be possible to sign off and import all change requests at the same time. After the start of production activities, the import queue of the production system may contain any of the following:

- Emergency fixes that require one or more change requests to be imported into production immediately (regardless of their position in the import queue sequence)

- Change requests that have been signed off and are ready for import into production

- Change requests that have not been signed off and are not yet ready for import into production

The TMS menu option *start import*, which imports all change requests waiting for import, cannot be used in such a situation. Instead, imports into the production system require you to check whether a change request has been signed off, and to import emergency fixes separately from other signed-off change requests. Thus, the import procedure involves careful manipulation of the import queue to determine the sequence in which change requests are imported into the production system.

Indicating Sign-Off after Testing   After business validation testing is completed, the tested change requests are signed off; that is, they are approved for transfer to the production system. When the affected change requests were imported into the quality assurance system, they were also added to the import queue of the production system. However, in releases before R/3 Release 4.6, the import queue of the production system cannot be used to indicate whether change requests have been formally signed off.

The sign-off process is often managed as follows:

- SAP Business Workflow® functionality is used to send a formal sign-off e-mail to the system administrator who will do the import.

- External to R/3, sign-off is recorded using the form shown in Figure 6.5, either on sheets of paper (one for each change request) or in a spreadsheet (as in Figure 6.7 later in this chapter) in a shared file.

- Verbal notification is provided by speaking with the system administrator who will do the import.

In R/3 Release 4.6, SAP has introduced the *QA Approval Process*, which provides a formal sign-off procedure for change requests waiting for import into an R/3 System. The process allows you to define which users are responsible for sign-off. Although a change request may be in the import queue of the production system, it cannot be imported until those people responsible for sign-off have approved the change request. The QA Approval Process is linked

FIGURE 6.5:

A sample production support change request form

Change and Transport Request Form				
Requestor		**Date**		
Source Client		**Target Client(s)**		
Source R/3 System	DEV	**Target R/3 System**		QAS
Change Request # ☐ Customizing ☐ Workbench			**Type of Change** ☐ Client-dependent ☐ Client-independent	
Description of contents				
Tasks/Request	☐ Change request released ☐ All tasks released ☐ To be released			
Special Requirements				
Approved by (please sign)				
IT Team USE ONLY				
Imported by			**Date**	
Transport Log Return Codes	☐ 0 Transport (export and import test) was successful. ☐ 4 Warning messages were generated. ☐ 8 Error messages were generated ☐ 12 Fatal error has occurred.			
Comments				
Exception handling-Corrected change request #			**Date** **Reason**	
Project Management Approval			**Date**	

with the CTS Project Management functionality in Release 4.6 so that the approval process is linked to change requests as a result of different projects. The approval process can be unique for the change requests of different projects.

Emergency Production Fixes   Typically, an emergency fix to correct a production problem is performed using a *preliminary import*. This imports the individual change request required to correct a problem, and retains that change request in the import queue of the production system to be reimported in sequence at a later time.

Figure 6.6 shows a sample import queue for a production system, PRD. The seventh and ninth change requests in the import queue have been signed off and are needed in the production system immediately. To achieve this, *preliminary import*s of change requests DEVK901633 and DEVK901638 will be performed.

FIGURE 6.6:

A sample import queue for a production system

Import Queue: System PRD			X
Request for PRD: 10/10			
Number	Request	Owner	Short Text
1	DEVK901532	KESTER	condition table for pricing
2	DEVK901561	HAMM	pricing agreements
3	DEVK901502	ROEHRS	foreign trade data
4	DEVK901514	SMITH	invoice lists
5	DEVK901585	SMITH	billing types
6	DEVK901592	HAMM	delivery scheduling
7	DEVK901633	SCHMIDT	FIX: shipping points
8	DEVK901543	KESTER	pricing rules
9	DEVK901638	SCHMIDT	FIX: shipping determination
10	DEVK901501	JAKOBI	new matchcode for billing

Importing Signed-Off Change Requests   Once signed off, change requests that are not part of an emergency fix are normally imported during the next scheduled import. There is a danger of incomplete functionality being imported if change requests that depend on other change requests do not receive sign-off at the same time.

Figure 6.7 gives an example of customer documentation showing an import queue, and also displays the status of the change requests and the dependencies among them. Change requests DEVK901633 and DEVK901638 have already been imported, possibly to provide an emergency fix, but should be imported again with the other change requests in the correct order. As revealed by the indicated dependencies, the change requests numbered 1, 2, 6, and 8 must be imported together to provide the desired functionality. Since they have all been signed off, you can assume that the functionality that will be imported is complete and fully tested. The third change request in the list has been signed off and is ready for import. Both the fourth and fifth change requests have not been signed off. If they are not signed off before the next scheduled import, they cannot be imported.

FIGURE 6.7:

Sample import queue documentation with sign-off status and dependencies

Number	Request	Status	Dependencies
1	DEVK901532	Approved	DEVK901561, DEVK901592, DEVK901543
2	DEVK901561	Approved	DEVK901532, DEVK901592, DEVK901543
3	DEVK901502	Approved	none
4	DEVK901514		
5	DEVK901585		
6	DEVK901592	Approved	DEVK901532, DEVK901561, DEVK901543
7	DEVK901633	Already Imported	
8	DEVK901543	Approved	DEVK901532, DEVK901561, DEVK901592
9	DEVK901638	Already Imported	
10	DEVK901501		

In such a situation, you should not perform an *import all* of the production import queue. To import the needed changes into the production system, either all change requests must be approved or the needed change requests must be imported individually.

TIP   To minimize the need for importing change requests out of sequence, SAP recommends that you ensure all change requests receive business validation and sign-off as soon as possible.

When you need to import change requests and cannot perform an *import all*, you have the following options:

- Set an end mark at a certain point in the import queue and *import all* change requests above the end mark.

- Perform a *preliminary import* for each individual change request.

- Perform *preliminary imports* for a group of individual change requests (available as of Release 4.5).

Either one or a combination of these import options can support the import of change requests into a production environment.

NOTE   Support of production activities requires experienced judgement in weighing the advantages of importing change requests in their original sequence against the advantages of performing imports out of sequence to provide emergency corrections to the production system.

To ensure consistency, change requests that are imported out of sequence are always imported again with all other change requests in the sequence dictated by the import queue. For example, after importing the signed-off change requests in Figure 6.7, the import queue would appear as shown in Figure 6.8. (Figure 6.8 no longer shows the first three change requests in Figure 6.7, since these were sequentially imported.) The change requests now numbered 3 through 6 (numbered 6 through 9 in Figure 6.7) will be imported again to ensure they enter the production system in the correct sequence.

FIGURE 6.8:

Import queue after
import of approved
change requests

Number	Request	Status	Dependencies
1	DEVK901514		
2	DEVK901585		
3	DEVK901592	Already Imported	DEVK901532, DEVK901561, DEVK901543
4	DEVK901633	Already Imported	
5	DEVK901543	Already Imported	DEVK901532, DEVK901561, DEVK901592
6	DEVK901638	Already Imported	
7	DEVK901501		

Scheduling Imports into the Production System

Importing change requests brings new Customizing settings and Repository object changes into the production system. These changes affect the runtime environment and have an impact on production activities. Imports into a live production system should be performed at times when online processing activity is low and scheduled background jobs have been completed. This is normally in the evening, when few or no users are in the system. For a global implementation, you can import at a time that represents the close of the business day for one region and the start of a new business day for another.

Before you perform imports, SAP recommends backing up the production system. If the import results in any unexpected problems, you can restore the R/3 System with the data preserved in the backup.

Responsibilities

The owner of a change request is responsible for that change request from the time it is created until it has passed through the quality assurance system and has been imported into production.

The business validation team takes over responsibility for the change request after it has been imported into the quality assurance system. The business validation team provides sign-off for the change requests (or collection of change requests), which can then be imported into the production system.

The actual import of change requests into the production system is the responsibility of the system administrator. The critical nature of changing a live production environment requires that the person performing the import must understand the current backup strategy, know when the R/3 System is carrying a low system load, and be able to react to any issues or errors that arise due to importing.

Business Validation

A well-managed change and transport process helps to ensure the success of your R/3 implementation. However, thorough quality assurance testing is what guarantees the successful addition of new and modified business processes to the production environment. Testing is only as good as the testing plans you devise, so design your testing plans carefully.

Several kinds of testing are required in the quality assurance system:

Business validation: The functional verification of your business processes.

Technical validation: Performance and stress tests ensure that the new business processes are optimized and supported by the hardware resources.

The technical validation required for production support is not covered in this book.

NOTE For more information on the technical validation of an R/3 System, see Hartwig Brand's *SAP R/3 Implementation with ASAP* (from Sybex).

Testing Procedures

Business validation is critical to the success of your R/3 implementation. It should always be performed before you import changes into the production system. Testing for production support may not be as time-consuming as the testing at the conclusion of an implementation phase, but it still requires business validation and sign-off. Standard, documented business validation procedures are required throughout the entire implementation process.

Business validation tests and verifies the following:

- New business processes and scenarios

- Existing core business processes (tested using regression testing)

- Customer developments and R/3 enhancements

The focus of business validation is on the R/3 application processes, but it may also include technical components such as interfaces, input and output methods, and print functions.

Designing a Test Plan for Business Validation

Like all other aspects of the R/3 implementation, business validation requires a defined procedure with assigned roles and responsibilities. A test plan should determine:

- The business scenarios and processes that require validation—for example, common business activities and core business transactions

- The testing methodology, including the different tools and user groups

- The people responsible for validating test results

R/3's sophistication ensures that there are always several ways of doing a business task. Therefore, it is not easy to define all possible scenarios. Project leaders in collaboration with end-user representatives can define the core business processes and common scenarios that require testing. Project leaders must also define the acceptance criteria that form the objective of the tests.

Evolution of a Test Plan   Your test plans will continuously change over time to deal with the variety of business processes being implemented. For example, your first phase of implementation may require business validation of the Financials components, a large number of data conversion routines, and interfaces to external systems. The subsequent introduction of the Logistics components does not require you to test any data conversion routines, but adds many more business processes and requires the verification of interfaces. In addition, in all testing procedures, you must test existing business processes through regression testing.

The Testing Cycle   Business validation involves the repeated testing of business processes in the quality assurance system until the acceptance criteria have been fulfilled. If the acceptance criteria are fulfilled, the change requests are signed off and are ready for import into the production system. If not, corrections are made in the development system *only*, and then the corresponding change requests are promoted to the quality assurance system for renewed testing.

During this cycle of business validation, it is common to "freeze" the quality assurance system—that is, to prevent the import of any new change requests and thus ensure the testing of a finite group of changes. Before freezing the system, you may wish to create a system backup. Because numerous transactions are run during testing—possibly creating unwanted data—it may be necessary to restore the system from a backup after testing. SAP recommends backing up data so that you can restore the R/3 System to its original state at any time.

Responsibilities

Business validation is process-oriented and should be set up and performed in consultation with experts from the business departments who are responsible for the particular process area. For the testing period, the project leaders' responsibilities include:

- Identifying the transactions that need testing (in conjunction with experts from the business departments)

- Defining the testing methodology that best suits the requirements

- Defining the acceptance criteria that form the objective of the tests

After the project leaders have defined the relevant transactions and methodology, the business validation team begins testing and verifying those transactions. The business validation team should represent different business departments and accordingly perform quality assurance tests for their respective R/3 settings, reports, and transactions. To enable the business validation team to check the import status for different projects, ensure that team members have display authorization for the Workbench Organizer and Customizing Organizer.

The R/3 system administrator should participate in setting up hardware and backups, and provide technical support during the actual testing.

R/3 Testing Tools

To achieve "perfect" business validation and performance testing, all employees would be required to spend a day or two in an R/3 System performing all their normal tasks. Since this procedure is too costly and inconvenient, project leaders generally use either or both of the following:

- Real users, representative of all the different user communities, running actual transactions

- Scripts that simulate R/3 transactions

The real-user approach is a simulation using actual, logged-on users. Although this approach allows you to test a realistic transaction mix while operating on actual user data, coordinating such tests may be difficult when many users are involved, especially when users are scattered all over the globe. In addition, such users may not always be available to test business validation when they are needed.

Scripting tools, on the other hand, provide a flexible method for testing a specific set of transactions. These tests are much easier to control, and therefore are easy to replicate. They also provide the option of simulating a different set of transactions and support business validation over time. To facilitate such testing, SAP provides testing tools as part of its core R/3 application. These tools make up the *Test Workbench* with its primary tool being the Computer Aided Test Tool (CATT).

The Test Workbench

Using the Test Workbench (Transaction S001; *Test > Test Workbench*), you can specify the applications to be tested by creating a *test catalog*. Within the test catalog, there are a series of scenarios that need to be tested, also known as *test cases*, which can be performed either manually or through scripting using a tool like CATT.

After creating different test cases, another tool, the *test organizer*, records which tests are necessary for the current business validation period. As testers perform the different tests in the test organizer, you can use this tool to track the status and results of the tests.

NOTE   For more information on the R/3 Test Workbench and on how to organize your business validation testing, refer to the R/3 online documentation.

Computer Aided Test Tool (CATT)

CATT is an R/3 tool integrated in the ABAP Workbench, which you can use to automate repeatable transactions in R/3 and record user activities for systematic testing. CATT can be used to perform the following tasks:

- Testing transactions

- Checking table values and database updates

- Setting up Customizing tables

- Testing the effect of changes to Customizing settings

- Creating test data

CATT includes the necessary functions to create, start, maintain, and log test procedures. When a CATT script is running, CATT validates user authorizations and produces a detailed result log that can be automatically archived. The CATT logs contain all information relevant to the test run and are stored centrally in the database of the executing R/3 System.

NOTE   For more information on how to build test scenarios with CATT, see R/3 online documentation.

Support for the SAP Standard

To provide an R/3 implementation with new and enhanced business functionality and support its customers' growing business needs, SAP periodically delivers new R/3 Releases. Existing R/3 customers obtain the new functionality in an R/3 Release upgrade. An upgrade replaces the current SAP standard objects—that is, the R/3 Repository—with new ones, while preserving customer data and developments.

In addition, SAP provides Support Packages and R/3 Notes, which allow the customer to integrate smaller-scale changes and repairs to the SAP standard. As with an R/3 Release upgrade, Support Packages and R/3 Notes ensure that the customer's data and Customizing and development changes will not be changed or lost. Your system landscape must be able to support all three forms of support, and your maintenance strategy should include the relevant procedures.

Support for an R/3 Release

SAP's Support Packages and R/3 Notes are R/3 Release–specific. Initially, SAP announces a correction for a particular R/3 Release and provides solutions in an R/3 Note. Then, to assist you in maintaining R/3, these corrections are bundled into Support Packages. A Support Package contains changes to source code and general improvements. A Support Package can in some ways be compared to an R/3 Release. For example, both change the R/3 standard. Each R/3 System not only has an R/3 Release level, but also a Support Package level that defines the status of the system's SAP standard.

To support your R/3 Systems at their current R/3 Release level, you must closely monitor the application of R/3 Notes and Support Packages and ensure that:

- You consistently transport changes that are based on R/3 Notes

- All R/3 Systems in your system landscape have the same R/3 Release level and the same Support Package level

- You do not overwrite modification adjustments that were imported to a system by subsequently applying a Support Package (see Chapter 15)

R/3 Notes

The solutions provided in R/3 Notes typically require you to make programming changes that modify the SAP standard, thereby creating what is known as a *modification*. To simplify applying these changes to your R/3 System, the corrections in R/3 Notes are bundled into Support Packages, which are available for download from SAPNet and can be automatically incorporated in your R/3 System without manual programming or the creation of modifications.

SAP recommends that you apply the corresponding Support Packages instead of making manual changes based on recommendations in an R/3 Note. However, you may still be required to make manual modifications for any of the following reasons:

Availability: A change documented in an R/3 Note has not been bundled into a Support Package.

Urgency: A correction documented in an R/3 Note is required as soon as possible. Rather than wait for the corresponding Support Package, you make the change in your development system according to the R/3 Note. The change request containing the modified SAP object is then transported to the quality assurance system and distributed to production after thorough testing and verification.

Verification: Making a single change according to an R/3 Note is much easier to verify than multiple changes. A single change requires only limited tests in contrast to the complete business validation of affected objects needed after applying a Support Package.

Dependencies: Support Packages must be applied in sequence. Because of this dependency, you cannot apply a Support Package until all of the previous Support Packages have been applied and verified. Additional dependencies may also exist if, for example, you are using industry solutions.

Performing a Modification   Before making modifications based on R/3 Notes, verify that the R/3 Note applies to your R/3 Release and that the symptoms documented in the R/3 Note correspond to the symptoms apparent in your R/3 System. In the case of uncertainty, SAP recommends contacting the SAP Hotline.

You should create all modifications of SAP objects in your development client. The change request containing the modification must then be transported to the quality assurance system for verification. Only after it has been thoroughly tested and signed off should you import the change request containing the modification into the production system.

For more information on the modification procedure, see Chapter 10.

Documentation Requirements   For every customer-changed SAP object, you will be required to perform a modification adjustment during R/3 Release upgrades and possibly also when applying Support Packages. To help speed up the modification adjustment process, you should document modifications when making them. Your documentation should include the R/3 Note number and R/3 Release dependencies. This information should be recorded in task documentation as well as in the short text of each change request. Then, when you begin a modification adjustment, you can recognize the corresponding change requests in the import queue.

Figure 6.9 shows how properly documented changes made as a result of an R/3 Note should appear in the import queue of a target system. Note that the relevant Support Package is also indicated.

This enables system administrators to decide whether the change request needs to be imported—it may be preferable to simply apply the corresponding Support Package to the target system.

TIP

Document all changes to SAP standard objects completely. If the change is based on an R/3 Note, include the R/3 Note number and relevant Support Package in the change request description.

FIGURE 6.9:

A sample change request resulting from an R/3 Note is waiting for import.

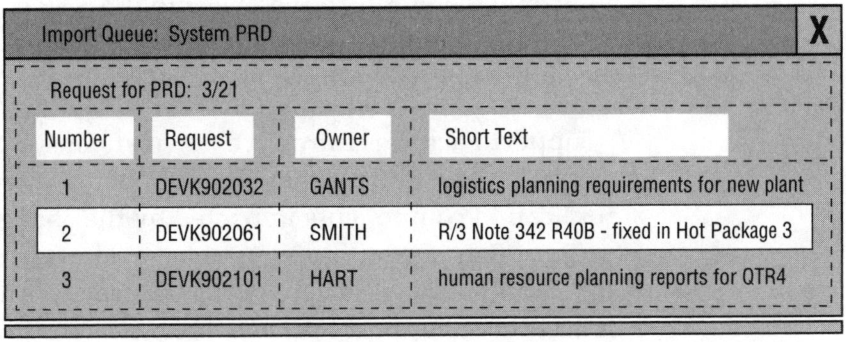
Import Queue: System PRD
X
Request for PRD: 3/21
Number
Request
Owner
Short Text
1
DEVK902032
GANTS
logistics planning requirements for new plant
2
DEVK902061
SMITH
R/3 Note 342 R40B - fixed in Hot Package 3
3
DEVK902101
HART
human resource planning reports for QTR4

Support Packages

SAP's Support Packages enable SAP to quickly and easily repair software errors in the R/3 Repository that require urgent attention. By applying Support Packages, you can maintain the latest corrections in your R/3 System and avoid making modifications to the SAP standard based on R/3 Notes. Support Packages keep your R/3 System up to date. However, you cannot apply Support Packages without considering:

- Possible conflicts with any modifications previously made to the SAP standard

- The impact of the corrections on your R/3 System, as well as the additional business validation tests required in the quality assurance system

When applying a Support Package, you may be asked to adjust any SAP objects you have modified manually, regardless of whether the modification was made according to an R/3 Note or to add customer-specific functionality. Modification adjustment involves choosing whether to retain the changes comprising the modification or delete them to regain the original SAP objects as contained in the Support Package. Ideally, the objective of this adjustment is to return the object to the SAP standard. SAP recommends limiting modifications to the SAP standard to simplify the application of Support Packages.

Support Packages introduce new versions of SAP standard objects into an R/3 System. The number of affected objects and application components impacted by the changes varies from Support Package to Support Package. However, since a considerable number of objects are changed, every Support Package (or collection of Support Packages) requires verification before being applied to the production system. Such validation testing is time-consuming and may not be possible within the current implementation plan.

SAP recommends that you apply all available Support Packages at the initial installation of your R/3 System or immediately following an upgrade. Subsequent Support Packages for the same R/3 Release level should be applied at the beginning of a new implementation phase to ensure that they are part of the business validation cycle.

Example: Applying Support Packages

An implementation phase has been undergoing business validation for a month. Initial business validation in the quality assurance system has begun to test newly implemented business processes. While large numbers of sales orders are being processed, a performance problem is detected. The system administrator looks for and finds a relevant R/3 Note. According to the R/3 Note, the solution is to either manually modify three different SAP standard objects or apply the next available Support Package.

Since final validation of the quality assurance system as a whole has not commenced, the customer has a choice—make manual modifications or apply the Support Package. If, however, the performance problem was detected in the middle of final business validation, the implementation schedule would probably cause the customer to decide to make the necessary modifications manually and apply the Support Package in a subsequent implementation phase.

R/3 Release Upgrades

Although Support Packages provide a select number of new Repository objects, an R/3 Release upgrade supplies a completely new R/3 Repository to obtain new R/3 functionality. The upgrade procedure requires a wider range of activities than those associated with Support Packages.

R/3 Release upgrades require:

- Downtime for each R/3 System during the import of the new R/3 Release
- Modification adjustment
- Customizing

The activities and tools required for an R/3 Release upgrade are covered in more detail in Chapter 15.

R/3 Release Upgrade Phase

Because of the changes associated with an upgrade, SAP recommends you dedicate an entire implementation phase to the upgrade process. An R/3 Release upgrade should not be part of an existing implementation phase that is required to introduce changes or creates business processes.

As with the rollout of new business processes, an R/3 Release upgrade also requires additional upgrade-specific Customizing activities known as *Release Customizing*. The successful implementation of this Release Customizing and the new R/3 Repository require:

- Technical changes to your R/3 environment, such as upgrades to operating system and database software, or to hardware

- Business validation testing

- Stable R/3 Systems—in particular, a stable production environment

Responsibilities

Although your system administrator is responsible for production support—for example, applying R/3 Notes, Support Packages, and R/3 Release upgrades—the impetus for applying such changes normally is one of the following:

- A problem arises for which there is a relevant R/3 Note or Support Package.

- Business departments want functionality contained in R/3 upgrades.

The decision-making process may involve people at many levels within your company.

Review Questions

1. Which of the following activities is *not* necessary for releasing and exporting a change request?

   A. Documenting every task in the change request

   B. Releasing every task in the change request

   C. Verification of the contents of the change request by the system administrator

   D. Unit testing the change request

2. Which of the following statements is correct in regard to the tasks used in change requests that record Customizing and development changes?

   A. Tasks belong to a change request.

   B. Tasks can be used by several R/3 users.

   C. Tasks are the direct responsibility of a project leader.

   D. Tasks record only client-specific changes.

3. Which of the following indicates that a change request has been signed off after quality assurance testing?

   A. The change request is released after unit testing.

   B. The change request is successfully imported into the quality assurance system.

   C. The change request is added to the import queue of all other R/3 Systems in the system landscape.

   D. The project leader communicates their approval of the change request.

4. Which of the following is *not* an SAP recommendation?

    A. Imports into the quality assurance and production systems should occur in the same sequence.

    B. Even if the import process is automatically scripted, a technical consultant or system administrator should review the results of the import.

    C. Project leaders should manually add change requests to the import queue of the quality assurance system.

    D. Change requests are imported in the same sequence that they were exported from the development system.

5. Which of the following is SAP's recommendation on how to rush an emergency correction into the production system?

    A. Make the change directly in the production system.

    B. Transport the change from the development system to the quality assurance system and production system using a *preliminary import*.

    C. Make the change and use a client copy with a change request to distribute the change to production.

    D. Make the change in the quality assurance system and transport the change using a *preliminary import*.

6. Which of the following transport activities is *not* typically the responsibility of the system administrator?

    A. Importing change requests into all clients within the system landscape

    B. Verifying the success of the import process

    C. Releasing change requests

    D. Assisting in solving either export or import errors

7. Which of the following does SAP provide as customer support?

   A. R/3 Release upgrades to provide new functionality

   B. Support Packages to correct identified problems in a specific R/3 Release

   C. R/3 Notes to announce errors and corrections for the reported problems

   D. All of the above

PART TWO
TECHNICAL TASKS

The first six chapters of this book have provided you with an overview of the change and transport concepts and recommendations for the implementation and maintenance of your R/3 system landscape. The next part of the book expands on the introduction to the transport mechanism, and outlines the technical tasks required to realize your system landscape. These tasks include:

- Setting up a transport directory at the operating system level

- Setting up the Transport Management System (TMS)

- Creating new clients

This part will be of most interest to those people who are directly responsible for setting up, upgrading, or extending a system landscape. This person is typically the implementation's system administrator.

Transport Setup Activities at R/3 Installation

To set up the capability for transporting R/3 change requests, you must perform certain activities when installing an R/3 System. These activities are explained in this chapter, and include:

- Specifying the system ID
- Setting up the transport directory
- Configuring the transport profile
- Performing activities within R/3 such as:
    - Initializing the Change and Transport Organizer (CTO)
    - Setting the system change option
    - Verifying the background jobs and background work processes required for transports

Specifying the System ID (SID)

When installing R/3, you must determine a name for the new R/3 System. The R/3 System name is known as the *system ID (SID)*. If you perform a standard installation, you must define a name for the R/3 System and the database at an early stage in the installation. If the new R/3 System is the result of a system copy, you must specify a new SID for the R/3 System and the database.

The SID of each R/3 System in the system landscape must be unique. When you specify a SID, especially when adding a system to an existing landscape, ensure that the new SID does not conflict with an existing SID.

NOTE   Under no circumstances may two R/3 Systems within a system landscape have the same SID.

Because of the need to set up transport routes early in the implementation of a system landscape, when you set up the development system, a placeholder or virtual system name is assigned—for example, to the production system, despite the fact that the production system has not yet been created. When you install further R/3 Systems in the system landscape, if a system has already been established within the Transport Management System (TMS) as a virtual system, use the name provided in the TMS and delete the reference to the virtual system. For more information on setting up transport routes and virtual systems, see Chapters 5 and 8.

SIDs that are reserved by SAP and may not be used by customers when naming new R/3 Systems include ADD, ALL, AND, ANY, ASC, B20, B30, BCO, BIN, COM, DBA, END, EPS, FOR, GID, INT, KEY, LOG, MON, NOT, OFF, OMS, P30, RAW, ROW, SAP, SET, SGA, SHG, SID, UID, and VAR.

NOTE   In addition to the names reserved by SAP, you cannot use a number as the first character of the SID.

Setting Up the Transport Directory

After starting the installation, you must specify the path to the system's transport directory. The transport directory is a file system located on the operating system level where the objects in change requests that were released and exported from that R/3 System are physically copied so that they can subsequently be imported to a target R/3 System. The transport directory is an integral part of transporting change requests from one R/3 System to another R/3

System. The transport directory enables you to perform the following tasks throughout your R/3 System landscape:

- Sharing changes, using change requests and client transports
- Applying SAP Support Packages

Because the files in the transport directory corresponding to the objects in the change request must be accessed by different R/3 Systems within the system landscape, often only one physical transport directory on one R/3 System is used, since it can be shared by all other R/3 Systems. This single shared transport directory is called the *common transport directory*. Every R/3 application server needs to have access to the common transport directory.

During installation, at least one physical transport directory has to be created on one R/3 System of your system landscape. Quite early in the installation process, you are asked to specify where the transport directory is to be created, or—if a transport directory has already been created—which host system serves as the *transport host*.

NOTE   The transport host is the system that physically contains the common transport directory.

All R/3 Systems that share the same transport directory make up a *transport group* (see Chapter 8). Figure 7.1 shows an example of a common transport directory. The transport host—the system containing the transport directory—is the development system, DEV. The quality assurance system (QAS) and the production system (PRD) share the transport directory of DEV. Together, all three systems—DEV, QAS, and PRD—are part of the same transport group.

NOTE   All R/3 Systems belonging to one transport group share the same physical transport directory, called the common transport directory.

FIGURE 7.1:

A common transport directory for a three-system landscape

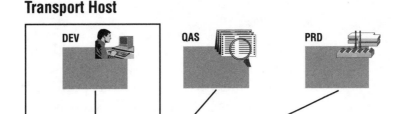

FIGURE 7.1:

A common transport directory for a three-system landscape

One or Many Transport Directories?

Standard practice is to have one common transport directory in a system landscape. However, it may be useful to have more than one transport directory if, for example:

- The network connection to an R/3 System is not fast enough.

- There is no permanent network connection between the different R/3 Systems of the system landscape.

- There are security reasons that prevent direct access to an R/3 System.

- There are different hardware platforms that do not allow a common transport directory.

If you require additional transport directories, you will need to use either further common transport directories (if more than one R/3 System share the directory) or a private one (if only one R/3 System uses the directory). For example, you can create a transport directory in the production system, and if this transport directory is not shared with other systems, it is called the *private transport directory* (see Figure 7.2).

When you create a new transport directory, a further transport group is added to your system landscape. Customizing and development work can be transported between different transport groups (see Chapter 13). However, transporting between different transport groups requires additional steps, time, and disk space due to the indirect transport through different transport directories.

FIGURE 7.2:

Two transport groups

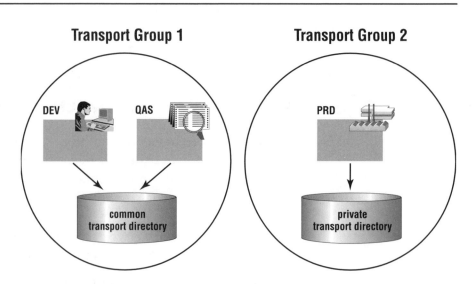

If you use several transport groups, bear in mind that:

- Log files generated during the export process can be displayed only in R/3 Systems that are in the same transport group as the source system. The source system is typically the development system.

- Log files generated during the import process can be displayed only in R/3 Systems that are in the same transport group as the target system. The target system is typically the quality assurance or production system.

- You must maintain the transport profile for each transport group.

Example of a System Landscape with Two Transport Groups

To provide a solid, 24-hour maintenance and support solution for a production R/3 System, a company outsources its system support for the production system. The internal technology team manages support for the development system and quality assurance system, both of which physically reside at the company headquarters. However, the production system is located in a different facility across town, and for this system, the external support vendor provides support.

While the production system is physically accessible from the company's headquarters through the network and the company's firewall, the production system does not share the same transport directory as the development system and the quality assurance system. The main reason for having separate transport directories is to avoid requiring an NFS (network file system) mount across the network and to protect the production system from nonrelevant transport activities. Consequently, there are two transport groups: one transport group for the development system and the quality assurance system, and another transport group for the production system (see Figure 7.2 earlier in this section).

Transport Directory Structure

The subdirectories in the transport directory store all the files needed for transports (see Figure 7.3). No user action is required to create the subdirectories—they are created automatically during the installation of an R/3 System.

FIGURE 7.3:

Transport directory structure

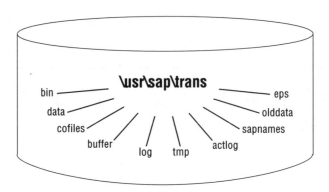

The subdirectories in the common transport directory include:

bin: This directory contains the transport profile, called TP_<domain>.PFL in R/3 Release 4.5 and TPPARAM in earlier R/3 Releases.

data: This directory stores the actual data files of the related change requests with the Customizing and development changes.

cofiles: This directory contains *control files,* or change request information files used by the transport tools on the operating system level. The information in the files includes data on transport types, object classes, required import steps, and return codes. These files contain the current status of the change request in the various systems of the transport group.

buffer: This directory contains an import buffer for each R/3 System in a transport group. These buffer files indicate which change requests are to be imported in the respective system. The import queues that have already been mentioned in Chapter 4 are the representation of the import buffers within R/3. Buffer files also provide information on the steps that must be performed for import, and the order in which requests are to be imported.

log: This directory includes all general log files, as well as all log files generated by the export and import of change requests or client copy activities.

tmp: This directory is needed to temporarily store log files and semaphores during transport activities.

actlog: This directory stores the log of user actions in R/3 for all change requests and tasks. This is the only subdirectory of the transport directory that is not accessed by the operating system *tp*. This directory is accessed only by the Change and Transport Organizer (CTO).

sapnames: This directory contains a file for each R/3 user working with the CTS. These files log transport activities for each change request.

olddata: This directory is needed when you clean up the transport directory. Old exported data that is to be archived or deleted is stored in this directory.

eps: This is the download directory for SAP Support Packages from SAPNet.

For more information on the files contained in these directories, see Chapter 14.

Procedure

To set up the common transport directory, you must provide a file system on the system that you have chosen to be the transport host before you run *R3setup* to start the actual installation. Many customers choose the development system as the transport host because it is typically the first system to be installed. When you run *R3setup* from the CDs, the transport directory is automatically created with its subdirectories.

Every computer of the transport group on which an R/3 instance is installed should have read access and write access to the transport directory. This is implemented through corresponding authorizations of the operating system user who owns the SAP instance—for example, <sid>adm on UNIX platforms. You should ensure that there is sufficient network availability between the systems that belong to the same transport group.

To set up your transport directory:

1. Create the following directory on the transport host:

   • /usr/sap/trans on UNIX and AS/400 platforms

   • \sapmnt\trans on Windows NT platforms

2. Mount this directory using operating system tools as part of the installation preparation on the hosts that belong to the same transport group.

3. Ensure that the correct path to the transport directory is stored in the parameter *transdir* in the transport profile as well as in the parameter *DIR_TRANS* in the instance profile.

Technical Requirements

The required free space on the transport directory highly depends on the transport volume. As a rule of thumb for estimating the required amount of disk space for your transport directory, proceed as follows:

• Estimate 100MB per R/3 instance that will be using the transport directory.

- Estimate 20MB for each user involved in Customizing and development.

- The minimum total amount of disk space for the transport directory deriving from the above two estimates should be 200MB.

- Add the estimated additional space needed for client exports. This amount of disk space depends on the data to be transported. (See also Chapter 9.)

- Add the estimated additional space needed for SAP Support Packages. (See also Chapter 15.)

The following sections cover how to set up the transport directory for UNIX, Windows NT, AS/400, and a heterogeneous environment.

Transport Directory on UNIX

To set up the transport directory on a UNIX platform:

1. Log on to the transport host as user *root*.

2. Create the file system for the transport directory.

3. Mount this file system as `/usr/sap/trans` (default value). Ensure that the directory belongs to the group *sapsys* and has the permission 775. After installation, you should restrict the permission to 771.

4. Export the directory using a tool such as NFS (network file system).

NOTE   Ensure that group *sapsys* has the same *group identification number* (GID) on all the computers of the network.

Next, perform the following steps on all other R/3 instances in the transport group:

1. Log on as user *root*.

2. Create a mount point, /usr/sap/trans.

3. Establish a network connection to the transport directory— for example, using NFS to mount the transport directory from the transport host.

NOTE   For details on the command syntax of the specific UNIX derivatives, see *R/3 Installation on UNIX-OS Dependencies*, one of the implementation guides accompanying the SAP R/3 installation package.

Transport Directory on Windows NT

To share a common transport directory, all application and database servers for an R/3 System either must be in the same Windows NT domain or, if the domains differ, you must specify an NT *trusted relationship* between them.

For Windows NT, you can choose any computer as the transport host. If you have chosen a computer that contains the R/3 central instance to be the transport host, skip the following three steps. Otherwise, if the computer chosen contains an R/3 dialog instance or no instance at all, perform the following steps before installation (that is, before running *R3setup*):

1. Create the directory \usr\sap\trans.

2. Set a global share *sapmnt* to point to the usr\sap file tree. This allows the transport directory to be accessed through the path \sapmnt\trans.

3. Grant NT access type *Full Control* for *Everyone* on this directory.

NOTE   The Windows NT access type *Full Control* is required for the transport directory only during R/3 installation. After the installation, for security reasons, you should restrict this access to write authorizations for operating system users.

You must define the transport host using the alias *SAPTRANS-HOST*. Whenever it is necessary to point to the transport host, this alias is used instead of the name of the transport host. Prior to R/3 installation, make this alias known to all Windows NT systems within the transport domain by using either of the following techniques:

- On the Domain Name Server (DNS), record the alias SAP-TRANSHOST for the transport host. This technique is recommended by SAP and creates what is known as the *central transport host*. Its main advantage is that you do not have to adjust the parameters of every system when moving the transport directory, but only the central record of the transport host on the DNS.

NOTE   For more information on the configuration of a central transport host, see R/3 Note 62739.

- If no DNS server is available, you can use the hosts file to record the alias SAPTRANSHOST. This file is located in the Windows NT default directory <drive>:\WINNT\system32\ drivers\etc. Use an editor to add the entry <IP_address> <hostname> SAPTRANSHOST. Ensure that this file is identical on all hosts where an R/3 instance is installed or will be installed.

Early in the R/3 installation process, you are asked to name the host that contains the transport directory. For a common transport directory, enter the alias SAPTRANSHOST. For a private transport directory, enter the host name of the computer that contains the transport directory.

Transport Directory on AS/400

To enable access to a common transport directory, use the integrated file server QFileSvr.400 on the AS/400 system to provide access to other file systems on remote AS/400 systems.

TIP   To avoid performance problems, use the QFileSvr.400 file server instead of NFS to connect the R/3 Systems on AS/400 platforms.

Prior to R/3 installation on AS/400:

1. For each host sharing the transport directory, create a subdirectory named with the respective host name in QFileSvr.400. To create such a subdirectory, execute the following command with the respective host name:

   MKDIR '/QfileSvr.400/<hostname>'

   Create the host directories with the startup program QSTRUP, because these directories no longer exist after the initial program load (IPL) of AS/400, and must be re-created.

2. Create the following operating system users on all AS/400 systems in the transport group:

   - SAP<nn> (as of R/3 Release 4.0; nn denotes the instance number)

   - <SID><nn> (as of R/3 Release 4.5; nn denotes the instance number)

   - <SID>OFR (for the R/3 System superuser)

   - <SID>OPR (for the R/3 System operator)

NOTE These users must have the same passwords on all computers and need *write* permission on the transport directory.

For each AS/400 R/3 System in the transport group, perform the following:

1. When installing the R/3 software, in the *R3setup* main menu (*R/3 Installation*), select option 3 to change the location of the transport directory /usr/sap/trans.

2. Specify the host name of the transport host. As a result, the transport directory can be accessed through /usr/sap/trans, which is a symbolic link that points to the directory /QfileSvr .400/<hostname>/sapmnt/trans.

For an R/3 installation with a private transport directory, perform a default installation for the transport directory. When the R/3 installation program asks for the location of the transport directory, agree to the default proposed settings. Accepting the default settings automatically creates the transport directory under /sapmnt/trans. The transport directory can be accessed through /usr/sap/trans, which is a link to the physical directory /sapmnt/trans.

NOTE R/3 Note 67213 provides more details on the transport directory for AS/400 platforms.

Heterogeneous Operating Systems

It is possible to use a common transport directory in heterogeneous operating system environments. The configuration depends on the operating systems. For example, you can set up the physical transport directory on a UNIX system and provide network access to AS/400 systems. You can also have the transport directory on an AS/400 server and access it from UNIX systems—although this configuration is more complex. In both cases, you must use NFS for the connection between the different platforms.

NOTE	For more information on setting up a central transport directory in environments with UNIX and AS/400 platforms, see R/3 Note 69429.

The implementation of a common transport directory in mixed environments with Windows NT and UNIX is more difficult. Some files in the transport directory are written in text mode. On UNIX platforms, a linefeed is written at each line end. On Windows NT, the line end is indicated by a carriage return followed by a linefeed. All R/3 Systems must be configured so that the transport directory files are written only in binary mode—the line end is indicated by a linefeed on both platforms.

There is no hierarchical file system on Windows NT platforms. It is not possible to create soft links to mount UNIX file trees on Windows NT systems, or links that mount Windows NT file trees on UNIX systems. To enable this access between the systems, you must install additional software such as SAMBA.

NOTE	For more information on setting up a central transport directory in environments with UNIX and Windows NT platforms, see R/3 Note 28781.

Configuring the Transport Profile

For each transport group, you need to set up and maintain a transport profile. The transport profile contains the settings needed to configure the transport control program *tp* and the transport program *R3trans*. The transport profile is stored in subdirectory *bin* of the transport directory.

In the transport profile, the following parameters must be maintained:

- Database-specific parameters:
    - *dbhost*
    - *dbname*
- Path-specific parameters:
    - *transdir*
    - *r3transpath*
- Parameters for heterogeneous environments

If you have more than one transport group, the transport profiles should all be identical. The only exception might be parameter *transdir*.

WARNING   In releases prior to R/3 Release 4.5, the parameters in the transport profile are specified in lowercase—for example, *transdir*. As of R/3 Release 4.5, they are specified in uppercase—for example, *TRANSDIR*. For simplicity, the transport profile parameters in this book are written in lowercase.

Transport Profile in R/3 Release 4.0

Up to R/3 Release 4.0, the transport profile is stored in the file TPPARAM, which is also known as the *global parameter file*. SAP delivers templates as sample profiles, which you have to adapt manually after R/3 installation.

The sample TPPARAM file is stored as TPPARAM.TPL in the installation directory—for example, in the UNIX directory \usr\ sap\<SID>\SYS\exe\run\INSTALL. To adapt the default transport profile, copy the template file—TPPARAM.TPL—as TPPARAM to subdirectory *bin* of the transport directory. To adapt TPPARAM to your system landscape, you must use a text editor on the operating system level.

Example of a Transport Profile TPPARAM for an NT Platform with R/3 Release 4.0

This example of a transport profile contains only the minimum required parameters:

```
##########################################################
# global Parameters                                      #
##########################################################
transdir = \\$(SAPTRANSHOST)\sapmnt\trans\
dbname = $(system)
##########################################################
# System specific Parameters                             #
##########################################################
##########################################################
# DEV #
DEV/dbhost = twdfmx01
# QAS #
QAS/dbhost = twdfmx02
# PRD #
PRD/dbhost = twdfmx03
```

Transport Profile in R/3 Release 4.5

As of R/3 Release 4.5, the file TP_<domain>.PFL is used as the transport profile. You no longer need to copy and adapt the profile on the operating system level. It is automatically generated the first time you call the Transport Management System (TMS) and contains the required transport parameter settings. This file is also stored in subdirectory *bin* of the transport directory. It is administered in the TMS.

WARNING As of R/3 Release 4.5, you do not modify the transport profile using a text editor on the operating system level.

The transport profile is maintained automatically when certain TMS functions are performed, such as adding a new R/3 System. If necessary, modify the transport profile from the R/3 initial screen:

1. Call Transaction STMS.

2. Choose *Overview* ➢ *Systems.*

3. Mark one system and choose *R/3 System* ➢ *Change.*

4. Choose the tab *Transport tool.*

Figure 7.4 shows how R/3 displays the transport profile TP_ <domain>.PFL for R/3 Release 4.5. You may change global, system-specific, and operating system specific parameters. Enter the changes directly in the *Value* column and choose *Save*. This creates a backup file by saving the previous version of the transport profile as TP_<domain>.BAK in the transport subdirectory *bin*.

FIGURE 7.4:

Transport profile
parameters

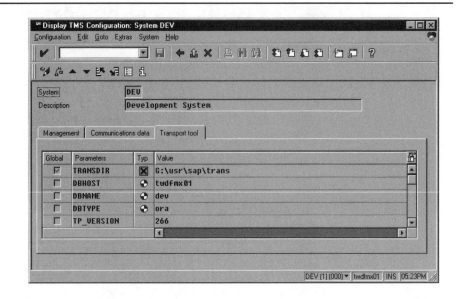

In the *Type* column, the symbols indicate the origin of certain parameters. To access the legend for these symbols, choose *Extras* ➤ *Legend* (see Figure 7.5).

FIGURE 7.5:

Legend for parameter
types

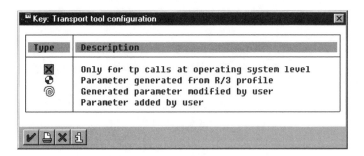

In Figure 7.4, the parameter *transdir* is the only parameter that is used explicitly on the operating system level. All database parameters—*dbhost*, *dbname*, and *dbtype*—have been automatically generated by the TMS. The *tp_version* parameter has been added automatically when implementing a current version of *tp*.

To list all the defined parameters and their values, in the screen *Display TMS Configuration: System <SID>*, choose *Goto* ➤ *TP parameters*.

Upgrading to R/3 Release 4.5

After an upgrade to R/3 Release 4.5, your R/3 System will contain two transport profiles: TPPARAM and TP_<domain>.PFL. The transport profile TP_<domain>.PFL is always used when calling *tp* from the R/3 System. A conflict may arise when you run *tp* on the operating system level if the formerly used transport profile TPPARAM still exists in the subdirectory *bin* after the upgrade. To start *tp* from the operating system, you must specify the location of the parameter file with the option pf=<path of TP_<domain>.PFL>. Otherwise, *tp* searches for the TPPARAM transport profile.

WARNING If both transport profiles—TPPARAM and TP_<domain>.PFL—exist, a conflict may arise when you run *tp* on the operating system level. Therefore, when starting *tp* on the operating system level, you must indicate which profile *tp* is to use.

Each R/3 System should be described in only one transport profile—for R/3 Release 4.5, this file is TP_<domain>.PFL. To achieve this, copy the settings in TPPARAM to TP_<domain>.PFL and then delete the entries in TPPARAM.

To copy the settings from the former transport profile, TPPARAM, to the new transport profile, TP_<domain>.PFL, proceed as follows:

1. Call Transaction STMS.

2. Choose *Overview* ➤ *Systems*.

3. From the screen *System Overview: Domain <domain>*, mark the R/3 System that is the source of the parameters to be copied.

4. Choose *R/3 System* ➢ *Change* and then the tab *Transport tool*.

5. Choose *Extras* ➢ *Copy configuration from TPPARAM*.

6. Choose *Save* and, as described in Chapter 8, distribute these changes to all R/3 Systems in the transport domain.

Profile Syntax

The parameters specified in the transport profile and their syntax are valid for both TPPARAM and TP_<domain>.PFL. The syntax for TP__<domain>.PFL corresponds to how it is represented on the operating system level; within R/3, the parameters are represented as depicted in Figure 7.4 (earlier in the chapter).

WARNING For R/3 Release 4.0, you must use a text editor on the operating system level to configure the transport profile parameters. For R/3 Release 4.5, these parameters are generated automatically. You do not need to set up the transport profile parameters for a minimum configuration. You can maintain and add transport profile parameters using TMS.

Parameter Types

Comment lines are preceded by # in the transport profile. All other lines contain parameter definitions, which can be any of the following:

- Global—that is, valid for all R/3 Systems in the transport domain

- R/3 System–specific—that is, valid only for one R/3 System

- Operating system–specific—that is, valid for all systems running a specific operating system

- Database-specific—that is, valid for all systems on a specific database platform

Table 7.1 shows the syntax for the different parameter types in the transport profile.

TABLE 7.1: Profile Syntax for TPPARAM

Parameter Types	Syntax	Possible Acronyms
Global	`<parameter>=<value>`	
R/3 System–specific	`<SID>/<parameter>=<value>`	
Operating system–specific	`<CPU>|<parameter>=<value>`	aix, axp (Open VMS), hp-ux, osf1, sinix, sunos, wnt (Windows NT), as4 (AS/400)
Database-specific	`<DB>:<parameter>=<value>`	ora (Oracle), inf (Informix), ada (SAP DB), mss (MS SQL Server), db2 (DB2 for OS390), db4 (DB2/400), db6 (DB2 for AIX)

If a parameter is not specified, the default value is used. SAP recommends grouping global settings at the beginning of the transport profile, because in general, the last setting for a given R/3 System, operating system, or database overrides previous settings.

Predefined Variables

Predefined variables can be used as part of the parameter values of the transport profile. They have the format $(<variable name>). If required, the brackets may be masked with a backslash (\). Table 7.2 lists all possible predefined variables.

TABLE 7.2: Predefined Variables

Variable	Description	Possible Values
$(cpu)	CPU name (important in heterogeneous system landscapes)	alphaosf, hp, rm600, rs6000 sun, wnt, as4
$(cpu2)	Acronym for the operating system	aix, hp-ux, osf1, sinix, sunos, wnt
$(dname)	Abbreviation for the day of the week	SUN, MON, ...
$(mday)	Day of the current month	01 to 31
$(mname)	Abbreviation for the name of the month	JAN, FEB, ...
$(mon)	Month	01 to 12
$(system)	System identifier (SID) of the R/3 System	For example, PRD
$(wday)	Day of the week	00 to 06 (Sunday = 00)
$(yday)	Day of the current year	001 to 366
$(year)	Year	For example, 1999
$(syear)	Short form of the year	For example, 99
$(yweek)	Calendar week	00 to 53

Example of Using Predefined Variables

Transport parameter *syslog* specifies the file *SLOG* that is used to monitor the transport activities of a specific R/3 System. The file is stored in subdirectory *log* of the transport directory and contains a general overview of performed imports. The name of this log file can be set in the transport profile using *syslog* as a global parameter. The default setting for the parameter *syslog* is SLOG<year><week>.<SID>.

The appropriate configuration is as follows:

- The parameter type is set to *global*.

Continued on next page

- The parameter is set using predefined variables to SLOG$(syear) $(yweek).$(system).

In week 31 of year 1999, this configuration instructs the system to log anything written to the file SLOG in the R/3 System QAS to a file called SLOG9931.QAS.

Table 7.3 contains the additional predefined variables that are available on Windows NT platforms.

TABLE 7.3: Additional Variables for Windows NT

Variable	Description
$(SAPGLOBALHOST)	Points to the host on which the central instance is installed
$(SAPTRANSHOST)	Points to the transport host

Required Parameters

For R/3 Release 4.0, to set up your system landscape for transporting, you must set a minimum number of parameters on the operating system level. These required parameters are automatically set during the setup of TMS in R/3 Release 4.5. The required parameters are described in this section. For information on further uses of these parameters and other transport profile parameters, see Chapter 14 and Appendix B.

Database Parameters

Database-specific parameters in the transport profile enable the transport control program *tp* to access the databases. The following parameters are required.

dbhost For each R/3 System within the transport group, configure the parameter *dbhost* (system-specific). This parameter specifies the host name—that is, the computer on which the database runs or, valid for Oracle and DB2 on AIX, on which the database processes run.

TIP
On Windows NT platforms, ensure that you use the TCP/IP computer host name as the value for parameter *dbhost*.

---

dbname Parameter *dbname* is used to specify the name of the database instance. Typically, the parameter is realized as a global parameter, and the value is specified using the variable *$(system)*. The transport parameter *dbname* passes over the name of the R/3 database, for which *tp* is called.

TIP
Note that parameter *dbname* is case sensitive on Informix platforms. For SAP DB as well as for DB2, this parameter has to be changed from lowercase to uppercase after the installation.

Exceptions are DB2/400 platforms and SAP standard installations on Oracle platforms. Standard installations use the name of the R/3 System for the name of the database instance and for the logical name of the database in the network. On these platforms, you do not need to specify parameter *dbname*.

Further Database Parameters Depending on your database platform, you must also set further parameters as listed in Table 7.4.

TABLE 7.4: Additional Parameters for Database Platforms

Platform	Parameter	Value
SAP DB	*Dbuserkey*	Name of the SAP instance
DB2/400 (only if opticonnect is used)	*Opticonnect*	1

TIP   For information on transport profile parameters required for a DB2 database on OS/390, see R/3 Note 77589.

Path-Specific Parameters

The parameters that ensure that the tools involved in the transport process use the correct paths are as follows:

- *transdir*
- *DIR_TRANS*
- *r3transpath*

The transport parameters *transdir* and *r3transpath* are specified in the transport profile. *DIR_TRANS* must be set in the instance profile.

transdir   The parameter *transdir* is located in the transport profile and specifies the name of the transport directory for *tp* as it has been mounted on all hosts of a transport group.

To set this parameter for R/3 Release 4.0 in a noncomplex landscape that has no special requirements such as special security demands:

1. Set the parameter *transdir* as a *global* parameter. It cannot be set *system-specific* or *database-specific,* but can be set as operating system–specific.

NOTE   For R/3 Release 4.0 in heterogeneous operating system environments, set the parameter type to operating system–specific. For example, `wnt|transdir = \\trans02\trans` specifies that for all Windows NT systems, the transport directory can be found on the host *trans02* in the directory *trans*.

2. Set *transdir* identically for all R/3 Systems within a single transport group.

3. Set the default values as listed for the respective platforms in Table 7.5.

TABLE 7.5 Operating System–Specific Values for *transdir*

Platform	Value for *transdir*
UNIX	`/usr/sap/trans`
AS/400	`/usr/sap/trans`
Windows NT (if you have configured a central transport host with alias SAPTRANSHOST)	`\\(SAPTRANSHOST)\sapmnt\trans`
Windows NT (without a central transport host)	`\\<transport host>\sapmnt\trans`

DIR_TRANS   The parameter *DIR_TRANS* is located in the instance profile. As with *transdir,* it points to the transport directory and is used by several programs, such as the R/3 kernel. Whenever the operating system transport tool *tp* is called from the R/3 System, the value of *transdir* is overridden with the value of *DIR_TRANS*.

NOTE   The transport parameters *transdir* and *DIR_TRANS* should always point to the same directory.

Example of the Parameters *transdir* and *DIR_TRANS* with UNIX

The following graphic illustrates how the transport directory is accessed using the parameters *transdir* and *DIR_TRANS* on a UNIX platform.

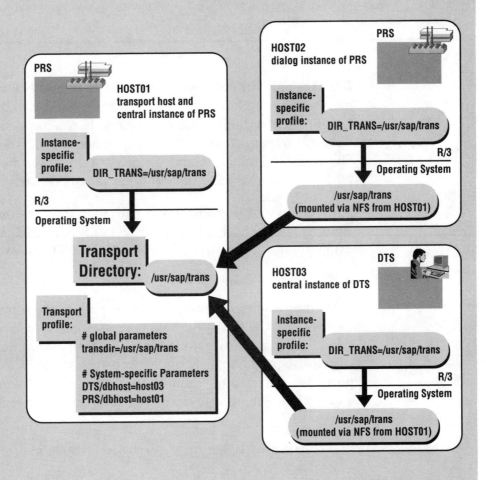

Continued on next page

This landscape consists of two R/3 Systems: the development-and-test system DTS and the production system PRS. DTS consists of a central instance (HOST03). PRS consists of a central instance (HOST01) and a dialog instance (HOST02). DTS and PRS share the same transport directory. HOST01 is the physical location of the transport directory /usr/sap/trans. In the instance profiles of all instances, the parameter *DIR_TRANS* is set to /usr/sap/trans. This directory is mounted on HOST02 and HOST03 using NFS from HOST01.

DIR_TRANS for Windows NT   In Windows NT environments, parameter *DIR_TRANS* points by default to directory \\\$(SAPGLOBALHOST)\sapmnt\trans. If you have configured a central transport host—that is, specified the alias SAPTRANS-HOST on the domain name server—you must set the value of *DIR_TRANS* to \\(SAPTRANSHOST)\sapmnt\trans.

If you have chosen a different path than the one specified by the share \sapmnt\trans, you must set parameter *DIR_TRANS* explicitly using the alias $(SAPTRANSHOST). For example:

```
DIR_TRANS = \\$(SAPTRANSHOST)\transport
```

Another way of defining the access path to the transport directory is to set the transport host that is specified in the domain name server to be overridden locally. This is recommended if all systems require a private transport directory. To cause the transport path stored in the domain name server to be overridden, add the following line to the directory \Winnt\system32\drivers\etc\hosts:

```
<IP address of private transport host> <TCP/IP name of private
transport host> SAPTRANSHOST
```

For example:

```
10.16.162.61      twdfmx05      SAPTRANSHOST
```

The entry in the file *hosts* has to end with a blank line. Keep in mind that the hierarchy governing which parameter value is determinant is as follows:

1. *DIR_TRANS* in the instance profile

2. Value of SAPTRANSHOST of the local hosts file

3. Value of SAPTRANSHOST of the domain name server

For example, *DIR_TRANS* will override SAPTRANSHOST.

TIP   When maintaining *DIR_TRANS* in the instance profile, you can also maintain parameter *DIR_EPS_ROOT*. This parameter points to subdirectory *eps* of the transport directory, which is used to deliver SAP Support Packages (see Chapter 15).

Example of Parameters *transdir* and *DIR_TRANS* with Windows NT

The following graphic shows an example of how the transport directory is accessed in a three-system landscape on Windows NT.

The landscape consists of the development system DEV on HOST01, the quality assurance system QAS on HOST02, and the production system PRD on HOST03. DEV and QAS share the same transport directory, whereas PRD has its own private transport directory due to special security demands. HOST01 is the physical location of the transport directory (c:\usr\sap\trans) shared by system DEV with system QAS. Directory c:\usr\sap on HOST01 is shared as sapmnt. DEV is also the domain name server of the Window NT domain, on which alias SAPTRANSHOST is set to HOST01. The instance profiles of DEV and QAS contain parameter *DIR_TRANS*, which is set to \\$(SAPTRANSHOST)\sapmnt\trans. Therefore, for both DEV and QAS, the parameters *DIR_TRANS* and *transdir*

Continued on next page

point to directory `c:\usr\sap\trans` on HOST01. Because PRD has its own private transport directory, both *DIR_TRANS* and *transdir* point to the private transport directory `c:\usr\sap\trans` on HOST03.

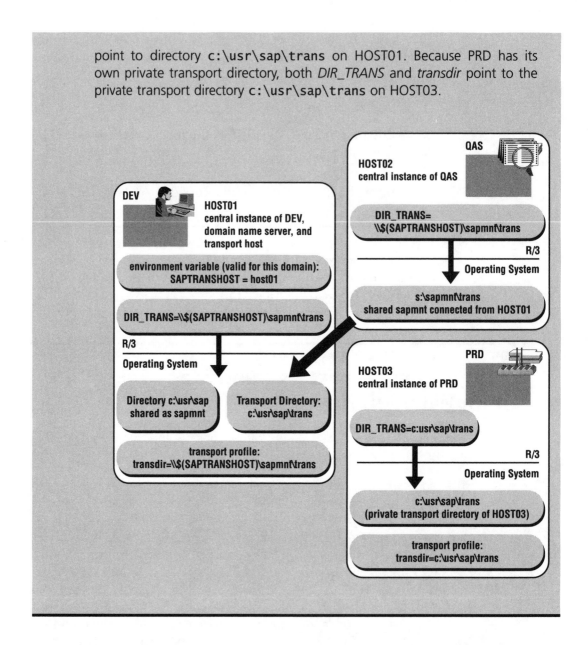

r3transpath   Parameter *r3transpath* specifies which platform-specific version of *R3trans* is used by *tp*. The default value—R3trans for UNIX and AS/400 platforms and R3trans.exe for NT platforms—

normally works. No explicit path is given. The path relies on the correct path definition of the user starting *tp*. In case of problems or in heterogeneous environments, make sure the specification is correct. Set the value for parameter *r3transpath* as described in Table 7.6.

TABLE 7.6: Specification of *r3transpath*

Platform	Parameter Specification	Value
UNIX, AS/400	*r3transpath*	R3trans
Windows NT	*Wntlr3transpath*	R3trans.exe

If the system landscape consists of R/3 Systems running on different database platforms, you must set the parameter to *system-specific* or *operating system–specific* to use different platform-specific versions of *R3trans*.

NOTE   See R/3 Note 83327 for more information on transporting in a heterogeneous environment.

Parameters for a Heterogeneous Environment with Windows NT and UNIX

If a transport group includes systems running on Windows NT and systems running on UNIX, additional settings are required.

For systems running on Windows NT, perform the following steps:

1. Set binary mode as the default mode for opening a file for tp.exe and R3trans.exe:

   A. For R/3 Release 4.0, on the operating system level, choose *Start* ➢ *Settings* ➢ *Control Panel* ➢ *System* ➢ *Environment* ➢ *User Variables* to set the environment variable `abap/NTfmode=b` in the user environment of the user under whom the kernel was started—that is, either <SID>ADM or SAPService<SID>. Afterward, you have to execute the program NTENV2REG.EXE, which is stored in the R/3 kernel directory. Then, start the SAP Service.

B. For R/3 Release 4.5, set the parameter *ababntfmode* in the transport profile to b.

C. For both R/3 Release 4.0 and 4.5, set the instance profile parameter *abap/Ntfmode* to b.

2. Make the following entries to the transport profile. Note that all of these entries are platform-specific for Windows NT and, with the exception of parameter *transdir*, they are also specific to a certain R/3 System:

   - `wnt|transdir = <path to the transport directory>`

   - `wnt|<SID>/r3transpath=\\<NTHOST>\sapmnt\`
     `<SID>\sys\exe\run\R3trans.exe`

   - `wnt|<SID>/sapevtpath=\\<NTHOST>\sapmnt\`
     `<SID>\sys\exe\run\sapevt.exe`

   - `wnt|<SID>/system_pf=\\<NTHOST>\sapmnt\`
     `<SID>\sys\profile\default.pfl`

3. Maintain parameter *DIR_TRANS* (and also *DIR_EPS_ROOT*) correctly in all instance profiles.

TIP   On Windows NT platforms, the transport profile TPPARAM is edited with SAP's editor SAPPAD, which is stored as `sappad.exe` in the R/3 executable directory `\usr\sap\<SID>\SYS\exe\run`. SAPPAD lets you save the settings using the UNIX formatting option.

Activities within R/3

After installation, the following activities from within R/3 are required for the setup of transport capabilities:

- Initializing the Change and Transport Organizer (CTO)

- Setting the system change option

- Verifying the background jobs and background work processes required for transports

Bear in mind that there are different types of "R/3 installations," and that how you perform the transport-related tasks described in this section will vary according to which type of R/3 installation you are working on. These installation types include:

SAP standard installation: An SAP standard installation is installed from the SAP CDs using the program *R3setup*.

System copy: A *system copy* or *database copy* as a technique for creating a new R/3 System was discussed in Chapter 5. The tools for creating system copies depend on the database and operating system platform and whether the system is to be migrated between platforms.

R/3 System upgrade: An R/3 System upgrade uses SAP CDs and the program *R3up* to upgrade an existing R/3 System Release to a higher R/3 System Release—for example, from R/3 Release 3.1G to 4.5B. (See Chapter 15.)

Unlike an SAP standard installation or an R/3 Release upgrade, a system copy requires you to manage entities carried over from the source system, such as:

- Clients

- Customizing data, application data, and user master data

- Open tasks or change requests

- The system name (SID) for customer-developed Repository objects that remain owned by the source system

Initializing the Change and Transport Organizer

After an R/3 installation by system copy, you must manually initialize the Change and Transport Organizer (CTO) with Transaction SE06. This causes the SID of the R/3 System to be stored in the appropriate database table, and establishes the initial value of the serial ID-number for change requests. This initialization is not required for an SAP standard installation, because when configuring TMS (see Chapter 8), the TMS automatically checks whether the CTO has been initialized, and, if not, initializes it.

To initialize the CTO manually, perform the following steps:

1. Log on to your R/3 System.

2. Call Transaction SE06.

3. Select *Database copy or migration* if the R/3 System is the result of a system copy.

4. To initialize the CTO, select *Execute*.

NOTE   To use Transaction SE06, you need the administration authorization S_CTS_ADMIN that is found in the authorization profile S_A.SYSTEM.

When initializing the CTO using Transaction SE06 and choosing *Database copy or migration,* Transaction SE06 not only initializes the CTO, it also provides functionality to handle change requests that have been copied into the new R/3 System. (Such change requests are not an issue for standard installations, because the SAP-delivered R/3 System contains no carryover change requests.)

Change requests that have been copied into the new R/3 System may cause problems when you upgrade or modify objects. The following activities take place:

- Initializing the control tables for change requests and the R/3 Release upgrade process.

- Detecting and listing all open tasks and change requests that existed in the originating R/3 System—including modifications—that are changes to the SAP standard. You will want to release these open tasks and change requests to delete the locks on the corresponding objects. For documentation purposes, these change requests remain recorded in the new system with the status released.

- Enabling you to decide whether the customer-developed Repository objects belonging to open change requests should be made original objects in the target system. If so, the original system for these objects, which are still "owned" by the source system after a system copy, is changed to the current system. (See Chapter 10.)

NOTE   For information on Repository object locks after system copy, see R/3 Note 62519. For information on original systems and Repository objects after a system copy in R/3 Release 4.5, see R/3 Note 146040.

Setting the Global System Change Option

The global system change option for each R/3 System determines whether Repository objects and client-independent (cross-client) Customizing objects can be changed. To set the system change option:

1. Call Transaction SE06 and choose *System change option*.

2. In the screen *System change option*, choose *Global setting*.

3. In the dialog box, choose either *Modifiable* or *Not modifiable* (see Figure 7.6).

The development system should be the only R/3 System within your system landscape in which changes to objects are allowed. From the development system, you can transport the changes into the other R/3 Systems of your landscape.

TIP   For the quality assurance system and the production system, SAP strongly recommends setting the global system change option to *Not modifiable.*

After setting the system change option to *Modifiable*, from the screen *System change option*, you can determine which specific namespaces and name ranges can be set to *Modifiable*. After selecting or deselecting *Modifiable* for a given namespace or name range, choose *Save*.

TIP   If you deselect the option *Modifiable* for a namespace or a name range, you will not be able to change objects of that namespace or name range even if the global system change option is set to *Modifiable*.

Figure 7.7 shows the system change settings for a development system DEV. The global system change option is set to *Modifiable*—this is indicated by the message *Global setting: Repository and client-independent Customizing can be changed.* Below this message, the column *Modifiable* indicates the objects in certain namespaces and name ranges that can be changed.

FIGURE 7.7:

Namespace and name range change option

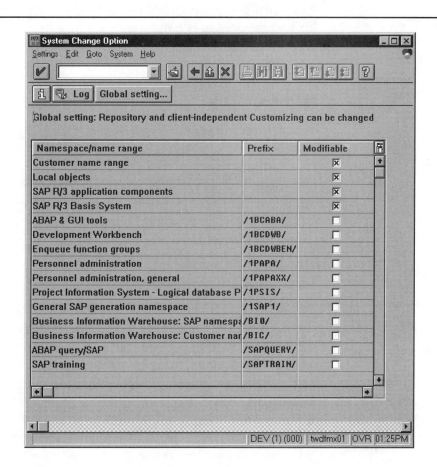

TIP   Deselecting *Modifiable* for a namespace or name range when changing is globally possible prevents changes in a particular namespace or name range.

When you save your changes to these settings, the new setting, date, time, and responsible user are logged. To display the log file, from screen *System Change Option,* choose *Log.*

In addition to the global change option and the change option for namespaces and name ranges, you can also set change options on a client basis. (See Chapter 3.)

Namespaces

A *namespace* is specified by a character set and a permitted name length. All names that match these criteria belong to the corresponding namespace. For example, as of R/3 Release 4.0, the namespace for programs covers all strings with up to 30 alphanumeric characters. Technically, a namespace is implemented by a template—that is, by a field in which all possible names can be entered. This field has a defined length and an integrated validation to check for allowed characters.

As of R/3 Release 4.0, customers can reserve development namespaces at SAP. This makes sense for customers who have a central development group that delivers developments to subsidiaries, as well as for companies that commercially develop add-ons for SAP customers. A reserved development namespace helps to prevent naming clashes that may occur when externally developed objects are imported to a given R/3 System.

NOTE   For more information on development namespaces for customers and partners, see R/3 Note 84282.

Name Ranges

A *name range* is a subset of a namespace—that is, an interval within a namespace. Each object type in the R/3 Repository has both an SAP name range and a customer name range. The SAP name range is reserved for objects delivered by SAP. Within the customer name range, customers can create and develop their own objects. The names reserved for customer objects typically start with "Y" or "Z."

NOTE   For more information on the customer name range, see R/3 Note 16466.

All customer developments must be made in the customer name range or in a customer namespace. This prevents customer developments from being overwritten during an R/3 Release upgrade. Objects in the SAP name range should not be changed unless to apply corrections of known errors in accordance with R/3 Notes if no corresponding SAP Support Package is yet available (see Chapter 15).

Example of Namespaces and Name Ranges

Software object names such as program names are assigned to a namespace when preceded by a prefix placed between slashes: /<prefix>/<object name>. This makes it possible to have objects with the same name belonging to different namespaces. Consider, for example, the object name ZABAP. The "Z" indicates that it belongs to the customer name range. Within the SAP training organization's namespace, there is another ZABAP program, which is distinguished from the customer report by being called /SAPTRAIN/ZABAP.

Verifying Required Background Jobs

To control the transport process, the transport control program *tp* requires various operating system programs and R/3 programs to run in the background. To run these programs in the background, the *transport dispatcher* RDDIMPDP must be scheduled as a periodic background job in each respective client. These jobs are named RDDIMPDP_CLIENT_<nnn>, where <nnn> specifies the client. In both R/3 Release 4.0 and 4.5, these jobs are automatically scheduled for all delivered standard clients or after a client copy for customer-created clients. The background jobs are scheduled *event-periodic*. They start to run as soon as they receive a certain event.

To help avoid transport problems, check whether the RDDIMPDP jobs are running:

1. Use Transaction code SM37. Alternatively, from the R/3 initial screen, choose *Tools* ➤ *CCMS* ➤ *Jobs* ➤ *Maintenance*.

2. In the screen *Select Background Jobs*, enter **RDDIMPDP*** in the field *job name*. Enter * in the field *user* and in the field *or start after event*.

3. To display a list of the jobs that match the search criteria, choose *Enter*. The RDDIMPDP jobs should appear in the list.

An alternative way of checking whether the RDDIMPDP jobs are running is to call *tp* on the operating system level with the following command:

```
tp checkimpdp <SID>
```

If, for any reason, you must schedule RDDIMPDP manually, you can do so by running program RDDNEWPP. To run this program, in the current client, access the ABAP Editor with Transaction code SE38, or, from the R/3 initial screen, choose *Tools* ➤ *ABAP Workbench* ➤ *ABAP editor*. In the field *program*, enter **RDDNEWPP** and choose *Execute*.

NOTE   For more information on the transport dispatcher RDDIMPDP, see also Chapter 14.

Verifying Background Work Processes

All systems from which data will be exported and/or imported require at least two background work processes to support the RDDIMPDP jobs. When importing changes into an R/3 System, the import dispatcher RDDIMPDP is triggered by *tp* and occupies one background work process. Depending on the type of objects to be imported, other background jobs need to run and are scheduled by the dispatcher. To guarantee that RDDIMPDP can monitor the status of the specific job runs, at least two free background work processes are needed.

Review Questions

1. The R/3 System ID (SID):

    A. Must be unique for each system sharing the same transport directory

    B. Must be unique for each system in the system landscape

    C. Can start with a number

    D. Can consist of any three-character combination

2. Which of the following statements is correct in regard to the transport directory?

    A. There can be only one transport directory in a system landscape.

    B. All R/3 Systems within a transport group share a common transport directory.

    C. In system landscapes using heterogeneous platforms, it is not possible to have a common transport directory.

    D. Only the production system can contain the transport directory.

3. The transport control program *tp*:

   A. Is stored in subdirectory *bin* of the transport directory

   B. Uses program *R3trans* to access the databases when transporting changes

   C. Cannot be used directly on the operating system level

   D. Depends on the settings of the transport profile

4. The transport profile:

   A. Is stored in subdirectory *bin* of the transport directory

   B. Contains comments and parameter settings that configure the transport control program *tp*

   C. Is managed from within TMS as of R/3 Release 4.5, but is modified with operating system text editors in earlier releases

   D. Contains only settings that are valid for all R/3 Systems in the system landscape

5. The initialization procedure of the CTO:

   A. Is especially required after a system copy

   B. Establishes the initial value for change request IDs

   C. Is not mandatory for the purpose of enabling transports

   D. Is performed automatically during R/3 installation by program *R3setup*

6. Which of the following statements is correct in regard to the settings governing changes to Repository objects?

   A. Only the customer name range should be modifiable in production systems.

   B. Developments are possible in an R/3 System only if you have applied for a development namespace from SAP.

C. If the global change option is set to *Not modifiable*, it is nevertheless possible to make changes in certain name spaces or clients that have their change option set to *Modifiable*.

D. The global change option should always be set to *Not modifiable* for the quality assurance system and the production system.

CHAPTER
EIGHT

8

Setting Up the TMS

After installing R/3, to enable change requests to be transported in your system landscape, you need to configure the Transport Management System (TMS). This chapter introduces the setup of the TMS and describes how to configure it in the following steps:

- Creating the transport domain
- Configuring transport routes
- Verifying the system landscape setup

This chapter also explains how to change the TMS configuration when adding more R/3 Systems, changing the role of an R/3 System, or upgrading to a new R/3 Release. As of R/3 Release 4.0, much of the existing transport functionality has changed. If you upgrade to R/3 Release 4.0 or 4.5 from an R/3 Release that does not have the TMS functionality, read this chapter to learn how to integrate an existing landscape in the TMS.

This chapter is aimed at people looking for general information on the TMS, as well as system administrators and technical consultants responsible for setting up the system landscape. If you are involved in development and Customizing, you will also want to familiarize yourself with TMS concepts and terminology.

This chapter does not outline the TMS functionality for performing transport activities, such as the importing of change requests. If you are responsible for transporting change requests, you should refer to Part 3 of this book.

TMS Terminology and Concepts

The TMS enables system administrators and technical consultants to centrally manage the transport configuration of multiple R/3 Systems by using a transport domain and defining transport routes. The TMS offers easy-to-use configuration tools to set up a transport domain and to set up and maintain transport routes.

> **NOTE** Besides enabling global transport maintenance and configuration, the TMS also provides an R/3 user interface for the transport tools at the operating system level. The TMS allows you to view change requests that are waiting for import and to perform and monitor imports from within R/3 (see also Chapter 13).

SAP introduced the TMS in R/3 Release 3.1H, and its use became obligatory as of R/3 Release 4.0. Note that when you employ the TMS, you can no longer use Transaction SE06, which was formerly used to configure transport routes. The tables used by Transaction SE06 are no longer used by the TMS.

Transport Domain

All R/3 Systems that you plan to manage centrally using the TMS form a *transport domain*. Within a transport domain, all R/3 Systems must have unique system IDs, and transport routes and associated settings are identical for all R/3 Systems.

The system landscape is the set of all R/3 Systems required to take your implementation from the development stages through production. Typically, your system landscape and your transport domain will contain the same R/3 Systems. However, you can have several system landscapes in one transport domain—centrally administered using the TMS. Figure 8.1 presents the transport domain of a multinational company that consists of two separate three-system landscapes, one for Asia and one for Europe. Both are administered centrally by system PR1.

Transport Domain

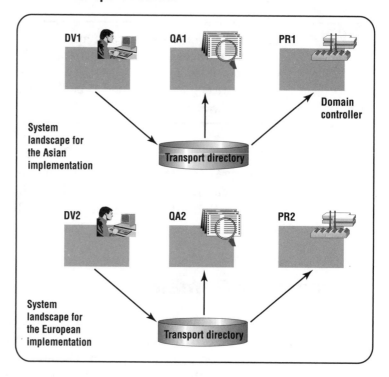

Transport Domain Controller

One of the great benefits of the TMS is the centralized configuration of the entire transport environment. One of the R/3 Systems in the transport domain holds the reference configuration, and all the other R/3 Systems hold copies of this reference configuration. The R/3 System with the reference configuration is called the *transport domain controller*—for example, system PR1 in Figure 8.1.

From the transport domain controller, you can manage the entire TMS configuration—the configuration of all included R/3 Systems, their roles, and their interrelationships. The centralized administration of the TMS ensures consistency throughout the transport domain.

Within a transport domain, each R/3 System can communicate with all other R/3 Systems through RFC connections that are generated when the TMS is configured. The transport domain controller, for example, uses RFC connections to distribute configuration changes to all other R/3 Systems in the transport domain.

Backup Domain Controller

To manage R/3 Systems and transport routes, every domain requires a transport domain controller. In addition, another R/3 System in the transport domain should be designated as the *backup domain controller*. (See Figure 8.2.) This backup domain controller enables you to perform necessary configuration changes to the transport domain when the transport domain controller is unavailable—for example, when that R/3 System is not running. In such cases, the backup domain controller can take over the role of the domain controller, and configuration changes to the transport domain can be made.

However, even if the transport domain controller is unavailable, you can use RFC links to perform transport activities such as viewing import queues and initiating imports from any R/3 System in the transport domain. The domain controller is required only for configuration changes to the transport domain.

FIGURE 8.2:

Central administration
from the transport
domain controller or
the backup domain
controller

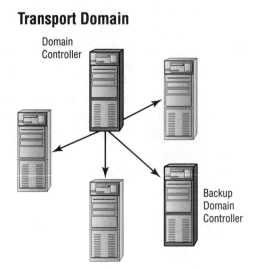

FIGURE 8.2:

Central administration from the transport domain controller or the backup domain controller

Transport Groups versus Transport Domains

A transport group is a collection of R/3 Systems that share the same transport directory (see Chapter 7). A transport group is a technical and physical setup because the involved R/3 Systems access a common transport directory. Rather than being a physical unit, a transport domain is purely an administrative unit for the TMS.

A transport domain may consist of several transport groups. However, a transport domain typically consists of only one transport group and involves only one common transport directory. Even when multiple transport groups are required (see Chapter 7), all R/3 Systems in the transport domain are managed centrally, regardless of whether they share the same transport directory.

Figure 8.3 depicts a more complicated transport domain composed of five R/3 Systems and two different transport groups. The transport domain controller manages the transport configuration of all five R/3 Systems. The transport routes that determine the flow of change requests are not shown in Figure 8.3. All R/3 Systems that regularly need to share change requests should be part of the same transport domain (but not necessarily the same transport group). To define transport routes, you first must establish the transport domain and transport groups.

FIGURE 8.3:

A transport domain
with two transport
groups

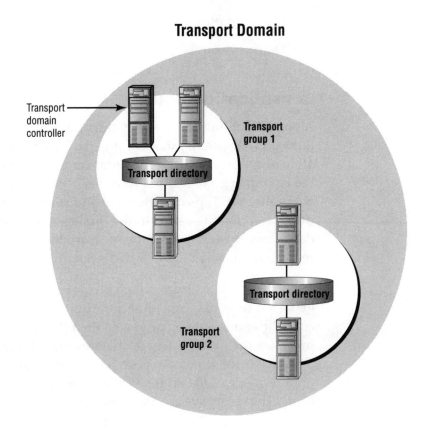

Transport Domain

Transport Routes

The terms *transport domain, domain controller,* and *transport group* concern only the physical environment. They do not include the transport relationship between the R/3 Systems, which is defined by the transport routes. Transport routes are used to indicate the role of each system and the flow of change requests. SAP distinguishes two types of transport routes:

- Consolidation routes
- Delivery routes

Consolidation Routes

A consolidation route defines the path (the successive R/3 Systems and/or clients) that is followed by change requests immediately after release. The consolidation route is used to accumulate the customer changes that have been integrated with the standard R/3 software. Typically, the consolidation route proceeds from the development system to the quality assurance system in a standard three-system landscape, or from the development system to the production system in a two-system landscape.

All R/3 Systems from which change requests are released and exported require a consolidation route. Such a source system in a consolidation route is known as the *integration system* because it provides the point at which changes are integrated into the R/3 System. At the time of export, a change request is added to the import queue of the target R/3 System defined by the consolidation route. The target system assumes the role of a *consolidation system*.

Development Classes and Transport Layers   Consolidation routes are closely associated with *development classes* and *transport layers*. Development classes are used to group R/3 Repository objects that are logically related, and act as containers to organize development work. All objects that belong to a development class are developed, maintained, and transported together.

A development class can be assigned to a transport layer. Each transport layer can be assigned to one consolidation route. The transport layer determines which consolidation route is valid for all objects of a development class. Development classes and transport layers enable you to specify a consolidation route for each R/3 Repository object. A consolidation route is defined by an integration system and a consolidation system and is associated with a specific transport layer.

NOTE   For information on using development classes and transport layers, see Chapter 10.

Standard Transport Layer   Because all Customizing changes must follow the same consolidation route, a *standard transport layer* is specified for each integration system. The standard transport layer is used for the transport of changes that have no concept of a transport layer, unlike Repository objects that belong to a development class. Assigning a standard transport layer to a consolidation route enables all Customizing changes made in the development system to be transported to the quality assurance system. A standard transport layer is a system attribute of integration systems.

NOTE   As of R/3 Release 4.5, transport routes can include not just R/3 Systems but also R/3 clients. Client-dependent changes do not always need to be transported using the standard transport layer, but can be transported using a client-specific transport route (see below, under "Extended Transport Control"), if the respective transport layer has been assigned to the client.

For each integration system, at least two transport layers are defined: the standard transport layer and the SAP transport layer (see below). There may also be several other transport layers. Each transport layer may have several development classes assigned to it. Although an integration system can be the source system for several consolidation routes, each consolidation route has exactly one transport layer assigned to it.

SAP Transport Layer   The transport layer *SAP* is the predefined transport layer for the development classes of all SAP standard objects. To modify standard objects in the R/3 System and to transport them along the same routes as development and Customizing changes, a consolidation route is assigned to the SAP transport layer. When setting up transport routes using the standard transport route configuration options, the consolidation route is generated automatically (see below, under "Standard Configurations").

Delivery Routes

Delivery routes are used to transport changes from the consolidation system to further R/3 Systems. Delivery routes are required only in a system landscape that consists of more than two R/3 Systems. In the standard three-system landscape, for example, a delivery route is specified between the quality assurance system and the production system. This enables changes to be transported to the production system after they have been tested and verified in the quality assurance system.

After change requests have been imported to the quality assurance system, a defined delivery route causes the change requests to be added to the import queue of the next R/3 System in the system landscape, the production system. While consolidation routes dictate which R/3 System receives the change request at export, a delivery route determines which R/3 System receives the change request after successful import. The definition of a delivery route specifies a source system and a target system.

Setting Up the Transport Domain

To set up a transport domain, first determine which R/3 Systems should be included in the transport domain. The transport domain should contain all systems in your system landscape and any other R/3 Systems that will be administered centrally using the TMS. One of these systems must be designated as the transport domain controller. You may later switch the role of domain controller to a different system, but during the R/3 implementation process, the first R/3 System for which the TMS is initialized is automatically designated as the transport domain controller.

TIP   To set up the transport domain, you require the authorization profile S_A.SYSTEM.

Figure 8.4 shows the components of a standard configuration. The transport domain includes system DEV as the development system, system QAS as the quality assurance system, and system PRD as the production system. DEV is designated as the transport domain controller. All systems use a common transport directory and thus form a single transport group.

FIGURE 8.4:

Example of a transport domain

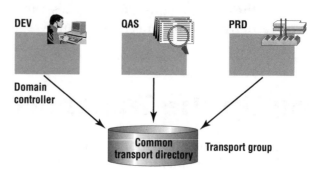

Setting Up the Domain Controller

Within a transport domain, the transport domain configuration—that is, the included systems, their roles, and the configured transport routes—is identical for all systems. The transport domain controller stores the reference domain configuration. All other systems in the transport domain have copies of the reference configuration. The advantage of the centralized administration of the transport domain is that it ensures consistency.

The development system is often initially designated as the transport domain controller, because the TMS must be set up to store the released development and Customizing requests in the import queues of the other systems that have not yet been installed.

Because the transport domain controller must provide high levels of system availability, security precautions, and maintenance, it is often subsequently moved to the production system or the quality assurance system. The system load generated by TMS configuration activities on a domain controller is quite low. The system load increases only briefly when the TMS configuration is changed.

Initializing the TMS

When using the TMS for the first time after R/3 installation, you are automatically prompted to initialize the TMS. To initialize the TMS for an R/3 System, proceed as follows:

1. Log on to the R/3 System that you have designated as the transport domain controller in client 000 with a user ID that possesses transport authorization profile S_A.SYSTEM, such as user SAP*.

2. Use Transaction code STMS or, from the R/3 initial screen, choose *Tools* ➤ *Administration* ➤ *Transports* ➤ *Transport Management System*.

NOTE   The first system of a transport group from which the TMS is called is automatically designated as the transport domain controller.

---

3. When starting the TMS for the first time, the dialog box shown in Figure 8.5 appears and prompts values for the creation of the new domain. For example, because the development system DEV is declared the transport domain controller in Figure 8.5, DOMAIN_DEV is suggested as the transport domain name.

4. You can accept the prompted name or enter a different name. Enter a short description and choose *Enter*. Subsequently changing the name of a transport domain requires deleting the TMS configuration and reconfiguring it—for all R/3 Systems in the transport domain. Only the short description can be easily changed at any time.

FIGURE 8.5:

Dialog box that appears
when you first use the
TMS in a transport
domain

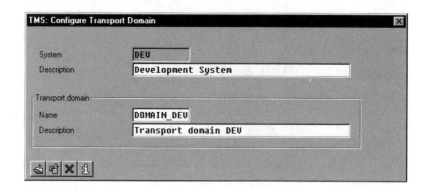

Initializing the TMS has several effects on an R/3 System (see
below, under "Technical Aspects of the Configuration Process").
During initialization, the basic settings of the TMS configuration
are stored in file DOMAIN.CFG in subdirectory *bin* of the transport
directory on the transport domain controller. These settings
include the transport domain name, the transport domain
description, and the system IDs (SIDs) of all R/3 Systems in the
transport domain. After you install an additional R/3 System that
shares the same transport directory as the domain controller, the
new R/3 System reads the already established configuration out
of file DOMAIN.CFG and automatically recognizes to which domain
the new system belongs.

After initializing the TMS, the TMS initial screen indicates which
transport domain contains the transport domain controller. Assuming your system landscape consists of only one R/3 System at this
point, if you now choose *Overview* ➢ *Systems* from the initial TMS
screen, you will see that the transport domain controller is currently the only system belonging to the transport domain.

To obtain detailed information on an R/3 System:

1. From the *Systems Overview* screen, choose *R/3 System* ➢
   Display.

2. Select an R/3 System and choose *Enter*.

3. The screen *Display the TMS Configuration: System <SID>* appears, providing you with details on the selected system. For example, under the tab *Communication data,* you can see that the system is not only assigned to the transport domain, but also to a transport group with the default name GROUP .<domain controller SID>. The screen also shows the generated address information used for communication between the different R/3 Systems in the transport domain (see below, under "Technical Aspects of the Configuration Process").

Extending the Transport Domain

When other R/3 Systems that will be part of an existing domain are ready for inclusion in the transport domain, you can extend the transport domain by adding these R/3 Systems.

Extending a transport domain is not restricted to physically installed R/3 Systems. Virtual systems are often included as placeholders for planned systems and are replaced by the planned system after it is implemented. In addition, you can extend the transport domain to include external systems—for example, an R/3 System from another transport domain.

New R/3 Systems

To add new systems to a transport domain, you must perform configuration activities on both the new R/3 System and the transport domain controller. Once you add systems to a transport domain, you should designate one R/3 System as the backup domain controller.

Requesting Inclusion from an R/3 System within the Same Transport Group To add a new R/3 System to a transport domain from within the same transport group, you must perform the TMS initialization process on the new system. Proceed as follows:

1. Log on to the new R/3 System in client 000 with a user that has complete transport authorization, such as user SAP*.

2. To access the TMS, use Transaction code STMS or, from the R/3 initial screen, choose *Tools* ➤ *Administration* ➤ *Transports* ➤ *Transport Management System*.

3. If the new system uses the same transport directory as the transport domain controller, the new system will read file DOMAIN.CFG in subdirectory *bin* of the transport directory and thus recognize the existence of a transport domain. When you're initializing the TMS on a new R/3 System, the dialog box shown in Figure 8.6 appears. The example in Figure 8.6 shows the quality assurance system QAS, which shares a transport directory with system DEV. Choose *Save*.

FIGURE 8.6:

Including an R/3 System in an existing transport domain

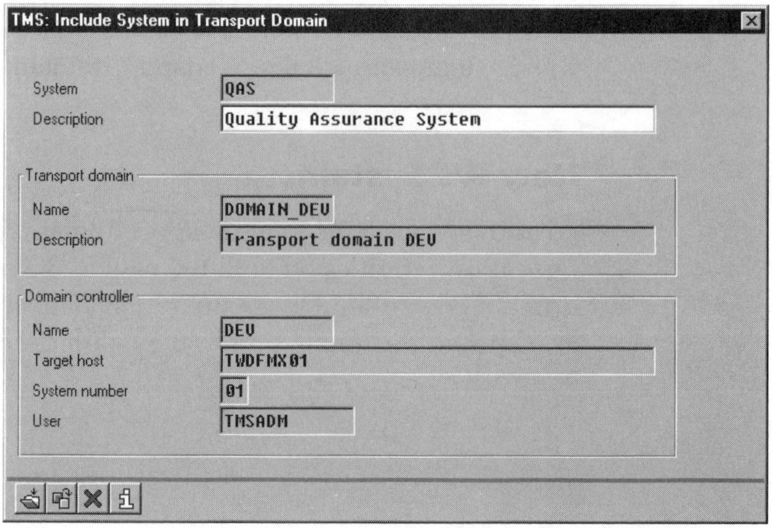

Requesting Inclusion from an R/3 System in a Different Transport Group   If the new R/3 System is the first system in a new transport group, and therefore does not share a transport directory with another R/3 System that is already part of the transport domain, the new R/3 System cannot recognize the transport domain in which it should be included. In this case, the TMS automatically tries to configure a new transport domain (see Figure 8.5 earlier in the chapter).

To add an R/3 System to an existing domain from a new transport group, you must proceed as follows:

1. In the dialog box *TMS: Configure the Transport Domain*, choose *Other configuration*. The dialog box *TMS: Include System in Transport domain* appears.

2. Specify the transport domain controller of the transport domain in which the system is to be included. Enter the *Target host* and the *System number* (instance number) of the transport domain controller.

3. Choose *Save*. Using RFC technology, the transport domain controller is automatically contacted for transport domain data from the file DOMAIN.CFG at the operating system level. The R/3 System to be included is now waiting for the transport domain controller to accept it in the transport domain.

If the R/3 System consists of more than one application server, you can choose one server as the target host. From the dialog box *TMS: Include System in Transport domain*, you can choose to list all possible servers. In R/3 Release 4.0, the server you are currently logged on to is automatically suggested as the target host. With R/3 Release 4.5, the central instance is automatically suggested as the target host. Ideally, you should choose the host system with the highest availability.

Acceptance of New R/3 Systems   You must explicitly accept new R/3 Systems into the transport domain controller. Prior to this, the new system is waiting for inclusion into the transport domain. As long as a system waits for inclusion, the *System Overview* screen of the TMS on this R/3 System displays only this system and the transport domain.

To accept an R/3 System that is waiting for inclusion, proceed as follows:

1. In the R/3 System that is the transport domain controller, from the initial TMS screen, choose *Overview* ➢ *Systems*. The *System Overview* screen appears. Position the cursor on the R/3 System that is waiting for inclusion and choose *R/3 System* ➢ *Accept*.

2. The dialog box *Accept system* appears. Choose *Enter*.

3. Note that acceptance causes a change in the TMS configuration. Such a change must always be distributed to all other systems in the transport domain. The dialog box *Distribute the TMS Configuration* now appears and asks if you want to distribute the new configuration immediately.

   • If you choose *yes*, the configuration is distributed immediately, and the TMS status of the new R/3 System is set to *active*.

   • If you decide to distribute the configuration later, you must distribute it explicitly. As long as the new configuration is not distributed, the TMS status of the new R/3 System remains *obsolete*. To distribute the new configuration and change the TMS status of the new system to *accepted*, from the *System Overview* screen in the domain controller, choose *Extras* ➢ *Distribute the TMS configuration*.

Whenever you change the TMS configuration, the dialog box *Distribute the TMS Configuration* appears by default to ask if you require immediate distribution. To change this default, from the initial TMS screen, choose *Extras* ➣ *Settings* ➣ *System overview* (or, from the *System Overview* screen, choose *Extras* ➣ *Settings*). You can change the default to either automatic distribution after a change or no automatic distribution. These options are shown in Figure 8.7.

FIGURE 8.7:

Settings for the distribution process

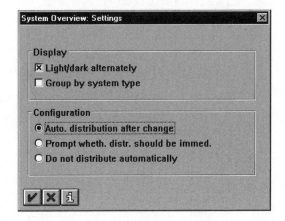

Virtual Systems

The TMS allows you to create—that is, enter in the list of R/3 Systems known to the TMS—R/3 Systems that are planned but not yet physically installed. These systems are referred to as *virtual systems*.

NOTE   To enable a virtual system to be replaced by an installed R/3 System, the virtual R/3 System must have the same SID as the subsequently installed R/3 System.

By creating virtual systems, you can model the transport routes of the planned system landscape and ensure that the import queues of subsequent systems already exist. In the initial life of an R/3 implementation, customers frequently have only the development system physically installed, and store the development and Customizing work in the import queues of the respective planned systems.

Creating a Virtual System   To create a virtual system, proceed as follows:

1. Log on to the transport domain controller with a user ID that has complete transport authorization.

2. From the initial TMS screen, choose *Overview* ➣ *Systems*. The *System Overview* screen appears. Choose *R/3 System* ➣ *Create* ➣ *Virtual System*.

3. In the dialog box *TMS: Configure Virtual System*, enter the name of the R/3 System and a description text. You also must specify an R/3 System as the *Communications system* for the virtual system. The communications system must be a system that is already part of the transport domain. It cannot be a virtual system or an external system. Choose *Save*.

4. Distribute the configuration change.

5. As of Release 4.5, in the transport profile, the default setting for the parameter *dummy*, which is the correct setting for this system, is TRUE. In R/3 Release 4.0, you must add <SID>/ dummy = TRUE to the transport profile manually.

Because no RFC address can be created for virtual systems, RFCs are accessed using the transport directory of an already existing R/3 System. This system acts as the *communications system*. A virtual system should always belong to the same transport group as the associated communications system. In the dialog box *TMS: Configure Virtual System*, the communications system proposed by default is the transport domain controller.

Replacing a Virtual R/3 System with a Real R/3 System

You can replace a virtual system when the corresponding planned system is realized—that is, it is either physically installed or has been upgraded to an R/3 Release with TMS functionality. This realized system is what is meant when referring to the *real* R/3 System in this context. On the transport domain controller, proceed as follows:

1. Delete the virtual system from the transport domain:

    A. From the initial TMS screen, choose *Overview* ➣ *Systems*. The *System Overview* screen appears. Position the cursor on the virtual system you want to delete.

    B. Choose *R/3 System* ➣ *Delete*. Confirm.

    C. Distribute the configuration change.

    As soon as the configuration change is distributed, the virtual system is deleted. The import queue in R/3 disappears. However, the import buffer at the operating system level remains unchanged.

2. Add the real R/3 System to the transport domain:

    A. Initialize the TMS on the real R/3 System and request the inclusion of that system in the transport domain.

    B. On the transport domain controller, accept the system.

    The existing import buffer at the operating system level is assigned to the real system. No change requests will be lost.

3. Distribute the configuration change.

TIP   After replacing a virtual system with the installed R/3 System, ensure the consistency of transport routes between all R/3 Systems in the transport domain.

External Systems

You can also add external systems to the transport domain that are not physically part of it. Like virtual systems, they are accessed using a communications system—a real R/3 System already included in the transport domain. Unlike virtual systems, external systems have their own transport directory. This transport directory, which must be explicitly defined, resides on a disk partition, is accessed by an R/3 System in another transport domain, or resides on an exchangeable data medium such as a CD-ROM. External systems are used for the following reasons:

- To write change requests to exchangeable data media
- To read change requests from exchangeable data media
- To provide an intermediate directory to enable you to send change requests to other transport domains (see Chapter 13)

To add an external system, proceed as follows:

1. From the *System Overview* screen, choose *R/3 System* ➤ *Create* ➤ *External System*. The dialog box *TMS: Configure External System* (shown in Figure 8.8) is displayed.

2. Enter the path to the transport directory of the external system, relative to the communications system (this is the path used by the communications system). The communications system proposed by default is the transport domain controller. In the example in Figure 8.8, the external system is DE2 (the development system of DOMAIN_DE2), and system DEV from DOMAIN_DEV is the communications system enabling transports between the two domains.

As of Release 4.5, the default setting in the transport profile for the parameter *dummy*, which is the correct setting for this system, is TRUE. In R/3 Release 4.0, you must add <SID>/dummy = TRUE to the transport profile manually. Also note that you must create the subdirectories of the external transport directory, which are not created automatically in the specified transport directory.

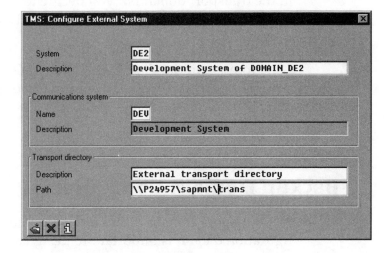

FIGURE 8.8:

Adding an external R/3
System to the transport
domain

Unlike virtual systems, external systems do not belong to an existing transport group in the transport domain, but are assigned to a new transport group whose default name is EXTGRP_ <transport domain controller SID>.

Changes to the Transport Domain

Changes to the TMS configuration correspond to changes to the transport domain—for example, when you:

- Move an R/3 System to another host
- Delete an R/3 System from the transport domain
- Cause an R/3 System to use another transport directory
- Change the transport profile settings

Such changes to the configuration of the transport domain can be performed only on the transport domain controller and must be immediately or subsequently distributed to the other R/3 Systems in the transport domain. If you decide to distribute a configuration change later, you must do so explicitly, using the following procedure:

1. From the initial TMS screen, choose *Overview* ➤ *Systems*. The *System Overview* screen appears. Choose *Extras* ➤ *Distribute the TMS configuration*.

2. In the resulting dialog box, choose *Yes*.

Backup Domain Controller

The transport domain controller is the source system for all configuration data. It is important to designate another R/3 System as the backup domain controller, because this gives you a way of performing configuration changes when the transport domain controller is not available. Once an R/3 System has been defined as the backup domain controller, you can activate that system as the transport domain controller.

NOTE   The system selected as the backup domain controller must be an existing R/3 System that is part of the transport domain. It cannot be a virtual or an external R/3 System.

Defining a Backup Domain Controller

To define an R/3 System in the transport domain as the backup domain controller, proceed as follows:

1. Log on to the R/3 System that is the transport domain controller. From the initial TMS screen, choose *Overview* ➤ *Systems*. The *System Overview* screen appears. Choose *R/3 System* ➤ *Change*.

2. The screen *Change the TMS Configuration* appears. Enter the name of an R/3 System in the transport domain that is not a virtual system or an external system.

3. In the field *Backup* (located in R/3 Release 4.5 in the tab *Communication data*), enter the SID of the R/3 System you want to designate as the backup domain controller.

4. Choose *Save*. Distribute the configuration change either immediately or subsequently.

Figure 8.9 shows the screen *Change TMS Configuration* for R/3 Release 4.5. In this screen, the system PRD has been entered as backup domain controller.

FIGURE 8.9:

Designating a backup domain controller in R/3 Release 4.5

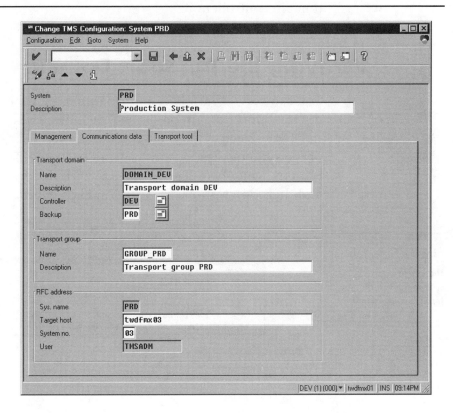

Activating a Backup Domain Controller

To use a backup domain controller to change transport domain configurations, you must activate it as the domain controller. To do this, proceed as follows:

1. Log on to the backup domain controller with a user that has complete transport authorizations.

2. From the initial TMS screen, choose *Overview* ➢ *Systems*. The *System Overview* screen appears.

3. Choose *Extras* ➢ *Activate backup controller*.

If the R/3 System that was previously the domain controller is available, it is automatically designated as the new backup domain controller.

Verifying the Transport Domain

You can view a variety of information about the R/3 Systems in the transport domain on the *System Overview* screen (from the initial TMS screen, choose *Overview* ➢ *Systems*). For an explanation of the symbols used, choose *Extras* ➢ *Legend*. The icons beside the SIDs indicate the roles of the respective R/3 Systems. These icons and their descriptions are listed in Figure 8.10.

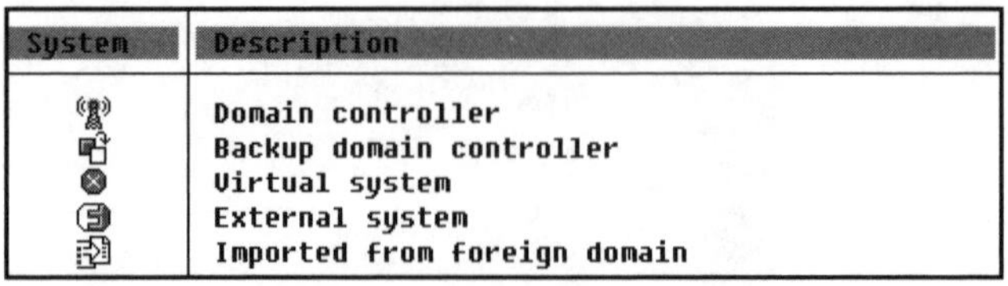

FIGURE 8.10:

The key to the icons for system roles in the *System Overview* screen

System	Description
	Domain controller
	Backup domain controller
	Virtual system
	External system
	Imported from foreign domain

System Status

The icons in the column *Status* of the *System Overview* screen indicate the status of each R/3 System (see Figure 8.11).

FIGURE 8.11:

The key to the icons for system status in the *System Overview* screen

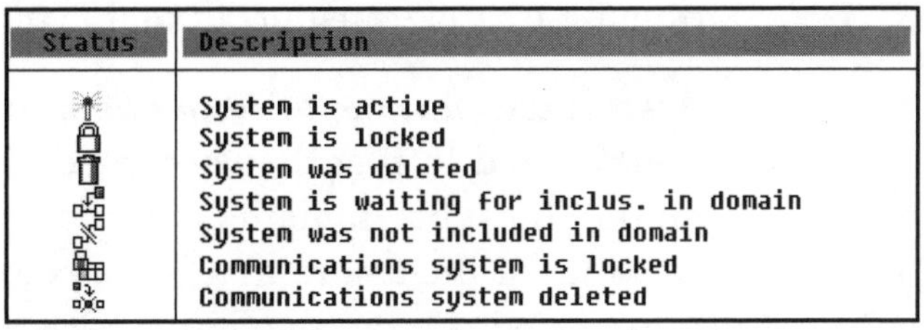

Status	Description
	System is active
	System is locked
	System was deleted
	System is waiting for inclus. in domain
	System was not included in domain
	Communications system is locked
	Communications system deleted

The system status indicated in the *System Overview* screen can be explained in more detail as follows:

System is active: This status means that the TMS has been initialized on this system, and that the system has been successfully included in the transport domain. A system must have this status to be integrated into the transport route configuration and included in the transport flow.

System is locked: From the domain controller, you can *lock* an R/3 System, thus preventing any TMS activity within the domain from accessing this system. You can do this, for example, to perform hardware maintenance. The TMS transport functionality is deactivated for a system with this status. To lock a system, position the cursor on the R/3 System in the *System Overview* screen and choose *R/3 System* ➢ *Lock*. To unlock this system, position the cursor on the locked R/3 System and choose *R/3 System* ➢ *Unlock*.

System was deleted: This status indicates that the system was deleted from the TMS domain configuration. Note that the import buffer file of a deleted system is not deleted.

Accessing the TMS on a system with this status displays a dialog box requesting the renewed inclusion of the system.

System is waiting for inclusion in domain: This status indicates that the TMS has been initialized on the R/3 System, and that this system has not yet been accepted into the domain by the transport domain controller.

System was not included in domain: This status indicates you rejected (rather than accepted) the system in the TMS on the transport domain controller. To reject an R/3 System waiting for inclusion (that is, to exclude it from the transport domain), from the *System Overview* screen, choose *R/3 System* ➤ *Delete*. The R/3 System disappears from the *System Overview* screen as soon as the deletion has been distributed to all R/3 Systems in the transport domain.

Communications system is locked: This status means the system is a virtual system and that the associated communications system has been manually locked, thus blocking access by the TMS of any other system in the transport domain.

Communications system deleted: This status means the system is a virtual system and the associated communications system has been deleted in the TMS on the domain controller.

Distribution Status

The background color in the column *Status* on the *System Overview* screen indicates whether the distributed configuration data for the transport domain, as recorded locally on the respective system, is up to date. The possible colors are as follows:

Green: This color means the configuration data on the system is up to date; that is, the configuration recorded on the system is identical with the reference configuration on the domain controller.

Yellow: Yellow means the recorded configuration data in the TMS of an R/3 System is obsolete; that is, it differs from the reference configuration stored on the domain controller. This may result because the TMS configuration has been changed on the transport domain controller but not yet distributed, or because the specific system was not available when a configuration change was distributed. If the status of a system is obsolete, you must distribute the transport domain configuration from the domain controller.

Red: This color means errors occurred while the RFC destinations were generated during the TMS initialization. If a system shows this status, use the Alert Monitor (see below) to identify the error. After eliminating the error, redistribute the TMS configuration to re-create the RFC destinations.

Purple: Purple indicates that errors occurred when the backup domain controller was being activated as the domain controller. Use the Alert Monitor (see below) to identify the error. After eliminating the error, restart the activation on the new domain controller.

If the TMS configuration has not yet been distributed to all R/3 Systems in the transport domain, a warning is displayed on the TMS initial screen in the R/3 System that is the transport domain controller.

Technical Aspects of the Configuration Process

Whenever you initialize the TMS on an R/3 System, several steps are automatically performed on that system:

- In client 000, CPIC user TMSADM is created.

- The RFC destinations required for the TMS connections are generated.

If the system you are initializing is the domain controller, the following additional steps are automatically performed:

- Certain basic settings for the TMS domain configuration are stored in the file DOMAIN.CFG in subdirectory *bin* of the transport directory. These settings include, for example, the transport domain's name and description, as well as the transport domain controller's host name, instance number, SID, and transport group.

- As of R/3 Release 4.5, the transport profile for the transport control program *tp* is generated (see Chapter 7).

NOTE   In R/3 Release 4.0, you must manually add the required entries for the R/3 System to the transport profile TPPARAM using an operating system editor (see Chapter 7).

If the system you are initializing is not the domain controller, the following additional steps are automatically performed:

- The address data of the system is sent to the transport domain controller, as part of the request for membership in the transport domain.

- As of R/3 Release 4.5, the profile parameter for configuring the transport control program *tp* is sent to the transport domain. If there are several transport groups in the transport domain, transport profiles are generated in the transport directory of every group.

NOTE   In R/3 Release 4.0, if you have several transport groups in the transport domain, you must adapt the transport profiles TPPARAM so that they are identical in all transport directories. Only the transport profile parameter *transdir* may differ from one transport group to another. (See also Chapter 7.)

RFC Connections

RFC connections are used for communication between the R/3 Systems in a transport domain. When you're initializing the TMS on an R/3 System, RFC destinations are generated to enable access between all involved R/3 Systems. There are two distinct types of access. One type is for *read* access and any *write* access that is not critical to security—for example, distributing the TMS configuration after a virtual system has been added from the domain controller to all R/3 Systems in the transport domain. The other type is any *write* access that is critical to security—for example, starting an import. This section explains the underlying techniques of the RFC connections used by the TMS.

Read Access and Noncritical Write Access   To set up the RFC destinations, user TMSADM of user type CPIC is generated in client 000 during TMS initialization. By default, TMSADM authorizations are limited to *read* and *write* authorization in the common transport directory, RFC authorization in the TMS, and display authorization in the CTS. This user is required for displaying import queues and for distributing the basic TMS configuration settings from the transport domain controller to all systems in the transport domain. For all R/3 Systems, to enable accesses that are not critical to security, the RFC connection TMSADM@ <SID>.<domain name> is generated. Figure 8.12 shows the RFC destinations that are generated during TMS initialization.

FIGURE 8.12:

RFC connections required for TMS *read* access and limited *write* access

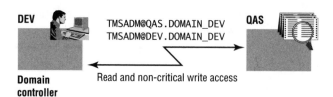

Transport Domain
DOMAIN_DEV

DEV

TMSADM@QAS.DOMAIN_DEV
TMSADM@DEV.DOMAIN_DEV

QAS

Domain controller

Read and non-critical write access

Critical *Write* Access   Since *write* accesses can cause changes in the target system—for example, changes to the import queue—the authorizations of user TMSADM are not sufficient to enable *write* accesses for certain activities. To execute a function that will result in a critical change in the target system—for example, starting an import into an R/3 System or changing transport routes—you must log on to this target system and possess sufficient authorization in the target system. The username and password for this RFC link should not be stored in the source system. The applicable security concept varies between R/3 Releases 4.0 and 4.5.

In R/3 Release 4.0, for each target system, a further RFC connection is generated with the address TMSSUP@<SID>.<domain name>. No username or password is automatically associated with this destination. Whenever you use this connection, you must log on to the target system. As of R/3 Release 4.5, the destination for critical accesses is calculated at runtime based on the address information stored in the TMS configuration. This concept avoids creating destinations for all targets, which may be very numerous as of R/3 Release 4.5 due to the new functionality for creating client-specific transport routes.

The realization of RFC connections technically differs somewhat between R/3 Release 4.0 and R/3 Release 4.5, but in both releases, the TMSADM connection is initially used for all accesses. If the authorizations of TMSADM do not suffice, a logon screen is automatically triggered for the target system, and a user with the proper authorizations must log on. If this procedure is too time-consuming—for example, if there is a large number of R/3 Systems —you may provide user TMSADM with the required authorizations through profile S_A.TMSCFG. If an R/3 System is accessed where the user TMSADM has sufficient authorizations, the logon procedure is suppressed.

WARNING When you extend authorizations for user TMSADM, an anonymous user can make system changes that are critical to security.

Configuring Transport Routes

Initializing the TMS and setting up the transport domain define the physical environment only in terms of the transport domain, the domain controller, and the transport group. Next, you must define the transport relationship between each of the R/3 Systems. Although the TMS has been initialized, you cannot perform transports until the transport routes have been configured and distributed.

Transport routes indicate the role of each system and the flow of change requests. The transport routes are what actually define your system landscape. The prerequisites for configuring transport routes are setting up the transport domain, including all involved systems, and configuring the transport control program *tp*. Configuring a transport route involves:

- Consolidation routes
- Delivery routes
- Target groups (only as of R/3 Release 4.5)

Procedure

To ensure consistency, transport routes can be configured only on the transport domain controller. To help define a transport route, the TMS provides a graphical editor and a hierarchical list editor, which can be used interchangeably. After you define a transport route, you must distribute it to all R/3 Systems in the transport domain and activate it.

SAP recommends creating transport routes as follows:

1. Use one of the standard installation options in the TMS editors. You can choose from a single-system, a two-system, or a three-system landscape. If your system landscape extends beyond a three-system landscape, begin with a three-system landscape and extend the setup using one of the TMS editors.

2. Distribute and activate the transport route configuration to all R/3 Systems in the transport domain.

NOTE   When you are using TMS, Transaction SE06 is no longer used to configure transport routes, and the tables used to store the transport route configuration are no longer TSYST, TASYS, and TWSYS.

Standard Configurations

The easiest way to create transport routes and thereby define a system landscape is to use one of the standard configuration options provided by both the hierarchical list editor and the graphical editor:

Single system: The option for a single-system landscape

Development and production system: The option for a two-system landscape

Three system group: The option for a three-system landscape

After you enter the names of the R/3 Systems that are to form the system landscape, R/3 automatically generates the necessary transport routes and transport layers. To create a more complex environment, initially use a three-system landscape and extend it later. To implement one of the above standard configuration options, proceed as follows:

1. Log on to the transport domain controller with a user that has complete transport authorization.

2. To access one of the TMS editors, from the TMS initial screen (Transaction STMS), choose *Overview* ➢ *Transport routes*.

3. Switch into change mode using *Configuration* ➢ *Display <-> Change*.

4. Regardless of which editor you are using, choose *Configuration* ➢ *Standard Configuration* and select one of the three standard configurations.

NOTE   By selecting one of the standard configurations, all existing transport routes are deleted. Existing transport layers and development classes are retained.

After selecting one of the three standard configurations, proceed as follows.

Single-System Landscape   Specify the SID of the R/3 System that is to be the single system in the system landscape. You also may specify a transport layer for local developments. For a single-system landscape, you do not need to define transport routes. (Imports can still be performed if necessary.) All object changes that you make in a single R/3 System are recorded in change requests of type *local* (see Chapter 10).

Two-System Landscape   Enter the SIDs of the development-and-test system and the production system. Choose *Save*. The following steps are performed automatically:

- The transport layer *Z<development-and-test system SID>* becomes the standard transport layer.

- A consolidation route is created from the development-and-test system to the production system through the transport layer *Z<development-and-test system SID>*.

- A consolidation route is created from the development-and-test system to the production system through the transport layer *SAP*.

As a result, all Customizing changes, all developments in development classes assigned to the standard transport layer, and all changes to SAP standard objects are recorded in change requests for transport to the production system.

Figure 8.13 shows a standard configuration of a two-system landscape with DTS as the development-and-test system and PRS as the production system. The standard transport layer ZDTS is automatically generated as well as the two consolidation routes, one for customer-developed objects belonging to the transport layer ZDTS and one for SAP standard objects.

FIGURE 8.13:

Components of the standard transport route configuration for a two-system landscape

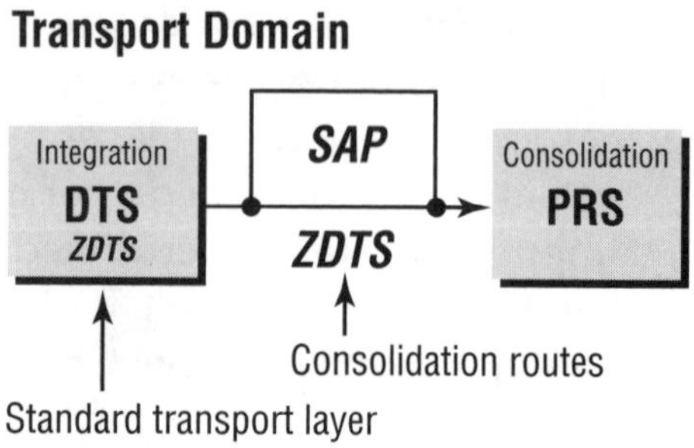

Transport Domain

Three-System Landscape   Assign SIDs to the development system, the quality assurance system, and the production system. Choose *Save*. The following steps are performed automatically:

- The transport layer *Z<development system SID>* becomes the standard transport layer.

- A consolidation route is created from the development system to the quality assurance system through the transport layer *Z<quality assurance system SID>*.

- To transport SAP standard objects, a consolidation route is created from the development system to the quality assurance system through the transport layer *SAP*.

- A delivery route is created from the quality assurance system to the production system. The production system is the recipient system for the consolidated changes.

As a result, all Customizing changes, all developments in development classes that are assigned to the standard transport layer, and all changes to SAP standard objects are recorded in change requests for transport to the quality assurance system for consolidation.

After consolidation, the change requests are delivered to the production system via the delivery route. Figure 8.14 shows a standard configuration of a three-system landscape with DEV as the development system, QAS as the quality assurance system, and PRD as the production system. ZDEV has been generated as the standard transport layer, and there are two consolidation routes, SAP and ZDEV. Additionally, there is a delivery route between QAS and PRD.

FIGURE 8.14:

Components of the standard transport route configuration for a three-system landscape

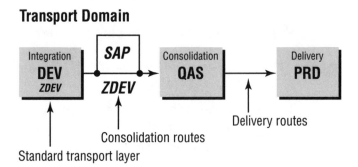

Distributing and Activating a Standard Configuration

Changes in configuration are not valid until manually distributed and activated. To distribute and activate the changes, from either the hierarchical list editor or the graphical editor, choose *Configuration ➤ Distribute and Activate*.

Extending and Changing a Transport Route Configuration

You can extend and change a transport domain's transport route configuration at any time using either of the TMS editors: the graphical editor or the hierarchical editor. The graphical editor is often easier to use for this purpose, because it provides a diagram of the existing environment into which you can "draw" your additions to the landscape.

The transport route configuration can be changed on the transport domain controller only with a user that has complete transport authorization. In either editor, to change the transport route configuration—that is, to add, delete, or modify transport routes—you must be in change mode. After making changes, always distribute and activate the changes by choosing *Configuration* ➤ *Distribute and Activate*. When activating a transport route configuration, you are prompted to log on to all involved R/3 Systems. To do this, you require a user that has complete transport authorization in each of the R/3 Systems.

Using the TMS Editors

Either editor can be used to add consolidation routes or delivery routes. To call an editor, from the TMS initial screen, choose *Overview* ➤ *Transport routes*. The default editor appears.

To change the default editor, proceed as follows:

1. From the TMS initial screen (Transaction STMS), choose *Extras* ➤ *Settings* ➤ *Transport routes*.

2. Select either the graphical or the hierarchical list editor.

3. Choose *Enter*.

Hierarchical List Editor   The hierarchical list editor lists all R/3 Systems, transport layers, and (as of R/3 Release 4.5) target groups in the transport domain in a tree structure. For example, Figure 8.15 shows the tree structure of the hierarchical list editor for the transport domain DOMAIN_DEV.

FIGURE 8.15:

The hierarchical list editor

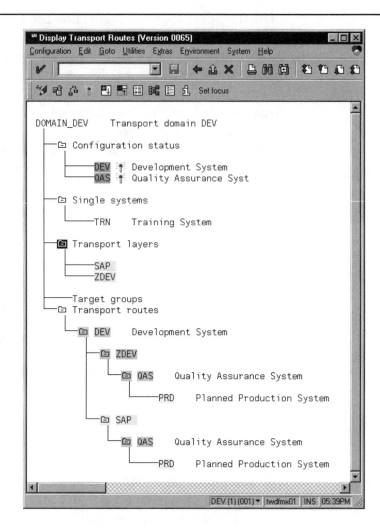

The system landscape diagramed in Figure 8.15 consists of two "real" R/3 Systems (the development system DEV and the quality assurance system QAS) as listed under the node *Configuration status*. The production system PRD has not yet been installed, but has already been configured as a virtual system to integrate it into the transport route configuration. Node *Single systems* lists the training system TRN, which has not yet been integrated in the transport route configuration. DEV, QAS, and PRD form a standard three-system landscape for which standard transport routes have been configured: two consolidation routes between DEV and QAS, one associated with transport layer SAP for SAP standard objects and one associated with the generated standard transport layer ZDEV for customer objects.

To add a new transport route using the hierarchical list editor, proceed as follows:

1. Log on to the transport domain controller with a user that has complete transport authorization.

2. From the TMS initial screen (Transaction STMS), choose *Overview* ➤ *Transport routes*.

3. Switch into change mode using *Configuration* ➤ *Display <->* *Change*.

4. Choose *Configuration* ➤ *Transport route* ➤ *Create*.

5. In the resulting dialog box (shown in Figure 8.16), select the type of transport route you require: either *Consolidation* or *Delivery*.

   A. For a consolidation route, you must specify an integration system, a transport layer, and a consolidation system. When a transport layer is assigned to a consolidation route, all objects belonging to the transport layer are assigned to this consolidation route.

   B. For a delivery route, you must specify a source system and a recipient system.

6. Choose *Continue* to confirm the settings and save the new transport route.

FIGURE 8.16:

Adding a new
transport route

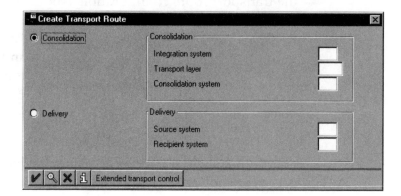

Graphical Editor   The display of the graphical editor is
divided into three areas, as seen in Figure 8.17. The left-hand area
at the top of the screen displays all objects that can be connected
via transport routes. These objects include all real, virtual, or
external R/3 Systems in the transport domain that have not yet
been integrated in transport routes. This area is called the
insertable objects area. Its objects can be inserted in the area below,
in the biggest part of the screen, which is called the *display area*,
containing a graphical representation of current transport routes
between R/3 Systems. This area also contains a legend (not
shown in Figure 8.17). The right-hand area at the top is the *navigation area*, which contains a simplified representation of the display area. In the navigation area, by using your mouse to drag,
you can determine the part of the landscape that is shown below
in the display area.

FIGURE 8.17:

The graphical editor

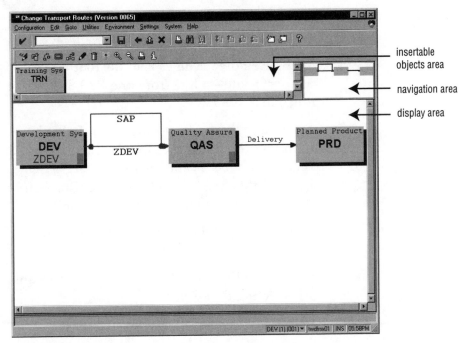

To add a transport route using the graphical editor, proceed as follows:

1. Log on to the transport domain controller with a user that has complete transport authorization.

2. From the TMS initial screen (Transaction STMS), choose *Overview* ➤ *Transport routes*. If necessary, switch to the graphical editor using the menu option *Goto* ➤ *Graphical Editor*.

3. Switch into change mode using *Configuration* ➤ *Display <-> Change*.

4. If a new R/3 System (or target group) is to be added to the transport route configuration, use the mouse to drag the R/3 System (or target group) out of the insertable objects area and drop it into the display area.

5. Choose *Configuration* ➤ *Transport route* ➤ *Create*.

6. The mouse now becomes a stylus that you can use to draw a transport route—a line from one R/3 System (or target group) to another.

7. After you draw a transport route, a dialog box similar to the one in Figure 8.16 (earlier in this chapter) appears. After you select either *Consolidation route* or *delivery route*, the graphical editor—unlike the hierarchical list editor—automatically enters some of the required information.

    A. For a consolidation route, you need to specify only a transport layer.

    B. For a delivery route, no further entries are required after selecting *Delivery*.

8. Choose *Enter*.

Additional Consolidation Routes

It is sometimes useful to consolidate specific Repository objects to an R/3 System outside the standard transport routes by creating an additional transport layer. Development projects that require this technique are called *multi-layered development projects*.

An Example of a Multi-Layered Development Project

A training system TRN is needed. This training system should be identical to the production system, but also requires special programs such as reset routines to return sample data to its original state. These programs only need to be consolidated to TRN, and should never be transported into the production system. To implement this, all training objects are assigned to a development class whose transport layer differs from the standard transport layer. This transport layer must be assigned to a consolidation route with TRN as the consolidation system.

Additional Delivery Routes

One technique for setting up additional delivery routes is known as using *multiple delivery routes*. This technique is frequently used by R/3 customers who have more than one delivery system. Multiple delivery routes have the same source system but different target systems. The concept of multiple delivery routes is also called *parallel forwarding*. The import queues of the target systems receive change requests in parallel as soon as the change requests have been imported into the source system of the delivery route.

Example of Multiple Delivery Routes

If you have a separate training R/3 System, TRN, which is used to train users working in the production system PR1, it makes sense to set up TRN in the same way as PR1 (see Figure 8.18 just below). Both the training and production systems should receive the same changes in parallel after these changes have been verified by quality assurance testing in system QAS. After a standard transport configuration has been created with DEV as the development system, QAS as the quality assurance system, and PRD as the production system, an additional delivery route may be created in the TMS editor with QAS as the source system and TRN as the target system.

Figure 8.18 combines the two examples given above: multi-layered development and multiple delivery systems. In addition, Figure 8.18 shows that a second production system, PR2, is delivered through the same transport flow as PR1.

FIGURE 8.18:

Multi-layered development and multiple delivery systems

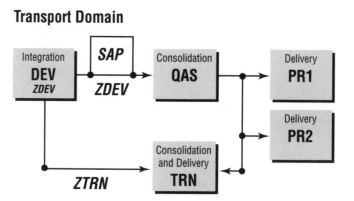

Another way of configuring more than one delivery system—not shown in the above diagram—is to use *multi-level delivery* or *multi-level forwarding*, which arranges the delivery routes in sequence. This is implemented by defining a recipient system for a recipient system—that is, defining a target system of a delivery route as the source system for an additional delivery route.

An example of multi-level delivery for a complex system landscape of an international company is shown in Figure 8.19. In this example, a standard transport flow exists between the global development system DEG, where global Customizing and development occur, and a global consolidation system QAG. After testing and verification in QAG, changes are delivered in parallel to the development systems of the two regional development systems, DEU for the United States and DEE for Europe.

Because each region requires its own specific Customizing and development, it has its own development system, quality assurance system, and production system. The global changes are delivered to the regional quality assurance systems, and thereafter, to the regional production systems. The concept of multi-level delivery here means that, between the regional development systems and quality assurance systems, there are three transport routes: one consolidation route for regional changes; one consolidation route for SAP objects; and one delivery route for global changes.

FIGURE 8.19:

A complex system landscape

FIGURE 8.19:

A complex system landscape

Transport Domain

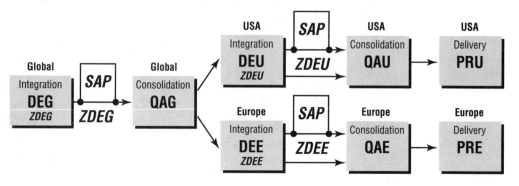

Version Control

The TMS provides a "version control" function for transport route configurations. Each activated configuration is stored with a sequential number and can be reactivated if needed. To reactivate a former configuration version from within the TMS editor, proceed as follows:

1. From the transport routes initial screen, choose *Configuration ➤ Get other configuration*.

2. Choose the source system—the system on which the configuration has been saved. If the transport domain controller was never moved from one R/3 System to another, only the transport domain controller can be entered in this field.

3. Choose the required version. You can use *F4* to display all available versions.

4. Choose *Enter*.

Extended Transport Control

As of R/3 Release 4.5, there are several additional features for transport route configuration that are summarized as *extended transport control*. Extended transport enables you to assign:

- Clients to transport routes

- Groups of clients (known as target groups) to transport routes

- Clients to transport layers

To take advantage of this functionality, in the transport profile, you must explicitly set parameter *ctc* to TRUE. The default value for this parameter is FALSE, which deactivates extended transport control. Before using extended transport control, you would ideally set parameter *ctc* to TRUE globally. After activating extended transport control, you can use either the normal, system-to-system transport routes or client-specific ones, but not a mixture of both types of connections in the same system landscape. If you are using a client-specific transport route, you must specify the clients when defining the source and target.

NOTE All R/3 Systems that are linked by transport routes must have either client-specific or client-independent source and target specifications, but not a mixture of both.

WARNING When you switch to extended transport control, if there are change requests in any import queue, those change requests will be highlighted red in the new column *Client* in the import queue, and cannot be transported until you specify a client for them (see Chapter 13).

Client-Specific Transport Routes

Extended transport control enables you to include R/3 clients in both consolidation and delivery routes (see Figure 8.20 just below). To create a client-specific transport route, proceed as follows:

1. Create an R/3 System–specific transport route as described above in the section "Hierarchical List Editor" or "Graphical Editor." In the dialog box *Create Transport Route* (see Figure 8.16 earlier), choose *extended transport control*.

2. Select either *Consolidation* or *Delivery*.

    A. For a consolidation route, enter the integration system and transport layer. In the field *Target system/client*, enter the SID of either an R/3 System and a client, or an existing target group.

    B. For a delivery route, enter a delivery source and a delivery system/client. The latter can be either an SID and a client, or an existing target group.

3. Choose *Enter*.

4. Choose *Save*.

5. Distribute and activate the new configuration.

Figure 8.20 shows a three-system landscape with client-specific transport routes as displayed in the hierarchical list editor. Changes in the development system DEV are transported to client 100 of the quality assurance system QAS. The target of the client-specific consolidation route is QAS.100. The delivery route from QAS to the production system PRD must also be client-specific. Client 100 of PRD is the production client, so the target of the client-specific delivery route is PRD.100.

FIGURE 8.20:

Client-specific
transport routes

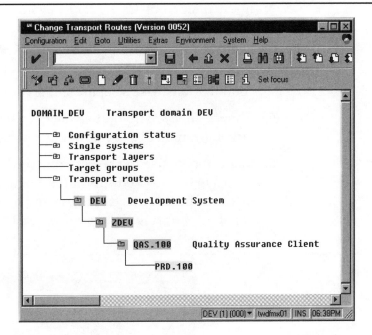

Target Groups

Extended transport control enables you to create *target groups* for
consolidations and deliveries. A target group is a group of target
clients. Each target client is specified in terms of an R/3 System
and a client ID within that system. When you release a change
request from the source system of a target group, the change request
is automatically added to the import buffers of all targets in the
target group. To define a target group, proceed as follows:

1. Access the initial screen of either the graphical or the hierarchical editor in change mode.

2. Choose *Configuration* ➤ *Target group* ➤ *Create*.

3. In the dialog box *Create Target Group* (shown in Figure 8.21), enter a name for the target group and a description. The name must begin and end with a forward slash (/).

4. Choose *Insert line*. Enter the required target system client combinations. Use a separate line for each client.

5. Choose *Transfer*. If you use the graphical editor, the created target group is displayed in the insertable objects area.

6. You can now use the target groups when defining transport routes in the TMS editors. After using a target group as part of a transport route, distribute and activate the changes as usual by choosing *Configuration* ➤ *Distribute and activate*.

FIGURE 8.21:

Creating target groups

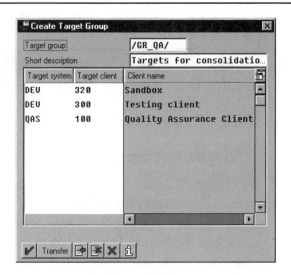

The use of target groups in a three-system landscape is shown in Figure 8.22. In this example, Customizing and development changes are made in client 100 in the development system DEV. Target group /GR_QA/ has been specified as the consolidation target for the consolidation route from the integration system

DEV. Changes are added in parallel to the respective import buffers for client 100 of the quality assurance system QAS, as well as for clients 300 and 320 of DEV. Target group /GR_PR/ has been specified as the delivery target of a delivery route with QAS.100 as the delivery source. After change requests are validated in QAS, they are transported into client 100 of the production system PRD as well as into training client 300 of QAS.

FIGURE 8.22:

Target groups in a three-system landscape

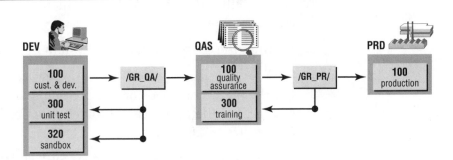

TIP   After you export change requests from the Customizing-and-development client, using target groups, you can transport change requests back into the other clients in the development system. This helps to ensure consistency among all clients in the development system.

Client-Specific Transport Layers

Extended transport control also enables you to give a client its own client-specific standard transport layer for client-dependent changes. Client-specific transport layers do not affect Repository objects. If no client-specific transport layer is created, each client uses the standard transport layer of the R/3 System to which it belongs.

With client-specific transport layers, the client in which a Customizing change is released determines the consolidation route. If a standard transport layer is defined for this client, the associated consolidation route is used. If no standard transport layer is defined for this client, the consolidation route is determined by the standard transport layer of the R/3 System.

To assign clients to transport layers, proceed as follows:

1. Access either the graphical or the hierarchical editor in change mode.

2. Position the cursor on the R/3 System in which the client resides.

3. For the hierarchical editor, choose *Configuration* ➤ *System* ➤ *Change*. For the graphical editor, choose *Configuration* ➤ *System reports* ➤ *Change*.

4. In the resulting dialog box *Change System Attributes*:

    A. To change the standard transport layer for the whole R/3 System—that is, for all clients—enter the name of the new standard transport layer.

    B. To assign clients to a transport layer, choose *Client assignment*. Choose *Insert line* and enter the required client and the transport layer combinations.

5. Choose *Transfer*.

6. Choose *Save*.

7. Distribute and activate the new transport route configuration.

Figure 8.23 shows a system landscape with client-specific transport layers using the graphical editor. In this example, there is a three-system landscape with a development system (DEV), a quality assurance system (QAS), and a production system (PRD). The R/3 application component for Financial Accounting (FI) is configured separately in client 200 in DEV and has its own separate R/3 Systems for quality assurance and production (QA2 and PR2). To consolidate all Customizing changes made for FI to QA2, these changes are made in client 200 in DEV (rather than in client 100), for which a client-specific standard transport layer (ZFI) has been defined.

Transport layer ZFI is assigned to a consolidation route with DEV as the integration system and client 100 in system QA2 as the consolidation target. This ensures that all client-dependent Customizing changes made in client 200 of DEV are consolidated to client 100 in QA2. To consolidate Repository objects to QA2, these objects must be created in development classes assigned to transport layer ZFI. Finally, all changes that have been imported into QA2 are delivered to PR2, the production system for FI.

FIGURE 8.23:

Creating client-specific standard transport layers

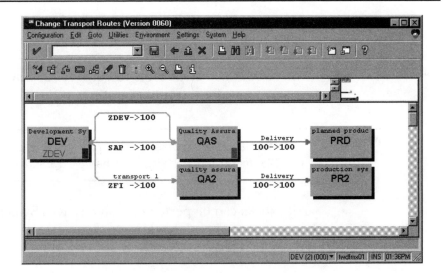

> **WARNING**   Although client-specific transport layers allow for the consolidation of client-dependent Customizing efforts to different target systems and clients, client-independent Customizing changes will follow only a single transport layer.

Verifying the System Landscape Setup

The TMS provides the following checks and monitor functions to help ensure that your system landscape is set up correctly:

- TMS checks

- Transport route configuration checks

- Alert Monitor

You should use these tools to verify your transport configuration and to perform troubleshooting.

> **NOTE**   For information on troubleshooting procedures and additional checks for TMS import functionality, see Chapters 13 and 14.

All checks can be performed on any R/3 System in the transport domain, not only on the domain controller.

Verifying the TMS Setup

To verify whether the TMS has been set up correctly, enter the *System Overview* screen (from the initial TMS screen, choose

Overview ➤ *Systems*). Choose *R/3 System* ➤ *Check*. The check is performed on all R/3 Systems unless you select a particular R/3 System by positioning the cursor on it. Choose one of the following checks:

- *Connection test*

- *Transport directory*

- *Transport tool*

During a connection test, the TMS tries to establish the RFC connection for the target hosts of all active R/3 Systems in the transport domain. The results list indicates whether the individual connections were successfully established and the time taken to establish the respective connection in milliseconds. A "backward check" is also performed to verify whether each target host can establish a connection back to the source system. To display details on a particular RFC connection, click the *status* field for a specific system.

When checking the transport directory, the TMS tries to create, read, and delete test files in all transport directories of the transport domain, including the transport directories of its external systems. The following subdirectories are covered in the check: *bin*, *buffer*, *cofiles*, *data*, *log*, *sapnames*, and *tmp*. From the results screen of this transport-directory check, you can run another check that tests whether a system is correctly assigned to a transport group. To run this check, choose *Goto* ➤ *Transport groups*.

The transport tool check gives an overview of the availability of the transport tools. This check may take some time. The check covers the *tp* interface, the transport profile, and the RFC destinations. It tests a *tp* call to every R/3 System of the transport domain. This *tp* call includes an RFC call, a database connect, and an offline call.

Verifying the Transport Route Configuration

To verify whether you have used TMS correctly to set up your system landscape, access one of the TMS editors. Unless you choose to run the check on a particular R/3 System (by positioning the cursor on it), the check is performed on all R/3 Systems in your system landscape. To start the check, choose *Configuration* ➢ *Check*. Choose one of the following checks:

- *Transport routes*

- *Request consistency*

A *transport routes check* investigates three things. First, it checks whether the transport flow provides deliveries from at least one consolidation system. Second, it checks whether the delivery is multi-level. If so, the check verifies that the parameter *multileveldelivery* is set in the transport profile for any R/3 Systems in the transport domain with an R/3 Release before 4.0. Third, if extended transport control is activated (that is, if parameter *ctc* is set to TRUE in the transport profile and the R/3 Release is 4.5 or higher), the check also verifies that the client-specific transport routes are not mixed with system-to-system transport routes for the same system landscape.

The *request consistency check* can be run either for the local system or for all systems. It checks whether transport routes associated with open tasks and requests are consistent with the current transport route configuration. If inconsistencies are found, it may be necessary to change the *type* of open requests—that is, either from *local* to *transportable* or vice versa, or from *repair* to *correction* or vice versa.

Open requests may also need a new transport destination if the original target system for these change requests does not correspond to the new configuration of the transport routes and does not provide a valid target system. This check also locates inconsistent change requests—change requests that contain invalid object combinations and make release impossible. After running the request consistency check, a list of all inconsistent change requests is displayed. To display details on the type of inconsistency and the required actions, position the cursor on a specific request and choose *Edit* ➤ *Display long text*.

The Alert Monitor

The TMS Alert Monitor enables you to monitor all actions that have been performed with the TMS. Highlighting is used to draw your attention to critical information. To access the Alert Monitor from the TMS initial screen, choose *Monitor* ➤ *Alert monitor*.

You can display either all messages or just warnings and error messages. The information is R/3 System–specific. To display the information corresponding to a different R/3 System, choose *TMS log* ➤ *Other system*. In the resulting dialog box, enter the appropriate SID in the field *Sys. Name* and choose *Enter*. To display the full text of a message, click the respective line.

The information provided by the Alert Monitor includes:

- Date and time of the activity
- Name of the user who performed the activity
- Related TMS function
- TMS messages, including error messages and warnings
- R/3 System and client where the TMS function was triggered

You should check the Alert Monitor if there are transport or TMS configuration problems, or to get detailed information to help you solve the problems.

Review Questions

1. Which of the following statements is correct in regard to the R/3 Systems belonging to a transport domain?

   A. They all share the same transport directory.

   B. They are managed centrally using TMS.

   C. They belong to the same transport group.

   D. They must run on the same operating system and database platform.

2. Which of the following statements is correct in regard to the domain controller?

   A. It must be the production system.

   B. It occurs once in a transport domain.

   C. It occurs in each transport group.

   D. It can only be the R/3 System that was originally designated as the transport domain controller.

   E. It should never be the production system due to the high system load that the domain controller causes.

3. Which of the following statements are correct in regard to the TMS?

   A. It needs to be initialized only on the transport domain controller.

   B. It needs to be initialized only on the transport domain controller and the backup domain controller.

   C. It must be initialized on every R/3 System.

   D. It must be set up before you can set up transport routes.

4. Which of the following statements are correct in regard to the RFC destinations for TMS connections?

    A. They are generated automatically when a transport route is created.

    B. They are generated between the domain controller and each R/3 System in the transport domain.

    C. They must be established manually before you can use the TMS.

    D. They are generated during the TMS initialization process.

    E. They are only needed for importing change requests.

5. How is the actual system landscape, including R/3 System roles and relationships, defined using the TMS?

    A. By including all R/3 Systems in the transport domain

    B. By configuring transport routes

    C. By assigning a role to each R/3 System during the TMS initialization process

    D. By designating real, virtual, and external R/3 Systems

6. Which of the following statements is correct in regard to a consolidation route?

    A. It is defined by an integration system and a consolidation system, and is associated with a transport layer.

    B. It is created in the TMS by defining only an integration system and a consolidation system.

    C. It is not necessarily required in a two-system landscape.

    D. It can be defined only once in a transport group.

7. Which of the following statements are correct in regard to client-specific transport routes?

   A. They are possible as of R/3 Release 4.0.

   B. They are possible only as of R/3 Release 4.5, and only if extended transport control is activated.

   C. They are only allowed for target groups.

   D. They may not be used in conjunction with client-independent transport routes.

CHAPTER
NINE

Client Tools

After R/3 installation, you need to set up R/3 clients so that users can log on to R/3 and perform Customizing and other tasks. Setting up the different clients for the R/3 Systems in your system landscape involves the following tasks:

- Defining the purpose of each client

- Enabling the appropriate users to access the client through user administration and authorization

- Preventing unwanted changes to Customizing settings and Repository objects in a client

- Providing all clients other than the source client CUST with the latest Customizing and developments in an organized and timely manner

- Populating a client with the necessary application data

To perform these tasks or subsequently modify clients to match your changing business needs, SAP provides the tools outlined in this chapter:

- Client maintenance tools (used to define a client and maintain its settings)

- Client copy tools (used to provide a client with the necessary data)

- Client delete tool (used to remove unwanted clients)

This chapter also explains the logging of Customizing changes affecting tables (table logging). Table logging is activated at the client level and needs to be considered when clients are set up.

Creating an R/3 Client

To create a client, you must make an entry for that client in table T000. Without this entry, you will not be able to log on to the client, import change requests into the client, or copy another client into the client. After creating the client entry, adjust the client settings to define the role of the client within the R/3 system landscape.

The newly created client is empty—it contains no client-dependent data. You must provide the client with the necessary user master data, application data, and Customizing data, so that users can log on to the client and perform, for example, Customizing activities or business transactions.

Client Entries

You can create, display, and change entries in table T000 using client maintenance (Transaction SCC4).

Creating a Client Entry

To create an entry in table T000 and thus create a new R/3 client, proceed as follows:

1. Access client maintenance by calling Transaction SCC4, or, from the R/3 initial screen, choose *Tools* ➢ *Administration* ➢ *Administration* ➢ *Client administration* ➢ *Client maintenance*.

2. The *Display View "Clients": Overview* screen appears. You are in display mode. Switch to change mode by selecting *Table view* ➢ *Display -> Change*.

3. A message box appears: "The table is client-independent (see Help for further info)". Choose *Continue*—you are now in change mode.

4. Select the button *New entries* or use the menu option *Edit* ➢ *New entries* to reach the screen *New Entries: Details of Added Entries* (see Figure 9.1).

5. Enter a three-digit client ID in the field *Client*. For example, to create client 145, enter **145** in this field. If this client ID is

already in use, the message "An entry already exists with the same key" will appear in the status bar. Provide a new and unique ID number.

6. Save your entry.

FIGURE 9.1:

The client maintenance screen

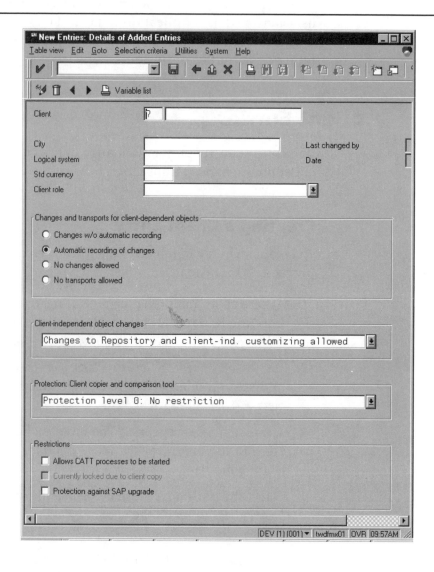

Maintaining a Client Entry

You can use client maintenance (Transaction SCC4) to view and change the settings for a client. From the screen *Display View "Clients": Overview*, you can do any of the following:

- Display the settings for a client by double-clicking the client ID

- Change client settings by choosing *Table view* ➢ *Display* -> *Change* to switch into change mode, then double-clicking the client ID

- Delete a client by selecting the client entry and then choosing *Edit* ➢ *Delete*

WARNING   You should avoid deleting a client entry from within client maintenance. Instead, use Transaction SCC5.

Deleting a Client Entry

When you delete a client entry from table T000 with client maintenance (Transaction SCC4), you can no longer log on to the client or update it using change requests. The deletion process, however, does not eliminate the data belonging to that client. This means the client-dependent data remains in your R/3 System, possibly without your knowledge, occupying valuable space in the database. To eliminate an R/3 client entirely—to delete both the client entry and the client-dependent data—use the client delete functionality (Transaction SCC5), which is explained below in "Deleting an R/3 Client."

Deleting a client entry with client maintenance allows you to temporarily lock the client. The deletion procedure preserves the data for that client, but prevents users from logging on to the client or accessing its data. By preventing logon, you can, for example, ensure that no users make changes during a client copy.

To restore the client and allow logon, re-create the client entry using client maintenance.

Client Settings

When you create a client entry, the only required input is a three-digit client ID. You can also make selections for the client settings or change previously selected settings. These settings are very important, because they further define and restrict the way the client is used. The different client settings include:

- Client name
- Client city
- Logical system name
- Standard currency
- Client role
- Client-dependent change option
- Client-independent change option
- Client protection against a client copy and client compare
- Restrictions

Assigning a name to a client provides you with a description that complements the client ID. The entry in the field *client city* is used to identify the physical location of the hardware for the R/3 System or the implementation team that is responsible for the client. Both the client name and city are optional. The other seven client settings provide more critical functions and deserve a more detailed explanation.

Logical System Name

You define a client within an R/3 System by creating an appropriate client ID. You may have other clients with the same client ID in your other R/3 Systems. For example, you may have a client 145 in both your development and quality assurance systems. To differentiate these two clients, you can provide them with unique 10-character logical system names. Logical system names are crucial for:

Application Link Enabling (ALE):   ALE is based on a distribution model that defines the message flow (or data exchange) between different logical systems. (See Chapter 4.)

SAP Business Workflow®:   SAP Business Workflow®, often simply referred to as *Workflow*, allows you to automatically control and execute cross-application processes within R/3. To define the steps and events in these processes, you need to know the logical system names of the clients where the events are initiated and performed.

ALE and SAP Business Workflow® recognize only logical system names, not client numbers or system IDs. These logical systems can be clients in the same or different R/3 Systems.

When creating a logical system name, follow these guidelines:

- Use a logical system name only once—each logical system name must be unique within your system landscape.

- Do not change a logical system name once it has been established or used by ALE or the SAP Business Workflow®.

WARNING   Avoid changing a logical system name. Such a change could result in the loss of ALE or SAP Business Workflow® documents.

Standard Currency

The standard currency is the default currency used for that client. It is entered as a three-letter code, such as USD for American dollars or EUR for the Euro dollar. For example, if you assign EUR as the client standard currency, whenever you enter a monetary value in that client, R/3 will assume that the currency is the Euro dollar unless you specify something different.

To be able to select a default currency for a client, currencies must be defined within the client or copied into the client from an SAP standard client. The SAP standard clients recognize over 100 different currencies. Other currencies can be defined using an IMG client-dependent Customizing activity.

Client Role

When you create a client, you normally assign a predefined role to it. The role reflects the purpose served by the client and can prevent or limit certain activities. The possible client roles include:

Production: A client with this role will not be deleted by a mistakenly initiated client delete or client copy. No client-independent changes can be imported into this client or into its R/3 System as part of a client copy. This prevents possible inconsistencies that could affect production. In addition, changing certain Customizing settings in a production client, such as currency exchange rates and posting periods, can be allowed in this client—despite the standard client-dependent change option that is used to prevent Customizing changes in a production client. These *Current Settings* (see Chapter 11) can be maintained in a production client without being recorded to a change request.

Test: A client with this role is protected against an R/3 Release upgrade by the appropriate client restriction (see "Client Restrictions" below).

Customizing: The factory calendar can be maintained in and transported from only the client with this role.

Demonstration: Setting up a demonstration client allows you to have a separate client for demonstration purposes.

Training/Education: Setting up a training client allows you to have a separate client for training purposes.

In future R/3 Releases, SAP plans to link additional functionality to the client roles to increase the scope of the protection they provide.

Client Change Options

These settings control the types of changes that can be made in the client and determine whether Customizing changes are recorded to change requests. The default change options for a client are as follows:

- *Automatic recording of changes*

- *Changes to Repository and client-independent Customizing allowed*

Because of the significance of these settings, the client change options were outlined in detail in Chapter 3.

Client Protection

When you select this client option—*Protection: Client copier and comparison tool*—on the client maintenance screen (see Figure 9.1 earlier in this chapter), the client is protected against being overwritten by a client copy. This option also ensures that sensitive data cannot be viewed from another client during client compares, an activity performed using the Customizing Cross-System

Viewer (Transaction SCU0; see Chapter 11). The levels of overwrite-protection you can select are as follows:

- *Protection level 0: No Restrictions*

- *Protection level 1: No overwriting*

  - This ensures that the client will not be overwritten by the client copy program. It also protects the client from the adjustment activities of the Customizing Cross-System Viewer. Use this setting for your Customizing-and-development client, as well as for clients that contain critical settings or data that should not be overwritten, such as your quality assurance client.

- *Protection level 2: No overwriting and no external availability*

  - This protects a client against being overwritten by a client copy and also against *read* access from another client using the tools of the Cross-System Viewer. Protection level 2 should be used for clients that contain sensitive data, such as your production client.

Client Restrictions

The following options enable you to restrict activities in clients:

Start of CATT process allowed: Select this option for a client such as the quality assurance test client where you wish to run the Computer Aided Test Tool (CATT) to perform scripted validity tests of application functionality. Since CATT scripts generate application data, they should not be run in every client.

Currently locked due to client copy: This option is automatically set by the R/3 System when you use the client copy tool. You cannot select it manually.

Protection against SAP upgrade: You can assign this option only to a client whose role is set to *Test*. This option prevents the introduction of new client-dependent Customizing changes into a client during an R/3 Release upgrade, thereby preserving the settings that existed prior to the upgrade. After an upgrade, the test client can be used in conjunction with the Cross-System Viewer to compare the client-dependent differences between the two R/3 Releases.

Providing an R/3 Client with Data

After you create a new client entry, the client will contain no data: no Customizing data, application data, or user master records. You must copy data into the new client to provide an environment where users can either customize, develop, test, or train, depending on the purpose of the client. A client copy is used to initially populate a client with base data from either the SAP standard client 000 or an existing customer client (see Chapter 5). Change requests are then used to distribute the latest Customizing and developments to the different clients.

The different client copy tools that can be used to initially populate a client with data include:

- Local client copy
- Remote client copy
- Client transport

Selecting a Client Copy Tool

To select the most suitable client copy tool in a given situation, you must consider the locations of both the source client and the target client, and the type of data to be copied. To copy a client in an R/3 System to another client in the same R/3 System, use a local client copy. Either a remote client copy or a client transport can be used to copy a client from one R/3 System to another R/3 System. (See Figure 9.2.)

FIGURE 9.2:

The three client copy tools

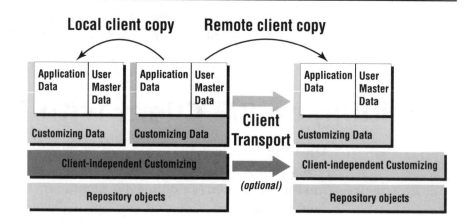

Advantages of a Client Transport

When you copy a client from one R/3 System to another R/3 System, you can use a client transport to:

- Preserve a copy of the client outside R/3 in files at the operating system level. A client transport involves writing a client to the transport directory (similar to the export process for a change request). This provides you with a copy of the client that you can use later, for example, to help create multiple clients based on one client.

- Copy client-independent Customizing. As of R/3 Release 4.6, this can also be done with a remote client copy.

- Schedule the two steps—data export and import—independently.

For these reasons, SAP recommends using a client transport when you cannot use change requests to build a new R/3 System (see Chapter 5). A client transport also provides a newly installed target system with the necessary client-independent and client-dependent data.

Note that you should not use a client transport to copy client-independent Customizing to a target system that already contains such Customizing, because the client transport will overwrite the existing client-independent Customizing objects in the target system. This causes inconsistencies when client-dependent data in other clients within the target system depends on the overwritten entries.

WARNING   Importing client-independent Customizing into an R/3 System that already contains such Customizing may affect the data and functionality of other clients in the system.

Advantages of a Remote Client Copy

If you do not need client-independent Customizing in your new client, SAP recommends using a remote client copy to provide the client with data. For example, a remote client copy is ideal if you wish to copy the user data from a unit test client in the development system to the training client in the quality assurance system. A remote client copy transfers data to another R/3 System using RFC technology. This client copy tool has the following advantages:

- It can prevent data loss. During a remote client copy, an automatic Repository consistency check is performed. The structure of each table to be copied is checked and compared with tables in the target system. If inconsistencies are detected—for example, tables are missing in the target system or fields are missing in the tables—the client copy is canceled, and an error message is displayed. This kind of check is not performed automatically during a client transport.

- It is faster than a client transport, because it can copy data not only sequentially but also in parallel.

- It does not require the multiple export and import steps required by a client transport.

- It does not generate files at the operating system level and therefore does not take up disk space in the transport directory. In contrast, the client transport of a production client may generate files larger than the available disk space or reach file size limitations set by the operating system.

Using Client Copy Profiles to Select Data

Regardless of the client copy tool you select, you must determine the type of data you wish to copy from a source client to a target client. A client copy profile determines the data to be copied. The data that can be copied includes:

- Client-dependent Customizing data

- Client-independent Customizing data

- Application data—both master data and transaction data

- User data, which is a combination of user master data and authorization profiles (see Chapter 4)

- *Variants*, which are sets of input values saved for programs that you often use

When you begin the client copy procedure, you select a particular client copy profile (see "Local and Remote Client Copy" and "Client Transport" below). The profiles delivered by SAP are displayed in Table 9.1. Note that you can copy application data only when you also copy Customizing data, because application data depends on the Customizing settings of the client, and is of no value without those settings.

TABLE 9.1: Client Copy Profiles for Selecting Data

Copy Profile	Client-Dependent Customizing Data	Application Data	User Data	Variants	Client-Independent Customizing Data
SAP_ALL	X	X	X	X	
SAP_APPL	X	X	X		
SAP_CUST	X				
SAP_CUSV	X			X	
SAP_EXBC*	X		X	X	X
SAP_EXPA*	X	X	X	X	X
SAP_EXPC*	X			X	X
SAP_UAPP	X	X	X	X	
SAP_UCUS	X		X		
SAP_UCSV	X		X	X	
SAP_USER			X		

*These profiles can be selected only for a client transport.

WARNING Before data is copied from the source client, the contents of the target client are deleted. This is true for all client copy profiles *except* the profile SAP_USER. In addition, if Central User Administration is active, you will not be able to copy user data, regardless of the client copy profile you select.

Example: Using Client Copy Tools to Support Training Needs

A company whose R/3 System has been in production for over a year decides to roll out additional business processes in the production system. This requires training for new users as well as those unfamiliar with the new business functionality.

To provide a training environment, a new client—client 300—is created in the quality assurance system. Client 300 is created as a client copy of the quality assurance client using a local client copy and the client copy profile SAP_ALL. The training staff cleans up client 300 by removing unnecessary data and providing base data for those business transactions the users must learn. Client 300 thus provides a basis that instructors can use to develop training materials.

Prior to the start of training classes, client 400 is created using a local client copy of client 300 with the client copy profile SAP_ALL. To verify profiles and help users feel comfortable in their accounts, user data is copied from the production client into client 400 on the quality assurance system. This is done using a remote client copy with the client copy profile SAP_USER. The training then begins in client 400.

Displaying Client Copy Profiles

You can display the R/3 client copy profiles from within the different client copy tools. For example, to display the client copy profile SAP_UCUS from within the local client copy tool, proceed as follows:

1. Use Transaction code SCCL or, from the R/3 initial screen, choose *Tools* ➢ *Administration* ➢ *Administration* ➢ *Client administration* ➢ *Client copy* ➢ *Local copy*.

2. Use the F4-Help to get a list of the different profiles. Select the profile SAP_UCUS.

3. Display the profile using *Profile* ➤ *Display Profile*.

Figure 9.3 shows the screen that appears. When you select this profile, Customizing and user data—but not application data—will be copied. This client copy profile also initializes and re-creates the target client—it deletes the target client prior to copying in data. It does not copy variants. This profile is valid for all client copy tools.

FIGURE 9.3:

Displaying client copy profile SAP_UCUS

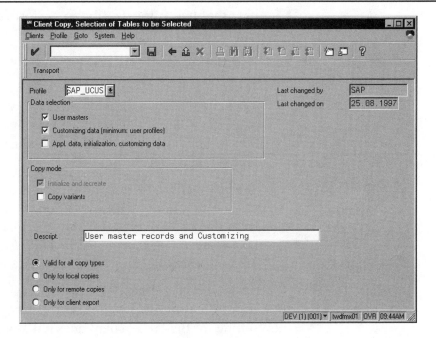

Local and Remote Client Copy

To perform either a local client copy or a remote client copy, proceed as follows:

1. Use client maintenance (Transaction SCC4) to ensure that the target client is defined in table T000.

2. Log on to the R/3 System in the target client.

   - If the target client is new and has no defined users, log on with the user SAP* and the password PASS.

   - If users are defined in the target client, log on with a user that has authorization to perform a client copy, such as the user SAP*.

3. Access the appropriate client copy activity.

   - To copy a client from the same R/3 System, access the local client copy tool using Transaction code SCCL or, from the R/3 initial screen, choose *Tools* ➢ *Administration* ➢ *Administration* ➢ *Client administration* ➢ *Client copy* ➢ *Local copy*.

   - To copy a client from another R/3 System, access the remote client copy tool using Transaction code SCC9 or, from the R/3 initial screen, choose *Tools* ➢ *Administration* ➢ *Administration* ➢ *Client administration* ➢ *Client copy* ➢ *Remote copy*.

   If a message box appears with the message "The client is locked for data import by client copy", the client protection setting for the target client does not allow overwriting.

4. Select the appropriate client copy profile. To see the available client copy profiles, use the F4-Help for the field *Selected Profile*.

5. Enter the source client information.

- For a local client copy, provide the client ID of the source client whose Customizing data, application data, and variant information should be copied. In the field *Source client user masters*, you may also enter a client ID for the source client whose user data should be copied. Usually the two source clients are the same, but you may wish to copy user data from a different client.

- For a remote client copy tool, you must provide an *RFC destination*. An RFC destination (maintained with Transaction SM59) is used to communicate with a client in another R/3 System for the purpose of sharing data. Using the F4-Help for the field *Source destinat.*, select the appropriate RFC destination. The name of the source R/3 System and the client ID of the source client are entered automatically. (See Appendix A for information on maintaining RFC destinations.)

If a message box appears with the message "Source client is protected against data export by client copy", the client protection setting for the source client does not allow external access and cannot be copied.

6. Choose *Execute* or *Execute in background* to start the client copy. Since a client copy is often very time-consuming, SAP recommends performing your client copy as a background job.

7. A *Verification* dialog box appears, which allows you to check and confirm the profile and source information. If everything is correct, choose *Yes* to start the client copy. Select *No* to cancel the procedure.

Client Transport

You can think of a client transport as a very large change request that contains the contents of an entire client. The multi-step process requires, first, a client export from the source client to files at the operating system level, and then the import of those data files into the target client. In addition, post-import processing is required to complete the procedure.

RFC System Check

An R/3 System consistency check is automatically performed before data is copied with a remote client copy. With a client transport, such a check is not automatic, but you can opt to perform one. The initial screen of the client transport tool (Transaction SCC8) has an *RFC system check* button that you can use to initiate this check.

The check program first determines what data is to be copied based on the selected client copy profile. RFCs are then used to locate the target system and client, and check whether all ABAP Dictionary definitions exist there in identical form. The check report usually confirms that all structures are consistent. If that is not the case, a list of the ABAP Dictionary table definitions missing in the target system is generated. This will help you to recognize in advance formal problems that may occur during the import of the source data.

TIP   To ensure the consistency of the ABAP Dictionary in the source and target R/3 Systems, SAP recommends performing an RFC system check before starting a client transport.

Client Export

A client export writes data files at the operating system level. These data files, unlike the data files that result from a standard change request, may be rather large. For this reason alone, SAP does not recommend copying large production clients using the client copy tools. A system copy may be more appropriate. In any case, prior to using a client transport, you should verify that there is enough available disk space in the transport directory using operating system tools.

NOTE   For information on how to copy large production clients, see R/3 Note 67205.

To perform a client export, follow these steps:

1. Log on to the R/3 System in the source client. Do not log on as user SAP*.

NOTE   Since the user SAP* cannot create a change request, it cannot perform the client export step in a client transport.

---

2. Access the client export tool using Transaction code SCC8 or, from the R/3 initial screen, choose *Tools* ➢ *Administration* ➢ *Administration* ➢ *Client administration* ➢ *Client transport* ➢ *Client export.*

3. Select the appropriate client copy profile. To view the possible client copy profiles, use the F4-Help for the field *Selected Profile.*

4. Enter the system ID of the target system. The exported files will be imported into this R/3 System. It must differ from the R/3 System in which you are initiating the client export. Only R/3 Systems defined in your transport domain may be selected. Proceed as follows in these special situations:

   • If the target R/3 System is not part of your transport domain, prior to the client export, use the TMS (Transaction STMS) to define the R/3 System as either a virtual or an external system.

- If the TMS is set up with extended transport control, you may provide an SID, a combination of an SID and a client ID, or a target transport group in the field for the target system.

5. Choose *Execute* or *Execute in background* to start the client export. Since this process can take a long time, SAP recommends performing the client export as a background job.

6. A *Verification* dialog box appears, which allows you to check and confirm the profile and source information. If everything is correct, choose *Yes* to start the client export. Select *No* to cancel the procedure.

7. An *INFO Client Export* message box will appear. This displays any change requests that may be generated as a result of the client export. Choose *Continue* to begin the client export.

Client Import

A client export generates up to three change requests for import into the target R/3 System. Table 9.2 displays the change requests for a sample client export. These change requests and files will be found in the transport directory for the fifteenth client copy performed in the development system DEV. Since this sample client export used the client copy profile SAP_EXPA, which includes all client-dependent and client-independent data from the source client, three change requests were generated. If the client copy profile SAP_USER, which selects only user data for export, had been selected for the sample client export, the DEVKO00015 change request would not have been created.

TABLE 9.2: Sample Change Requests from a Client Export

Change Request	Data Contents	Data File	Command File
DEVKO00015	Client-independent data	RO00015.DEV	KO00015.DEV
DEVKT00015	Client-dependent data	RT00015.DEV	KT00015.DEV

Continued on next page

TABLE 9.2: Sample Change Requests from a Client Export (Continued)

Change Request	Data Contents	Data File	Command File
DEVKX00015 (None prior to R/3 Release 4.5)	Client-dependent text, such as SAPscripts	RX00015.DEV (SX0015.DEV prior to R/3 Release 4.5)	KX00015.DEV None prior to R/3 Release 4.5)

Note that the client export files have a naming convention distinct from Customizing and Workbench change requests. Like those change requests, the ID number for client export files begins with the system ID of the source system (here, DEV), and ends with a sequential five-digit number. In the middle, however, there is a combination of the letters K and O (for client-independent data), T (for client-dependent data), or X (for client-dependent texts). These letters allow you to quickly distinguish a client export change request from standard change requests when viewing an import queue.

As a result of the client export, the change requests are added to the import queue of the target system. To view the import queue of a system, call Transaction STMS and choose *Overview* ➢ *Imports*; then, double-click the system ID.

Figure 9.4 shows a sample import queue. A total of seven change requests are waiting for import, three of which resulted from a client export initiated by user DRENNAN. Since client export change requests are special requests that, in most cases, delete and re-create a client as well as provide a client with new data, they cannot be imported using standard import commands (in Transaction STMS: *Start import* or *Preliminary import*). They must be imported as individual change requests. Such change requests are highlighted in a different color to indicate that they will not be imported. To determine the meaning of the different icons and colors, use the *Legend* button on the import queue screen.

FIGURE 9.4:

A sample import queue
with client export
change requests

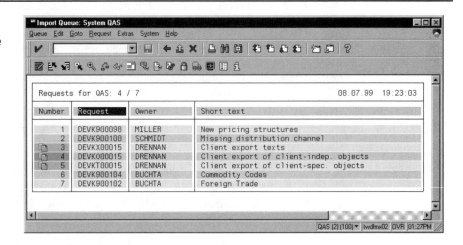

All change requests, including those released as a result of a
client export, should be imported in their correct order—the order
in which they appear in the import queue. (See Chapter 5.) Before
you import change requests as part of your client export process,
import those change requests higher up in the import queue. For
example, in Figure 9.4, the first two change requests should be
imported before the client export.

As of R/3 Release 4.5   If your R/3 System is at R/3 Release
4.5 or higher, follow these steps to import the client data that has
been exported and is waiting in the import queue:

1. Call Transaction STMS and then choose *Overview* ➣ *Import*.
   Double-click the target R/3 System of the client export to display its import queue.

2. Select the first client export change request waiting for
   import and choose *Request* ➣ *Import*. By selecting this change
   request, you initiate the import for all the client export
   change requests.

3. The screen *Client Import*, as shown in Figure 9.5, will appear. It lists the names of the change requests to be imported. Enter the client ID of the target client.

4. Execute the import by selecting the *Import* button. The import of the change requests occurs as a background job.

FIGURE 9.5:

The client import screen as of R/3 Release 4.5

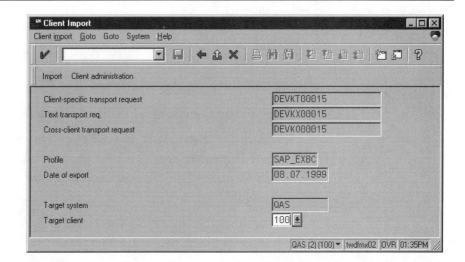

Prior to R/3 Release 4.5   For systems with releases prior to R/3 Release 4.5, use the following procedure to import change requests resulting from a client export:

1. Call Transaction STMS and then choose *Overview* ➢ *Import*. Double-click the target R/3 System of the client export to display its import queue.

2. If the client export has created a client-independent change request—for example, in Figure 9.4, DEVKO00015—import this change request first.

A. Select the change request and choose *Request* ➢ *Import*.

    B. Enter the client ID of the desired target client.

    C. Because the import may be time-consuming, schedule the import to occur in the background by selecting the button *Expert mode* and choosing *Start import in background*.

    D. To start the import of the change request, choose *Start import*.

  3. Import the client-dependent change request—for example, DEVKT00015.

    A. Select the change request and choose *Request* ➤ *Import*.

    B. Provide the client ID of the desired target client.

    C. Because the import may be time-consuming, schedule the import to run as a background job by selecting the button *Expert mode* and choosing *Start import in background*.

    D. To start the import of the change request, choose *Start import*.

Since a change request does not exist for text files in releases prior to R/3 Release 4.5, they will not be involved in the import process. Instead, they are included in post-import processing.

Post-Import Considerations   For all R/3 Releases, after successful import, the client export change requests remain in the import queue of the target system. You should delete these change requests by individually selecting each change request in the import queue and choosing *Request* ➤ *Delete*.

Client export change requests do not continue along the standard transport routes. In other words, if you import a client into the quality assurance system, the change requests will not be added to the import queue of the production system. If the client export is to be imported into other R/3 Systems or clients, you must add the change requests to the import queues accordingly.

Post-Import Processing

No one should work in the client until the necessary post-import activities have been performed successfully. The only exception to this is when you perform a client import that contains only user data. Post-import processing includes:

- Deleting data from certain imported tables, including tables with delivery class "L" (explained in more detail below in "Table Delivery Classes")

- Importing texts (prior to R/3 Release 4.5)

- Generating reports, screens, and other Repository objects

- Adjusting number ranges

To perform post-import processing:

1. Log on to the target R/3 System in the target client.

2. Use Transaction code SCC7 or, from the R/3 initial screen, choose *Tools* ➢ *Administration* ➢ *Administration* ➢ *Client administration* ➢ *Client transport* ➢ *Post-process import*.

3. The screen *Client import - postprocessing* appears (see Figure 9.6). It shows the name of the client-dependent change request from the client import process. The name of the profile used during the client export is also displayed. To begin post-import processing, choose either *Execute* or *Execute in background*.

4. If client-independent Customizing objects were copied, you will be prompted to process the cross-client Customizing changes. If the R/3 System contains none of its own unique client-independent Customizing, choose *Yes*.

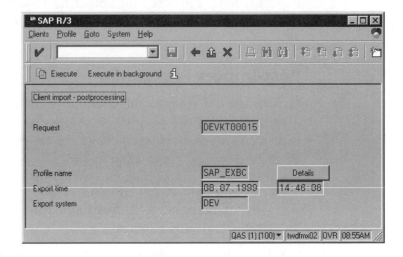

Post-import processing needs to be performed only once. If you try to restart post-import processing, one of the following messages will appear in the status bar:

- "A physical client transport with tp has not taken place". This message appears when post-import processing has been completed.

- "Client has not yet been generated by a data import". This message appears when a client import has not occurred or the import of the client data was not successfully completed.

Monitoring and Verifying a Client Copy

While a client copy is running, throughout the rather long procedure, you can view the status in the *Client Copy Log*. After the procedure is complete, you can also use the log to verify whether the client copy was a success or failure before you begin working in the target client.

To access the Client Copy Log, use Transaction code SCC3 or, from the R/3 initial screen, choose *Tools* ➤ *Administration* ➤ *Administration* ➤ *Client administration* ➤ *Copy logs*. The screen displays the current status of all local and remote client copies, listed by the target client number. Figure 9.7 shows a sample screen indicating client copy logs for three different target clients. The column *Number Runs* indicates how many client copy log files exist for the target client. The most important column, *Status text*, displays the status of the last remote or local client copy. Possible status texts include:

- *Initializing*
- *Processing*
- *Successfully completed*
- *Completed with errors*
- *Canceled*
- *R3trans export (see SE01)*

These texts are also valid for a client transport. In fact, the last text is client transport–specific and is explained below in "Special Transaction for Client Transports."

With Transaction SCC3, you can also monitor the client export and import activities that make up a client transport. In R/3 Releases prior to Release 4.5, the client export log files are displayed on the initial screen of Transaction SCC3 with "EXP" in the column *Target Client*. With these Releases, import logs can only be found using the Transport Organizer (Transaction SE01). To view import logs as of Release 4.5, from the initial screen of Transaction SCC3, you can choose either *Client exports* or *Client imports*.

FIGURE 9.7:

Client Copy Log Analysis screen

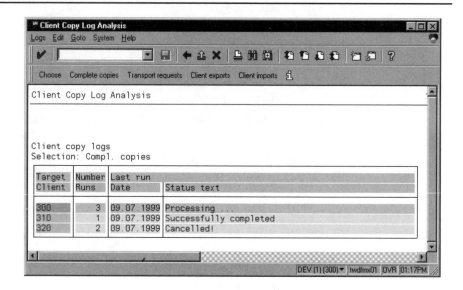

To access the logs for a particular target client, double-click that client ID. A list of all available log files for that client will be displayed. A sample screen is shown in Figure 9.8. The table on this screen contains a variety of information, including the client copy profile (column *Profile*) and the client copy type (column *Mode*). In the column *Test*, the entry "R" indicates that a resource check was run, and "X" refers to a simulation (explained below in "System Resources"). By double-clicking a particular log file, you can obtain the following information:

- For client copy logs resulting from a test run (an entry in the column *Test*), you have detailed access to the tables impacted by the copy as well as an estimated resource analysis.

- For client copies that have the status *Processing*, you can see the table whose data is currently being processed and the number of tables still to be copied.

- For client copies with the status *Successfully completed*, you can verify the tables that were copied and the number of table inserts and deletes.

- For client copies with the status *Canceled* or *Completed with errors*, to determine the cause of the error, you can view the log files.

FIGURE 9.8:

Client copy runs for a single R/3 client

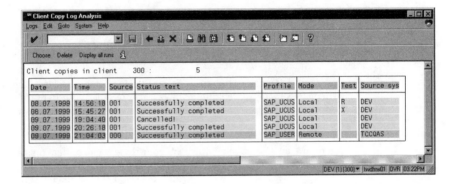

Special Transaction for Client Transports

When data is being extracted for a client export, the status for the client copy log in this transaction will read "R3trans export (see SE01)". Because client transports use *R3trans*, a database tool external to R/3 (see Chapter 7), you can view only limited log files within Transaction SCC3.

To see all the export and import log files generated during a client transport process, access the Transport Organizer by calling Transaction SE01. From the initial screen, select *Client transports* as the request type, and click *Choose*. This displays client transport change requests in the same hierarchical manner used for standard change requests in the Customizing Organizer or Workbench Organizer.

Restarting a Canceled Client Copy

Table 9.3 lists the most common reasons why a client copy is terminated, and presents possible solutions.

TABLE 9.3: Common Causes and Fixes for a Failed Client Copy

Cause of Termination	Solution
A user stops the program.	Restart the client copy.
A user shuts down the R/3 System, or the system fails.	Restart the client copy.
The program terminates due to inadequate storage space in the database.	To monitor the database fill level and size of objects such as tablespaces or tables, use Transaction DB02. Using database tools such as SAPDBA, increase available space and restart the client copy.
You receive an ABAP dump with the error cause *timeout*.	Either increase the maximum online runtime (profile parameter *rdisp/max_wprun_time*) and restart the client copy, or perform the client copy in the background (covered below in "Background Scheduling of a Client Copy").
The program terminates due to an error in an EXIT module. You receive an ABAP dump.	Review the copy logs to determine which program failed. Using SAP's Internet site, SAPNet, search for R/3 Notes related to the failed program to find a correction. Correct the problem or contact the SAP Hotline for further support.
An inconsistency occurs between the database and the R/3 System. You receive an ABAP error message noting a database inconsistency.	Data cannot be copied properly because table structures in the source and target systems differ. Correct the inconsistencies and restart the client copy. (Refer back to "RFC System Check.")

After correcting the problem, restart the client copy by again calling the appropriate client copy transaction (Transaction SCCL, SCC9, or SCC8). Since the initial client copy failed, the *Restart* option will be proposed by default. For example, if a local client copy failed because of inadequate tablespace, you would remedy the problem and then call Transaction SCCL. The parameters you initially used for the canceled client copy would still be present (see Figure 9.9), and the field *Restart mode active* would be selected. To run the client copy from the point of failure—that is, to begin copying the table where the failure occurred—choose either *Execute* or *Execute in background*. To perform a completely new client copy, choose *Restart <-> New start*.

FIGURE 9.9:

The restart option for a canceled client copy

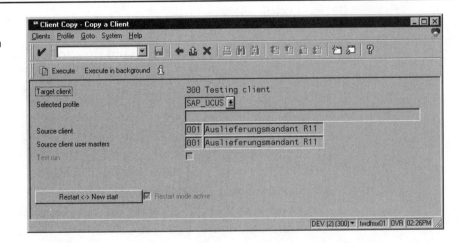

TIP   If a terminated client copy was a recent run, which will be indicated in the status line, SAP recommends restarting the client copy from the time of the termination. This will save the time required for recopying data that has already been successfully copied.

Additional Tools

In addition to reviewing the client copy logs, you can also monitor and verify a client copy with the following tools:

- Analyze a client copy error by calling Transaction SM21 (*System Log*) and checking the system log. This indicates whether database problems are responsible for the client copy error. Correct any database problems and then restart the client copy.

- Check the status of a client copy started as a background job by calling Transaction SM37 (*Background Job Overview*). This indicates whether a background client copy job has started, is active, or has been completed.

- Monitor the progress of a particular client copy by using Transaction SM30 (*View Maintenance*) to access view V_CCCFLOW. This view contains, for example, the runtime and processing status of a local client copy, the number of already copied tables, and the name of the table currently being copied.

- View the log files physically stored in the transport directory at the operating system level. Log files are named CC<number> .<SID>, where <number> is the six-digit serial client copy number, and <SID> is the source system ID. For example, the twenty-first client copy on the development system will generate the log file CC000021.DEV.

Considerations for a Client Copy

The client copy process impacts not only the performance, memory, and database resources of the involved R/3 System (or systems), but also the availability of the source and target clients. Before starting a client copy, you must evaluate the system resources and client availability in your system landscape. In addition to technical issues, you must also consider the impact a client copy has on certain data, including number ranges and address data.

Client Impact

Unless you are copying only user data, a client copy or client import reinitializes the target client by deleting it. The key entries of the tables corresponding to the target client are deleted.

To ensure data consistency in the target client during the client copy or client import, the target client's restriction *Currently locked due to client copy* is activated automatically, and only the users DDIC and SAP* can log on to the target client.

No user should work in the source client during the copy procedure. This prevents possible inconsistencies, particularly in the number ranges, resulting from changes in tables that are being copied. You should schedule a client copy for a time when the source system's usage is minimal—for example, in the evening.

TIP   Users should not make changes in a source client while it is being copied.

Background Scheduling of a Client Copy

The client copy program has a long runtime. Therefore, it should always be started in the background. This has the following advantages:

- The client copy will not use or block work processes required for online processing.

- The client copy will not be terminated if it exceeds the allowed execution time. This is important when very large tables are involved in the copy. Although the maximum execution time for online work processes (profile parameter *rdisp/max_wprun_time*) is usually too short to allow a complete client to be copied, this runtime restriction does not apply to background processing.

- Changes to tables during online processing are not blocked. (While the client copy is in progress, to prevent possible inconsistencies, no changes can be made to tables in the source client.)

To perform a client copy as a background job, choose *Execute in background* when initiating the client copy. Next, schedule the job as immediate or specify a start time, preferably a time when the system is not being used. Provide the print parameters for the spool output. Once you save these parameters, the client copy is scheduled for background processing.

> **NOTE** For more information on background processing, see Chapter 9 of Liane Will's *SAP R/3 System Administration* (from Sybex).

System Resources

As pointed out in Chapter 3, every client requires both hardware and administrative resources. To copy a client, you must ensure that adequate space is available in the target R/3 System. In other words, the target R/3 System database must have enough free storage space available in existing tables for the client copy to succeed. In addition, you need enough system memory to process the copying of data. Without the required system resources, a client copy will fail.

Tablespace Requirements   For an R/3 System whose database management system (DBMS) is Oracle, Informix, SAP DB, or DB2—not MS SQL Server—you can determine whether the database space for each table suffices by performing a test run of the proposed client copy. After a test run, you receive a list of all database areas (tablespaces) that will be extended during the copy. In addition, since these test runs are logged, you can use the log to check how much space the entries require.

To perform a client copy as a test run, simply execute the client copy with the option *Test run* selected. A test run can be executed either online or, more appropriately, as a background job. To start the test run, choose either *Resource Check* or *Simulation*. These two types of test runs differ as follows:

- A resource check estimates the required database space by counting the records to be copied. It is faster than a simulation.

- A simulation estimates the required database space by reading all records to be copied without updating them in the database.

There is no way to exactly determine the range of free storage space available in existing tables. For every table copied, the number of required inserts is calculated. However, since database deletions are not possible in some databases until after reorganization, these deletions are not taken into account. This means the forecasted database requirements may be considerably larger than the actual requirements. If a resource check or a simulation indicates that you have enough tablespace to perform a client copy, you can be certain the client copy will not fail because of a lack of tablespace.

Memory Requirements   A client copy requires a great deal of system memory. If your system memory is limited, you should not perform any other activities in the system during the copy procedure. In this case, SAP recommends running the client copy as a background job at a time when the normal activity of the system is greatly reduced.

Table Delivery Classes

By selecting a particular client copy profile, you determine which data is copied in a client copy. In turn, the R/3 System uses table delivery classes to determine which data corresponds to the client copy profile.

A table delivery class indicates the type of data housed in a table—application data, Customizing data, or some type of system data. Every table in the ABAP Dictionary is assigned a table delivery class. R/3 Release upgrades and the client copy tools use this information to determine which table data to copy to target clients.

Table 9.4 displays the different table delivery classes and indicates when the different classes are copied. For example, if you select the client copy profile for client-dependent Customizing data only, the client copy will select the client-dependent data from those tables with the delivery class "C." In addition, the client copy selects the client-dependent data from system tables with the delivery classes "G," "E," and "S."

TABLE 9.4: The Role of Table Delivery Classes in a Client Copy

Table Delivery Class	Type of Table	Copied* When?
A	Application data	When selected
C	Customizing data	When selected
L	Temporary table	Never
G	Customizing table protected during an upgrade	Always
E	Control table	Always
S	System table that you cannot maintain	Always
W	System table	Never

*It is assumed that the copy mode is set to *Initialize and recreate*.

You do not need to select particular delivery classes, because they are tied to the client copy profile. However, when you are debugging, the table delivery class may help you discover why a certain data type was not included in a client copy. For example, if data is stored in a table with the table delivery class "W," you know the data will not be part of any client copy. However, if you selected a profile that included application data, and the data from a table with delivery class "A" was not included in the copy procedure, one of the following has occurred:

- The data was entered into the source table after the client copy.

- The data was deleted from the target client after the client copy was completed.

- The table containing the data is assigned to the temporary development class $tmp. Data in tables that are assigned to a temporary development class is not copied during a client copy.

- There is a programming problem. In this case, check SAP's Internet site, SAPNet, for a specific R/3 Note, or report the problem to the SAP Hotline.

To view the delivery class of a table, use Transaction code SE11 or, from the R/3 initial screen, use *Tools* ➤ *ABAP Workbench* ➤ *Dictionary*. Enter the name of the table and select *Display*.

Number Ranges

When performing Customizing activities within the IMG, you often adjust *number ranges*. A number range is the set of consecutive numbers that can be assigned to business objects—or their sub-objects—of the same type. Examples of such objects include addresses, business partners, general ledger accounts, orders, posting documents, and materials. Number ranges are assigned to application data—master data in the case of business partners or transaction data for orders. When working with multiple R/3 clients and using client copies to create new clients, you should evaluate the status of your number ranges. For example, you may wish, for the purpose of testing, to use different number ranges in different clients, or perhaps the same number ranges for certain master data but not necessarily for transaction data.

If you copy only Customizing data, the target client will contain no application data after the completion of the client copy. In this case, the number ranges will be automatically reset to default values during the copy procedure. In all other cases, the number range status remains unchanged or is copied from the source client.

TIP   After a client copy, SAP recommends that you evaluate number ranges in the target client and reset them when necessary.

NOTE   Address number ranges can be problematic when information is shared between clients. For more details on avoiding possible address inconsistencies in your system landscape, see R/3 Note 25182.

Deleting an R/3 Client

When you delete an R/3 client from your system landscape, you have to remove:

- All of its associated client-dependent data

- Its entry in table T000

Deleting a client is a permanent step. The client can be reinstated only by restoring the entire database of the R/3 System from a backup.

WARNING   Once you have deleted an R/3 client, you cannot simply undo the procedure. A restore of the R/3 System database is the only way to bring back a client.

To delete a client's data and its entry in table T000:

1. Log on to the R/3 client you wish to delete.

2. To access the client delete tool, use Transaction code SCC5 or, from the R/3 initial screen, choose *Tools* ➤*Administration* ➤ *Administration* ➤ *Client administration* ➤ *Special functions* ➤ *Delete client*.

3. Select a client delete option. Choose from either:

   Test run: To simulate the deletion process and see what table entries will be deleted

   Delete entry from T000:   To delete the client ID from client maintenance

4. Select the button *Delete online* or *Background* to start the procedure.

Table Logging for an R/3 Client

Table logging is different from recording changes to change requests. Logging table changes made in a client provides an audit trail that allows you to verify who made exactly what change to the data and when. For example, if a user changes the company name associated with a company code:

- A change request would record that the key value—in this case, the company code—has been changed by a particular user.

- Table logging would indicate the actual field that changed in a table and would store the original company name. It would record who made the change and when.

When you log table changes made as a result of Customizing activities, you can pinpoint the actual change. For example, you can determine whether data in a particular field was changed or whether a new record was added to a table. In releases prior to R/3 Release 4.5, all table logging is displayed at the table level. Beginning with R/3 Release 4.5, you can also display table logs at the Customizing-activity level. To activate table logging, see below.

Resource Constraints

Table logging saves a "before image" by documenting the complete set of table entries before a change is made. Each time a Customizing change is made, a new before image is created. Therefore, table logging will constrain your system resources in the following way:

- Each before image requires storage space in the database of your R/3 System. Table logging is not suitable for recording or managing large quantities of data.

- Activating table logging causes twice as many database updates as before, resulting in a higher database memory load and reduced system performance. However, as long as table logging is restricted to Customizing tables (not application data tables), performance should not be greatly reduced.

This tool has the potential to produce large amounts of data, more than you may be able to actually review and evaluate. For all of these reasons, SAP recommends using table logging only in those clients where Customizing changes must be closely monitored. Most Customizing changes occur in the Customizing-and-development client. However, it should suffice to rely on the information provided by change requests in this client. Table logging is more appropriate in the production client, providing you with a complete audit of any immediate changes to Customizing settings or changes that usually occur in the production client, such as adjustments to currency exchange rates.

Activating Table Logging

To activate the logging of table changes for Customizing, the R/3 System profile parameter must be set to `rec/client = <client ID>`. To change the R/3 System profile, use Transaction code RZ10 (*Maintenance of profile parameters*) or, from the R/3 initial screen, choose *Tools* ➤ *CCMS* ➤ *Configuration* ➤ *Profile maintenance*.

For example, to activate the recording of table changes in the production client 400, the profile for the production system requires the entry `rec/client = 400`. Possible variations of the profile parameter include the following:

- `rec/client = 300, 400` activates logging in two clients, 300 and 400.

- `rec/client = OFF` deactivates logging for all clients.

- `rec/client = ALL` activates logging in all clients within the R/3 System.

TIP	For changes in the R/3 System profile to take effect, an R/3 System must be restarted.

Activating Logging during Imports

When you activate table logging using the *rec/client* profile parameter, you ensure that table changes made within the client or clients will be logged. However, since Customizing changes may also be imported into the client, you can record them by setting the transport parameter `recclient = <client ID>` in the transport profile (see Chapter 7).

The transport parameter should have the same setting as the R/3 System profile parameter *rec/client*. In other words, if you have activated table logging for client 300 and client 400 by setting the profile parameter (`rec/client = 300,400`), the transport profile should be identical (`recclient = 300,400`).

Logging imported change requests as well as table logging in the R/3 System provide a comprehensive, collective audit of all Customizing changes. If you do not have logging turned on during import, you can always use change requests in conjunction with table logging to get a similar audit history. In fact, this may be a more viable alternative, since logging imported changes can negatively impact system resources and unnecessarily inflate the amount of data collected.

Log Data Changes **Option**

SAP has predetermined the tables that are logged. These tables contain Customizing settings and were chosen because of their significance to the flow of business processes within R/3. When you activate table logging for a client, a history of changes will be collected for those tables in the ABAP Dictionary selected by SAP. Technically, these are the tables for which SAP has activated the *Log data changes* option in the ABAP Dictionary. To check if a specific table will be logged when you activate table logging, display that table in the ABAP Dictionary Maintenance (Transaction SE11); then, choose *Technical Settings* to see if *Log data changes* is indicated for that table.

Starting with R/3 Release 4.5, logging has advanced beyond the table level to the Customizing-activity level. Technically, logging still occurs at the table level using the *Log data changes* option in the ABAP Dictionary. However, from within each IMG Customizing activity, you can view the tables associated with each Customizing activity and learn which have table logging activated.

Using Table Maintenance (Transaction SE13), you can change the technical settings for a specific table, including changing the *Log data changes* option for a table. However, SAP does not recommend altering this setting. If you deactivate logging for an object, an analysis of changes will result in inconsistencies. Activating table logging for a table may also negatively affect system performance. This applies particularly to application tables, due to the frequent changes to application data.

Viewing Table Logs

After you have activated table logging in a client, changes to tables are saved to *change documents*, often referred to as *change logs*. Using the tools provided by R/3, you can view these change documents in detail and compare older change documents with present table entries to obtain a before and after picture of your Customizing settings.

Table Log Analysis

To view the audit history for tables, use Transaction code SE38 (*ABAP Editor*) and execute the ABAP program RSTBHIST. Alternatively, from the R/3 initial screen, choose *Tools* ➢ *Business Engineer* ➢ *Customizing* ➢ *Tools* ➢ *Table History*. From the resulting screen, you can do any of the following:

- List all logged Customizing changes that occurred on the current day (only before R/3 Release 4.5)

- List all logged changes that occurred during a given time period (for example, over the last 15 days), or only those in a specific table

- List all tables for which table logging is active

- Compare the present contents of a table (for which logging is active) with its contents at a previous date and time

For example, to compare the current exchange rates (table TCURR) in an R/3 System with the values on June 13, 1999, you would:

1. Log on to the client whose data you wish to analyze.

2. Access the table history tool by using Transaction code SE38 and executing program RSTBHIST. Alternatively, from the R/3 initial screen, choose *Tools* ➤ *Business Engineer* ➤ *Customizing* ➤ *Tools* ➤ *Table History*.

3. To compare the current values of the table with its contents in the past:

   - In releases prior to R/3 Release 4.5, choose *Comparison*.

   - As of R/3 Release 4.5, select *Comparison: History <-> Current*, and choose *Function* ➤ *Analyze change documents*.

4. Provide the name of the table whose values you want to compare—in our example, table TCURR. Enter the date (June 13, 1999) and, if you wish, a time.

5. Choose *Compare* to begin the comparison.

Figure 9.10 shows the sample outcome for this comparison. Of particular interest is the first column, *Status*. The possible entries in this column include:

Status "M":   The current value and the past value are different.

Status "C":   A current table entry did not exist in the table at the past date.

Status "S":   A table entry at the past date no longer exists in the current table.

No status: The values for the table entries are identical.

FIGURE 9.10:

Results of a table log
analysis

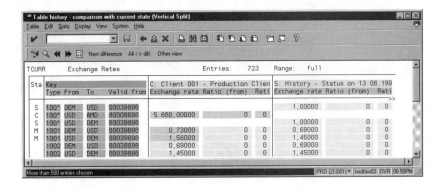

Customizing Activity Logging

Starting with R/3 Release 4.5, you can also analyze table logs from within a Customizing activity. This allows you to see the changes to tables that are part of a Customizing activity without knowing the specific names of the tables involved. Using Customizing activity logs from within an IMG activity, you can:

- Examine the tables involved in the current Customizing activity and determine which of the involved tables have table logging activated

- View the current changes that have been logged for the Customizing activity

For example, to see which tables are affected by the Customizing activity *Define condition types* for Pricing and, of those tables, which are being logged, you would proceed as follows:

1. Access the IMG (Transaction SPRO) and choose *Implement. projects* ➤ *SAP Ref. IMG*. Then, drill down the tree structure: *Enterprise Controlling* ➤ *Profit Center Accounting* ➤ *Transfer Prices* ➤ *Pricing* ➤ *Define Condition Types*.

2. Choose *Utilities* ➢ *Change logs* to view the table logging information for the activity.

3. Select the button *Logging: Display status* to display the logging status of the current client and the tables that are being logged in the current Customizing activity.

The results of this analysis are shown in Figure 9.11. The tables involved in this activity are T685, T685A, and T685T. Note that the text table (T85T) does not have table logging activated, while the more critical data tables (such as T685) do have table logging activated.

FIGURE 9.11:

Customizing activity logging status in R/3 Release 4.5

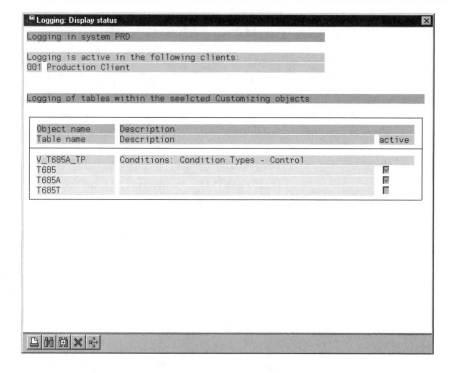

You can also view the actual changes that have been recorded for a particular IMG Customizing activity. To do this, begin the Customizing activity and then choose *Utilities* ➢ *Change logs*. For example, to view the changes that have taken place in a production system for the Customizing activity to change currency exchange rates, proceed as follows:

1. Access the IMG (Transaction SPRO) and choose *Implement. projects* ➢ *SAP Ref. IMG*. Then, drill down the tree structure: *Global Settings* ➢ *Currencies* ➢ *Enter Exchange Rates*.

2. Choose *Utilities* ➢ *Change logs* to view the table logging information for the activity.

3. Enter the time frame you wish to view.

4. Select the button *Execute* to display the logged information for the current Customizing activity during the specified time frame.

Figure 9.12 displays the results of this analysis. The column *Key fields* shows the table entries that were adjusted. The actual changes are shown in the second column, *Function fields, changed*. Here, you can see whether the entry was changed, deleted, or newly created.

Removing Change Documents

As more and more Customizing changes impact different tables, the number of change documents increases over time and occupies valuable space in the database. Therefore, it is important for you to manage the growth of change documents. R/3 provides you with two alternatives: You can either delete change documents that contain table logging data or archive the documents for retrieval and analysis at a later date in time. Archiving is the ideal method for preserving a complete audit history.

FIGURE 9.12:

Change documents for
a Customizing activity

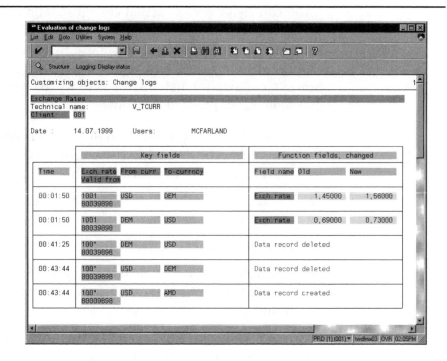

To delete unnecessary change documents, proceed as follows:

1. Log on to the client where you wish to delete change
    documents.

2. Access the table history tool by using Transaction code SE38
    and executing program RSTBHIST; or, from the R/3 initial
    screen, choose *Tools* ➢ *Business Engineer* ➢ *Customizing* ➢
    Tools ➢ *Table History*.

3. To delete change documents:

    -   In releases prior to R/3 Release 4.5, choose *Administra-
        tion* ➢ *Delete documents*.

    -   As of R/3 Release 4.5, choose *Edit* ➢ *Change docs* ➢ *Delete*.

4. Enter a date. All change documents prior to and including that date will be deleted.

5. Provide the name of the table or tables for which change documents should be deleted. To delete all change documents regardless of the table name, leave this field blank.

6. Choose *Execute* or *Program* ➤ *Execute in background* to delete the selected change documents.

To archive change documents, use the archiving management tool (Transaction SARA). To archive change management documents that resulted from table logging, use the archive object for database log files, BC_DBLOGS. As of R/3 Release 4.5, you can also select archived change documents for inclusion in a Customizing activity log analysis.

NOTE For more details on using R/3 data archive tools, see Chapter 12 of Liane Will's *SAP R/3 System Administration* (from Sybex).

Authorization Profiles for Client Tools

To provide a method for controlling access to the different client tools, SAP delivers its R/3 software with standard authorization objects. In addition to these authorization objects, you can rely on the client protection setting defined for each client to protect its data from being overwritten or accessed externally. Once a client has this setting, no matter how many authorizations a user has, that person cannot overwrite the data in the protected client by performing a local client copy.

Table 9.5 provides a list of the authorizations delivered by SAP that are relevant for the client copy tools. It also indicates whether that authorization is required for the user account in the target client and/or the source client. For example, in a remote client copy, the source client's user is defined by the RFC destination used during the client copy. To perform a remote client copy, the user referenced in the RFC destination must at least have the authorization S_ TABU_RFC.

TABLE 9.5: Authorization Objects Needed in Source/Target Clients when Using the Client Copy Tools

Authorization Object	Description of Permitted Activities	Local Client Copy	Remote Client Copy	Client Transport
S_TABU_CLI	Maintaining client-independent tables	Target	Target	Source and target
S_TABU_DIS	Maintaining the client copy control table CCCFLOW	Target	Target	Source and target
S_DATASET_ALL	Writing log files to the operating system level	Target	Target	Source and target
S_CLIENT_IMP	Importing data into a client	Target	Target	Source and target
S_TABU_RFC*	Performing a remote client copy		Source	
S_TRNSPRT	Exporting data			Source
S_USER_PRO	Copying user profiles	Target	Source and target	Source
S_USER_GROUP	Copying user data	Target	Source and target	Source

*Required as of R/3 Release 4.5

A client entry and its settings are stored in table T000. Since this is a client-independent table, a user needs the authorization object S_TABU_CLI to maintain client entries using Transaction SCC4. To delete a client, you must have three authorization objects: S_TABU_CLI, S_TABU_DIS, and S_DATASET_ALL. Analyzing table logs and Customizing activities requires two authorization objects: S_TABU_CLI and S_TABU_DIS.

TIP User SAP* has complete authorization to use all client tools. However, because SAP* cannot create a change request, SAP* cannot perform the client export step in a client transport.

Review Questions

1. After you create a new client entry in table T000, which of the following activities enables you to provide the client with data?

   A. A remote client copy to populate the client with data from a client in another R/3 System

   B. A client transport to import data from a client in another R/3 System

   C. A local client copy to import data from a client within the same R/3 System

   D. All of the above

2. Which of the following *cannot* be used to restrict a client from certain activities?

   A. The client role

   B. The client-dependent change option

    C. The client ID-number

    D. A client restriction

    E. The client-independent change option

3. Which of the following tasks can be performed using the client copy tools?

    A. Merging application data from one client into another client

    B. Copying only application data from one client to another client

    C. Copying only Customizing data from one client to another client

    D. All of the above

4. Which of the following tasks can be performed using the client copy profiles?

    A. Scheduling a client copy to occur at a time when system use is low

    B. Selecting the subset of application data that will be copied when a client copy is executed

    C. Providing required user authorization for the use of client tools

    D. Determining the data that will be copied when a client copy is executed

5. Which of the following statements is correct in regard to table logging?

- **A.** Table logging should be used instead of change requests whenever possible.

- **B.** Table logging provides an audit history of who made what changes and when.

- **C.** Table logging does not negatively impact system resources.

- **D.** All of the above.

PART THREE

TOOLS

Part 1 of this book provided an overview of the change and transport concepts and recommendations for your R/3 System landscape. Part 2 covered the technical requirements and setup of these tools. Part 3 will explain in detail how to use the following change and transport tools:

- Workbench Organizer (Chapters 10 and 12)

- Customizing Organizer (Chapters 11 and 12)

- Transport Management System (TMS) (Chapters 13 and 14)

- Transport control program (Chapter 14)

- SAP Patch Manager (Chapter 15)

- R/3 Transactions for modifications and adjustments (SPDD and SPAU) (Chapter 15)

The first four chapters of Part 3, Chapters 10–13, will be of most interest for those people who are directly involved in making changes to the R/3 System—the customizers and developers—as well as for those responsible for importing change requests.

The final two chapters, Chapters 14 and 15, will particularly benefit system administrators who are responsible for troubleshooting transport problems. Chapter 15 will also be of interest to project leaders who need a better understanding of the upgrade process.

Managing Development Changes

Technically, development changes in an R/3 System are changes to R/3 Repository objects using the tools of the ABAP Workbench. These changes are recorded to Workbench change requests, which are then managed using the Workbench Organizer. Development changes include creating and changing customer-developed or SAP-delivered objects.

Proper management of development changes, which ultimately ensures that all changes can be validated and distributed to all R/3 Systems in the system landscape, can be divided into the following areas:

- Development prerequisites

- Change requests and tasks

- Repairs and modifications

- The Object Directory

Development Prerequisites

As prerequisites to performing development, ensure that:

- The client-independent change option and the system change option allow changes to R/3 Repository objects

- Each developer has the appropriate R/3 authorizations and obtains an SAP Software Change Registration (SSCR) key

- Development classes and object names are used that enable the transport of new R/3 Repository objects

A user with developer authorizations can perform development work only if the current R/3 client allows for client-independent changes—changes to R/3 Repository objects. In addition, the system change option must allow the relevant types of objects to be changed—for example, local objects, customer-developed objects, or SAP-developed objects.

NOTE   See Chapter 11 for more information on developer authorizations, Chapter 9 for information on client-independent changes, and Chapter 7 for information on the system change option.

SSCR Registration of Developers

Any R/3 user who wishes to use the ABAP Workbench to create, change, or delete R/3 Repository objects (including customer-developed objects) in the R/3 System must be registered using the *SAP Software Change Registration* (SSCR) key. Such users are often referred to as *development users* or *developers*.

The first time that development users attempt to create or change an object, the R/3 System displays the *Add developer* dialog box, which asks for their access key (see Figure 10.1). To obtain this access key, enter the developer's user ID and the R/3 System's installation number in the SCCR area in SAPNet. Copy the resulting 20-digit key into the appropriate field in the *Add developer* dialog box.

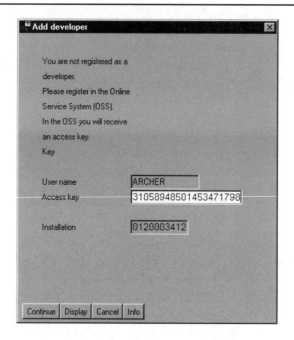

FIGURE 10.1:

SSCR key for a
developer

After a developer has been registered through SSCR, the R/3 System will not request an SSCR key for that developer's subsequent attempts to create or change R/3 Repository objects.

Development Classes

To group development objects and facilitate transport, all R/3 Repository objects, whether delivered by SAP or created by the customer, are assigned to a *development class*. For example, SAP has assigned the program RDDNEWPP to the development class SCTS_EXE and the table T000 to the development class STRM.

These two development classes are examples of *SAP-delivered development classes* set up by SAP's developers to group development objects of the same functional areas.

Customers must also assign any objects they create to development classes known as *customer development classes*. For example, all conversion routines can be grouped in a development class called ZCONVERSION, while new sales reports can be grouped in a development class called ZSALESREPORTS. The names of customer development classes must fall within the customer name range—for example, they begin with either Y or Z.

In addition, if a customer has reserved a namespace, the development class should fall within that namespace (see Chapter 7). For example, if the namespace /COMPANY/ has been reserved, the development class /COMPANY/REPORTS can be created, and all objects that belong to that development class must also begin with the namespace /COMPANY/.

Creating a Customer Development Class

To create new programs, screens, or tables for transport to other R/3 Systems, your development system must have at least one customer development class. To create a new development class for your development environment, proceed as follows:

1. Access the R/3 Repository Browser using Transaction code SE80 or, from the R/3 initial screen, by choosing *Tools ➤ ABAP Workbench ➤ Repository Browser*.

2. From the *Repository Browser: Initial Screen*, select *Development Class*.

3. Enter a name for your new development class. The name can be up to 30 characters long and must fall within the customer name range or namespace. For example, use a name in the

form Y<name> or Z<name> where <name> is a short descriptive name for the development class.

4. Choose *Display*. The system checks whether the development class exists and then asks if you want to create it. Choose *Yes*.

5. The *Create Development Class* screen is displayed (see Figure 10.2). Enter the following information:

   - A descriptive short text of your new development class.

   - A transport layer—normally, you should use the standard transport layer that is provided.

   - As of R/3 Release 4.5, you can also assign an application component to the development class if the objects saved to the development class will all be for the same business application area.

6. Choose *Save*. The R/3 System requests a change request ID. Provide the change request ID by either:

   - Entering the change request ID of an existing change request.

   - Choosing *Create request* to create a new change request. The system displays the *Create Request* screen (see Figure 10.6 later in this chapter). Enter a descriptive name for the change request.

7. Choose *Save*. The screen *Repository Browser: Development Class <development class>* appears, showing your new development class at the top of the development class list. Since the development class is new, it will not yet have any R/3 Repository objects assigned to it.

FIGURE 10.2:

Creating a new
development class

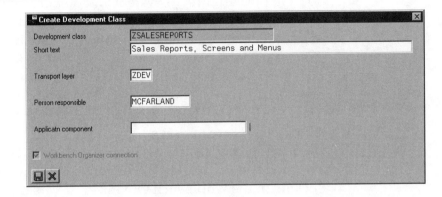

Types of Development Classes

To facilitate transport, one or more development classes are
assigned to a *transport layer*. When a change request is released
and exported, the TMS uses this transport layer to determine
which transport route is used for the objects recorded in the
change request (see Chapter 8). The transport layer determines
the system to which the objects in a change request are consolidated. Objects in a single change request must consolidate to the
same R/3 System.

The default transport layer is the *standard transport layer*, which
is used, for example, for change requests of type *Customizing*—
usually transporting them from the development system to the
quality assurance system. Typically, you assign the standard
transport layer to a customer development class so that all objects
of that development class consolidate to the quality assurance
system. Two other, less commonly used, types of development
classes, which are not associated with a transport layer, are the
local development class and the *test development class*.

A local development class is used for creating *local objects* and
begins with a $. Local objects are R/3 Repository objects that are

local to the current R/3 System and do not require transport to other R/3 Systems, such as a program created to clean up local master data records and that is not required in other R/3 Systems. To create a local object, choose *Local object* instead of providing a development class for the new R/3 Repository object (see Figure 10.3). This object is assigned the SAP-delivered development class $TMP. $TMP is often called the *temporary development class*. $TMP objects are not saved to change requests. Like the objects of all development classes beginning with a $, $TMP objects are not connected to the Workbench Organizer and hence have no object locking in the Workbench Organizer or version history in the version database.

NOTE All new R/3 Repository objects must be assigned to a development class or saved as a local object.

FIGURE 10.3:

Creating a new R/3 Repository object requires assigning a development class or choosing *Local object*.

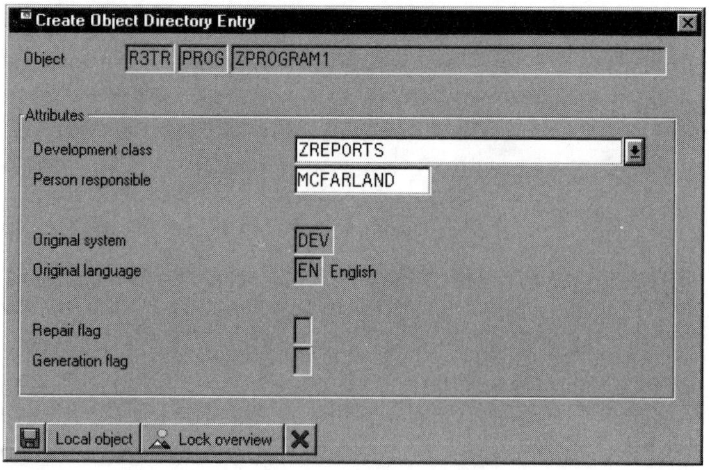

A *test development class* begins with the letter T. Although the objects of this development class are not transported, they can be linked to the Workbench Organizer—that is, saved to change requests and supported by object locking and version history. Objects in a change request are locked and can be modified only by users who have tasks in the change request. In addition, releasing a change request causes a version of the object to be created in the version database.

Restricting Customer Object Names

To ensure that your objects are not overwritten by SAP-delivered objects during the import of Support Packages or an upgrade, SAP has reserved name ranges for customer-developed objects and SAP-delivered objects. When creating a new R/3 Repository object, SAP developers must use the SAP name range, and you must use the customer name range.

> **NOTE** For more information on customer name ranges, naming conventions, and examples of names, refer to R/3 online documentation.

> **WARNING** SAP delivers a few system objects with names that fall within the customer name range. To avoid using these names, consult the list in table TDKZ.

Most R/3 implementations feature a single development system in which all customer developments are created. Performing all development work in a single R/3 System ensures that each object name can be used only once for a program, table, or other object type.

Performing development efforts in multiple R/3 Systems may cause difficulties if there are objects created with the same name in various R/3 Systems. This may happen, for example, when development changes are made centrally at a company's headquarters and then delivered to its subsidiaries. An attempt to import an object into a development system that already contains an object with the same name will fail, because, by default, objects in their original systems cannot be overwritten. If the target system is not a development system, the imported object will overwrite an object that has the same name in the target system. This may cause inconsistencies if the objects were originally developed in different systems.

You may not notice that there is a naming conflict until you transport your development work. At this late stage, resolving the conflict requires renaming the objects and all references to them. To avoid this type of conflict:

- Define naming conventions in the view V_TRESN (as described below) in all R/3 Systems. The ABAP Workbench will prevent you from creating objects with the same names in different systems.

- Register a namespace with SAP through SAPNet. Large corporate implementations or development partners may require a unique namespace to use for developing objects. This ensures that, when centrally developed objects are delivered to other R/3 Systems, they will not conflict with locally developed objects.

Defining a Naming Convention   The first characters in the name of an object correspond to a naming convention in the ABAP Workbench. You can define a naming convention for a development class. The Workbench Organizer refuses to create an object if the developer tries to assign it to a development class other than the one dictated by the naming convention. This ensures, for example, that all R/3 Repository objects beginning with the naming convention ZSALES are assigned to the development class ZSALESREPORTS. Naming conventions are stored in the view V_TRESN.

To define a naming convention for a development class:

1. Use the View Maintenance screen (Transaction SM30). Enter the view name **V_TRESN**. Choose *Maintain*. The *Change View "Naming Conventions in the ABAP Workbench": Overview* screen appears.

2. Choose *New entries*. The *New Entries: Details of Added Entries* screen appears.

3. Enter data in the respective fields as follows:

Field	User Entry
Program ID	R3TR or R3OB.
Object type	To select the object type for which the naming convention applies, position the cursor in the field and use the possible entries arrow.
Name range (generic)	Enter the naming convention to be used—that is, specify the first characters of all object names that are to correspond to the development class.
Devel. Class	Enter the development class that is to correspond to the naming convention.
Reservation type	Retain the default value D, which indicates a standard name range reservation.

Field	User Entry
Person responsible	Enter the name of the person responsible for reserving the name range.
Short description	Enter a short text to describe why the naming convention was assigned to a particular development class.

4. Choose *Save*.

For consistent naming protection, the view V_TRESN must be the same in all R/3 Systems in the system landscape. New entries to V_TRESN should be recorded to a change request and distributed to all R/3 Systems in the system landscape.

Example: Naming Conventions for Development Classes

In a system landscape connecting company subsidiaries in various countries, the corporate headquarters creates a standardized package of Customizing settings and development objects such as reports in the development system COR.

The two regional headquarters that receive the package, Asia and Europe, each have their own development systems. The Asian development system is ADV, and the European development system is EDV.

To avoid having R/3 Repository objects with the same name on the various development systems (COR, ADV, and EDV), the following entries are added

Continued on next page

to the view V_TRESN on the development system COR and transported to all other R/3 Systems in the system landscape:

PgId	Obj	Name Range	Type	Dev. Class	Descriptions
R3TR	PROG	Y	D	ZCORPORATE	Programs
R3TR	TABL	Y	D	ZCORPORATE	Tables
R3TR	DOMA	Y	D	ZCORPORATE	Domains
R3TR	PROG	ZA	D	ZASIA	Programs for Asia
R3TR	PROG	ZE	D	ZEURO	Programs for Europe

These entries ensure that centrally developed programs, tables, and data domains beginning with a Y belong to the development class ZCORPORATE. Programs for the Asian region will begin with ZA and receive the development class ZASIA; programs for the European region will begin with ZE and receive the development class ZEURO.

Workbench Change Requests

When you create or change a nonlocal R/3 Repository object, the object is recorded to a *Workbench change request*. To manage Workbench change requests, use the Workbench Organizer (Transaction SE09).

Unlike Customizing change requests, Workbench change requests are divided into the following types:

- Transportable
- Local
- Unclassified

Unless specified, a change request is created as an unclassified change request. When an R/3 Repository object has been recorded to a task in a change request, the change request becomes either a transportable change request or a local change request. The development classes of objects recorded to tasks in the change request determine the type of change request. For example, any object whose development class uses a transport layer that does not have an associated transport route in TMS is recorded to a local change request.

Transportable Change Request

Since most changes are created with the aim of transporting them to other R/3 Systems, the transportable change request is the most commonly used type of Workbench change request.

A transportable change request is a change request that can be released and exported for transport to other R/3 Systems. It contains R/3 Repository objects that can be transported—that is, R/3 Repository objects with a development class that is assigned to a valid transport layer. A transport layer is considered valid by the TMS if the R/3 System in which the object is created or changed is the source system of a designated consolidation route. For example, in Figure 8.18 (see Chapter 8), the training transport layer ZTRN is the consolidation route from the development system to the training box TRN. If the TMS is set up according to Figure 8.18, all R/3 Repository objects with a development class whose transport layer is ZDEV, SAP, or ZTRN can be recorded to transportable change requests.

NOTE   R/3 Repository objects that are to be consolidated to different R/3 Systems must be recorded to different change requests. For example, an object with the transport layer ZTRN cannot be recorded to the same change request as an object with the transport layer ZDEV. The export cannot occur because the target systems differ; the same change request cannot be simultaneously consolidated to the training system and the quality assurance system. (See also Chapter 8.)

Local Change Request

Changes to R/3 Repository objects whose transport layer is invalid are automatically recorded to local change requests. A transport layer is invalid if it is not assigned to a consolidation route that includes the current system as the source system. For example, the TMS typically does not list a consolidation system for the quality assurance system and the production system. Therefore, there is no valid transport layer for these systems. A change to an R/3 Repository object in a quality assurance system or production system is not transportable and will be recorded to a local change request.

A local change request can be released, but not transported. To transport the objects in a local change request, release the change request and then either:

- Create an appropriate transport layer for the object's development class. For example, to transport a change made to an SAP-delivered object in the quality assurance system to the production system, use the TMS to add the consolidation route from the quality assurance system to the production system for the transport layer *SAP*.

- Using Transaction SE80 (see below, under "Displaying or Changing an Object Directory Entry"), assign the object to another development class or change the development class for the object and assign it to a valid transport layer for the current R/3 System.

Tasks

As long as no changes have been recorded to a task, its status in the Workbench Organizer (see below) is *Not assigned*. This status is also referred to as *unclassified*. When an R/3 Repository object is first recorded to a task in a change request, the task is classified as either:

- *Development/correction*
- *Repair*

Most changes are recorded to *development/correction* tasks, which contain changes to objects that originated in the current R/3 System.

A *repair* is a change to an R/3 Repository object that originated on an R/3 System other than the current R/3 System. The object can be an SAP-delivered object or a customer-developed object. For example, since all SAP-delivered objects are defined as belonging to the R/3 System *SAP*, if you change such an object, the change is regarded as a repair. As another example, consider a customer-developed program, ZPROGRAM, created in the development system DEV. If you try to change this program in the training system TRN, you are automatically required to save the change to a task of type *repair* since the object does not originate in TRN.

TIP   Changing an object on a system other than the system in which it was originally created will be recorded in a task of type *repair.*

To complete your development activities, you may need to include both types of tasks—*development/correction* tasks and *repair* tasks—in a change request. For example, after creating a new R/3 Repository object and saving it to a task in a change request, if you try to add a repair to the same change request, a *Create Task* dialog box automatically appears to indicate that a new task must be created in the change request—a task of type *repair*.

TIP   In releases prior to R/3 Release 4.5, the objects listed in a task of type *repair* can be changed only by the person who has ownership of the task. As of R/3 Release 4.5, all users with a task in a change request can also change objects listed in the task of type *repair*.

Viewing Workbench Change Requests

To view Workbench change requests and the associated tasks, access the Workbench Organizer by using Transaction code SE09 or, from the initial R/3 screen, by choosing *Tools ➤ ABAP Workbench ➤ Overview ➤ Workbench Organizer*. Figure 10.4 shows the initial screen of the Workbench Organizer. Enter your selection criteria to determine which change requests will be displayed. These selection criteria include the user who created the change request and its type. The default selections are as follows: transportable change requests and local change requests that are modifiable (that is, not released). Under *Last changed*, you can enter dates to limit the displayed change requests to those that were last changed in a certain period.

FIGURE 10.4:

Initial screen of the Workbench Organizer

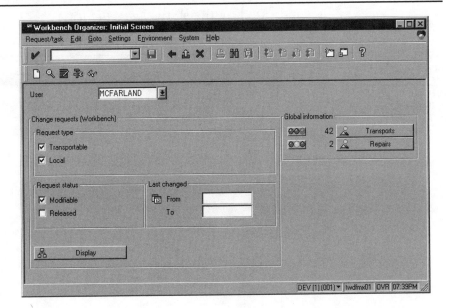

To accept the selection criteria and display the corresponding change requests, choose *Display*. The screen *Workbench Organizer: Requests* appears, showing a tree structure containing change requests and tasks (see Figure 10.5). The change requests listed include both change requests that were created by the user whose name you entered on the initial screen and the change requests in which that user is assigned to a task. To see the tasks associated with a particular change request, expand the list using the + sign beside the ID number of the change request.

The example in Figure 10.5 shows the display of all change requests for user MCFARLAND. As indicated in the list, both DEVK900180 and DEVK900110 are transportable change requests, while change request DEVK900188 is a local change request. User BUCHTA owns change request DEVK900180. In this change request, user MCFARLAND owns task DEVK900181, which records two changed R/3 Repository objects: the development class ZREPORTS and the program ZPROGRAM. User DRENNAN also has a task in the change request, but has not yet recorded any changes to it (as indicated by the status *Not assigned*).

FIGURE 10.5:

Hierarchical display in the Workbench Organizer

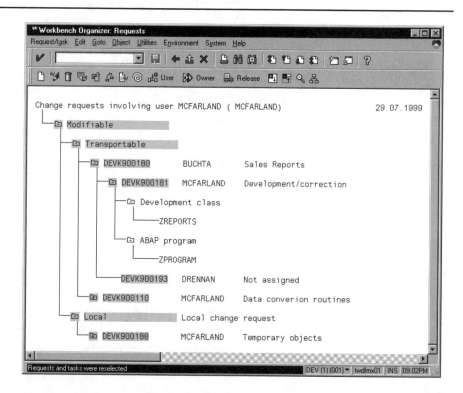

Creating a Workbench Change Request

A Workbench change request can be created either prior to or during development work. To simplify project management, SAP recommends creating change requests before starting development work. This makes it easier for developers from the same development project to record their changes to a single change request that can be released and exported as a testable unit. A project team leader or development manager should be responsible for creating the change request and assigning the various developers to it. To create a change request, you require the authorization profile S_A.CUSTOMIZ (see also Chapter 11).

To create a transportable Workbench change request in the Workbench Organizer (Transaction SE09), proceed as follows:

1. In the screen *Workbench Organizer: Requests*, choose *Request/Task* ➢ *Create*.

2. In the resulting dialog box, select *Transportable change request*. Choose *Enter*.

3. The dialog box *Create Request* appears (as shown in Figure 10.6):

   - In the field *Short description*, enter a short text to identify the development project, describe the functionality, indicate the urgency of the change, or indicate whether the change is a modification.

   - In the fields under *Tasks*, enter all users who will be contributing development changes to this change request. For each user listed, a task will be created in the new change request.

4. Choose *Save*.

FIGURE 10.6:

Creating a change request and assigning initial tasks

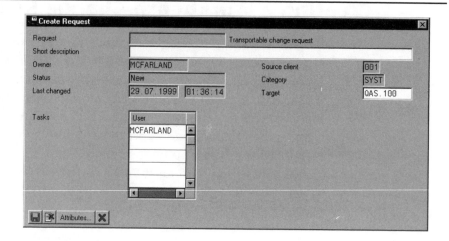

When creating a Workbench change request, there are some default settings you cannot change. These include:

- Name of the R/3 user who created the change request
- Status
- Date and time stamp
- Category
- Source client in which the change request was created

The change request category is always SYST, indicating that this change request is a Workbench change request.

The source client is always the client in which the change request was created. It is only from within this client that you can perform the following activities:

- Recording changes to the change request
- Changing the owner of the change request or of its tasks
- Adding additional tasks to the change request
- Releasing the change request

Adding Further Users to a Workbench Change Request

To add further users to a Workbench change request you previously created, proceed as follows:

1. In the screen *Workbench Organizer: Requests*, position the cursor on the appropriate change request ID and choose *Request/ Task* ➢ *Create*.

2. The *Add user* dialog box appears. Enter the name of the user for whom you wish to create a task. To find a user, you can use the possible entries arrow (or place the cursor in the user-name field and choose F4).

3. Choose *Enter*.

NOTE   You can add users only to a change request that has not been released. A change request or task cannot be changed after it has been released.

Changing Ownership of Change Requests and Tasks

Every change request and task is owned by an R/3 user. When a user creates a change request, that user automatically receives ownership of the change request and a task in the change request. The owners of all other tasks in the change request are those people assigned to a task by the owner of the change request. Only the owner of a change request can perform the following activities for either change requests or tasks:

- Deleting tasks in the change request

- Changing the object list

- Releasing (exception: a user with the authorization profile SAP_ALL)

- Changing attributes, such as the short description
- Changing the owner

The owner of a change request can specify another person as the owner of the change request or the tasks it contains. To do this, proceed as follows:

1. In the *Workbench Organizer: Request* screen, position the cursor on the ID of the change request or task whose ownership you want to change. Choose *Request/Task ➢ Change owner.*

2. In the *Change owner* dialog box, enter the username of the new owner, or use the possible entries arrow to select a user.

3. Choose *Enter.*

Protecting a Workbench Change Request

You can protect a Workbench change request to ensure that only the creator of the change request can add users to the change request. This even prevents users with the authorization profile S_A.CUSTOMIZ from adding users to the change request (see also Chapter 11).

To protect a change request you have created, in the *Workbench Organizer: Request* screen, position the cursor on the ID number of the change request that you want to protect, and choose *Request/Task ➢ Request ➢ Protect.*

To remove this protection from the change request, choose *Request/Task ➢ Request ➢ Remove protection.*

Recording R/3 Repository Objects to Change Requests

When creating or changing an R/3 Repository object, you will be required to specify the Workbench change request to which the object can be recorded unless:

- The object is already recorded in a change request that has not yet been released.

- The object is assigned to a local development class, such as $TMP, whose objects are not recorded in a change request.

Figure 10.7 shows the dialog box that appears for recording a new or changed object to a change request. There are three ways to specify the change request ID:

- Manually enter your change request ID.

- Choose *Own requests*. From this list, double-click the change request to which you wish to record the object. This list will display only change requests to which this object can be saved.

- Choose *Create request*. (You require the appropriate authorization.) In the *Create Request* screen, enter the required data (see Figure 10.6 earlier in the chapter).

After specifying a change request, choose *Continue*. The object is recorded to this change request.

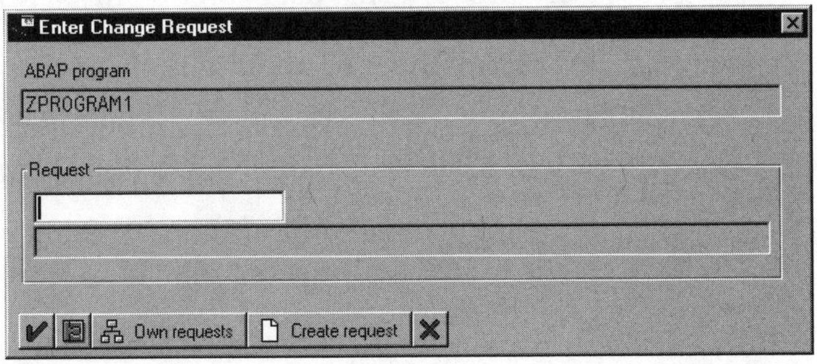

FIGURE 10.7:

Recording an R/3 Repository object to a change request

When recording the development change to a Workbench change request, you must select a change request:

- In which you have a task or the authorization to create a task

- With the correct type, either transportable or local

You must save the change to a transportable change request if the object's development class is associated with a defined transport route. Otherwise, you should record the change to a local change request. The correct type of change request for development work matches the Repository object's defined transport layer and the associated transport routes for the current R/3 System as defined in the TMS.

Object Locking

When you record a new or changed R/3 Repository object to a task, the Workbench Organizer locks the object so that only those users who have tasks in the change request can modify the object. Another kind of locking—through an R/3 enqueue—ensures that only one user can change an object at one time.

When the Workbench Organizer locks an object, this prevents users outside the development team from changing any of the objects in the change request. For example, if a user does not own a task in change request DEVK900586, but tries to edit the program ZABAP using the ABAP Editor, that person receives the error message "Object ZABAP locked by request/task DEVK900586". This user can do only one of three things:

- Display the object, but not make changes to it

- Have a new task created for the user in change request DEVK900586 by someone with authorization to create tasks

- Change ownership of the task containing the locked object to the user wanting to change it

If you try to change an object that is already being held by an enqueue lock, you receive the error message "User ARCHER is currently editing ZABAP". This ensures that only one user at a time can modify an object in the system.

Object List of Change Requests and Tasks

An *object list* records objects that have been changed and shows what will be transported when the change request is released and exported. Each changed object has an entry in the object list. The object list of a change request is filled after the tasks in the change request have been released (see also Chapter 12). The entries in the object list correspond to the entries in the *Object Directory* described later in this chapter.

The ABAP Workbench tools that record your changes to tasks automatically include the corresponding objects in the object list. Workbench Organizer tools also enable you to manually include or delete objects in the object list. In certain situations, you may wish to manipulate an object list by, for example, removing the only listed object that is not ready to be released. When you remove an object, it is no longer in a change request. It is not locked by the Workbench Organizer and will not be transported. In addition, the Workbench Organizer no longer indicates that this object has been changed. Therefore, manual changes to the object list should only be made with caution.

WARNING   Use caution when making manual changes to the object list.

To display the object list, in the *Workbench Organizer: Request* screen, double-click the change request or task ID. In the sample object list in Figure 10.8, each object that has been recorded in the task is represented by a combination of entries in the columns *PgmID* (program identification), *Obj* (object type), and *Object name*. The object represented in the row R3TR DEVC ZREPORTS is the development class ZREPORTS. The ABAP program ZPRO-GRAM is represented in the row R3TR PROG ZPROGRAM.

FIGURE 10.8:

An object list

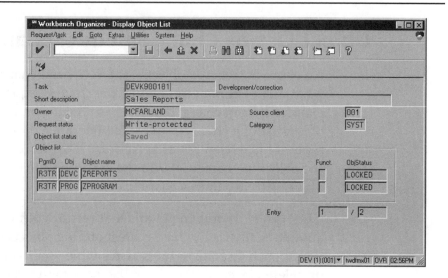

In the object list in Figure 10.8, the entry in column *ObjStatus* for each object is LOCKED. This refers to locking by the Workbench Organizer. In other words, the program ZPROGRAM and the development class ZREPORTS can be changed only by the users specified in the change request DEVK900180. These users are indicated in Figure 10.5 (earlier in the chapter) as users MCFARLAND, DRENNAN, and BUCHTA (the owner of the change request). The Workbench Organizer locks the objects in the request until the entire change request is released.

The change request or task does *not* contain the actual table entries or the object content that has changed. A change request or task does *not* even record whether the change was an addition, modification, or deletion. A change request or task only *lists* the changed objects. Each row in the object list is a pointer to the actual objects—programs, tables, data domains, views, and so on—that are physically located in the R/3 Repository. As an example, task DEVK900181 is a result of creating, modifying, or deleting the program ZPROGRAM and the development class ZREPORTS.

NOTE A change request or task only lists—it does not actually contain objects. The objects exist outside the change request in the R/3 Repository.

Manual Additions to the Object List

There are times when the standard, automatic procedure for recording new or modified R/3 Repository objects or Customizing changes to a change request is too cumbersome and time-consuming. Situations in which you may instead need to manually add objects to a new or existing object list include the following:

- A change request did not transport properly and needs to be rereleased and reexported. After a change request is released, it cannot be rereleased. Instead, you can include its object list in a new change request and then release the new change request.

- You want to transport an entire development class to another R/3 System. Instead of changing each object so that they are recorded to a change request, you can create a new change request and enter the objects in its object list. (See procedure below.)

- You would like to combine several change requests to form a single new change request—for example, to bundle change requests that were imported into the development system or need to be copied to another client within the current system using the function *Client copy according to a transp. request* (Transaction SCC1). (See procedure below.)

- Objects may need to be added to special change requests such as *relocation transports* (see below, under "Transporting Objects Using the Transport Organizer").

Including all Objects of a Development Class   To transport some or all objects of a particular development class, proceed as follows:

1. Create a transportable change request. To do this, from the *Workbench Organizer: Request* screen (in Transaction SE09), choose *Request/Task* ➢ *Create*. In the resulting dialog box, choose *Transportable* and then choose *Enter*. A second dialog box appears—enter a short description and choose *Enter*.

2. Position the cursor on the newly created change request and choose *Request/Task* ➢ *Object List* ➢ *Include objects*. Select *Freely selected objects*. Choose *Enter*.

3. The *Object Selection* screen is displayed. Enter the name of the development class for which you would like to display the object list. Choose *Execute*.

4. A tree structure is displayed containing all objects that belong to the development class. Position the cursor on individual objects or collections of objects and choose *Select/deselect*.

5. When all the required objects have been selected, choose *Save in request*. All selected objects will be added to the object list of the new change request.

NOTE   You can include objects in the object list of a change request, but not a task, using the *Include objects* functionality.

Combining Several Object Lists into a Single Change Request To merge a copy of an existing object list from one or several change requests into a new change request, proceed as follows:

1. Create a transportable change request. To do this, from the *Workbench Organizer: Request* screen (in Transaction SE09), choose *Request/Task* ➤ *Create*. In the resulting dialog box, choose *Transportable* and then choose *Enter*. A second dialog box appears. Provide a short description and choose *Enter*.

2. Position the cursor on the newly created change request and choose *Request/Task* ➤ *Object List* ➤ *Include objects*. Select *Object list from multiple requests*. Choose *Enter*.

3. The *Merge Object lists in request <change request ID>* screen appears. Enter selection criteria for the change requests and tasks whose object lists are to be included in the new change request. Examples of selection criteria include:

Field	User Entry
Owner	Name of a particular user or users.
Date	Begin dates and end dates. This entry selects all change requests that were last modified during a specified time period or periods.
Request type	Use the possible entries arrow to specify the type of change requests and tasks to be included—for example, transportable change request.

4. In the same screen, select the status of the change requests and tasks to be included from the following options:

   - *Modifiable*

- *Open (faulty status)*

- *Released*

5. Choose *Execute*.

6. A list of all change requests matching the selection criteria is displayed. Select the individual requests or collections of change requests that you require by choosing *Select/deselect* (or F7).

7. Once you have selected the required objects, choose *Merge object lists*. A dialog box appears asking "How should action be performed?" Proceed as follows:

    - To combine a small number of change requests, choose *Online*.

    - To combine a large number of change requests, choose *In background*. You are automatically asked to schedule the merger as a background job.

8. Choose *Enter*. All selected objects are added to the object list of the new change request.

Changing an Existing Object List   You can manually change the object lists of change requests or tasks by adding or deleting objects. A user should not need this function often, since almost all changes to objects are automatically recorded to change requests. Occasionally, expert users with a detailed knowledge of the respective objects may need to add or remove them manually.

To change an existing object list, from the *Workbench Organizer: Request* screen (in Transaction SE09), position the cursor on the task or change request to be changed and choose *Request/task* ➤ *Object list* ➤ *Change object list*. You can then do the following:

- To add entries to the object list, choose *Insert line*. Enter the program name, object name, and object type. To make manual additions to the *Change object list* option, you must be familiar with certain technical data for an object, including the program ID, object type, and other objects that may be affected. You may prefer the procedure described above under "Including All Objects of a Development Class" to add individual objects to the object list.

- To delete objects in the object list, choose *Delete line*. Before deleting entries from the object list, use your knowledge of the objects to ensure that the deletion does not jeopardize other dependent objects.

WARNING SAP does not recommend deleting objects from an object list, because it may jeopardize consistency between your R/3 Systems.

Locking and Unlocking Objects in Object Lists

Adding an object manually to the object list does not automatically lock the object. Any other user can record this object to a change request and perform changes on it. To prevent this, after adding objects to an object list, you are advised to manually set a lock on the objects as follows:

1. In the *Workbench Organizer: Requests* screen (in Transaction SE09), position the cursor on the change request you want to lock.

2. Choose *Request/task* ➤ *Object list* ➤ *Lock objects*.

You may receive an error message indicating that one or more objects are already locked in another change request or task. If the objects are locked, you may need to release the change request containing the locked objects.

To manually unlock an object in a change request, you require the authorization S_CTS_ADMIN, which is provided in the authorization profile S_A.SYSTEM. When you have this authorization, you can unlock an object in a change request using the *Organizer Tool* (Transaction SE03). In the tree structure under

Objects in Requests, access the function *Unlock objects*. Enter the request or task you wish to unlock and choose *Execute*.

Repairs and Modifications

Every R/3 Repository object has an *original system*, which is the R/3 System in which the object was created and should be edited. If you change an object in a system that is not the original system, you are changing a *copy* of the object and not the original itself; this is called a *repair*. In the production system, for example, if you change a copy of a program that originated in the development system, the changed object is considered a repair.

The original system for all SAP-delivered objects is defined as *SAP*. A change to an SAP-delivered object is a special type of repair known as a *modification*.

Certain risks are associated with repairs and modifications. For example:

- If you did not create the original object, you may not be able to guarantee application functionality after changing the object.

- The repair can be overwritten by imports if it has been confirmed (and therefore the repair flag is no longer set).

- Performing an upgrade is more complex if there are modifications in the pre-upgrade system.

Making a repair requires two steps that are not required when changing an object in the original system:

- Setting a repair flag for the object

- Monitoring and controlling the changes made to the Repository object with the *Modification Assistant* (available as of R/3 Release 4.5)

Setting a Repair Flag

When you change an R/3 Repository object in an R/3 System that is not its original system, regardless of whether it is an SAP-delivered object or a customer-developed object, the *Set Repair Flag* dialog box will appear. To continue, you must choose *Object for repair*. This sets the repair flag for this object.

The repair flag protects an R/3 Repository object from being overwritten if it is subsequently reimported from the source system. When the repair flag is set, an error message appears during import indicating that the object has not been imported because it was repaired in the target system.

If necessary, it *is* possible to reimport an object after it has been repaired in the target system. To reimport a repaired object, do one of the following:

- *Confirm* a repaired object when releasing it (see Chapter 12).

- *Confirm* a repaired object that was previously released. (Select the task or change request that contains the repaired object. In the *Workbench Organizer: Requests* screen, choose *Request/task ➢ Confirm repair*.)

- When importing the change request containing the object, use the import option *Overwrite objects in unconfirmed repairs* (see Chapter 13) from within TMS or the appropriate unconditional mode if importing using *tp* directly (see Chapter 14).

Example of the Effect of Repair Flags

A customer-developed program, ZDATAPUT, caused critical problems in the production system. Because it was disrupting the work of many users, the program's developer was asked to quickly resolve the problem in the production environment. The developer resisted this suggestion at first, knowing that

Continued on next page

making programming changes in the production environment is not a good idea. However, he finally agreed since the development system was unavailable due to hardware maintenance, and because it was a two-system landscape, there was no quality assurance system.

After getting senior-level approval and having the system administrator temporarily change the client and system change options, the developer successfully repaired ZDATAPUT in the production system and recorded the change to a local change request. The system administrator reestablished the client and system change options for the production system.

Later, the developer returned to the development system and made the same correction to ZDATAPUT that he had made on the production system. This time the change was saved to a transportable change request and released and exported. This and other change requests were imported into the production system. The change request containing ZDATAPUT failed during import because, according to the production system, the object ZDATAPUT had been repaired. The developer returned to the production system and confirmed the object in the Workbench Organizer. The import of the change request was performed again, this time successfully.

Modification Assistant

As of R/3 Release 4.5, the ABAP Editor offers the Modification Assistant to guide you during repairs to objects that are not in their original system. Although the name *Modification Assistant* may imply that it is used only to make modifications, this tool is designed to help manage the repair of any object, whether it is SAP-delivered or customer-developed.

The Modification Assistant ensures that repairs to an object outside its original system are made using only the options *Insert*, *Replace*, and *Delete*. This preserves a record of the original form of objects, and indicates the change request that is used to make the change. For example, using the Modification Assistant, you can no longer simply change an existing line of code in a program. You must use the *Replace* option. This option inserts an asterisk to preserve the original line of code as a commentary (as in line 221, in Figure 10.9). The option *Modification undo* simplifies undoing all changes made during the repair.

NOTE
The Modification Assistant preserves a copy of that part of an object that was changed in a repair or modification.

FIGURE 10.9:

The ABAP Editor when used with the Modification Assistant

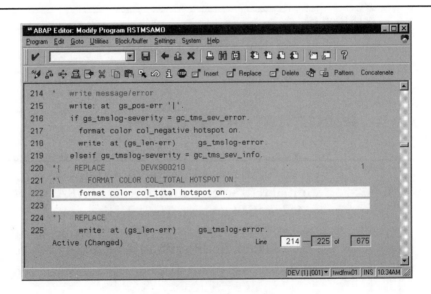

This detailed documentation provided by the Modification Assistant in the ABAP Editor helps to dramatically reduce the amount of effort needed to apply Support Packages and upgrade your R/3 System.

Occasionally, you will have to disable the Modification Assistant—for example, to upload a program into the ABAP Editor. To disable the Modification Assistant, before making changes, from within the ABAP Editor choose *Edit* ➤ *Modifications* ➤ *Disable assistant*. Repairs and modifications made when the Modification Assistant is deactivated will still be registered as repairs in the Workbench Organizer. However, you lose the pre-change documentation provided by the Modification Assistant. When performing modification adjustments during an upgrade or when applying a Support Package, to gain insight into changes that were made without the Modification Assistant, you will have to use the version management functionality of the ABAP Workbench (see Chapter 12).

WARNING   To simplify future upgrades, SAP recommends having the Modification Assistant activated at all times.

Modification Browser

To display a tree structure listing all repairs and modifications in the Modification Browser, use Transaction code SE95 or, from the initial R/3 screen, choose *Tools* ➤ *ABAP Workbench* ➤ *Overview* ➤ *Modification Browser*. The selection screen of the Modification Browser appears, which enables you to specify the criteria for the repairs and modifications to be displayed. For example, you can select:

- All repairs, or only the repairs for a specific development class and/or time period

- Repairs made with and/or without the Modification Assistant

- Modifications to SAP objects that may subsequently need to be adjusted during an upgrade or Support Package application (see Chapter 15)

In the Modification Browser, to access the ABAP Workbench tool relevant to a particular object type (such as the ABAP Editor for a program), position the cursor on a specific object and choose *Display* or *Change*.

To undo repairs made with the help of the Modification Assistant, in the Modification Browser, place your cursor on a specific object and choose *Reset to original*. Using this function returns the Repository object to its original state and causes the object to be deleted from the Modification Browser.

Modifications

Modifications are a specific type of repair—they are changes to the SAP standard. Modifications may be made in the following ways:

- By applying the corrective coding provided to customers in an R/3 Note

- By adapting R/3 to your specific business needs

WARNING A modification is a change that is more serious than a repair. Making a modification changes the functionality delivered by SAP and may negatively impact the performance and functionality of the R/3 System.

Prior to making modifications based on R/3 Notes, ensure that the R/3 Note is applicable to your R/3 Release and that the symptoms in the R/3 Note are the symptoms apparent in your R/3 System. In the case of uncertainty, contact the SAP Hotline.

Before making modifications with the goal of adapting R/3 to your specific business needs, you should be well-acquainted with the existing construction and flow logic of the application component. This knowledge will help you evaluate modification possibilities and enable you to decide on a sensible modification design.

This knowledge will also help you determine when SAP enhancement technology provides a better alternative to performing a modification.

When you make a modification, in addition to setting a repair flag and preferably using the Modification Assistant as of R/3 Release 4.5, you need:

- An SSCR key so that the SAP-delivered object can be modified

- Documentation in change requests and attached to the affected objects to assist the modification adjustment process during the application of future Support Packages or R/3 upgrades

- Correct timing for transporting the modification in relation to the time when Support Packages are applied (see Chapter 15)

TIP   SAP recommends that you perform all modifications to SAP-delivered objects in the Customizing-and-development client.

SSCR Key for Modifications

The first time an SAP-delivered Repository object is changed, the ABAP Workbench prompts the developer for an object-specific SAP Software Change Registration (SSCR) key through the dialog box shown in Figure 10.10. You can obtain the key from SAPNet (using the procedure described above under "SSCR Registration of Developers").

After you enter the key in the dialog box shown in Figure 10.10, the key is automatically added to the table ADIRACCESS in the current R/3 System. The SSCR key is specific to the program ID and object type of the R/3 Repository object, as well as to the installation number and R/3 Release of the R/3 System. Therefore, you have to register the R/3 Repository object that you want to modify only once per R/3 System and R/3 Release level.

FIGURE 10.10:

The ABAP Workbench requests an SSCR key when you try to modify SAP objects.

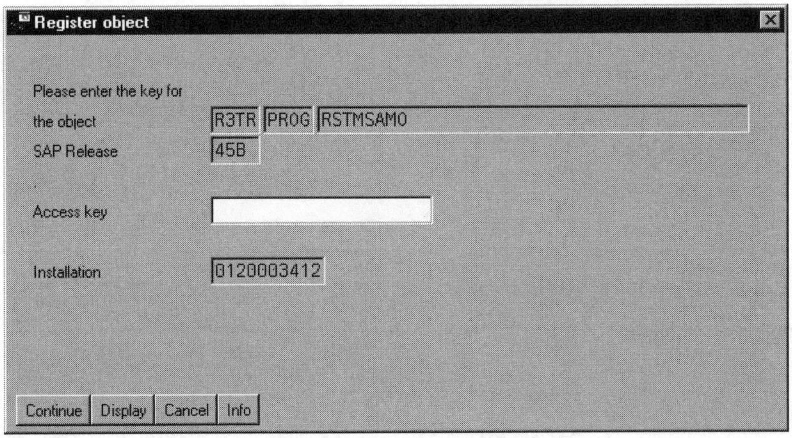

NOTE R/3 Repository objects that do not require SSCR registration include matchcodes, database indexes, buffer settings, customer objects, and objects generated through IMG Customizing activities.

Documentation Requirements

Creating modifications makes R/3 Release upgrades or the application of Support Packages more complex due to the need for a modification review and possible adjustments during upgrade. To simplify decision making during this review process, when creating modifications, you should document all changes thoroughly in both the change request and the documentation attached to the object.

Include the R/3 Note number and R/3 Release dependencies in the field *Short description* when you create the relevant change request and in the task-specific documentation (under *Goto ➤ Documentation* in the Workbench Organizer). The change request description, for example, will then inform the person performing the upgrade that the modification was made as a result of an R/3

Note and can be safely overwritten by the new R/3 Release. The short description of the change request will also be recognizable in the import queue. This is shown in Figure 10.11, where the R/3 Note number and the relevant Support Package number indicate that the second change request does not have to be imported if Hot Package 3 has already been applied.

FIGURE 10.11:

A sample import queue with a change request that is the result of an R/3 Note

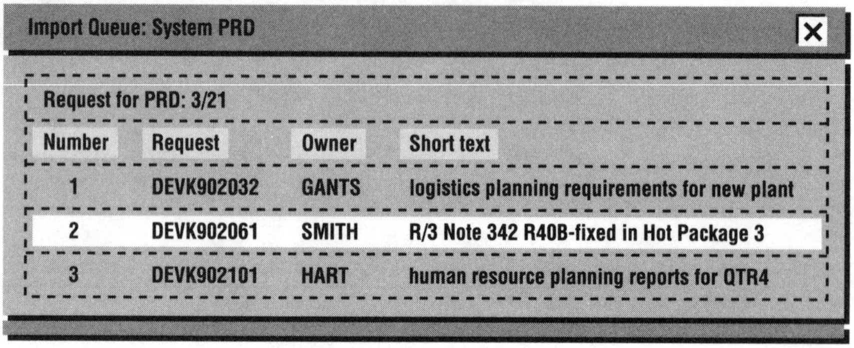

Import Queue: System PRD			☒
Request for PRD: 3/21			
Number	**Request**	**Owner**	**Short text**
1	DEVK902032	GANTS	logistics planning requirements for new plant
2	DEVK902061	SMITH	R/3 Note 342 R40B-fixed in Hot Package 3
3	DEVK902101	HART	human resource planning reports for QTR4

TIP   All changes to SAP standard objects should be well-documented in the relevant change requests and tasks. If the change is a result of an R/3 Note, be sure to include the R/3 Note number as part of the change request description.

The Object Directory

When you create an object, a corresponding Object Directory entry is also created. The key data for this entry is visible in the object list for each change request or task. Although this information is created automatically, there may be situations in which it is useful to display and possibly change the Object Directory entry for a particular object.

The Object Directory in the table TADIR is a catalog of all R/3 Repository objects in the R/3 System, including the SAP standard objects that are delivered with R/3 Systems and all objects you create using ABAP Workbench tools. These objects include ABAP programs, module pools, function groups, and ABAP Dictionary objects (domains, data elements, and tables).

The primary key of the table TADIR comprises the following fields:

- Program identification (PgmID)
- Object type (Obj.)
- Object name

For the majority of Repository objects, the PgmID is R3TR. The object type classifies the object—for example, PROG denotes an ABAP program, and TABL denotes a dictionary table structure. Examples of common object entries are listed in Table 10.1.

TABLE 10.1: Sample Object Entries

PgmID	Object Type	Description
R3TR	PROG	ABAP programs
R3TR	DEVC	Development class
R3TR	VIEW	Table view
R3TR	FORM	ABAP form
R3TR	CMOD	Customer enhancement
R3TR	TABL	Table structure
R3TR	DTEL	Data element
R3TR	DOMA	Domain
R3TR	TRAN	Transaction
R3TR	FUGR	Function group

When reviewing the object list of a task or change request, you may see the entry LIMU in the column PgmID. LIMU indicates that the object is a sub-object of either an R3TR or an R3OB object. These sub-objects do not have their own Object Directory entry, but, instead, they are included in the entry for the respective object. Sub-objects can be transported separately so that the entire R/3 Repository object does not have to be transported every time a change is made.

When, for example, the ABAP program ZPROGRAM is created, the corresponding Object Directory entry R3TR PROG ZPROGRAM is automatically created. This entry is then used in the object list of the task and, when the task is released, in the object list of the change request. After an object is initially created, all of its components are transported. Subsequent changes to the object transport only the changed sub-objects. Sample sub-objects for an ABAP program are listed in Table 10.2.

TABLE 10.2: Typical Sub-Objects for ABAP Programs

PgmID	Object Type	Description
LIMU	REPS	Program source
LIMU	DOCU	Documentation
LIMU	REPT	Text elements of the report
LIMU	VARI	Program variants
LIMU	ADIR	Object directory entry

Object Attributes

The Object Directory also contains the *object attributes* of each R/3 Repository object. You can display these attributes as described in the next section. They include:

- Development class
- Original system
- Person responsible for object
- Original language
- Generation flag
- Repair flag

You can change the attribute *original system*—the system in which the object was created—by making a *relocation transport* in Transaction SE01 (described below). In general, if there are problems with a particular object, consult the person indicated in the attribute *person responsible for object*.

The *original language* attribute is an attribute for the language-specific components of each object, such as text elements, and is equivalent to the logon language in which the object was created. If you are developing in more than one language, the system asks you whether you want to change the original language when you log on in another language and proceed to edit the object.

If an object is flagged as *generated*, it was automatically created as an indirect result of other user activities, such as particular Customizing transactions (see "Client-Independent Customizing Activities" in Chapter 11).

Displaying or Changing an Object Directory Entry

There are several ways of displaying Object Directory entries. The most common way is to use the Repository Browser, which lets you display and change the Object Directory entries for R/3 Repository objects in the current R/3 System. To display objects in the Repository Browser, proceed as follows:

1. Use Transaction code SE80 or, from the R/3 initial screen, choose *Tools* ➢ *ABAP Workbench* ➢ *Repository Browser*.

2. In the resulting selection screen, the upper and lower screen areas enable you to perform the selection in two different ways:

   • In the top half of the screen, you can generate an object list and then select the particular object you wish to display. To do this, mark one of the radio buttons offered and, in the adjacent field, enter the corresponding development class, program, function group, or user. Choose *Display*. Expand the object list if necessary, and position the cursor on a particular R/3 Repository object.

   • The lower half of the screen enables you to display an individual object. Select the type of object and choose *Edit*. A new selection screen appears. Enter the object name and choose *Execute*.

3. To display the object's directory entry, select *Edit* ➢ *Object directory entry*. The dialog box *Change Object Directory Entry* appears (see Figure 10.12), enabling you to view the Object Directory entry, or to change the development class or person responsible.

FIGURE 10.12:

Displaying or changing the Object Directory entry

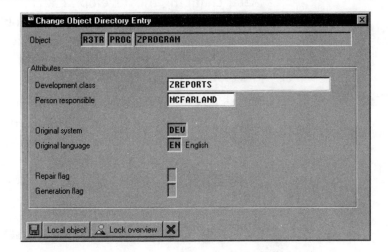

For example, when you want to transport an object with development class $TMP, you would use this dialog box to change the development class to a customer development class. You can also change the owner of an object—for example, if a developer has left the project and all of his or her objects need to be assigned to another developer.

Some attributes cannot be changed from this dialog box in the Repository Browser. For example, if you need to assign the current R/3 System as the original system of an object, use Transaction SE03. A tree structure is displayed listing various tools. Choose *Object directory*, and double-click an entry to perform the respective Object Directory task.

No matter which method you use to change Object Directory entries, keep the following points in mind:

- With authorization profile S_A.SYSTEM and Transaction SE03, you can modify all attributes except original language.

- After changing the development class, responsible person, generation flag, or repair flag for an object, you must save your changes to a change request. Exceptions include objects local to the current system such as those assigned to the development classes $TMP.

- When changing the development class of an object that has already been released and exported, the new development class ideally has the same transport layer as the previous one. This helps to ensure that the affected objects continue to be transported along the same transport route.

Transporting Objects Using the Transport Organizer

The *Transport Organizer* (Transaction SE01) is used for all non-standard transports—that is, for transports that are not performed using the Workbench Organizer and the Customizing Organizer. In particular, the Transport Organizer enables you to create change requests to perform the following kinds of transports:

Transports of copies: Used to transport a collection of R/3 Repository objects and Customizing objects to a specified R/3 System. The Object Directory entry of the objects remains unchanged in both the source and target system.

Relocations without development class change: Used to change collections of objects in another R/3 System on a temporary basis—for example, to make special developments that do not interfere with the normal development environment. The original system of the objects becomes the target system. The same type of relocation transport is later used to return the objects back to the source system.

Relocations with development class change: Used to change the development system of individual objects on a permanent basis. The original system of the objects becomes the target system. Assign a development class that ensures the objects will be associated with the right transport route after import into the target system. Once the objects have been imported into the target system, you can record them to a transportable change request without making any further changes to their Object Directory entry.

Relocations of complete development classes: Used to permanently change the transport layer of a development class and the original system of the objects. The object list of the change request for this transport is set up automatically and contains all objects in the development class.

To perform any of these four types of Transport Organizer transports, proceed as follows:

1. Enter Transaction code SE01 or, from the initial R/3 screen, choose *Tools* ➤ *Administration* ➤ *Transports* ➤ *Transport Organizer*.

2. Select *Transport of Copies, Relocation* and then press *Choose*.

3. Choose *Create*. In the resulting dialog box, select one of the following:

   - *Transport of copies*

   - *Relocation of objects w/o dev. class change*

   - *Relocation of objects with dev. class change*

   - *Relocation of a complete development class*

4. Choose *Enter*. The dialog box *Create request* appears, enabling you to create an appropriate change request as follows:

Field	User Entry
Short description:	Enter a short text describing the change request.

Field	User Entry
Target:	Enter the name of the target system (or, if extended transport management is active, the target system and client). The target system must be one that is defined in the TMS.
Target dev. Class:	This field appears if you selected *Relocation with dev. class change.* Enter the name of the target development class for the Repository objects. The development class must be defined in the current R/3 System and assigned to a transport layer specific to the target R/3 System.
Development class and *Target transp. layer:*	These fields appear if you selected *Relocation of a complete development class.* Enter the name of the development class for the objects to be copied, and the target transport layer for the development class.

5. After completing the required entries, choose *Save.*

6. The *Display request* screen appears, showing the newly created change request. To modify the details you entered in the previous dialog boxes, position the cursor on the change request and choose *Request/task* ➢ *Display/change.*

Unless the change request is a relocation for an entire development class, the newly created change request does not contain any R/3 Repository objects. To add objects to the change request, in the *Display request* screen, select the change request and choose *Request/Task* ➢ *Object List* ➢ *Include objects.* Then, proceed as described above, under "Object List of Change Requests and Tasks." After adding objects to the change request, you can release and export the change request.

Example of Using *Relocation of a complete development class*

A large pharmaceutical company implementing R/3 initially wants a standard three-system landscape (DEV, QAS, and PRD). Due to the development and testing requirements of Internet interoperability, however, the company decides to create a second development system, NET, to be used solely for the development needs of SAP's Internet Transaction Server. DEV will still be used for traditional forms of development work such as the creation of special reports and legacy conversion routines.

The R/3 System NET is created as a system copy of the current development system. The TMS and transport routes for NET are configured as shown in the following diagram:

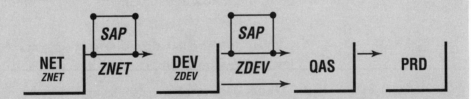

New Repository objects that support Internet activities are created in NET and assigned to the development class ZINTERNET, whose transport layer is ZNET. These objects are recorded to change requests and transported to DEV. The delivery route between DEV and QAS ensures that changes from NET are subsequently delivered to the quality assurance system and ultimately to the production system.

To ensure that objects created in NET and DEV have unique names, naming convention entries are added to the view V_TRESN. Only an object whose name begins with "ZNET" should receive the development class ZINTERNET. New objects on DEV cannot be named using "ZNET."

Continued on next page

The R/3 System NET helps to bring Internet transactions to the production environment. Over time, the need for NET disappears, and all Internet development is to be concentrated in DEV. To support the switch from NET to DEV, all Repository objects created on NET (those objects with the development class ZINTERNET) are copied from NET to DEV by relocating the entire development class. The development class is assigned the new transport layer ZDEV. DEV then solely supports all development efforts, including those required for Internet functionality.

Review Questions

1. Which of the following statements is *false* in regard to development classes?

   A. Development classes facilitate project management by grouping similar Repository objects.

   B. All Repository objects are assigned to a development class.

   C. A development class determines the transport route that a changed Repository object will follow.

   D. A local object does not need a development class.

2. Which of the following kinds of changes are transported using Workbench change requests?

   A. Client-independent changes

   B. Modifications to SAP-delivered objects

   C. Changes made using the ABAP Editor and ABAP Dictionary

    D. Repairs to R/3 Repository objects that originated in another R/3 System

    E. All of the above

3. Which of the following data is *not* contained in the object list of a task?

    A. The actual change made to the objects listed in the task

    B. The list of changed objects recorded to the task

    C. Whether the objects recorded to the task are locked

    D. The complete Object Directory entry for the object

4. Which of the following statements are correct regarding repairs and modifications?

    A. Repairs are changes to SAP-delivered objects; modifications are changes to any object that originated on an R/3 System other than the current R/3 System.

    B. A repair flag protects an R/3 Repository object against being overwritten by an import.

    C. All repairs are saved to Workbench change requests.

    D. A modification is a change to an SAP-delivered object.

    E. All of the above.

CHAPTER
ELEVEN

Managing Customizing Changes

This chapter explains the tools that enable you to perform Customizing and manage the change requests containing Customizing changes. Proper management of Customizing changes can be divided into the following areas:

- Customizing prerequisites
- Customizing change requests
- Nonstandard Customizing activities
- Support tools for Customizing

Customizing Prerequisites

To enable Customizing activities in R/3:

- Ensure that Customizing changes occur only in a single R/3 client in your system landscape.
- Ensure that Customizing changes are recorded to change requests.
- Assign user authorizations to the Customizing team.
- Set up the necessary Project IMGs.

To ensure that Customizing changes occur only in a specific R/3 client, use the client and system change settings to allow or disallow Customizing in each R/3 System and client. As described in Chapter 3, to enable Customizing changes in a specific client, the client settings for that client in Transaction SCC4 should be as follows:

- The client-dependent change option allows changes and is preferably set to *Automatic recording of changes*.

- The client-independent change option allows changes to client-independent Customizing objects.

- The client's role is not *production*.

In addition to providing the client settings, to enable Customizing, you must set the system change option for the R/3 System to *Modifiable* to support client-independent Customizing (see Chapter 7).

To limit who can create and release change requests and tasks, assign user authorizations based on the following authorization profiles:

S_A.CUSTOMIZ: This profile is for project leaders and enables them to create and release change requests, and to assign tasks to team members.

S_A.DEVELOP: This profile is for team members and enables them to perform Customizing and development activities, and to work with the Customizing and Workbench Organizers. Team members can release their tasks after unit testing, but they cannot release the change request.

You can use SAP-delivered authorization profiles as templates for creating your own authorizations.

NOTE   For information on the authorization objects and authorizations related to the profiles S_A.CUSTOMIZ and S_A.DEVELOP, see R/3 online documentation.

Setting Up Project IMGs

Customizing management during R/3 implementation is ideally realized using Project IMGs (introduced in Chapter 2). Project

IMGs subdivide the functionality of your R/3 application components, enabling you to focus your Customizing on particular areas. Project IMGs also provide project management capabilities that enable project leaders to monitor the status of their project and review relevant documentation. After you have generated Project IMGs, the Customizing team can begin its work.

To create Project IMGs, you must first generate the Enterprise IMG by selecting the desired application components and compiling the list of required Customizing for the selected components. To generate the Enterprise IMG, proceed as follows:

1. Use Transaction code SPRO or, from the R/3 initial screen, choose *Tools* ➤ *Business Engineer* ➤ *Customizing*.

2. Choose *Basic Functions* ➤ *Enterprise IMG* ➤ *Generate*. Enter a distinctive title for the Enterprise IMG and choose *Continue*.

3. Choose all countries or, to focus on country-specific activities, only the countries relevant for your company. Choose *Confirm*.

4. A tree structure is displayed showing SAP's entire application components list (the SAP Reference IMG). Select the R/3 components that your company requires. Choose *Generate*.

After generating the Enterprise IMG, you are ready to create the various Project IMGs by dividing the Enterprise IMG into several parts, as well as filter the Project IMGs to create various *views* based on task priority. To create a Project IMG and the associated views, proceed as follows:

1. Use Transaction code SPRO or, from the R/3 initial screen, choose *Tools* ➤ *Business Engineer* ➤ *Customizing*. Choose *Project Management*. The *Project Management* screen appears.

2. Choose *Project* ➤ *Create*. Enter a unique number for the new project and choose *Continue*. The *Change Project* screen appears (see Figure 11.1).

3. Enter a descriptive name, a default project language, a project owner, a start date, and an end date. Select the desired project management and documentation options. Choose *Generate Project IMG*. The dialog box *Generate Project IMG* appears.

4. Choose *Select countries and application components* and select *Continue*.

5. In the resulting dialog box, choose all countries or only the countries relevant for your project. Choose *Continue*. The *Select business application components* screen appears, showing the list of application components in the Enterprise IMG.

6. Select the application components you want to include in the Project IMG. Choose *Generate*. The dialog box *Generate views of the Project* is displayed.

7. Select the project views to be created and choose *Generate*.

Project IMGs provide project management capabilities that are not contained in the Enterprise IMG. These include time scheduling, status maintenance, documentation, and Customizing task priority. The project leader should create Project IMGs for the respective implementation phases.

FIGURE 11.1:

Creating a Project IMG

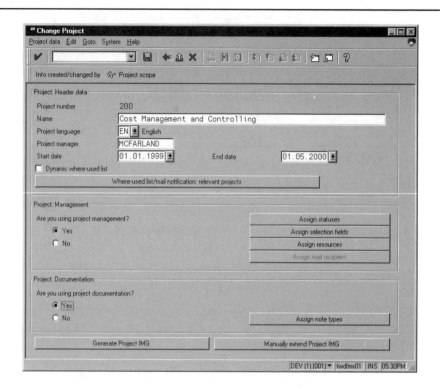

You can subsequently extend the Enterprise IMG and regenerate it without losing the originally selected components. This is necessary, for example, after R/3 Release upgrades, because new releases include new application components and new Customizing activities. To re-create the Enterprise IMG, repeat the above procedure for creating the Enterprise IMG. After generating the Enterprise IMG, regenerate each Project IMG as follows:

1. Use Transaction code SPRO or, from the R/3 initial screen, choose *Tools* ➢ *Business Engineer* ➢ *Customizing*. Choose *Project Management*. The *Project Management* screen appears.

2. To regenerate a single Project IMG, select the Project ID and choose *Project* ➢ *Change*. Choose *Generate Project IMG*. Alternatively, to regenerate all existing Project IMGs, choose *Project* ➢ *Bulk regeneration*.

Customizing Change Requests

Customizing is performed in the activities specified in a Project IMG. After an activity has been completed, the changes should be recorded to change requests so they can be transported to other R/3 Systems and clients. Most Customizing activities of the IMG are client-dependent and affect only the current R/3 client. These changes are recorded in a Customizing change request. Client-independent Customizing changes require Workbench change requests.

Project leaders are responsible for creating Customizing change requests (and, if necessary, Workbench change requests) and assigning tasks within those change requests to Customizing team members (see Chapter 6).

Viewing Customizing Change Requests

To view the Customizing change requests that a user owns, as well as the Customizing change requests in which that user owns a task, proceed as follows:

1. Access the Customizing Organizer using Transaction code SE10 or, from the R/3 initial screen, by choosing *Tools* ➢ *Business Engineer* ➢ *Basic functions* ➢ *Change Requests (Organizer)* ➢ *Create Requests/tasks* ➢ *Customizing Request Management*. The initial selection screen of the Customizing Organizer appears (see Figure 11.2).

2. Select the user ID of the change request or task owner, as well as the types of change requests you would like to view, and choose *Display*. The default selection displays only the *modifiable* change requests for your user ID. Modifiable change requests are Customizing change requests that have not been released. Additional selection options include Workbench change requests, released change requests, and change requests corresponding to a *last changed* time period that you specify.

3. The screen *Customizing Organizer: Requests* is displayed, showing a tree structure listing all change requests that match the selection criteria. To expand the tree structure, click a folder icon. If the folder icon you click is beside a change request ID number, a list of the associated tasks is displayed. If the folder icon you click is beside a task, a list of the objects recorded in the task is displayed.

FIGURE 11.2:

The initial selection screen of the Customizing Organizer

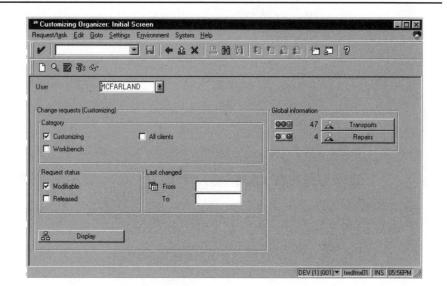

Figure 11.3 shows a sample tree structure view containing all modifiable Customizing change requests related to the user MCFARLAND. MCFARLAND owns the task DEVK900256 in a change request owned by ROEHRS (DEVK900255). MCFARLAND also owns change request DEVK900250, in which users ARCHER, MCFARLAND, and DRENNAN have tasks. DRENNAN's task contains changes to the view V_T685A, which consists of the tables T685, T685A, and T685T.

FIGURE 11.3:

Tree structure in the Customizing Organizer listing change requests and tasks

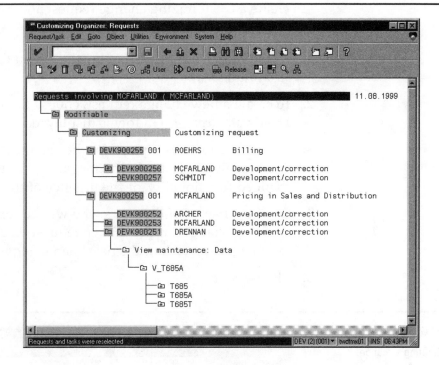

Creating Customizing Change Requests

The project leader uses the Customizing Organizer to obtain an overview of all Customizing changes in their respective tasks and is responsible for releasing change requests. Therefore, the project leader should be the one to create change requests and assign project team members to them. Ideally, this should be completed well before project team members begin performing Customizing activities. SAP recommends recording all Customizing activities for a particular project objective to a single change request, thereby enabling their subsequent release and export as a testable unit.

To create a Customizing change request and assign project team members to tasks, proceed as follows:

1. From Transaction SE10, display the screen *Customizing Organizer: Requests*.

2. To create a new change request, choose *Request/Task* ≻ *Create*. The *Create Request* window is displayed (see Figure 11.4).

3. Provide a short description for the change request including, for example, project information, a description of the changed functionality, or the urgency of the change.

4. Enter the names of the users who will be contributing Customizing changes to the change request. Each user automatically receives a task in the new change request.

5. Choose *Save*.

FIGURE 11.4:

Creating a change request

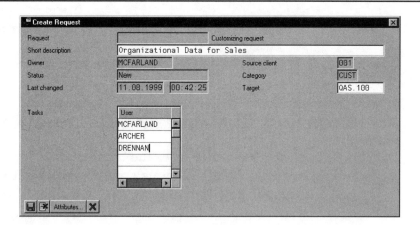

When creating a Customizing change request, you cannot change the following default settings:

• Name of the R/3 user who created the change request
• Status

- Date and time stamp
- Source client in which the change request was created
- Change request category

The source client is always the client in which the change request was created. Only from within this client can you perform the following activities:

- Recording changes to the change request
- Changing the owner of the change request or of its tasks
- Adding additional tasks to the change request
- Releasing the change request

The change request category is always CUST, indicating that this change request is a Customizing change request and can record only client-dependent changes.

Adding Additional Users to a Change Request

You can add users to a change request at any time in the interval between creating and releasing a change request. To add users to an existing Customizing change request, thereby creating a task for these users, proceed as follows:

1. From Transaction SE10, display the screen *Customizing Organizer: Requests*.

2. Position the cursor on the change request ID to which you wish to add a user. Choose *Request/Task* ➤ *Create*. The *Add user* dialog box is displayed.

3. Enter the name of the user, or use the possible entries arrow to select a user.

4. Choose *Copy*.

> **TIP**   After it is released, a change request or task cannot be changed. For example, you cannot add a user to a released change request.

Changing the Owner of Change Requests and Tasks

Each change request and each task have an R/3 user defined as its owner. By default, the user who creates a change request becomes its owner, and a task for that user is automatically created. If other users are assigned to the change request, tasks are automatically created for those users.

You may wish to change the owner of a change request or task—for example, to reassign it to another user or to become its owner so that you can change its attributes or delete an empty task. To change the owner of a change request or task, proceed as follows:

1. In Transaction SE10, access the screen *Customizing Organizer: Requests*.

2. Position the cursor on the ID of the appropriate change request or task. Choose *Request/Task* ➢ *Change owner*.

3. Enter the name of the user, or use the possible entries arrow to select a user.

4. Select *Confirm*. The new user now owns the change request or task.

Customizing in Project IMGs

To perform Customizing as a member of the project team, proceed as follows:

1. Use Transaction code SPRO or, from the R/3 initial screen, choose *Tools* ➤ *Business Engineer* ➤ *Customizing*. The *Customizing* screen is displayed, showing the Project IMGs that have been created. (If the dialog box *First Customizing Steps* appears, choose *Continue* or *Skip this in future*.)

2. Choose the project you need to customize by double-clicking the Project ID. The Project IMG tree structure is displayed.

3. To display Customizing activities for the Project IMG, expand the tree structure (see Figure 11.5).

FIGURE 11.5:

Project IMG tree structure

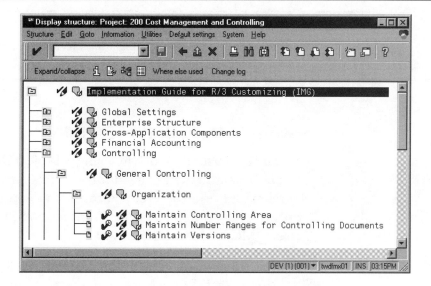

Double-clicking the appropriate icon to the left of the description of each Customizing activity takes you to various related tasks.

- The large check mark takes you to the relevant Customizing transaction. In Figure 11.5, for example, the large check mark to the left of the Customizing activity *Maintain Controlling Area* takes you to the maintenance transaction for defining or changing controlling areas.

- The pencil-and-check-mark icon lets you assign status information to this Customizing activity.

- The pencil-and-paper icon takes you to the screen for entering project documentation.

Double-clicking the Customizing activity name itself accesses related R/3 online documentation.

NOTE   Customizing activities are performed in the Project IMG tree structure. These activities include maintaining project status information, project documentation, and Customizing settings.

Setting a Default Project IMG

Customizers usually work in a single Project IMG over a period of time. To eliminate the need for selecting the Project ID to access the relevant tree structure, you can set a default Project IMG that appears every time you access Transaction SPRO. To set a default Project IMG, proceed as follows:

1. Use Transaction code SPRO or, from the R/3 initial screen, choose *Tools* ➢ *Business Engineer* ➢ *Customizing*. The *Customizing* screen is displayed, showing the Project IMGs that have been created.

2. Position the cursor on the Project IMG you want as your default Project IMG and choose *Implement. Project ➢ Default project/view ➢ Define.*

The Project IMG you select as your default Project IMG appears on the *Project Management* screen (from within Transaction SPRO) in red.

Customizing Using Views

Most Customizing transactions in R/3 are defined so that the Customizing settings for you to change correspond to the settings in views rather than the tables themselves. Views are logical tables in the ABAP Dictionary that group together fields from physical tables to create a uniform business context. Using views to perform Customizing activities masks the physical table structures and presents the constituent fields in a meaningful arrangement. Using table views wherever possible for Customizing has the following advantages:

- You need only one view to Customize several tables.

- You see only those fields from the physical tables that are relevant to the business object.

- The presentation and your processing of Customizing data are standardized.

Some business objects, such as material types and document types, cannot be represented in a view and are considered complex Customizing objects. Rather than having standardized maintenance transactions, these objects are maintained using special transactions, which can differ from object to object and, instead of views, use object-specific screen sequences.

TIP   Customizing objects, whether standard or complex, are defined by SAP and can be viewed using Transaction SOBJ.

Recording Customizing Changes

Customizing changes performed in the respective Customizing transactions can be either automatically or manually saved to a change request for transport to other clients and systems.

SAP recommends that the client in which you make Customizing changes has its client-dependent change option set to *Automatic recording of changes*. In Figure 11.5 (earlier in this chapter), for example, when you create a new controlling area and save the change, you will be automatically required to save it to a change request.

If the client in which you are performing Customizing changes is not set to *Automatic recording of changes*, you can manually record the change to a change request, either after saving the change or at a later time.

NOTE　Certain Customizing activities, referred to in this chapter as *manual transport* Customizing activities, are not automatically recorded to a change request, even if the client is set to automatic recording. These Customizing activities are transported using a method that varies according to the activity.

Automatically Recording Changes to Change Requests

If the setting for client-dependent changes in your Customizing-and-development client is set to *Automatic recording of changes*, when you save a Customizing change, you must indicate a change request to which the change can be recorded. The dialog box *Enter Change Request* is displayed (see Figure 11.6). In this dialog box, you can do one of the following:

- Enter the change request ID of a change request in which you have a task.

- Choose *Own requests* and select a change request from the change requests offered (see Figure 11.7).

- Choose *Create request* and (assuming you have the appropriate authorization) create a new Customizing change request in which you automatically also have a task.

- Choose *Cancel* and thereby not save your Customizing changes.

FIGURE 11.6:

Recording a change to a change request

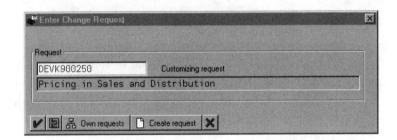

FIGURE 11.7:

Selecting from a list of available change requests

Manually Recording Changes to Change Requests

If a client is not set to automatically record Customizing changes to a change request, you can save Customizing changes without recording them to a change request. Subsequently, you can manually record the existing Customizing changes to a change request. Manual recording of Customizing settings can also be used to record existing entries that, while they already may be in a change request, should be transported together in a single change request. To manually record existing Customizing entries, proceed as follows:

1. Use the IMG (Transaction SPRO) to access the Customizing activity. Click the large check mark to display the existing Customizing data you wish to manually record to a change request.

2. Select the Customizing entries to be recorded to the change request. To do this, select all entries using *Edit* ➤ *Selections* ➤ *Select all*, and then deselect individual entries by clicking the adjacent selection buttons.

3. Choose *Table view* ➤ *Transport*. The dialog box *Enter change request* is displayed.

4. Enter the ID number of the change request to which the selected entries will be recorded. Choose *Continue*. You return to the screen displaying the Customizing data.

5. Choose *Include in request*. This records all the Customizing entries you selected to the defined change request. Choose *Save*.

Not all Customizing activities allow changes to be manually recorded to a change request. When you display such Customizing settings, the menu option *Table view* ➤ *Transport* is not available. To transport such Customizing, you may need to activate automatic recording of changes and edit the existing entries to force them to be recorded to a change request.

Setting Your Default Change Request

When using automatic recording of change requests, you can set a default Customizing change request to eliminate the need for specifying the change request. As a result, whenever you save a client-dependent Customizing change, it is recorded to your default change request. To set a default change request, proceed as follows:

1. In Transaction SE10, access the screen *Customizing Organizer: Requests*.

2. Position the cursor on the change request you want as your default change request and choose *Request/task* ➢ *Standard request* ➢ *Set*. The change request appears in the *Customizing Organizer: Requests* screen in a different color.

When you have a default change request and try to save your Customizing changes, no dialog box appears to ask you to indicate a change request. Your default change request is valid for one week unless you change the validity period. To change the validity period, choose *Request/task* ➢ *Standard request* ➢ *Set validity period*.

If you no longer want a particular change request to be the default change request, from the *Customizing Organizer: Requests* screen, position the cursor on the default change request and choose *Request/task* ➢ *Standard request* ➢ *Reset*.

Object Lists for Customizing Change Requests

The object list records objects that have been changed and shows what will be transported when the change request is released and exported. Each changed object has an entry in the object list. The object list of a change request is filled only after the tasks in the change request have been released (see also Chapter 12).

By expanding the hierarchical structure of a Customizing change request, you are able to see the list of objects recorded to a change request. For example, Figure 11.8 shows the Customizing objects (values in tables) that were changed in task DEVK900266. This task is owned by the user DRENNAN, and the change request to which the task belongs is owned by the user MCFARLAND. In the diagram, you see that changes were recorded to the tables ADDRESS and OVXK and to the view V_TVKO. View V_TVKO has been expanded, so you can see the tables (TVKO and TVKOT) that this view is based on and the primary keys of the table entries changed through Customizing. For example, for the table TVKO, the primary key recorded in this change request is 001PRNT.

FIGURE 11.8:

Objects in the tree structure for Customizing change requests

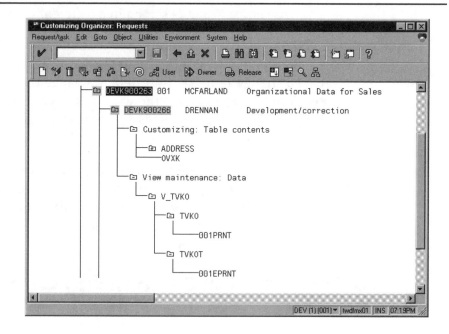

To see more information on these objects, access the object list by double-clicking the task ID. The resulting object list for the task DEVK900266 is shown in Figure 11.9. The program identification

PgmID and the object description *Obj* indicate the type of objects that were changed. *R3TR VDAT* indicates view data, and *R3TR TDAT* indicates table data. Note that a *K* (for key value) is present in the *Funct.* column for V_TVKO, ADDRESS, and OVXK. This *K* indicates that a primary key has been recorded for these particular objects. When a primary key is recorded, not all rows of the specified table or view need to be transported; instead, only the individual rows matching the key definition are transported.

FIGURE 11.9:

Object list for a
Customizing task

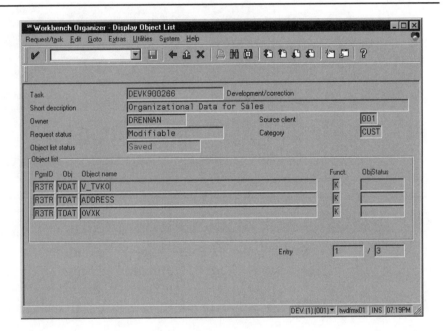

To better understand the primary key recorded for the changed Customizing entry, in the screen *Workbench Organizer—Display Object List* (see Figure 11.9), double-click the object name in the object list and then double-click the primary key value. A screen appears such as that shown in Figure 11.10, which shows the key data for the table TVKO. In Figure 11.10, you can see that the name of the primary key 001PRNT is composed of 001, which is the ID number of the client in which the changes were made, and PRNT, which is a sales organization. When released and exported, this change request will extract the current table entry values for the sales organization PRNT in client 001.

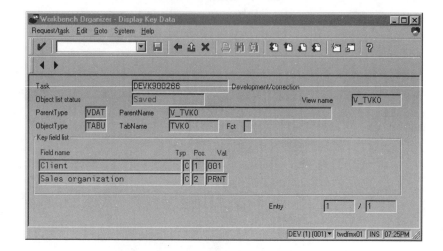

Customizing change requests contain only client-dependent Customizing objects. For changes recorded in a Customizing change request, the client ID number is included in the primary key value. At the time of release and export, the primary key is used in an SQL SELECT statement to access the changed table entry.

A change request does *not* contain the actual table entries or the object that has changed. A change request does not even record whether the change was an addition, modification, or deletion. All that is recorded in a change request is the list of the objects (views, tables, and/or key values) that have changed. For example, the objects in task DEVK900266 in Figure 11.9 (earlier in the chapter) may be the result of creating sales organization PRNT, or they may be the result of modifying or deleting the sales organization PRNT.

> **NOTE** A Customizing change request records, but does *not* contain, the actual table entries that have changed.

The Customizing Organizer does not lock changed objects in change requests. For example, if the user DRENNAN makes a change to the sales organization PRNT, the Customizing Organizer does not prevent other users from also modifying this Customizing setting while it is in an unreleased change request. Since Customizing objects in R/3 are shared between different application components, it is important that the Customizing Organizer cannot lock entire tables or single table entries. Otherwise, Customizing could not be performed by more than one user in a client.

> **NOTE** Changes recorded to a Customizing change request are not locked by the change request and can be changed and recorded to other change requests.

Identifying Change Requests with the Same Object

Unlike Workbench change requests, Customizing change requests do not lock objects. It is possible for more than one person to change the same Customizing settings. If this shared access to Customizing objects creates a misunderstanding among project team members, it may be necessary to see which users are changing the same Customizing object.

To view all tasks or change requests that include the same Customizing object, proceed as follows:

1. Access the Workbench Organizer Tools by using Transaction SE03.

2. The *Workbench Organizer: Tools* screen will appear, listing the available tools in a tree structure. Expand the node *Objects in requests*.

3. Double-click the option *Search for objects in requests/tasks*. The screen *Search for Objects in Requests/Tasks* appears (see Figure 11.11). This is a selection screen where you can define the object for which you are searching.

4. Select the appropriate object type and then, in the adjacent field, enter the name of the object. For example, if the object is in a view, enter the object type VDAT and then enter the name of the view.

5. Other selection criteria include the type of change requests, whether the change requests have been released, the owners of the change requests, and a time period in which the objects were last modified. If you are searching for Repository objects, the option *Also search for sub-objects* will display tasks and change requests containing LIMU entries (see Chapter 10).

6. After making your selections, choose *Execute*. A list of change requests and tasks containing the object is displayed.

Nonstandard Customizing Activities

Customizing activities are typically client-dependent changes to views and tables that are made by a user through IMG activities. However, an implementation phase usually includes other Customizing activities that are considered nonstandard because they have one or more of the following characteristics:

- They are client-independent and, therefore, affect not only the current R/3 client but all clients within the R/3 System.

- They require a manual method for transport instead of being automatically recorded to a change request.

- They can be performed both in the IMG and by alternative means (since they commonly need to be performed in the production client).

FIGURE 11.11:

Searching for change requests or tasks with common objects

FIGURE 11.11:

Searching for change requests or tasks with common objects

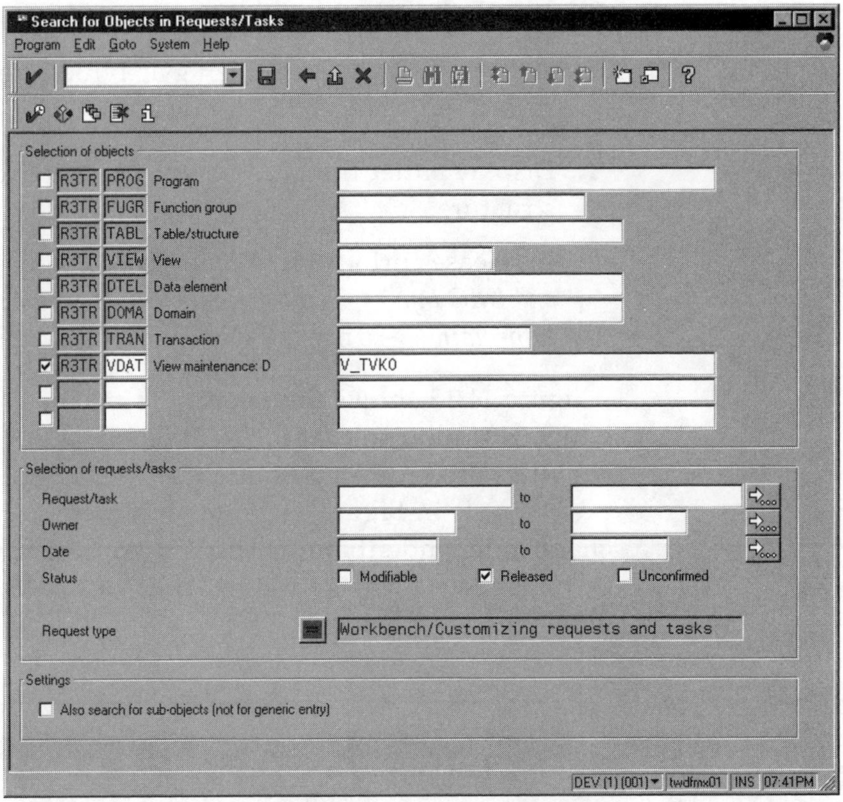

Client-Independent Customizing Activities

Although most Customizing objects of type CUST are client-dependent and are recorded in Customizing change requests, client-independent Customizing objects are of type SYST and are recorded in Workbench Organizer change requests. Changes to client-independent Customizing settings can also create ABAP Workbench objects (known as *generated objects*).

Determining whether a Customizing Activity Is Client-Independent

To determine which Customizing activities are client-independent (or cross-client), proceed as follows:

1. Display either the Enterprise IMG or a Project IMG tree structure.

2. In releases prior to R/3 Release 4.5, choose *Information* ➤ *Title and IMG info* ➤ *Client-dependency*. As of R/3 Release 4.5, choose *Information* ➤ *Title and IMG info* ➤ *Whether client-specific*.

Figure 11.12 shows the resulting screen as of R/3 Release 4.5, which is similar to that for R/3 Release 4.0. Cross-client IMG activities are indicated on the right-hand side of the screen. In the example in Figure 11.12, the maintenance of calendars is client-independent and requires a Workbench change request to be transported. The activity *Check Units of Measurement* is client-dependent.

FIGURE 11.12:

Displaying cross-client Customizing activities in the IMG

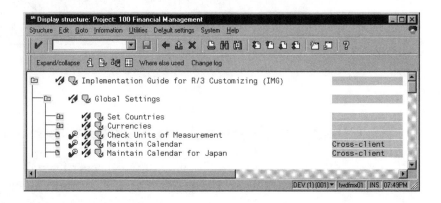

Recording Client-Independent Customizing Changes

When you save changed Customizing settings that are client-independent, a dialog box always appears requesting you to record your change to a Workbench change request, regardless of the client settings. You can either select a Workbench change request from a list after choosing *Own requests* or create a new Workbench change request with *Create request*.

Assigning Generated Customizing Objects to a Development Class

Cross-client Customizing activities sometimes result in the automatic generation of new R/3 Repository objects. Before these are generated, in the relevant Customizing transaction, you are required to provide a name for the new object. Next, a dialog box appears requesting a development class. Finally, a dialog box appears requesting a change request of type Workbench. The development class determines whether the objects can be transported. Most likely, you will want to transport all Customizing changes that trigger the creation of new R/3 Repository objects, and will therefore need to assign a customer development class with a valid transport layer (see Chapter 10).

Example: Objects Generated Automatically during Customizing

An example of a client-independent Customizing activity that results in the creation of new Repository objects is defining pricing condition tables. To access this Customizing activity in the IMG, choose *Sales and Distribution* ➤ *Basic Functions* ➤ *Pricing* ➤ *Pricing control* ➤ *Define pricing dependencies*

Continued on next page

(condition tables). Performing this Customizing activity automatically generates a pricing table, which stores various pricing criteria. After specifying the object name (such as 601, which automatically generates the object name A601) and defining pricing criteria in the relevant dialog boxes, you must assign a development class and save the object to a Workbench change request. After saving the generated object to a Workbench change request, if you access the object list corresponding to the change request, the list will show the objects recorded to the change request as the result of creating the pricing condition table A601:

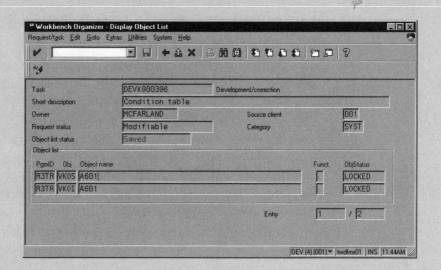

The two objects in the object list are not the pricing condition table A601, but rather the information required to generate that table. The definition of the object to be generated and not the object itself is recorded in the change request and subsequently transported. After export and during import into the quality assurance and production systems, the definition information is used to generate the required object.

Continued on next page

To check whether the object has been generated, use Transaction SE11, enter **A601** beside *Database table*, and choose *Edit* ➢ *Object directory entry*. The screen displayed is the one shown below. This screen shows A601 flagged as a generated object whose original system is SAP. Since its development class does not begin with a Y or a Z, it is an SAP-delivered development class. The field *Generation flag* contains an X; therefore, the object was generated by SAP.

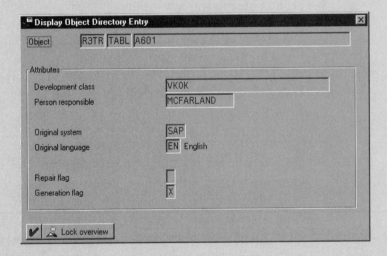

The objects defining the generated pricing condition table that are recorded in the change request are assigned to a customer development class. They do not appear as generated objects, and their original system is the customer's development system. To verify this, use Transaction SE11 to display the above screen for the objects in the change request.

Generated Customizing objects often are not transported. The definitions and instructions for the creation of the required Customizing object are transported.

Manual Transports and Other Transport Types

For most IMG Customizing changes, if the client setting specifies automatic recording of changes, the changes are automatically saved to a change request. However, there are some Customizing activities for which automatic recording to a change request is not possible. Such Customizing activities are considered *manual transport* Customizing activities.

Automatic recording to a change request is generally not possible when the entries for a Customizing object cannot be transported individually—the entire object (all of its entries) must be transported as a unit. Changes to such critical Customizing settings require a manual method of transport when the project leader recognizes that the entire object is ready for transport.

To determine which Customizing activities require manual transport, from either the Enterprise IMG or a Project IMG tree structure, choose *Information* ➤ *Title and IMG info* ➤ *Transport type*. A screen like that shown in Figure 11.13 is displayed. The right-hand side of the screen indicates the transport method for each Customizing activity. The transport methods may include:

Automatic transport: If the client is set to automatic recording of changes, the changes as a result of the Customizing activity will be recorded to a change request when saved.

Manual transport: Individual changes to the Customizing activity will not be recorded to a change request. To transport the Customizing settings, the changes must be transported using a special menu option found in the Customizing transaction.

No transport: Changes to the Customizing activity cannot be transported. This often applies to R/3 System–specific changes that are of a technical nature and not related to

Customizing. It also applies when the IMG activity is a check routine that enables you to verify settings and data in the current R/3 client. These IMG activities are not changes to Customizing settings and therefore do not require transport.

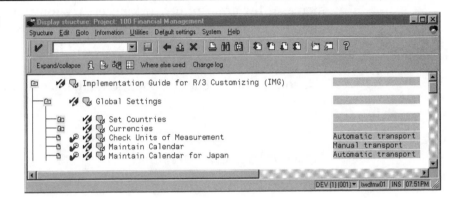

In Figure 11.13, the transport method *Automatic transport* is assigned to the Customizing tasks for checking the units of measurement and maintaining the calendar for Japan. The Customizing activity *Maintain Calendar* requires a manual transport. To transport changes to the calendar, use the *Transport* button in the Customizing transaction, which will transport not just the most recent change but the entire calendar.

Customizing in a Production Client

For your production client, SAP recommends setting the client-dependent change option to *No changes allowed*, thereby ensuring that all Customizing and development occur in the development system. However, some Customizing activities in the IMG concern minor changes that a customer may need to make on a regular basis. Examples of these changes include interest rates, health insurance premiums, pension schemes, tax schemes, and currency exchange rates. These types of changes are known as *data-only* Customizing changes.

Making such changes in the development system and transporting them regularly to the production system is tedious and increases the amount of work necessary for maintaining import queues and monitoring import logs. To avoid having to use change requests for these changes, SAP has introduced the *Current Settings* function. This function enables Customizing in a production client for client-dependent changes that do not impact the business flow.

Activating *Current Settings*

As a prerequisite for using the *Current Settings* function, the following settings must be made in Transaction SCC4 for the production client:

- The client role is *Production.*

- The client-dependent change option is *No transports allowed.*

NOTE	For more information on using *Current Settings* in a production client, see R/3 Note 77430.

Customizing Activities in *Current Settings*

The Customizing activities that can be performed in a production client using the *Current Settings* function are listed in the database table CUSAMEN.

As of R/3 Release 3.1H, you can add Customizing activities to table CUSAMEN, allowing you to perform them in the production client with the *Current Settings* function. SAP recommends that you add Customizing activities to CUSAMEN only if it is necessary and only if the changes resulting from these activities are data changes that:

- Are required on a regular basis

- Do not require a formal quality assurance sign-off

- Are not required in the other clients within the system landscape to maintain consistent Customizing environments

Adding an entry to table CUSAMEN results in a modification. (See Chapter 10.)

TIP   For more information on adding Customizing activities to the table CUSAMEN so that they can be performed using the *Current Settings* function, see R/3 Note 135028.

An alternative to adding Customizing activities to the table CUSAMEN is using ALE to distribute Customizing data. ALE enables you to distribute a change to all R/3 clients without the need for a change request. This requires ALE development, because SAP does not provide ALE scenarios for Customizing activities (see also Chapter 4, under "Transferring Master Data between R/3 Systems").

Support Tools for Customizing

To enable you to compare Customizing settings in different clients, R/3 provides the following tools:

- *Client compare* (as of R/3 Release 4.5, the Customizing Cross-System Viewer)

- View/Table Comparison

- Business Configuration Sets
- Customizing Transfer Assistant

To use any of these tools, you must:

- Have a user authorization that includes authorization S_CUS_CMP in both the logon client and the comparison client. To compare client-independent objects, you also need the authorization S_TABU_CLI.

- Create an RFC connection between the logon client (RFC target client) and the comparison client (RFC source client). To find out how to create an RFC connection, see Appendix A. When you create the RFC connection, the user you are required to define should be a user whose authorization in the target client does not exceed the authorization required to use these tools. For example, you can define a CPIC user who has only the authorization S_CUS_CMP.

- Set client protection in the comparison client to either *Protection level 0* or *Protection level 1*. (See "Client Protection" in Chapter 9.)

- To transfer Customizing settings from a comparison client, set the client protection in the logon client to *Protection level 0*.

Comparing Customizing in Two Clients

To compare the Customizing settings of two clients, in releases prior to R/3 Release 4.5, use the function *client compare*. As of R/3 Release 4.5, use the Customizing Cross-System Viewer, which is an improved version of the *client compare* function.

Using either of these tools enables you to compare Customizing objects and tables in one R/3 client (comparison client) against the settings in the current client (logon client). The result is an overview screen, showing differences between the two clients. In this screen, you can drill down the listed items to display the corresponding Customizing entries. To change these entries, you can use direct links to the corresponding IMG activity or a function that allows you to adjust the differences between the entries.

During R/3 implementation, you often need to compare the contents of tables or views located in the same R/3 System or in different R/3 Systems. Comparing clients can help you to:

- Identify the differences between the Customizing settings of two R/3 clients, or verify that both clients have consistent Customizing settings

- Compare current Customizing settings to those of a reference client such as client 000

- Compare Customizing settings delivered from a central corporate development system with the local Customizing settings

When you access either of the comparison tools (*client compare* or the Customizing Cross-System Viewer) using Transaction SCU0, a selection screen like the one shown in Figure 11.14 appears. This selection screen shows the kinds of objects you can compare. It contains the following selection options:

IMG activities: This option selects Customizing objects related to an entire Project IMG or Enterprise IMG.

Application components: This option selects Customizing objects related to one or more branches of a business application component.

Customizing object list/transport: This option selects all Customizing objects recorded in an object list or a change request. This option is available as of R/3 Release 4.0.

Business configuration set: This option is available only in the Cross-System Viewer. It selects all objects recorded in the Customizing snapshot known as a Business Configuration Set.

Manual selection: This option selects the Customizing objects and ABAP Dictionary tables that you specify.

FIGURE 11.14:

Selection screen of the
Cross-System Viewer
(containing options
similar to those on the
selection screen for
client compare)

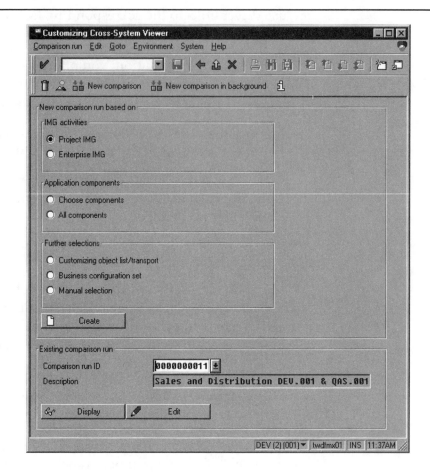

Releases Prior to R/3 Release 4.5: The *Client Compare* Function

To perform a client comparison in releases prior to R/3 Release 4.5, proceed as follows:

1. Access the *client compare* functionality by either using Transaction code SCU0 or, from the R/3 initial screen, choosing

Tools ➤ Business Engineer ➤ Customizing ➤ Tools ➤ Customizing objects ➤ Contextual comparison.

2. Select the criteria for comparison and choose *Create*. Other dialog boxes may appear, requesting additional information, such as the specific Project IMG, the specific application components, or a change request ID.

3. After you completely define the selection criteria for the comparison, a further screen appears requesting data for the comparison:

   - To schedule the comparison as a background job, select *Background execution*.

   - To include client-dependent Customizing objects, select *Client-dependent*.

   - To include client-independent Customizing objects, select *Client-independent*.

4. Choose *Difference List* to see what differences exist between two clients. Alternatively, choose *Object list* to get a list of objects that can be compared so that you can limit the comparison to particular objects.

5. Provide an RFC connection to the comparison client.

6. Choose *Continue* to begin the comparison.

As of R/3 Release 4.5: The Customizing Cross-System Viewer

To perform a client comparison as of R/3 Release 4.5, proceed as follows:

1. Access the Customizing Cross-System Viewer. To do this, use Transaction code SCU0 or, from the R/3 initial screen, choose *Tools ➤ Business Engineer ➤ Customizing ➤ Tools ➤ Customizing objects ➤ Object comparison.*

2. The selection screen for the Cross-System Viewer is displayed. Select the criteria for comparison and choose *Create*. You may need to indicate, for example, the Project IMG, the different application components, or a change request ID.

3. After you choose *Create*, a *comparison run ID* (a sequential value also referred to as the *worklist ID*) is automatically generated. A *Selection by:* screen appears:

   • Enter a description for the comparison. The description should enable you to remember what selection criteria you are using. Note that, to subsequently display the results of the comparison, you will need the comparison run ID.

   • To include client-dependent Customizing objects, select *Client-specific*.

   • To include client-independent Customizing objects, select *Cross-client*.

   • Provide an RFC connection to the comparison client.

TIP   From the *Selection by:* screen, choosing *Extra* ➢ *Extended Settings* allows for further detail in the selection criteria for the comparison. These options are not required for most comparisons.

---

4. To schedule the comparison as a background job, choose *Total comparison in background*. To begin the comparison immediately (if the comparison involves only a few objects), choose *Total comparison*. Alternatively, to get a list of Customizing objects that can be compared so that you can limit the comparison, choose *Object overview*.

Displaying the Results of a Client Comparison

The results of the comparison are the starting point for the display and subsequent adjustment of the differences between the logon client and the comparison client.

In releases prior to R/3 Release 4.5, the results of a *client compare* can be displayed on-screen immediately or scheduled to run in the background and result in spool output. Spool output displays the results of the comparison, but does not allow you to perform the analysis that is possible with the on-screen display of Customizing differences, such as viewing more details or linking to the relevant IMG activity.

WARNING   In releases prior to Release 4.5, background scheduling of client comparisons results in spool output that may be viewed but that cannot be used for further on-screen processing.

To display the results of a client comparison, proceed as follows:

- As of R/3 Release 4.5, use Transaction SCU0. In the field *Existing comparison run*, enter the worklist ID (the comparison run ID) for the client comparison you wish to display. Choose *Display*.

- In releases prior to R/3 Release 4.5, if the comparison was not created as a background job, the results are automatically displayed at the completion of the comparison run.

- In releases prior to R/3 Release 4.5, if the comparison was created as a background job, to display the results, use Transaction SM37. Identify your background job in the selection screen and choose *Enter*. Position the cursor on the comparison job and choose *Spool list*. Double-click the job to display the comparison results.

The results screen shows the differences for each compared object, a description of the object, and the *comparison status* in the column *Comp*. The comparison status indicates the equivalence or nonequivalence of the object in the respective clients. In releases prior to R/3 Release 4.5, this column is the first column. As of R/3 Release 4.5, it is the fourth column.

As of R/3 Release 4.5, the comparison results of the Cross-System Viewer are known as a *worklist*. You can use the worklist to review completed comparisons and maintain status information. The worklist also uses traffic-light icons to indicate processing status information—whether you are still analyzing or have already corrected found differences.

Figure 11.15 displays sample differences between the logon client, client 001 of system DEV, and the comparison client, client 001 of system QAS. The Customizing view V_TVKO and the view V_TVKOS_AU (namely, table TVTA) differ in the two clients. The right-hand side of the screen compares the number of entries for this object in both clients.

FIGURE 11.15:

The result of comparing two R/3 clients (R/3 Release 4.5)

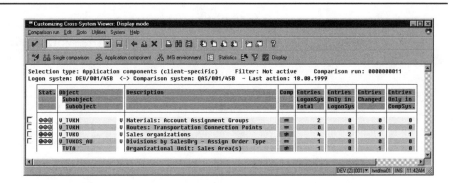

Comparison Status   The column showing the comparison status, *Comp*, may indicate the following:

- Contents are identical.

- Contents are not identical.

- Contents are identical, but the ABAP Dictionary structure of the object differs.

- Contents are not identical, and the ABAP Dictionary structure of the object differs.

- Contents could not be compared.

To display the legend for the symbols in this column, choose *Legend*.

There are several reasons why a comparison may not be possible. For example:

- The table or view does not exist in a local or a remote client.

- The sum of the length of all fields in the table or view exceeds the byte limitations of the standard compare tool (this is very rare).

- The structure of the table or view is not consistent between the two clients. For example, the primary key differs, or a field in one client is defined as a character field, while being defined as numeric in the other client. This can occur when the clients have different R/3 Release levels.

- The table is a system table and is therefore excluded from comparison.

Processing Status Shown as Traffic Light (Release 4.5)

The processing status indicated as a traffic light in Release 4.5 enables you to distinguish those objects that have already been processed from those that still need to be processed. Red indicates *not processed,* yellow indicates *in process,* and green indicates *completed.* Initially, the process status is set as a result of the comparison so that all red traffic lights indicate a difference in the two clients or the inability to compare the object. A green traffic light indicates that the comparison found no differences.

The processing status can be set manually—for example, from red to yellow to green. To do this, choose *Comparison run* ➤ *Display* <-> *Change* and then click the traffic light until the desired color indicator is displayed. Remember to save the changes. By manually setting the processing status, you can track your progress as you analyze and possibly adjust the differences for each object.

For example, in Figure 11.15 (earlier in this chapter), during the review of table V_TVKO, the status for this object can be changed to yellow to indicate to other members of the Customizing project that the difference is currently being analyzed. During your analysis, you may discover that the difference is simply due to the fact that a change request has not yet been transported from client 001 of DEV into the quality assurance system. In this case, the difference will be resolved when that change request is imported, and no adjustment is required in the comparison results screen. You can change the processing status from red to green.

Analyzing Differences   To analyze the differences between two clients, you can:

- Filter the comparison results screen according to various criteria for processing status, comparison status, and object type
- Display a statistical overview showing differences and object types
- Display the relevant IMG activity for particular objects
- Display the application component for a particular object in the application component hierarchy
- Perform a single comparison, as described below

Performing a Single Comparison

To view the corresponding records of the table or view, display the comparison results list, position the cursor on an object, and choose *Single comparison* for R/3 Release 4.5 or *View/table* for earlier releases. The screen *Overview comparison* is displayed. To make the differences easy to identify, the entries of the respective views of each object are shown consecutively. The results of the comparison are color-coded. For an explanation of the colors, choose *Legend*. The different comparison statuses are shown in Table 11.1.

TABLE 11.1: Single Comparison Status Indicators

Status	Description
<blank>	The listed entry is identical in both clients.
ML	The entries are not identical; the listed entry is the logon client entry.
MR	The entries are not identical; the listed entry is the comparison client entry.
L	Entry exists only in logon client.
R	Entry exists only in comparison client.
(M) or (E)	Differences only in fields that you have hidden from the comparison (for example, you may wish to exclude a noncritical field such as *LastChangedAt* from comparison).

An example of the results of a single comparison for the object V_TVKO is displayed in Figure 11.16. The different sales organizations are displayed as follows:

- Sales organization 0001 is different in the logon client and the comparison client, and both entries are displayed. The column *Ref. S Org* shows referencing sales organization values. The value for this Customizing setting is 0005 in the logon client, but does not exist in the comparison client.

- Sales organization 0005 is identical in both clients.

- Sales organization 0020 exists only in the comparison client.

- Sales organizations COMP and PRNT exist only in the logon client.

FIGURE 11.16:

A single comparison
for a view

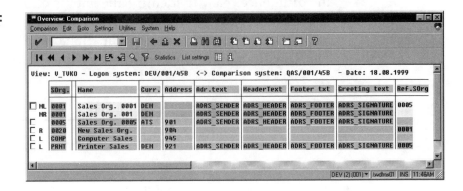

Performance Considerations   As of R/3 Release 4.5, when
you analyze a particular Customizing object by performing a single comparison, the window *Restrict selection set* appears, asking
whether you would like to compare all values or restrict the comparison. To optimize performance, you may wish to restrict the
comparison. If the object to be detailed does not contain a lot of
table entries—for example, fewer than 500—you do not need to
restrict the comparison.

In releases prior to R/3 Release 4.5, the comparison is restricted
by default, and the corresponding selection screen, *Restrict Comparison Using Selection Criteria*, always appears. Enter the appropriate selection criteria and choose *Single comparison* or *View/table*.
The single comparison is displayed.

Adjusting the Customizing Differences between Clients

To adjust the Customizing differences between clients, you need
to transfer view and table entries or the contents of individual

fields from a comparison client to the logon client as described below. Keep the following points in mind:

- Table and view entries can be changed only in the logon client, not in the comparison client.

- The adjustment can be performed for only one object at a time.

- The adjustment can be performed for only the tables and views that can be maintained using Table Maintenance (Transaction SM30). Other objects can be compared, but not adjusted.

- The data transferred to the logon client is subjected to the standard validation checks, which may prevent you from saving the transferred data. This may occur, for example, if you transfer a row, and part of the data comprising the primary key is missing in the logon client.

- Customizing objects cannot be adjusted for Business Configuration Sets.

WARNING   Some differences as the result of a comparison cannot be adjusted for technical reasons.

You can transfer the following kinds of data from the comparison client to the logon client:

- An entire row in a view or table. If the entry is present only in the comparison client, it is added to the logon client. If the row is present, but different in the two clients, it is copied into the logon client.

- A specific field in a row. Only the contents of the field you select are copied. The contents of all other fields are not affected.

- All entries of a table or view in the comparison client.

- An entire column of data (as of R/3 Release 4.5). In this way, values are only added, not replaced.

In addition, you can delete entries in the logon client to resolve a difference.

Adjustments in R/3 Release 4.5   As of R/3 Release 4.5, you can access the tools for performing adjustments in the Cross-System Viewer. To perform an adjustment, from within the client you wish to adjust, proceed as follows:

1. In Transaction SCU0, access the worklist for which you wish to initiate a transfer by providing the worklist ID and choosing *Display*.

2. The screen *Customizing Objects: Difference list* appears. In this screen, to switch to change mode, choose *Display <-> Change*.

3. Position the cursor on the Customizing object to be adjusted and choose *Edit* ➤ *Interact. Copy*.

4. The screen *Overview: Comparison* appears. Position the cursor on the entry you wish to adjust and choose *Adjust*.

5. The screen *Detail View: Adjust* appears. Choose the type of adjustment to be made. For example, to copy an entry from the comparison client to the current client, choose *Entry*.

6. At this stage, the data has been transferred but not saved (entered into the database). Choose *Back* to leave the adjustment tool. You will be prompted to save your changes. To save them, choose *Yes*. Choosing *No* returns the table or view to its original state.

7. If automatic recording of changes is active, you are prompted for a change request.

Adjustments in Releases Prior to R/3 Release 4.5   As of R/3 Release 3.1H, to initiate the comparison of a table or view and then perform an adjustment, from within the client you wish to adjust, proceed as follows:

1. Access *Table/View Maintenance* (Transaction SM30). Provide the name of the specific table or view to be adjusted, and choose *Maintain* ➢ *Utilities* ➢ *Adjust*.

2. Provide the required RFC connection and choose *Enter*.

3. A detail screen appears, similar to the one in Figure 11.16 (earlier in the chapter), displaying each table or view entry. Select the entry to be adjusted and choose *Adjust*.

4. Choose the type of adjustment to be made. For example, to copy an entry from the comparison client to the current client, choose *Entry*.

5. Choose *Back* to leave the adjustment tool. You will be prompted to check your changes. To check them, choose *Yes*. Choosing *No* terminates the transfer of data.

6. At this stage, the data has been transferred but not saved (entered into the database). To preserve your changes, choose *Save*.

7. If automatic recording of changes is active, you will be prompted for a change request.

Single Comparison with Transaction SCMP

The Customizing Cross-System Viewer and the *client compare* tool are useful for comparing many objects at once—for example, when comparing objects from a project or application perspective. However, you may wish to simply compare a single Customizing object or table. Since the Customizing Cross-System Viewer and the *client compare* tool are specifically designed for Customizing objects, you cannot use them to compare tables that are not considered Customizing objects. Such non-Customizing objects include, for example, tables that contain application data.

WARNING   Single comparisons read the view or table contents into memory before performing a comparison. Therefore, views or tables with a lot of entries, such as an application table, will negatively impact system performance.

To compare a single R/3 object or a non-Customizing object, the simplest option is to use Transaction SCMP. To do this, proceed as follows:

1. Use Transaction code SCMP or, from the R/3 initial screen, choose *Tools* ➤ *Business Engineer* ➤ *Customizing* ➤ *Tools* ➤ *Customizing objects* ➤ *Object comparison* (or *Single comparison* in releases prior to Release 4.5).

2. The screen *View/Table Comparison* appears (see Figure 11.17). Enter the name of the view or table to be compared and the name of the RFC destination (R/3 connection).

   • To limit the comparison to specific key values, select *Enter selection requirements*.

   • To see only entries that differ between the two clients, select *Display differences only*.

   • To schedule the comparison as a background job, select *Background execution*—the results will be available as spool output only.

   • To limit the CPU required for the comparison, select *Restrict fields to be compared*.

3. To run the comparison, choose *Single comparison* (or *View/table* in releases prior to R/3 Release 4.5). Depending on what you selected in the previous step, you may be prompted for information regarding selection requirements or the restriction of the number of fields that will be compared.

4. The comparison list is displayed. The results are identical to those of a single comparison from within the Cross-System Viewer. For example, the status *L* indicates that the entry exists only in the current logon client and not in the comparison client.

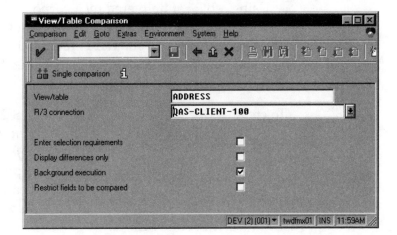

WARNING   In single comparisons using Transaction SCMP, restrict the number of fields to be compared if more than 500 entries are involved.

Business Configuration Sets

To create a reference of documented and proven settings, as of R/3 Release 4.5, you can preserve a copy of Customizing settings to a Business Configuration Set (BC Set) using Transaction SCPR2. A BC Set is useful, for example, in the following situations:

- During the testing of a new implementation phase, a BC Set from the previous implementation phase can be compared with current settings to highlight the differences and identify

Customizing settings that may impact existing processes in production.

• Customizing standards established by a corporate R/3 development system are often provided to subsidiaries in change requests. Because Customizing cannot be locked or protected, a local subsidiary can change corporate-delivered standards. Using a BC Set delivered by a corporate system, subsidiaries can periodically compare their current Customizing settings with the corporate standards recorded in the BC Set. Any discrepancies discovered must be resolved both locally and with the corporate development system.

To create a BC Set, use Transaction code SCPR2 or, from the R/3 initial screen, choose *Tools* ➤ *Business Engineer* ➤ *Customizing* ➤ *Tools* ➤ *Customizing objects* ➤ *Business Configuration Sets*. In the resulting IMG tree structure, select and copy the relevant Customizing activities. BC Sets can also be created on the basis of existing change requests. To create and display existing BC Sets, use Transaction code SCPR2.

NOTE   For more information on creating and changing Business Configuration Sets, see R/3 online documentation in R/3 Release 4.5. See also "Enhancements in Customizing: Business Configuration Sets, the Customizing Cross-System Viewer, and the Activity Log" by Matthias Melich in *SAP Professional Journal* (November/December, 1999).

Customizing Transfer Assistant

A new R/3 tool as of Release 4.5, the Customizing Transfer Assistant (Transaction SADJ) lets you compare the client-dependent changes that have been imported by a change request with the settings of the current client. The Customizing Transfer Assistant imports changes into a temporary, "holding" client and allows you to avoid importing individual changes that you may not want in the current client. This is useful in the following situations:

- An international implementation often involves the delivery of changes from a central development system to each of the subsidiaries. Because there is no protection against the overwriting of Customizing settings during import, a subsidiary may choose to import the changes from the central development system to a holding client and check the new settings against the client-dependent settings in the subsidiary's Customizing-and-development client. If the changes do not conflict with the local settings, they are transferred to the local Customizing-and-development client.

- Customizing efforts for a new implementation phase have been made in another R/3 System, such as a predevelopment system. To eliminate the need to redo these changes in the Customizing-and-development client in the development system, the Customizing changes from the predevelopment system are imported into a holding client, and the Customizing Transfer Assistant is used to adjust the settings in the Customizing-and-development client.

- During production support, emergency changes are made in the production system. These changes need to be made in the development system to ensure consistency. To avoid overwriting the changes currently being created in the development system for the next implementation phase, the production system changes can be imported into a holding client and checked with the Customizing Transfer Assistant.

WARNING   When importing changes to the holding client, ensure that you do not overwrite client-independent changes that apply to the entire R/3 System.

Before using the Customizing Transfer Assistant, set up an appropriate holding client. The Customizing Transfer Assistant creates a *worklist* to enable you to compare the Customizing objects in a change request of type *Customizing* that has been successfully imported into the holding client and therefore has the status of *released*.

After importing the change request to the holding client, to create the worklist, proceed as follows:

1. Log on to the client into which you will transfer Customizing changes.

2. Start the Customizing Transfer Assistant using Transaction code SADJ or, from the R/3 initial screen, by choosing *Tools ➢ Business Engineer ➢ Customizing ➢ Tools ➢ Customizing objects ➢ Customizing Transfer Assistant*.

3. Provide the change request ID that will be used to create the worklist. This change request ID must be a change request that has already been imported into the R/3 System in the comparison/holding client.

4. Choose *Create* to create the worklist.

5. The screen *Create New Worklist for Request to be Imported* appears, indicating the worklist ID (which you need, for example, to obtain the comparison results when the worklist is generated as a background job).

   • Provide a description for the worklist.

   • Provide the RFC connection to the comparison client.

6. To display the differences between the changes imported into the holding client and the corresponding Customizing entries in the logon client, choose *Determine status*. If the change request contains a large number of Customizing objects and will therefore require a lot of processing time, choose *Determine status in background*. Alternatively, to display a list of

objects that will be compared so that you can selectively initiate the comparison for particular objects, choose *Object list*.

Displaying and Transferring Differences

If not scheduled as a background job, the worklist is displayed immediately following the execution of the comparison. If the comparison has been scheduled in the background, to subsequently display the worklist, enter the worklist number in the Customizing Transfer Assistant (Transaction SADJ) and choose *Display*.

As when using the Customizing Cross-System Viewer, you can display more details by choosing *Single comparison*; you can display statistics; and you can filter the list. The first column of the resulting worklist, *Stat.*, indicates the *copy status* for each Customizing object. The copy status shows whether the object can be automatically transferred or, if the transfer is complete, whether it was successful. For an explanation of copy statuses, choose *Legend*.

By switching into change mode using *Display <-> Change*, you can copy entries from the comparison client to the current client. Copy options available from the menu using *Edit ≻ Copy* include:

Interactive: You perform the adjustment of single entries manually as described above, under "Adjusting the Customizing Differences between Clients."

Automatic direct: All differences are automatically transferred.

Autom. Background: Automatic adjustment is performed as a background job.

Review Questions

1. Which of the following requirements must be met before you can change both client-dependent and client-independent Customizing settings in a client?

   A. The client settings must allow for changes to client-independent Customizing objects.

   B. The client role must be *Production.*

   C. The system change option must be set to *Modifiable.*

   D. The client settings must allow for changes to client-dependent Customizing.

2. Which of the following statements are correct when project leaders and project team members receive only the recommended authorizations?

   A. Only developers can create change requests.

   B. Only project leaders can create change requests, and are therefore responsible for assigning project team members to change requests.

   C. Project team members can create and release change requests.

   D. Project leaders can release change requests.

3. Which of the following statements are correct with regard to Project IMGs?

   A. The Project IMG provides access to the Customizing activities defined for a particular project.

   B. Customizing is performed in the Project IMG tree structure.

   C. The Project IMG enables you to display project status information and document Customizing activities.

   D. All of the above.

4. Which of the following activities are performed using the Customizing Organizer?

   A. Viewing all Customizing change requests related to a particular user

   B. Viewing all Workbench change requests related to a particular user

   C. Viewing all change requests related to a particular user

   D. Managing change requests you own or reviewing change requests in which you have assigned tasks

5. Which of the following statements is correct in regard to Customizing?

   A. All Customizing activities in the IMG are client-dependent.

   B. All changes resulting from IMG activities can be transported.

   C. All Customizing changes are automatically recorded to a change request if the client change option is set to *Automatic recording of changes.*

   D. A Customizing activity may involve the creation of client-independent objects and therefore requires a Workbench change request.

6. Which of the following activities are performed using client comparison tools?

   A. Comparing the Customizing settings of two R/3 clients in the same R/3 System or in a different R/3 System

   B. Adjusting the Customizing differences between two different R/3 clients

   C. Transporting Customizing settings into the production client

   D. Comparing the objects listed in the object list of a change request with an R/3 client

CHAPTER
TWELVE

12

Promoting Change Requests

When you *promote* a change request, you release and export it. Often, the words *export* and *release* are used interchangeably. Technically, however, they are two different processes:

- The *release* process acts as a sign-off for the development or Customizing work in the task or change request. This process verifies ownership and user authorization for the respective changes—first at the task level, and then at the change request level. It also causes the respective Repository objects to be locked by the Workbench Organizer and copies a version history of them to the version database. You can release a change request only if all tasks belonging to the change request have been documented and released. Before releasing the change request, ensure that the changes it records have been unit tested and verified.

- The *export* process physically copies the objects and tables referred to in the change request from the R/3 database of the development system to a file in the transport directory at the operating system level. In addition, this process adds the change request to the import buffer of the target system defined by the relevant transport route.

This chapter covers the release process and export process, as well as documentation, unit testing, and version management. The topics are covered in the chronological order in which the activities are performed.

Documenting Change Requests and Tasks

SAP recommends that you write thorough documentation for all tasks in a change request while performing Customizing and development. This makes it easier to reconstruct the configuration process if necessary. The documentation is transported with the changes, thus becoming available in the quality assurance system, and is also a requirement for releasing the change request in the development system. In your documentation for change requests and tasks, you should include the following information:

- The purpose of the development or Customizing project
- The current status of the project (IMG status information is maintained within the Project IMG, not within change request documentation)
- Areas of responsibility and the people responsible, as well as contact people
- Sources of other documentation or instructions
- The expected impact of the changes on the implementation
- Interdependencies between this and other projects

The object lists of change requests and tasks indicate the objects that have changed. Action logs recorded by the R/3 System give you information on various activities, such as who created, released, or changed the ownership of a change request or task. The object list and documentation together with the action logs provide a detailed audit history of all changes made.

Creating and Changing Documentation

To create or change documentation for a task or change request, proceed as follows:

1. In the Customizing Organizer (Transaction code SE10) or the Workbench Organizer (Transaction code SE09), choose *Display*. The screen *Customizing Organizer: Requests* (or *Workbench Organizer: Requests*) is displayed, listing the change requests and tasks related to your user ID.

2. Position the cursor on the task or change request for which you want to write documentation. Choose *Goto* ➤ *Documentation*. The documentation maintenance screen is displayed.

3. Enter the detailed documentation and choose *Save*.

4. Choose *Back* to return to the change request hierarchy.

You can release a task only if it has been documented. Before a task or change request has been released, you can add documentation to it at any time. Once the task or change request is released, documentation cannot be changed.

When the task is released, the associated documentation is copied to the documentation of the change request containing the task. The documentation of the change request then contains its own documentation and the documentation of any of its released tasks. For example, suppose that there are two tasks in a change request, and both have been documented and released. Until the change request is released, the documentation for both tasks can be viewed and changed within the documentation of the change request.

Action Logs for Change Requests

In the *action log* of each change request, the R/3 System automatically logs the occurrence time and user responsible for the following actions in regard to that change request or any of its tasks:

- Creation
- Ownership change
- Deletion
- Release

To see the action log for a particular change request, position the cursor on the change request in the screen *Customizing Organizer: Requests* (or *Workbench Organizer: Requests*) and choose *Goto ➤ Action log*.

The action log of each change request is physically located as a separate log file in the transport directory *actlog*. The name of this log file is `<SID>Z<change request ID number>.<SID>`, where SID is the system ID of the system on which the change request was created. The change request ID number is a six-digit number beginning with 9. For example, the log file for the change request DEVK900747 is `DEVZ900747.DEV`. This log file is located at the operating system level and can be accessed from any R/3 System within the same transport group.

Unit Testing

Before releasing a change request or task, it should be unit tested as described in Chapter 6. For a change request, this means unit testing the combined contents of all tasks as a unit.

If unit testing is to occur in a unit test client, before performing testing, you must copy the client-dependent changes to the unit test client. Client-independent changes automatically impact all clients within the R/3 System and therefore can be verified by simply logging on to the unit test client and performing verification. As explained below, client-dependent changes may be of the following types:

- Client-dependent Customizing
- SAPscript styles and forms
- Variants

Client-Dependent Customizing

To unit test client-dependent Customizing changes in a client other than the one in which the changes were originally recorded to change requests, copy the changes into the applicable client using the client copy transaction *client copy according to a transp. request* (Transaction SCC1). This transaction enables you to verify the contents of your tasks before release. The owner of a change request can also use this transaction to verify the contents of the change request and all of its tasks before release.

You can only use Transaction SCC1 to copy the changed objects recorded in a change request or task from one client to another client in the same R/3 System.

Although Transaction SCC1 can be used to copy objects recorded in tasks and change requests that have been released, you should not release the respective change requests and tasks before using the transaction to perform unit testing. If unit testing reveals missing or incorrect Customizing settings, you can still record additional changes to the unreleased task or change request.

Copying Changes with Transaction SCC1

To use Transaction SCC1 to copy changes, you require the necessary authorizations in the unit test client for testing the relevant business processes, as well as the user authorization S_CLNT_IMP. Once you have the proper authorizations, log on to the unit test client—the client into which you wish to copy the recorded changes of a particular change request or task—and proceed as follows:

1. Use Transaction code SCC1 or, from the R/3 initial screen, choose *Tools* ➢ *Administration* ➢ *Administration* ➢ *Client Administration* ➢ *Special Functions* ➢ *Copy transport request*. The screen *Copy as per Transport Request* is displayed (see Figure 12.1).

2. Enter the source client ID number, as well as the ID of the change request or task to be copied.

3. If copying a change request, select the option *Incl. tasks for request* to ensure that changes recorded in unreleased tasks are also copied.

4. To start copying the change request, choose either *Execute* or *Execute in background*.

5. If you choose *Execute*, a dialog box appears indicating the number of objects to be copied. If this number is zero, no changes will be copied. In that case, choose *Cancel* and retry this procedure using a different change request or task ID.

FIGURE 12.1:

Client copy according to a transp. request (Transaction SCC1)

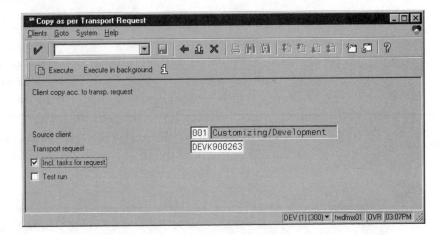

Reviewing the Log Files for Transaction SCC1

To review the log files generated by Transaction SCC1, proceed as follows:

1. Access the Client Copy Log using Transaction code SCC3 or, from the R/3 initial screen, by choosing *Tools* ➢ *Administration* ➢ *Administration* ➢ *Client administration* ➢ *Copy logs*.

2. Choose *Transport requests.* The screen displays the current status of all client copies based on a transport request (that is, a change request). These client copies are listed by the ID number of the target client.

3. Double-click the ID number of the client into which you copied changes using Transaction SCC1. The various log files for the copied change requests are displayed. The column *Transport* indicates the change request or task IDs.

4. To see more information on a client copy based on a change request, double-click the related change request or task ID.

SAPscript Styles and Forms

SAPscript is the word-processing functionality of R/3. At its core, there are *forms* (often referred to as *layout sets*) and *styles*. Forms are used to control page layouts. Styles are format definitions for paragraphs and characters that can be used to format the text itself. Although SAPscript styles and forms are client-dependent, when they are created or changed, they are recorded to a Workbench change request. To unit test styles and forms as of R/3 Release 4.0, you should use Transaction SCC1 to copy the styles and forms in the Workbench change request.

NOTE   In releases prior to R/3 Release 4.0, you cannot use Transaction SCC1 to copy SAPscript styles and forms from one R/3 client to another.

Alternatively, to copy SAPscript styles and forms from one client to another in the same R/3 System, use the *Copy from client* functionality provided by SAPscript. To do this in releases prior to R/3 Release 4.5, choose *Tools* ➢ *Word processing* ➢ *Form* ➢ *Utilities* ➢ *Copy from client.* As of R/3 Release 4.5, choose *Tools* ➢ *SAPscript* ➢ *Form* ➢ *Utilities* ➢ *Copy from client.*

Copy from client works only if the objects to be copied are not locked in a change request. By default, all Repository objects in a change request are locked. Before using *Copy from client*, you must either unlock the recorded objects or release the change request containing the objects. However, unlocking the recorded objects is time-consuming, and releasing the relevant change request prevents you from being able to add corrections to the change requests. For these reasons, as of R/3 Release 4.0, SAP recommends that you use Transaction SCC1 to copy SAPscript styles and forms from the client in which they are created to the unit test client.

Report Variants

Although R/3 programs (often referred to as *reports*) are client-independent, *report variants* are client-dependent. Report variants are used to record data that is supplied to an ABAP program so that you do not need to enter the same selections repeatedly. When report variants are created or changed, by default, they are not recorded to a change request. Since report variants are usually localized to the current environment and have little value for other clients, they are not usually transported. If needed, variants can be copied to other clients. In some cases, the variants must then be added to a change request for transport.

To copy variants to a unit test client, use one of the following techniques:

- From the unit test client, execute the program RSDBVCOP. This program copies variants from another client within the same R/3 System.

- In the client in which the variant was created, manually add the variant to a change request by creating the object-list entry LIMU VARX <program name><variant name>. Then, use Transaction SCC1 to copy the recorded variants in the change request to the unit test client.

| **NOTE** | For more information on how to transport variants, see R/3 Note 128908. |

Releasing a Task

Promoting changes recorded in a change request begins with releasing the relevant tasks. Releasing a task indicates that the owner of the task has completed his or her Customizing or development work, that unit testing was successful, and that the appropriate documentation is complete. The technical requirements for releasing a task are as follows:

- The task contains a recorded object.
- The task has been documented.
- You own the task (or you have authorization S_A.SYSTEM).

To release a task, proceed as follows:

1. To list the change requests that you are working on, in either the Workbench Organizer (Transaction code SE09) or the Customizing Organizer (Transaction code SE10), choose *Display.* The request overview is displayed.

2. To view all the tasks assigned to a particular change request, expand the tree structure. Position the cursor on the task you wish to release and choose *Release.*

3. If you have not yet entered documentation for the task, the documentation maintenance screen appears. Document your changes, save the documentation, and choose *Back.* (For more information on providing documentation, see "Creating and Changing Documentation" above.) If the task is successfully released, in the status bar, you will receive the message "Task <task ID> has been released to request <change request ID>."

4. Released tasks are highlighted with a particular color in the request overview. To see the color key, choose *Utilities* ➤ *Key*.

Release Errors

If the task cannot be released, an error message appears in the status bar to indicate, for example, that:

- The task can be released only by the owner of the task (or a user with the authorization profile SAP_ALL).

- The task cannot be released because it contains no recorded objects and has been classified as *Not Assigned* (as opposed to *Development/correction* or *Repair*).

If there is a more serious error, no message will appear in the status bar. Instead, the screen *List of entries cannot be locked* is displayed. Such errors may occur with development work in tasks belonging to Workbench change requests. Examples of these errors include:

Object locked in another request/task: Prior to release, all Repository objects in a task or change request require a Workbench Organizer lock. This message indicates that the Workbench Organizer cannot lock (and therefore release) objects in the task because the objects are already locked in another task or change request.

Transport object to target system <SID> only: The development class and its transport layer for objects in the task do not consolidate to the target system defined when the change request was created. For example, an object has a development class that consolidates to the quality assurance system, but the target for the change request is the training system. This means that, after the object was recorded to a task, someone manually changed the target system for the change request, or changed the transport routes for the development system using the TMS.

Correcting these errors may require you to:

- Modify the object list of a change request to acquire proper Workbench Organizer locks

- Change the target system for the change request

- Change the transport routes defined within the TMS

To remedy the problem, the owner of the task may need the assistance of the system administrator.

Releasing a *Repair*

When you release a task of type *repair*, a dialog box appears (see Figure 12.2), asking you whether the repair should be automatically confirmed. When a repair is confirmed, the repair flag for the objects in the task is deactivated. This allows the objects in the repair to be overwritten by future imports (see Chapter 10, under "Repairs and Modifications"). Confirming a repair implies that the changes comprising the repair have also been applied to the respective objects in the original system (or, for SAP objects, that they have been corrected by SAP). If you release a repair without automatic confirmation, you can confirm it at any subsequent time by choosing *Request/task* ➤ *Task* ➤ *Confirm repair* in the request overview. In the request overview, unconfirmed repairs are highlighted with a special color.

FIGURE 12.2:

The *Confirm repair automatically* option removes the repair flag automatically.

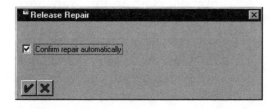

After a task of type *repair* is released, its objects can be edited by other users working in the same change request. In releases before R/3 Release 4.5, only the owner of a task containing a repair can change the repair object. To enable someone else to repair the object, either the task containing the repair must be released or the owner of the task must be changed.

Impact on the Change Request

When you release a task, the task object list and the relevant locks and documentation are automatically copied to the object list of the change request that contains the task. Before a task is released, the object list of a change request is empty (unless objects have been added manually).

Figure 12.3 demonstrates these processes. The task DEVK900266 in the Customizing change request DEVK900263 has been released. Prior to its release, no objects were listed at the change request level. After the release of the task, a *Comment* is added to the request overview, which, when the relevant node is expanded, indicates when the task was released.

You can also see this information in the object list of the change request. For example, in Figure 12.4, the object list entry *CORR RELE DEVK900181 19990813 001406 MCFARLAND* indicates that the task was released on August 8, 1999. The other two entries, the development class ZREPORTS and the ABAP program ZPRO-GRAM, are the contents of that task. In the column *ObjStatus*, these two Repository objects are indicated as locked. When a task containing R/3 Repository objects is released and its contents are transferred to its change request, the Workbench Organizer retains the locks on the respective objects.

FIGURE 12.3:

Upon release, the object list of a task is copied to the object list of its change request.

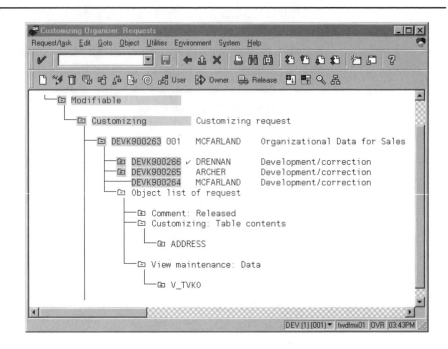

FIGURE 12.4:

Object list of a change request showing the released task and locked Repository objects

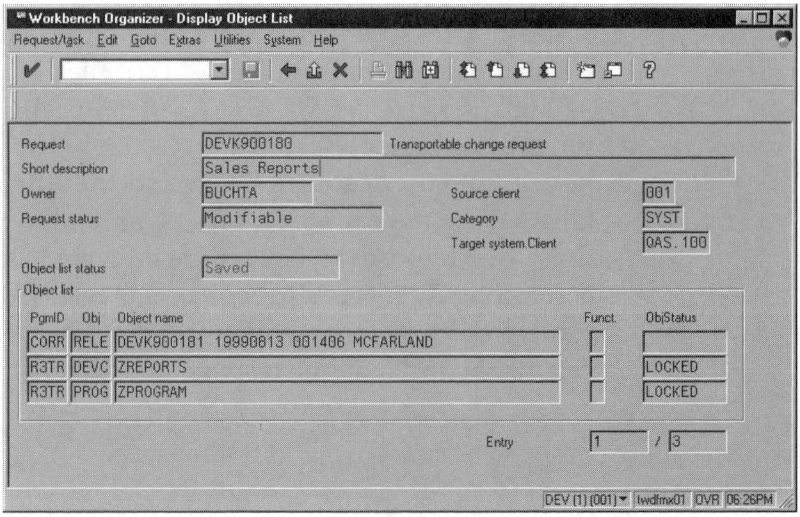

Releasing a Change Request

By releasing a change request, you indicate that it has sufficient documentation, the changes recorded in it have been unit tested, and the changes are ready to be transported using the TMS transport routes. During the export process triggered by the release, the objects recorded in the change request are copied from the R/3 database to a file external to R/3. This copy "freezes" the objects in their present state. In addition, a record of the change request is automatically added to the import queue of the defined consolidation system.

Releasing and exporting a single change request generates export logs and import logs. Testing in the quality assurance system and sign-off are necessary before import into the production system. To support the validation process and limit the technical and administrative overhead, SAP recommends merging change requests of a project prior to export.

Merging Change Requests

Combining multiple change requests into a single change request to create a testable unit is useful only if the change requests for a particular project are ready to be transported at the same time. This is usually the case when the change requests are related and need to be tested together.

To merge two change requests, the following requirements must be satisfied:

- You must own both change requests.
- The change requests must be of the same type—for example, a Customizing change request can be merged with only another change request of type *Customizing*.
- The change requests cannot have been released.

NOTE You cannot merge a task with a change request. A change request can be merged with only another change request.

To merge an unreleased or *modifiable* change request with another modifiable change request, proceed as follows:

1. In the Workbench Organizer (Transaction code SE09) or Customizing Organizer (Transaction code SE10), choose *Display*. The request overview is displayed, showing the change requests and tasks related to your user ID.

2. Position the cursor on the change request you wish to include in another change request. Choose *Request/Task ➢ Merge*. The *Merge Request/Task* window is displayed (see Figure 12.5).

3. Enter the change request ID of a second change request in the field *Include in request*. This change request will contain both merged change requests at the end of the merging process. Choose *Continue*.

FIGURE 12.5:

Merging two change requests

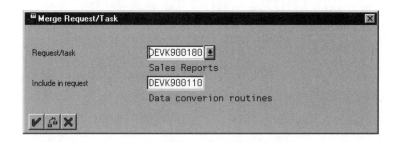

Only change requests of the same type can be merged using the above procedure. However, you can also combine a Customizing change request with a change request of type *transportable* (see Figure 12.6 in the next subsection).

Procedure for Releasing a Change Request

To release a change request you own, proceed as follows:

1. In the Workbench Organizer (Transaction code SE09) or Customizing Organizer (Transaction code SE10), choose *Display*. The request overview is displayed, showing the change requests and tasks related to your user ID.

2. Position the cursor on the change request you wish to release and choose *Release*. Depending on the type of change request, this results in the following:

   - For a Customizing change request, the window *Release Customizing Request* is displayed (see Figure 12.6). Select *Direct release and export* and choose *Continue*. (The other two options in the window are explained below.)

   - For a transportable change request, if the release is successful, this automatically starts the export process.

   - For a local change request, if the release is successful, this automatically results in the following message in the status bar: "Local request released (objects no longer locked)." The request is not exported.

3. When the export process starts, the screen *Overview of Transport Logs* appears, showing the transport logs specific to the change request. The export process has the status *In process*. You can wait for the export to complete or choose *Back* to return to either the Customizing Organizer or the Workbench Organizer. (Reviewing the transport logs to verify the success of an export process is explained below under "Transport Logs.")

FIGURE 12.6:

The three release
options for a Customiz-
ing change request

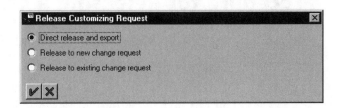

When you release a Customizing change request, the dialog box
Release Customizing Request (see Figure 12.6 just above) offers
three release options. Normally, you select *Direct release and
export*. Alternatively, you can release the change request to either
a new change request or an existing change request. The latter
options both prevent changes to the object list of the change
request, since the object list cannot be changed after a change
request is released. In addition, they combine the object list of this
change request with the object list of a *transportable* change
request. This is helpful, for example, if:

- A transportable change request was generated for the project
  as a result of client-independent Customizing activities, and
  you want to include the client-dependent Customizing
  changes in this change request.

- You wish to combine multiple Customizing change requests
  in a single transportable change request when you release
  them (this provides an alternative to the merge procedure
  described above).

TIP   A Customizing change can be merged into a transportable change
request at the time of release.

Release Errors

If a change request cannot be released, an error message will appear in the status bar indicating, for example, one of the following situations:

- There are tasks in the change request that have not been released. Before the change request can be released, all tasks in the change request must be released.

- The change request can be released only by the owner of the change request (or a user with the authorization profile SAP_ALL).

- Not all Repository objects in the request could be locked. The Workbench Organizer cannot lock an object that is already locked in another task or change request. Before the change request can be released, all R/3 Repository objects in the change request must have a Workbench Organizer lock.

- The transport routes defined from within TMS have changed since the change request was created. The target system for the change request is not defined in the TMS as a consolidation system; therefore, the change request cannot be released. To change the target system for the change request, in the request overview, position the cursor on the change request and choose *Request/task* ➢ *Display/change*.

- The development class and its transport layer for an object listed in a transportable change request no longer consolidate to the target system defined when the change request was created. To solve this problem, change the development class of the object, change the target system defined for the change request, or delete the object in the object list of the change request.

- A system administrator has disallowed release from the R/3 System. If you create the file T_OFF.ALL or T_OFF.<SID> in the transport directory *bin*, the release of change requests for either all R/3 Systems in the transport group or a specific R/3 System can be prevented. This option is useful when the target R/3 System is being upgraded or problems at the operating system level have been reported. If the export of change requests has been disallowed, the change request will not be released and exported, and will require the owner to release and export the change request later.

Object Checks

When you release either a transportable or a local Workbench change request, you can activate object checks that identify and display errors such as program syntax errors. This reduces the risk of importing "bad" Repository objects that will not be able to be activated or generated in the target systems.

If activated, these checks automatically run when you release a Workbench change request. They include a program check with Transaction SLIN, as well as an ABAP Dictionary check to verify that all ABAP Dictionary objects in the request have the status *Active*.

Activating Object Checks   As a user with the CTS administration authorization (S_CTS_ADMIN), you can either:

- Activate or deactivate the object checks for all users
- Leave it up to the user to decide whether to activate or deactivate the checks

To activate or deactivate the object checks, proceed as follows:

1. Use Transaction code SE03 or, from the R/3 initial screen, choose *Tools* ➢ *ABAP Workbench* ➢ *Overview* ➢ *Workbench Organizer* ➢ *Goto* ➢ *Tools*.

2. Expand the *Administration* hierarchy and double-click *Global Customizing Workbench Organizer*. The screen *Global Customizing Workbench Organizer* is displayed (see Figure 12.7).

3. Under *Object checks at request release*, select one of the following:

   Globally activated: This activates automatic checking of all objects before release.

   Globally deactivated: This deactivates automatic checking of all objects before release. A user cannot set the automatic checking of objects before release as an individual default.

   Can be set for specific user: This enables a user to use Transaction SE09 to set automatic object checking as their user default.

4. To save your settings, choose *Continue*.

FIGURE 12.7:

Global activation of transport error display and object checks in Transaction SE03

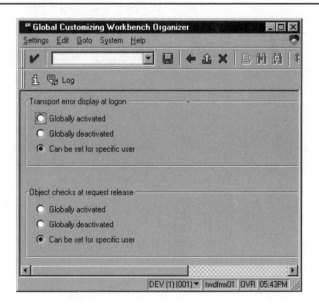

If the global option *Can be set for specific user* is set, individual users can activate or deactivate the checks themselves. From the initial screen of either the Customizing Organizer (Transaction SE10) or the Workbench Organizer (Transaction SE09), the user chooses *Settings* ➢ *Change & Transport Organizer* and selects *Check objects on request release.*

TIP   Regardless of whether object checks are activated globally, you can check the objects in a change request at any time. To do this, from the request overview of the Workbench Organizer, position the cursor on the appropriate change request or task and choose *Request/task* ➢ *Overall checks* ➢ *Objects (syntax check).*

If you have activated object checks, the objects in a Workbench change request are automatically checked at change request release. When you release the change request, if no previous object check for this change request has been run, the *Object checks* window appears (see Figure 12.8). You have the following options:

- Run the object check in the background. If the objects contain no errors, the release process is started automatically in the background. When the background processing is completed, a dialog box tells you that errors were found or that the change request was released.

- Run the object check in the foreground, which automatically displays the results of the checks. After this, you must complete the release of the change request manually.

- Cancel the object check and do not release the change request.

FIGURE 12.8:

Automatic object check prompt when releasing a Workbench change request

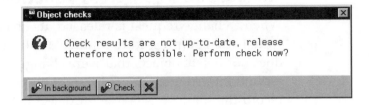

When the object check is finished, a *Results* dialog box informs you of any errors that were found. You can then:

- Continue the release process despite the errors

- Display the errors by double-clicking the specific check that generated the error

- Cancel the release process

Figure 12.9 shows a sample dialog box indicating the line of code in the ABAP program ZPECA that has produced an error.

FIGURE 12.9:

Object check reveals syntax errors in an ABAP program.

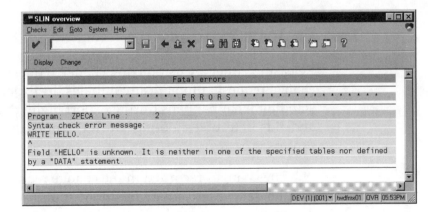

The *Sort and Compress* Function

When a change request is released, its object list is automatically sorted and compressed to remove duplicate entries. This process does not delete objects that were changed, but simply deletes redundant listings. Often, different users of a change request record the same objects in their object lists because they are pursuing overlapping objectives within the same Customizing or development project. Suppose, for example, that two tasks of a change request contain the object entry R3TR TABL ZNEWTABLE. When the tasks are released, the object list of the change request shows the entry twice. After the change request is released, thanks to the *sort and compress* function, the object occurs in the object list only once.

You can also manually initiate a *sort and compress* at any time. If you do this prior to releasing the change request, it may speed up the release process or prevent release failure due to a long runtime. To manually initiate a *sort and compress*, from the request overview in either the Customizing Organizer or the Workbench Organizer, choose *Request/Task* ➤ *Object list* ➤ *Sort and compress*.

The Export Process

Releasing either a Customizing change request or a transportable change request automatically initiates the export process. Understanding what happens during export highlights its significance and aids in troubleshooting. During export, the following processes occur:

1. The changes recorded in the change request are copied from the database to a data file in the transport directory at the operating system level. In addition, a control file and an export log file are created and written to the transport directory (see Table 12.1).

2. The change request is added to the import queue of the target system, which is typically the quality assurance system.

3. By default, a "test import" is performed in the target system. The test import verifies the connection to the target system's database and checks the objects to be imported.

4. The Workbench Organizer lock is removed for the objects in the object list of the exported change request, thus enabling them to be included in other change requests.

Table 12.1 provides details on the three files created in the transport directory: the data file, the control file, and the export log file.

TABLE 12.1: Transport Directory Files Created during the Export of a Change Request

Naming Convention	Transport Sub-Directory	Contents	Example: Files Created for Request DEVK900747
R<request #> .<SID>	data	Data file containing exported data	R900747.DEV
K<request #> .<SID>	cofiles	Control file with instructions for import and import history for the change request	K900747.DEV
<SID>E<request #> .<SID>	log	Log file with details about the success of the export process	DEVE900747.DEV

*The request # is the six-digit request number from the change request ID. By default, it begins with the number 9.
**The SID is the system ID for the source R/3 System from which the change request is released.

The programs *tp* and *R3trans* are used during the export process. The program *tp* manages the export of a change request and issues calls to *R3trans*. *R3trans* physically extracts the recorded changes from the database of the source R/3 System and writes the data file and the control file. Because the data files written to the transport directory are in *R3trans* format and not a database-specific format, the data file can be imported into any other R/3 System regardless of its database platform.

After writing the data file and the control file for a change request to the transport directory, the transport control program *tp* adds the change request to the end of the import buffer—to the file <SID> in the transport subdirectory *buffer*, where SID is the system ID of the target system. The target system is the consolidation system defined for the change request (typically, the quality assurance system).

Exported Data

Change requests record only what has changed and do not contain actual changed objects. The export of the change request physically copies the changed objects in their current state to a file in the transport directory at the operating system level. The data can be either an R/3 Repository object or table entries associated with Customizing.

To return to the example in Figure 11.8 (see Chapter 11), one of the Customizing changes recorded in the change request was a change to the sales organization PRNT. Exactly which table entries are copied by the export is determined by the primary key values recorded in the change request. The primary key of table TVKO consists of the client and the sales organization. The primary key values recorded in this change request are 001PRNT (where 001 is the client and PRNT is the sales organization). These values identify the table row that will be extracted during export.

Customizing change requests record table entries rather than entire tables. Since table entries are not locked, two users may change the same table entry. Regardless of whether the change was a creation or an edit, the primary key and the object list in each of the change requests will be identical. When the change requests are released and exported, the table row corresponding to the primary key will be extracted from the database. The data from this row as it appears at the time of export is saved to the transport directory and eventually imported into the downstream system. This is illustrated in the following example.

Example: Exporting Customizing Changes with the Same Primary Key

The user THOMAS creates a new plant called PHL1 with the description *Philadelphia*. Later, the user JANE decides to change the description of the plant PHL1 to *Philadelphia West*. Both users have saved their changes to different change requests.

What happens when user THOMAS releases and exports his change request depends on whether he releases and exports his change request before JANE makes her change.

- If the change request of THOMAS is released and exported before JANE makes her change, the data file in the transport directory will contain the description *Philadelphia* for plant PHL1.

- If THOMAS releases and exports after JANE has made her change, the data file in the transport directory will contain the description *Philadelphia West* for the plant PHL1.

Test Imports

In addition to entering the exported change request in the import buffer of the target system, by default, the transport program *tp* initiates a test import in the target system. The test import is not an attempted import so much as a screening of the objects to be imported. The test import process connects to the database of the target R/3 System and reviews the objects listed in the object directory. An error is indicated in the transport log file for the change request if (for any Repository object):

- The target system is the original system

- A repair flag is set in the target system

- The table into which data will be imported does not exist in the target system

If the error occurs because the target system is the original system, you may need to perform a nonstandard import or choose not to import the object to prevent overwriting the corresponding object. If a repair flag is the source of the error, this can be corrected by confirming the repair prior to importing the change request. A missing table in the target system is a serious problem and will require the transport of the table from the development system before the import of the change request that contains data for that table.

To perform a test import, the transport program *tp* must be able to connect to the target system's database. This is not possible if, for example, the target system has not been installed and is simply a virtual system, or if the target system is in a different network for security purposes. In such situations, you may wish to deactivate the test import functionality.

To deactivate the test import as the default setting, set the transport profile parameter *testimport* to FALSE. This parameter can be set either globally—for all R/3 Systems in the transport domain— or for a specific R/3 System. When setting the parameter for a specific system, set it in the source R/3 System and not in the target R/3 System. For example, to deactivate test imports into the quality assurance system, proceed as follows:

- In releases before Release 4.5, add the entry DEV/testimport= FALSE to the TPPARAM file.

- As of R/3 Release 4.5, use the TMS to set *testimport* in the transport parameter to FALSE for the development system (Transaction STMS; choose *Overview* ≻ *Systems*).

Authorizations

The release and export process is critical because it initiates the transport process for changed objects. Therefore, SAP recommends that only specific users be authorized to release change requests. As explained in Chapter 11, the relevant user authorization profiles are S_A.CUSTOMIZ (for the project team leader) and S_A.DEVELOP (for project team members). These authorizations enable a project leader to create and release change requests, and a team member to change and release only their own tasks.

Example: Using Authorizations to Control the Release and Export Process

A company initially allows all users in the development system to create and release change requests. The users inform the system administrator when a released change request is ready for import. The sequence in which change requests were imported is not taken into account.

During an important testing period, the quality assurance validation team reports several consistency problems with regard to the organization and functionality of basic business processes. After analyzing several problems, they discover that—since change requests are being imported on demand, out of sequence, and partly not imported—the quality assurance system has older versions of settings and is missing Customizing. Everyone agrees that the change requests require better management.

The idea of restricting the creation and release of change requests to the project leader is regarded as unrealistic. For this R/3 implementation, project

Continued on next page

leaders are focused on planning and are unavailable to handle the day-to-day activities of creating change requests. It is decided that all users should be able to create change requests. However, only specific users receive the authorization to release change requests or change the ownership of a change request and then release it. To release a change request, other users contact a power user, define the purpose of the change, and ask the power user to release the change request.

As a result of this new procedure, change requests are imported into the quality assurance system in the same order in which they are released—not simply whenever someone asks for a change request to be imported. This prevents older versions of settings from replacing the latest versions.

Transport Logs

The release and export of a change request is the beginning of its transport process, which is when the first transport log file—the export log file—is automatically generated. Transport log files reside in the transport directory and can be displayed within R/3 as follows:

- A system administrator can view all transport log files for a change request in an import queue. To do this, display the import queue of a particular R/3 System (Transaction STMS; *Overview* ➤ *Imports* ➤ *Import Queue* ➤ *Display*). Position the cursor on the change request and choose *Request* ➤ *Display* ➤ *Logs*.

- Any user can view all transport log files relating to a specific user. To do this, access either the Customizing Organizer (Transaction SE10) or the Workbench Organizer (Transaction SE09). Enter the relevant user ID and, under *Global information*, choose *Transports*.

- Any user can view all transport logs for a particular change request. To do this, call the Organizer Tools (Transaction SE03), drill down under *Request/task,* and choose *Display transport logs.* Enter a change request ID and choose *Enter.*

After you use any of these methods, the screen *Overview of all Transport Logs* is displayed (see Figure 12.10). This screen shows a tree structure of released change requests and the respective export and import processing steps, grouped according to target systems. The success of individual steps is indicated by the highlighting color, comment, and return code. (For more information on return codes for exports and imports, see Chapter 14.) If the change request was imported, the import log files for the various R/3 Systems are displayed.

Figure 12.10 shows the export steps for change request DEVK-900263. The operating system check finished without errors (*Ended OK*), as did the export of changes from client 001. In the quality assurance system, however, the test import was cancelled by the transport control program *tp* and therefore was not successful.

To see more information about the failure of a processing step, you can drill down to the associated error message or warning.

FIGURE 12.10:

Transport logs displayed in R/3

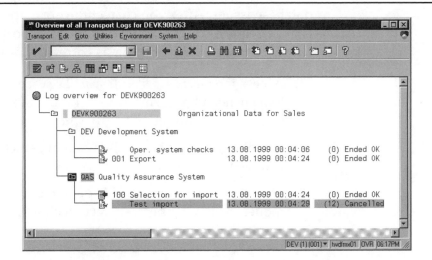

Managing Transport Logs

Managing the transport logs involves reviewing errors and possibly marking them as *corrected*, and deleting unnecessary transport logs.

If an error occurs in relation to either export or import, the corresponding change request receives the transport log status *Incorrect*. Incorrect change requests can easily be identified when you look at the overview of your transport logs—the incorrect change requests are flagged in red and appear at the top of the hierarchical list.

Over time, the number of transport logs associated with the various change request owners will increase. The only transport logs of interest are the most recent logs, not the logs either of the last implementation phase or that have received quality assurance sign-off. To facilitate your transport log analysis, you can delete old change requests from a user's list of transport logs.

Marking a Change Request as *Error Corrected*

To correct an error, the owner of the change request may have to release an additional change request, or a system administrator may have to intervene if the error concerns operating system or database issues. After you correct the error, the attribute of the change request can be changed in the transport log to *Error corrected*. To mark a transport log as corrected, proceed as follows:

1. Access the *Overview of Transport Logs* screen in either the Workbench Organizer (Transaction SE09) or the Customizing Organizer (Transaction SE10). Choose *Transports*.

2. Position the cursor on a change request whose error has been resolved and choose *Error corrected*.

3. The screen *Error corrected?* is displayed. To mark the change request as having been corrected, choose either *Yes* or *Yes*,

delete. If you choose *Yes, delete*, the change request will no longer appear in the overview of transport logs. If you choose *No* or *Cancel*, the status of the change request will not change.

If you choose *Error corrected* without reviewing the log file associated with the change request, a message is displayed indicating that the error has not been analyzed, and you will not be able to mark the error as corrected. This is a safety mechanism provided by SAP to ensure that you review the cause of all errors.

Marking a Change Request as *Tested*

After change requests have been successfully imported into the quality assurance system and tested, you should mark them in the transport logs as *Tested*. To do this, in the screen *Overview of Transport Logs*, select the change request and choose *Tested*. The change request can be either marked as tested or marked as tested and automatically removed from the transport log display.

Deleting Transport Logs

After a change request has been successfully imported into all R/3 Systems in the system landscape, there is no longer any need for the owner to review the change request's transport logs. Such logs should be periodically deleted by the owner of the change request. To delete an individual change request, in the screen *Overview of Transport Logs*, position the cursor on a change request and choose *Delete from display*. If you do not select a particular change request before choosing *Delete from display*, all tested or corrected change requests will be deleted.

TIP   Only change requests with the attributes *Error corrected* or *Tested* can be deleted from the transport log list.

When a user deletes the transport logs of a change request, they are only eliminated from the user's display. All log files associated with a change request will still reside in the transport directory at the operating system level and can be viewed within the R/3 System.

Displaying Transport Errors at Logon

By changing a default setting, you can cause transport errors to be automatically displayed when you log on to an R/3 System within the transport domain.

The release and export process is the responsibility of the person who released the change request. Therefore, it is the responsibility of the owner of the change request to monitor and correct transport errors, even if this requires the help of a system administrator. SAP recommends that you use the default setting that automatically informs users of failed exports and imports at the time of logon.

The dialog box that appears at logon to indicate the transport errors is shown in Figure 12.11. In this dialog box, you can select:

- *Continue* or *Cancel* to bypass viewing the errors and access the R/3 initial screen instead

- *Display* to see a list of transport logs for the affected change requests

- *Workbench Organizer* to go directly to the Workbench Organizer (Transaction SE09)

FIGURE 12.11:

Transport error notifi-
cation at logon

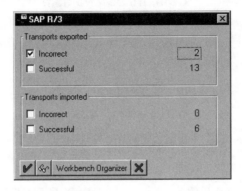

Activating the Automatic Display of Transport Logs at Logon

By default, errors during export or import are not displayed when a user logs on to an R/3 System. You can globally activate or deactivate the automatic display of transport errors at logon for all R/3 users, or you can allow users to make the automatic display one of their individual default settings.

If you are the system administrator (a user with the CTS administration authorization S_CTS_ADMIN) and you want to globally activate or deactivate the transport logs at logon, proceed as follows:

1. Use Transaction code SE03 or, from the R/3 initial screen, choose *Tools* ➢ *ABAP Workbench* ➢ *Overview* ➢ *Workbench Organizer* ➢ *Goto* ➢ *Tools*.

2. Drill down in the tree structure at *Administration* and double-click *Global Customizing Workbench Organizer*.

3. The screen *Global Customizing Workbench Organizer* appears (see Figure 12.7 earlier in this chapter). Choose one of the following options under *Transport error display at logon*:

   Globally activated: Transport errors will be automatically displayed at logon for all users.

Globally deactivated: The automatic display of transport errors is deactivated. A user cannot set the automatic display of transport logs as an individual default.

Can be set for specific user: Users can select the automatic display of transport errors as one of their individual default settings.

4. To save your settings, choose *Continue*.

If the option *Can be set for specific user* is set, to make the automatic display of transport errors one of your individual default settings, from the initial screen of the Customizing Organizer (Transaction SE10) or the Workbench Organizer (Transaction SE09), choose *Settings* ➢ *Change & Transport Organizer*. Select *Display transport errors at logon* and choose *Enter*.

Versioning for Repository Objects

When a change request is released, a version of each R/3 Repository object in the change request is added to the version database. This enables the release process to provide a complete change history for all Repository objects. Another automatically created version is the *active* version, which displays the current state of all active objects in the R/3 System. In addition to the automatically created versions, you can also create versions at any time, which are known as *temporary* versions.

The different types of versions are stored in two different sets of tables (two different databases) in the R/3 System database:

- The *version database*, which stores versions saved as a result of a released change request and temporary versions

- The *development database*, which stores the active version of an object (its current state in the R/3 System)

The version database is maintained in the development system, since this system is where R/3 Repository objects are created, changed, and released. If you discontinue a development system, you will lose all version history for all customer developments and modifications to SAP objects made in that system.

Version Management

You can access version management for a particular Repository object using any of the following:

- Repository Browser (Transaction SE80)

- Workbench Organizer (Transaction SE09)

- Display and maintenance transactions for Repository objects, such as the ABAP Editor for ABAP programs and the ABAP Dictionary for tables, domains, and data elements

For example, to view the versions maintained for the ABAP program ZPROGRAM, proceed as follows:

1. Access the ABAP Editor using Transaction code SE38 or, from the R/3 initial screen, by choosing *Tools* ➤ *ABAP Workbench* ➤ *ABAP Editor*.

2. Enter the name of the ABAP program whose versions you wish to view.

3. Choose *Utilities* ➤ *Version management*. The versions stored for the ABAP program are displayed (see Figure 12.12).

FIGURE 12.12:

Versions of an ABAP program

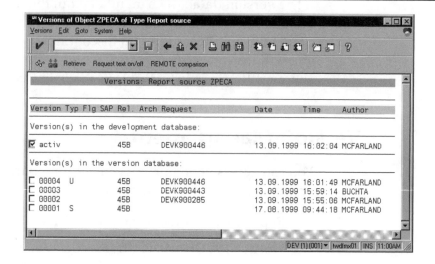

The display of versions for a Repository object includes both the version in the development database and the versions in the version database. If, as in Figure 12.12, a change request ID is indicated for the active version, the object is currently locked by the change request and was changed by the indicated user. If no change request ID appears for the active version, the object is currently not recorded to a change request and not locked by the Workbench Organizer.

Versions in the version database are numbered starting with 0001. The first version for a customer object will always be of type *S*, indicating that it is the original creation of the object. Because most versions in the version database are the result of a released change request, the change request number and owner of the change request are also indicated.

Temporary versions are indicated as type *U*. These versions are created if, when maintaining an object, you use the option *Generate version*. In the ABAP Editor, for example, you would choose *Program ➤ Generate version*. Temporary versions are deleted when a change request is released, since releasing a change request writes a permanent version to the version database.

From the display of versions for an R/3 Repository object, you can:

- Display a particular version by selecting the version and choosing *Display*.

- Compare two different versions by selecting the two versions and choosing *Compare*. A split screen will show the differences between the two versions.

- Restore a version by selecting the version and choosing *Retrieve*. This causes the currently active version to be overwritten by the older version you select. If the object is not already recorded to a change request, you must record the change to a change request. To use *Retrieve*, the Repository object's maintenance screen must be in change mode.

Versions in Nondevelopment Systems

By default, R/3 Repository objects are not versioned upon import. This restricts version histories to the development system. The quality assurance and production systems have only the currently active version for each Repository object. This version indicates the change request that caused the import of the object, but cannot be used to display or compare older versions.

Versions cannot be transported between R/3 Systems. Because versions reside only in the development system, if the development system is removed from the system landscape, all versions in the version database are lost.

WARNING In releases prior to R/3 Release 4.5, versioning stored in the development system cannot be preserved if the development system is removed from the system landscape or overwritten with a database copy from another R/3 System.

As of R/3 Release 4.5, you can create versions at import, enabling you to preserve your version history for all Repository objects if the development system is removed from the system landscape or overwritten with a database copy. If versioning upon import is activated, when you import change requests into an R/3 System, versions of the imported objects are added to the version database of that R/3 System.

Versioning at import can be achieved by setting the transport parameter *vers_at_imp* to either C_ONLY or ALWAYS. The value C_ONLY causes only relocation transports (see Chapter 10) to create versions in the target system. The value ALWAYS makes all imports create versions. This transport parameter can be set specifically to an R/3 System or globally for all systems.

NOTE Activating versioning at import increases the number of import processing steps during the import of a change request. To minimize the amount of time required for import into the production system, you may wish to avoid activating versioning at import for that system.

Review Questions

1. Which of the following is a prerequisite for copying client-dependent changes to a unit test client using a *client copy according to a transp. request* (Transaction SCC1)?

    A. The change request has been released.

    B. The tasks have been released, but the change request has not.

    C. The tasks have been released after successful unit testing by the owner of the task.

    D. The change request has not been released.

2. Which of the following are the result of releasing a task?

   A. A data file is created in the transport directory and contains the objects recorded in the change request.

   B. The object list and documentation for the task are copied to the change request.

   C. All objects recorded in the task are locked.

   D. You can no longer save changes to that task.

3. Which of the following are the result of releasing and exporting a change request?

   A. A data file is created in the transport directory to contain copies of the objects recorded in the change request.

   B. Versions are created in the version database for all R/3 Repository objects in the object list of the change request.

   C. All repairs recorded in the change request are confirmed.

   D. You can no longer save changes to that change request.

4. When you release a Customizing change request, you have the option to do which of the following?

   A. Release the change request to another Customizing change request.

   B. Schedule the release of the change request for a later time.

   C. Release the change request to a transportable change request.

   D. Initiate immediate release and export.

5. Which of the following is a prerequisite for releasing a transportable change request?

   A. There are no syntax errors in the ABAP programs recorded to the change request.

   B. You must own the tasks in the change request.

C. All Repository objects in the change request are locked by the change request.

D. The change request has documentation.

6. The export process initiates which of the following activities?

    A. The creation of files in the transport directory

    B. The automatic import of change requests into the target system—for example, the quality assurance system

    C. The addition of the exported change request to the import buffer of the target system

    D. The deletion of the change request within the R/3 System

7. Which of the following activities result in a version history for all Repository objects?

    A. A Repository object is recorded to a change request.

    B. Change requests are imported into an R/3 System, and the transport parameter *vers_at_imp* is activated.

    C. A task containing a Repository object is released.

    D. A change request containing a Repository object is released.

CHAPTER
THIRTEEN

Importing Change Requests

The Transport Management System (TMS) provides customers with a tool for importing change requests from within R/3. Although transports using operating system tools cannot always be avoided at R/3 Release 4.0, improvements in R/3 Release 4.5 almost completely eliminate the need for transports at the operating system level.

The information in this chapter prepares you to:

- Understand import queues

- Perform imports

- Manage import queues

- Schedule imports

- Monitor imports

- Transport between transport groups and transport domains

NOTE   Before reading this chapter, you may wish to reread the sections related to imports and TMS in Chapters 6 and 8.

Understanding Import Queues

The most important tools for performing imports using the TMS are the *import queues,* which reflect the same information in R/3 as the system-specific *import buffers* at the operating system level. (For more information on import buffers, see Chapter 14.) The import queue displays the change requests that are to be imported, in the order of their export.

In the TMS (Transaction STMS), you will find two screens that are relevant to the import queues: *Import Overview* and *Import Queue.*

Import Overview

The *Import Overview* screen shows the import queues of all R/3 Systems in the transport domain (see Figure 13.1). To access the import overview, from the TMS initial screen (Transaction STMS), choose *Overview* ➤ *Imports*.

FIGURE 13.1:

The import overview

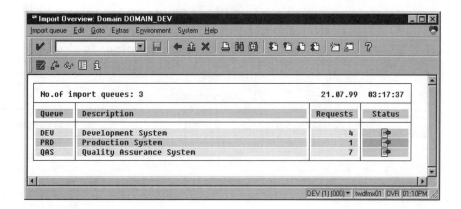

In the import overview, the column *Requests* contains the number of change requests ready to be imported. This number may differ from the total number of requests listed in the import queue for the following reasons:

- The change requests occur after an end mark in the import queue. The system administrator can set the end mark to separate the change requests that will be transported in the next import from those change requests that will not be included in the next import.

- The change requests are excluded from being imported due to certain parameter settings in the transport profile; for example, the transport profile parameter *sourcesystems* in the transport profile for the target system is set and does not include the source system for some of the change requests in the import queue. (See Appendix B for more information on the transport parameter *sourcesystems*.)

- The change requests have already been imported—for example, change requests that belong to a client copy—and have not yet been deleted from the import queue.

The column *Status* in the *Import Overview* screen indicates the current status of each import queue in the transport domain. For an explanation of the colors and symbols indicating the status, from the *Import Overview* screen, choose *Extras* ➢ *Legend*. Each combination of colors and symbols is also explained in Table 13.1.

TABLE 13.1: Status Information of Import Queues

Symbol	Color	Status	Explanation
	Green	Import queue is open.	New change requests can be added and will be imported during the next import.
	Green	Import queue is closed.	The import queue is closed, and the system has set an end mark. All change requests before the end mark will be imported during the next import.
	Green	Import is running.	All change requests before the end mark are currently being imported.
	Yellow	Errors occurred during import.	Errors occurred during import, but the import did not terminate.
	Red	Import was terminated.	Serious errors occurred during import, and the import terminated.
	Red	Import queue could not be read.	To determine why an import queue could not be read, click the symbol. One reason may be that certain files could not be accessed on the operating system level.

Import Queue

To display the import queue of an R/3 System, in the *Import Overview* screen, position the cursor on the R/3 System and choose *Import Queue* ≻ *Display*. The import queue lists the change requests in the order in which they will be imported; as a rule, this is the order in which they have been exported. The owner and the related short text are also indicated for each change request (see Figure 13.2).

FIGURE 13.2:

Import queue for a particular R/3 System

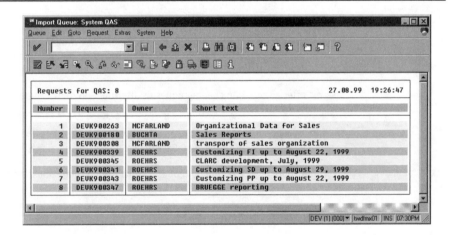

The colors and symbols used in the *Import Queue* screen indicate the status and type of change request. For an explanation of these colors and symbols, choose *Extras* ≻ *Key* (Release 4.0) or *Extras* ≻ *Legend* (Release 4.5). Although the colors and symbols differ from R/3 Release 4.0 to 4.5, the available status information is the same (see Table 13.2).

TABLE 13.2: Status Possibilities for Change Requests in an Import Queue

Status	Explanation
Request waiting to be imported	The change request will be imported during the next import.
Request was already imported	The change request is displayed in the import queue, but will not be imported with the next import—for example, because it was already imported with a client import or as an individual import with the preliminary import option deselected (see below, under "Preliminary Imports").
Request was already transported	The change request was already imported as a preliminary import. To ensure consistency, it will be imported again during the next import of the entire queue.
Request will not be imported	The settings for specific transport profile parameters prevent import of the change request. For example, if the transport profile parameter *k_import* is set to FALSE, all Workbench change requests are excluded from the import, but will still be displayed in the import queue.
Request after end mark	The change request is after the end mark. Therefore, the change request will not be imported during the next import.
SAP Hot Package	The change request is an SAP Support Package that can only be applied using the SAP Package Manager (Transaction SPAM). (See Chapter 15.)
Client transport	The change request results from a client transport and must be imported individually (see Chapter 9).

Additional Display Options

For further information about the import settings for change requests, in the *Import Queue* screen, choose *Edit* ➤ *Display more*. The screen displays two additional columns (see Figure 13.3 later in this section):

- Column *I*, which contains the data known as the *tp* import flag
- Column *U modes*, which indicates the import options related to each change request

In column *I*, the value of the *tp* import flag (also known as the tp *import indicator*) is specified. It reflects the type of change request and under what conditions a change request is or is not imported. To display a short description of the various import flags, position the cursor in column *I* and choose **F4**. The most common import flags are a *w* indicating a Customizing change request and a *k* representing a Workbench change request. If either of these letters is capitalized, it indicates that the change request is excluded from transport.

To prevent the import of Workbench change requests into an R/3 System—for example, to supply client-dependent changes back to a client in the development system without impacting client-independent efforts—you would set the transport profile parameter *k_import* to FALSE. All Workbench change requests added to the import queue for the development system would have the import flag *W*. (See Appendix B for more information on the transport profile parameter *k_import*.)

On the operating system level and in R/3's TMS, you can assign *import options* to your imports to override specific rules of the Change and Transport System (CTS). These import options are also known as *unconditional modes.* You can access these import options in the TMS through the *expert mode* (see below). In Figure 13.3 (later in this section), the single character in the column *U modes* denotes the import option assigned to a change request. For details on import options on the operating system level, see Chapter 14.

R/3 Release 4.5 display Settings   In R/3 release 4.5, to display information on the import status, from the *Import Queue* screen, choose *Extras ➢ Settings ➢ Display return code.* The result of an import for a change request is indicated by the *maximum return code* as depicted in column *RC* in the *Import Queue* screen (see Figure 13.3). Every import activity results in a return code in the TMS. The return code may warn you about problems with the target R/3 System or about an error that has occurred during import. The system collects all the return codes and displays the *maximum* return code—the code with the highest numerical value. For example, the return code 0004 represents a warning, whereas 0000 indicates that the import was successful. If you import the entire queue and these two return codes are collected, the 0004 will be displayed to alert you of the warning (see Chapter 14).

To display the source client in column *N* of a change request, from the *Import Queue* screen, choose *Extras* ➤ *Settings*➤ *Display source client*.

If the transport domain is running with extended transport control in R/3 Release 4.5, the *Import Queue* screen also shows the target client in the column *Clt* (see Figure 13.3).

Display Details of a Change Request   In addition, if you position the cursor on a change request and choose *Request* ➤ *Display* in the *Import Queue* screen, you can display further details about the import queue, such as:

- *Object list*

- *Owner*

- *Documentation*

- *Logs* (export and import log files)

Bear in mind that not all log files can be displayed when you are dealing with different transport groups (see Chapter 7). See also the section "Transporting between Transport Groups" later in this chapter.

FIGURE 13.3:

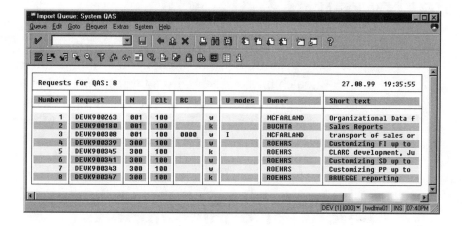

FIGURE 13.3:

Additional display
options in the import
queue

Refreshing the Import Queue

To improve performance, data is read from the transport directory only the first time you access the TMS. After that, the data in
the import overview and import queue is buffered in the database
of the R/3 System. The time stamp in the screen indicates how
recent the data is. The internal buffers of the TMS become invalid
each day at 0:00.

To refresh the data in the display, from either screen, choose *Edit*
➤ *Refresh*. It may be more convenient to have the data refreshed
periodically in the background. To do this, schedule the report
RSTMSCOL to run at regular intervals in the R/3 Systems in
which you frequently use the TMS. SAP recommends scheduling
RSTMSCOL to run hourly.

Performing Imports

Importing is when you bring exported R/3 changes into another R/3 System. Because there is no automatic mechanism for importing a change request into a target system, you have to use the tools provided in the TMS or on the operating system level. The procedure for using the TMS is covered in this chapter. For information on performing imports at the operating system level, see Chapter 14.

Before Performing Imports

Before starting an import, you should ensure that the transport environment is set up to properly fulfill your particular import needs. By taking certain precautions, you can facilitate the import procedures and avoid unnecessary work.

You should always check the import queue for SAP Support Packages and change requests resulting from client transports. The changes included in a Support Package and a client transport depend on their sequence in the import queue and should be imported accordingly. However, they are not imported using standard *import all* or preliminary import steps. For example, Support Packages have to be imported using the SAP Package Manager (Transaction SPAM) as described in Chapter 15. Change requests resulting from a client transport are imported together and should always be imported before you import the change requests that follow in the import queue (see Chapter 9).

Setting a Target Client

During import, change requests are by default imported into the client that has the same client ID as the source client. For example, change requests released from client 110 in the development system are by default imported into client 110 in the quality assurance system. If this does not satisfy your import needs, you must specify the required target client ID during the initial steps of an import. At that time, a dialog box appears—either *Import Transport Request* for individual requests or *Start Import* for imports of entire queues—allowing you to enter a target client ID.

NOTE   If you have not set the target client, the change requests will be imported into the client that has the same number as the source client.

Target Clients with Extended Transport Control

When extended transport control is activated, there is no need to specify the target client's number in the dialog boxes *Import Transport Request* and *Start Import*. Extended transport control with R/3 Release 4.5 requires that transport routes specify client and system combinations; therefore, every change request in the import queue will have associated with it the client ID into which it needs to be imported. You do not have to provide a target client. Figure 13.3 (earlier in the chapter) displays an import queue for the system QAS. The fourth column, *Clt*, indicates the target client and also tells you that extended transport control is currently activated for this system landscape.

When extended transport control is activated, there is the possibility that change requests in an import queue do not have a target client specified. For example, if you activate the extended transport control while there are still change requests in any of the import queues, the requests will not have a target client specified. The column *Clt* will be highlighted in red. You cannot perform any operations on the import queue until you specify a target client for these old requests.

To set a target client for a change request:

1. From the *Import Queue* screen, mark the respective change request.

2. Choose *Request* ➤ *Target client* ➤ *Set*.

3. Enter the target client ID and choose *Enter*.

To change a specified target client before starting an import, proceed as follows:

1. From the *Import Queue* screen, mark the respective change request.

2. Choose *Request* ➤ *Target client* ➤ *Change*.

3. Enter the target client ID and choose *Enter*.

The advantage of extended transport control is that you can ensure change requests are delivered to all clients in your system landscape in their correct sequence. Because change requests now have an additional indicator in the import queue—the target client—you can choose to specifically import only the change requests destined for a particular target client by setting a *target client filter*.

To set a target client filter, follow these steps:

1. From the *Import Queue* screen, choose *Edit* ➤ *Target client filter*.

2. Enter the target client ID and choose *Enter*.

Closing the Import Queue by Setting an End Mark

You can close an import queue and set an end mark at the end of the import queue. All change requests that are released after the import queue is closed are added to the end of the import queue in their correct sequence—but after the end mark. This will prevent these recently released change requests from being imported during the next import activity. When an import of all waiting requests is started, all the change requests before the end mark will be imported. SAP recommends freezing certain states of development and Customizing using this closing technique.

To close the import queue, from the *Import Queue* screen, choose *Queue* ➤ *Close*. Similarly, to open an import queue, choose *Queue* ➤ *Open*. This removes the end mark.

If you do not close the import queue manually, the initial step in the import procedure is to close the import queue. The transport control program will automatically close the import queue and set the end mark. After the import, the queue is opened again automatically, and the end mark is removed. Setting an end mark at the end of the import queue is necessary to protect the import process from additional change requests while in the middle of performing import steps.

Import All

Once you have verified the target client settings and have closed the import queue, you are ready to start your import. To initiate an import, use the TMS option *Start import* (explained below), which is also referred to as *import all* because it imports all change requests waiting to be imported. Importing a collection of change requests waiting to be imported ensures that the objects are imported in their correct sequence—the sequence in which they were released and exported from the development system. (See the section "Sequence in Import Queues" in Chapter 4 and "Importing Change Requests" in Chapter 6.)

Imports can be started from any R/3 System in the transport domain. If you start the import from an R/3 System other than the target system, you will be required to log on to the target system. Following logon, the TMS starts the transport control program *tp* in the target system. For the duration of the import, *tp* continues to run in the background so that the user session is not blocked.

After the import, the queue is opened again automatically, and the end mark is removed.

To import all change requests waiting to be imported in the import queue of an R/3 System, perform the following steps:

1. From the TMS initial screen (Transaction STMS), choose *Overview* ➤ *Imports*.

2. Mark the system into which you want to import, and choose *Import queue* ➤ *Display*.

3. From the *Import Queue* screen, choose *Queue* ➤ *Start import*.

4. The dialog box *Start Import* appears. If necessary, enter the target client number.

5. If special import options are required, choose the *Expert mode* icon (see below).

6. Choose *Continue* to initiate the import procedure.

Once change requests have been imported successfully into a system defined as the source system of a delivery route, the change requests are automatically added to the import queues of the respective target R/3 Systems. The transport route configuration specifies which change requests are automatically delivered to which target systems.

Expert Mode

The *expert mode* for an *import all* allows you to handle special import requirements, such as reimporting change requests and overwriting objects. To use the expert mode, select one of the following required import options in the *Start Import* dialog box (mentioned above) and then choose *Continue:*

Select all requests for new import (or Flag all requests for further import for releases prior to R/3 Release 4.5):
When you select this option, all imported change requests

are kept in the import queue after the import instead of being deleted immediately. In this way, they can be imported into further clients in the R/3 System (see the section "Importing into Multiple Clients"). This import option is similar to the preliminary import option when importing single change requests (see below).

Overwrite originals: If a change request contains objects that originate in the target system, the import overwrites the existing original in the target system.

Overwrite objects in unconfirmed repairs: If a change request contains objects that are currently being repaired in the target system and not yet confirmed, the import ignores the repair and overwrites the object in the target system.

WARNING   SAP recommends using expert mode options only when necessary. Expert mode selections should not be used during every import of an import queue.

Preliminary Imports

As an alternative to importing entire import queues, you can also import single change requests. This is called a *preliminary import* because it enables you to send one change request as a preliminary through the defined transport route. To minimize the risks associated with preliminary imports, the request remains in the import queue and is reimported the next time the entire import queue is imported. This helps to ensure that export and import sequences are always the same.

> **WARNING** To ensure object dependencies and consistency, SAP strongly recommends importing all or a collection of sequenced change requests. You should limit your use of preliminary imports to exceptional situations.

In R/3 Release 4.0, individual change requests can only be imported as preliminary imports using TMS. As of R/3 Release 4.5, the default setting for importing individual change requests is to perform preliminary imports—although you also have the option of deselecting this function in expert mode (see below).

To import a single change request, perform the following steps:

1. In the *Import Queue* screen, mark the change request to be imported.

2. Choose *Request* ➤ *Import*.

3. The dialog box *Import Transport Request* appears. If necessary, enter the target client number.

4. If you wish to select special options, choose the *Expert mode* icon (see below).

5. Choose *Continue*.

Multiple Change Requests

As of R/3 Release 4.5, you can select multiple change requests to be imported using a preliminary import. Choose the change requests you wish to import by positioning your cursor on the change request and either choosing *Edit* ➤ *Select* ➤ *Select Request* or pressing **F9**. Once the change requests have been selected, perform a preliminary import as described above. Each highlighted change request is imported one after the other—they are not imported as a collection of change requests as with an *import all* (see the section "*tp* Processing Sequence" in Chapter 14).

TIP
If a transport domain contains at least one R/3 System of R/3 Release 4.5A or higher, the import of multiple change requests in a preliminary import is possible for the R/3 Releases prior to Release 4.5A as well.

Expert Mode

If you have special import requirements for your preliminary import, use the expert mode. The expert mode for preliminary imports allows you to specify:

- *Import options*
- *Execution type*

WARNING Setting import options during the import of change requests should be done in exceptional situations only.

Import Options   In expert mode, you can select the following import options:

Prelim. Import of transport req **(as of R/3 Release 4.5):** When performing a preliminary import, the default setting is that the change request remains in the import queue and is reimported when you import the entire queue. This import option is selected by default. In releases prior to R/3 Release 4.5, you cannot deselect this option; therefore, all individually imported change requests from within TMS are left in the import queue for reimport. However, with R/3 Release 4.5, you are able to deselect this option. The change request remains in the import queue, but is not imported again with the next import of all waiting requests. To remove such a change request, you must manually delete the change request from the import queue.

WARNING To ensure consistency and object dependencies, SAP strongly recommends that you do not deselect the preliminary import option.

Ignore that the transport request was already imported:　If a change request has already been imported into the target system, this option allows you to import it again without error.

Overwrite originals:　If a change request contains objects that originate in the target system, the import overwrites the existing original in the target system.

Overwrite objects in unconfirmed repairs:　The import ignores any repairs and overwrites unconfirmed objects in the target system (see above, under "Import All").

Ignore invalid transport type:　This option overrides the transport profile parameters that exclude a transport type. For example, if the transport profile parameter *k_import* is set to FALSE, Workbench change requests (type *k*) are excluded from being imported. If this option is selected, transport profile parameters restricting the type of imports will be ignored, and, in this case, imports of Workbench change requests will be possible.

Execution Types　In the expert mode for preliminary imports from within TMS, there are two selections for the execution of the import:

- *Start import in foreground*

- *Start import in background*

By default, individual imports are set to start in the foreground. It is unlikely that performing an import in the foreground will exceed the dialog work process runtime (300 seconds), because work process time is consumed only for receiving and displaying *tp* status messages, not for the entire time *tp* is actually running. Therefore, starting the import in the background makes sense only if you do not want to have the user session locked.

Managing Import Queues

To help manage single and multiple change requests, additional functionality is provided from within the *Import Queue* screen. To use the selection option, choose *Edit* ➤ *Select*. You can use the following functionalities:

- Forwarding a change request

- Deleting a change request from an import queue

- Adding a change request to an import queue

- Moving the end mark in an import queue

- Performing checks on the import queue

TIP As of R/3 Release 4.5, you are able to select multiple change requests in an import queue prior to performing different functions on those change requests. In earlier releases, only a single change request can be selected.

Forwarding a Change Request

The TMS enables you to manually forward a change request. When you *forward* a change request, you add it to the import queue of a selected R/3 System. The target of a forwarded change request can be an R/3 System or—with extended transport control in R/3 Release 4.5—a specific client within an R/3 System. Forwarding of a change request is used to add a change request to an import queue outside the predefined transport routes and therefore should be used only in exceptional cases.

To forward a change request to a target system outside the predefined transport routes, proceed as follows:

1. From the *Import Queue* screen, mark the respective change request.

2. Choose *Request* ➤ *Forward* ➤ *System* (or *Request* ➤ *Forward* for R/3 Releases prior to Release 4.5). Provide the name of the R/3 System to which the change request should be forwarded. If extended transport control is active, you will be required to forward the change request to a client and system combination.

As of R/3 Release 4.5, you can forward a request into a specific client of the same system. To do this, from the *Import Queue* screen, choose *Request* ➤ *Forward* ➤ *Client*.

If the source and the target systems belong to different transport groups, you must adjust the import queue of the target system. For more details on adjusting import queues, see the section "Transporting between Transport Groups" later in this chapter.

Example: Forwarding a Change Request

A company has a four-system landscape that consists of the systems development, quality assurance, production, and training. The development system consolidates to the quality assurance system. A delivery route is specified between the quality assurance system and the production system, and then between the production system and the training system.

A program included in a change request is imported into the quality assurance system. It is urgently needed in the training system, but an import into the production system is not possible at this time. A manual forward of the change request that contains the respective program is performed to rush it to the training system before it has been imported into the production system.

Deleting a Change Request from an Import Queue

To delete a change request from an import queue, mark the change request in the *Import Queue* screen and choose *Request* ➢ *Delete*.

Object dependencies may cause inconsistencies in the target system after the next import. For example, if you delete a request containing a new data element, all other requests containing tables that depend on that data element will fail.

WARNING   To avoid inconsistencies, you are strongly advised not to delete individual change requests. Make your corrections in the development system and release a new request instead.

There are situations in which deleting change requests from an import queue is necessary. These situations include:

- Change requests from a client transport. After successful import of a client transport, the change requests for that client transport still remain in the import queue and will need to be deleted (see Chapter 9).

- In R/3 Release 4.5, if you have deselected the preliminary import option when importing a single change request, the change request will remain in the import queue and will need to be manually deleted after import. To do so, from the *Import Queue* screen, select the change request that has the status *Request was already imported* and choose *Extras* ➢ *Delete imported requests*.

Adding a Change Request to an Import Queue

If you have manually copied a change request to the transport directory or if you wish to reimport a change request that is no longer in the import queue, you must manually add the change request to the respective import queue. To do this, choose *Extras* ➤ *Other requests* ➤ *Add*. Provide the change request ID for the change request to be added and choose *Enter*. Note that if extended transport control is active, you will also have to enter a target client ID.

Moving an End Mark

When an import queue is closed, an end mark is added at the very end of the import queue. To move the end mark to another position within the import queue, position the cursor on a change request and choose *Edit* ➤ *Move end mark*. The end mark will then be positioned above the selected change request. For example, Figure 13.4 shows the result of selecting change request DEVK900345 and then performing a *Move end mark*.

FIGURE 13.4:

Moving an end mark

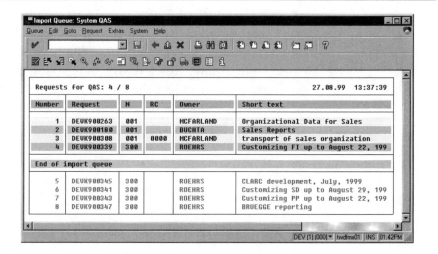

Performing Checks

To ensure that your import runs smoothly, you should run checks on the import queue before performing the import. To start these checks, from the *Import Queue* screen, choose *Queue* ➢ *Check*. Then, choose one of the following checks:

- *Consistency*
- *Transport tool*
- *Critical objects* (as of R/3 Release 4.5)

Consistency Check for the Import Queue

This check function verifies that all data files and control files that belong to a change request exist in the transport directory and can be read.

To run this check, from the *Import Overview* screen, choose *Import Queue* ➢ *Check* ➢ *Consistency*. The *Check Import Queue* dialog box appears.

- By default, this dialog box is set to *No*. If you choose *No*, the system displays whether the corresponding files are available in the transport directory and whether they are readable. Consistent files are indicated by a check mark on the right side of the screen *TMS: Import Queue Check* that appears. If the corresponding files are not available or are not readable, the system marks the files or the directory with an *x*. If an error occurred, you can access more information by clicking the *x*.

- If you choose *Yes* in the *Check Import Queue* dialog box, the size of the files and directories is displayed in addition to information concerning the consistency of the directories.

Transport Tool Check

Before starting an import, it is also helpful to check the transport tools to ensure that they can function and have the appropriate settings for performing imports. You can check the transport tools for one or all R/3 Systems within a transport domain (except for virtual systems and external systems). The check examines the following:

tp interface: The status of the transport control program

Transport profile: The readability of the transport profile at the operating system level

RFC destination: The status and success of required RFC calls to the transport control program

tp call: The status of the communication link between the transport control program and the database of the R/3 System

To perform a transport tool check, from the *Import Queue* screen for an R/3 System, choose *Queue* ➢ *Check* ➢ *Transport tool*. The screen *TMS: Check Transport Tool* appears and will indicate whether the transport tools have the appropriate settings for performing imports. To display more information about the individual tools and potential errors, expand the tree structure. A green check mark indicates a successful test. If a particular check is marked with an *x*, its check was not successful, indicating either an error at the operating system level or a problem with the current transport profile parameters.

Critical Objects

As of R/3 Release 4.5, the TMS can search for objects that you have defined as critical. A *critical object* is an object that you expect to cause problems during import or an object that is critical for security. By defining critical objects, you can help to protect against the import of objects into certain R/3 Systems that may cause serious errors or damage settings in the R/3 System.

An example of a critical object is authorization profiles created in the development system that you do not want to transport into the production system for security reasons. You can define authorization profiles as critical objects in the production system. (The critical object list is specific to each R/3 System in the system landscape—you have to define the critical objects for each target system within your landscape.) Once the authorization profiles are defined in the critical object list, to ensure that change requests including authorization profiles are not accidentally imported, you need to perform a check for critical objects prior to each import.

To define critical objects, proceed as follows:

1. From the *Import Overview* screen, choose *Extras* ➢ *Critical transport objects*.

2. Choose *Enter*.

3. To add an object to the table, switch to change mode by choosing *Table view* ➢ *Display <-> Change*.

4. Choose *Edit* ➢ *New Entries*.

5. Specify the critical objects. You can define an object as critical only if its Object Directory entry has the PgmID *R3TR* (see Chapter 10).

6. Save your entries.

NOTE   If you have defined critical objects for a system, you should always run the critical objects check on the import queue of that system before importing.

To start the check for critical objects in the import queue, from the *Import Queue* screen, choose *Queue* ➢ *Check* ➢ *Critical objects*. The system then searches the object list of the import queue for critical objects in the table of critical objects (see Figure 13.5). The results of the search are displayed in the screen *TMS: Critical Objects in Requests*.

Bear in mind that this check offers only a display function. Neither the check nor the definition of critical objects automatically prevents you from importing change requests that include critical objects. It is the responsibility of the system administrator to ensure that the respective change requests are not imported. He or she must also reexport any noncritical objects that are contained in the list of change requests into another change request from the source system. This must be done in a way that preserves the original sequence of the change requests.

> **WARNING** The critical objects check is only a display function. It is the responsibility of the person performing imports to manage critical objects located during a critical object check.

FIGURE 13.5:

Scanning for critical objects

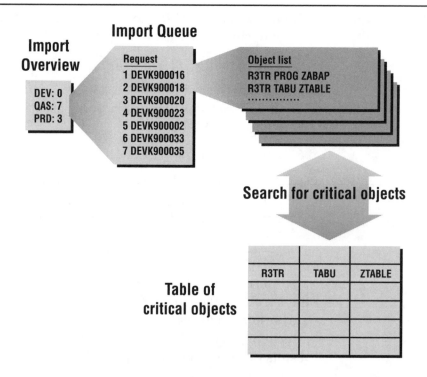

Scheduling Imports

After export, a change request is not automatically imported. To import the change requests, you have two options: You can perform an import manually, or you can set up a scheduling program on the operating system level to perform the import.

NOTE Using a scheduling program does not prevent you from checking the import results for problems.

When planning imports, ensure that you include enough time to accommodate post-import tasks such as quality assurance testing. SAP recommends performing imports of entire import queues (*import all*) at regular intervals—for example, monthly, weekly, or daily. A more frequent import rate is not advisable.

Because imports into a production system affect the runtime environment, you should schedule them for times when they are least likely to affect running transactions and programs (see Chapter 14). This is especially important when you import data into a production system, because an import can invalidate some R/3 buffer contents, forcing them to be reloaded and consequently reducing performance. You should schedule imports into production systems to run at night in the background, or perform a detailed check on the jobs that would be running at the same time and monitor the effects carefully. Before importing into a production system, perform a complete R/3 System backup.

Ideally, no users should be working in an R/3 System when change requests are imported. This is particularly important when importing into the production system. For this reason, you should make sure that you choose appropriate times and send a system message telling users to log off.

Importing into Multiple Clients

Often, a customer wishes to import change requests into multiple clients throughout the system landscape—a procedure that poses certain problems. These problems and their possible solutions are outlined in more detail in this section.

Figure 13.6 shows an example of transport route requirements for imports into multiple clients. After the release of change requests from the CUST client, the changes are to be imported into not only the TEST client and the SAND client in the development system, but also into the QTST client and a DATA client in the quality assurance system. Once the change requests are imported into the QTST client, the change requests will be transported to the TRNG client and the PROD client in the production system.

FIGURE 13.6:

Transporting into multiple clients

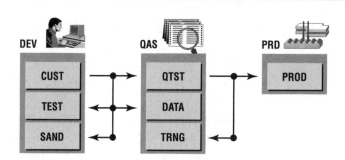

As of R/3 Release 4.5, you can rely on extended transport control to ensure that all clients in the system landscape contain the latest changes that originate in client CUST. The change requests are automatically placed in the import queues of specified R/3 Systems and clients. Extended transport control also ensures that client-independent objects in a change request are imported into an R/3 System only once, protecting newer versions of objects from being overwritten. For example, if a change request that contains an ABAP program is released from the CUST client, the program itself is imported into the quality assurance system only once, while the change request may be in the import queue for multiple clients. On the other hand, client-specific changes are imported into each client.

NOTE   As of R/3 Release 4.5, you can use extended transport control to set up client-specific transport routes, which allows you to import into multiple clients in a single R/3 System at the same or different times. (See Chapter 8.)

Importing into Multiple Clients without Extended Transport Control

If extended transport control is not available (releases prior to R/3 Release 4.5) or if extended transport control is not activated, you cannot take advantage of client-specific transport routes. Instead, you must manually import the change requests that originate in client CUST to all the clients in the system landscape. Although it is possible to import change requests into the quality assurance client and then wait to import them into the other clients in the same system at a later time, this requires complex management of change requests and import queues.

NOTE   Without client-specific transport routes defined using extended transport control, you have to manually import the change requests several times, once for each client in an R/3 System.

The standard is that at the end of an import of the entire queue, the imported change requests are removed from the import queue of the target system. If you wish to import change requests into another client, you will want to import the change requests and keep the change requests in the import queue in their prescribed order. This can be accomplished by using the preliminary import option during import.

Importing change requests using the preliminary import option requires you to determine the next client to which the change request should be imported, and you must ensure that the change requests are imported into all the different R/3 clients in the system. Managing imports into multiple clients at different times requires you to track change requests outside of R/3 and its transport tools.

SAP recommends that you import change requests into multiple clients in a sequential process. This ensures consistency in the import queues and ensures that all clients have received the latest change requests. If this is not possible, use client copy tools to assist in maintaining the consistency of different clients in the target system. For example, a data conversion test client could be re-created periodically as a copy of the quality assurance test client. Or, the training client could receive the latest Customizing changes on a weekly basis through *client copy according to transp. request.*

The easiest way to support imports into multiple clients is to schedule them for a time when a group of change requests are sequentially imported into all clients within the quality assurance system, starting with the quality assurance client. In this way, the change requests are imported first into the quality assurance client, and the other clients sequentially receive the imports.

Importing an Import Queue into Multiple Clients   To manually perform the import of a collection of change requests into multiple R/3 clients, first close the import queue of the target system. Then, to keep the change requests in the import queue in their correct order for imports into other clients, import into all the target clients except the last target client using a special import option for preliminary imports. When you perform the import into the last target client, perform an *import all* with no import option.

To perform a preliminary import into multiple clients, proceed as follows:

1. From the *Import Queue* screen, choose *Queue ➤ Start import*.

2. In the *Start Import* dialog box, enter the respective target client.

3. To perform preliminary imports of the entire queue, choose *Expert mode* and:

   - For R/3 Release 4.0, select the import option *Flag all requests for further import*.

   - For R/3 Release 4.5, select the import option *Select all requests for new import*.

4. Choose *Continue*.

For the last client to receive the change request, you should perform the import without selecting the expert mode option for a preliminary import. This final import will then remove the change requests from the import queue of the target system.

Importing Single Change Requests into Multiple Clients

For all the target clients except the last target client, to transport a single change request originating in client CUST to all other clients within the system landscape, follow these steps:

1. From the *Import Queue* screen, select the change request to be imported.

2. Choose *Request ➤ Import*.

3. In the *Import Transport Request* dialog box that appears, enter the respective target client number.

4. Choose *Continue* to initiate the import.

Remember that by default single imports are set to *Prelim. Import of transport req* in the expert mode. Therefore, you do not need to specify the expert mode. For the last client to receive changes, you will have to change the expert mode. To change the expert mode for the last target client and thus remove the change request from the import queue of the quality assurance system:

1. From the *Import Queue* screen, select the change request to be imported.

2. Choose *Request* ➤ *Import*.

3. In the *Import Transport Request* dialog box that appears, enter the respective target client number.

4. Choose the *Expert mode*. Deselect the import option *Prelim. Import of transport req.*

5. Choose *Continue* to initiate the import.

Monitoring Imports

The TMS provides several tools for monitoring the transport activities in your transport domain. Bear in mind that to open these tools, you must branch into them successively from the previous tool.

Additional information on TMS activities is provided by the Alert Monitor, which was discussed in Chapter 8. For details on monitoring and troubleshooting, see Chapter 14.

Import Monitor

To display status information about currently running and completed imports, start the *Import Monitor*. To access the Import Monitor for a specific R/3 System, from the *Import Overview* screen, position the cursor on the system and choose *Goto* ➤ *Import monitor*. The Import Monitor displays the information for each *tp* import command, regardless of whether it imported a single change request or the entire queue. The information includes

- *tp* command
- Start mode (online or offline)
- Start time (date and time)
- *tp* process ID
- Last change (date and time)
- *tp* status (current status of the *tp* command)
- Maximum return code
- *tp* message

In the *TMS Import Monitor* screen, to update the display of a currently running import in the import monitor, choose *Edit* ➢ *Refresh.* If you notice that the last change date of an import has not changed in a long time and the status of the *tp* command is *still running,* it may be due to one of the following reasons:

- The data volume of the change request(s) is large.
- An error has occurred that is shown in the TP System Log.
- *tp* has been terminated with operating system tools.

The *tp* message indicates the step currently being processed and then either the successful completion of the import or the last error that occurred.

TP System Log

The TP System Log displays an overview of the transport activities for the current R/3 System—for example, all *tp* calls and errors, as well as the return codes, which indicate the success of each import. To branch to the TP System Log, from the *TMS Import Monitor* screen, choose *Goto* ➢ *TP system log.* The *tp System*

Log screen appears. The information displayed is stored in a file on the operating system level in the subdirectory *log* of the transport directory. This file is also known as the *SLOG*.

Action Log File

The *action log* contains the transport activities and the return codes for all transport activities. Each transport group has its own action log file. To branch to the action log, from the *tp System Log* screen, choose *Goto* ➢ *Transport steps*. The *Transport Step Monitor* screen appears. The information displayed is stored in a file on the operating system level in the subdirectory *log* of the transport directory. This file is also known as the *ALOG*.

Single Step Log Files

For each transport activity, the system writes a log file, called the *single step log file*. If an error is indicated in the Import Monitor, you can branch to the TP System Log and the action log. From the *Transport Step Monitor* screen, you can open the single log file to analyze the error. To open the single log files, on the action log file screen, position the cursor on a change request and choose *Request* ➢ *Logs*. Double-click a specific import activity to view its related log file. (See Chapter 14 for the name and location of the single step log files.)

Transporting between Transport Groups

Usually, all R/3 Systems in a transport domain share a common transport directory. In certain situations, multiple transport directories may be required (see Chapters 7 and 8), and the transport domain will consist of multiple transport groups, one for each transport directory that is used. The TMS supports transports between transport groups. Each transport group reflects the configuration of the transport domain; that is, each transport group includes import queues for all R/3 Systems belonging to the transport domain. Nevertheless, change requests can be imported into a target system only if they exist in the import queue of the transport group to which the target system belongs.

NOTE   If more than one transport group exists, each transport group contains a local import queue for each R/3 System belonging to the transport domain.

After a change request has been released, it is stored in the transport directory of the source system and recorded in the local import queue of the target system, where *local* means that this import queue belongs to the transport group of the source system.

If the source and the target system belong to different transport groups, the import queue of the target transport group has to be adjusted. Figure 13.7 depicts a simplified example of this process, based on the R/3 Systems DEV and QAS.

FIGURE 13.7:

Transporting between
transport groups

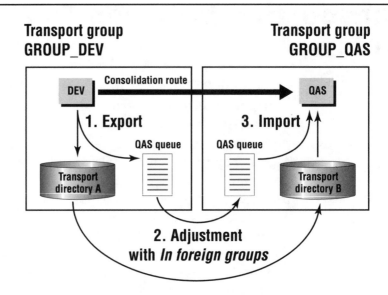

Figure 13.7 shows a system landscape with two transport groups: GROUP_DEV and GROUP_QAS. Customizing and development changes are performed in the development system DEV. A consolidation route is defined between DEV and the quality assurance system QAS. When a change request is released and exported from DEV, the data file and control file are created on the transport directory local to DEV—the transport directory for GROUP_DEV. Also, the change request is added to the import queue of QAS—the import queue that is local to the development system. For an import of the change request to take place, the data file and control file as well as the import queue entry need to be local to the quality assurance system. In other words, the files need be adjusted from the transport group GROUP_DEV to GROUP_QAS. The process for moving the required files and entries from one transport group to another is known as *adjusting*.

NOTE   In R/3 Release 4.0, ensure that the parameters in the transport profile—except for *transdir*—are the same for all transport groups. As of
R/3 Release 4.5, this is guaranteed by TMS.

Adjusting Transports

Before change requests can be imported into a system whose
transport group is different from its delivering system, the different transport groups need to be adjusted. The TMS adjusts the
import queue in the target system's transport group to search for
change requests waiting for import into the target R/3 System,
which are stored in transport directories belonging to other transport groups, and to add these change requests to the transport
directory of the target system's transport group.

There are three steps to perform when transporting between
R/3 Systems that belong to different transport groups (as depicted
in Figure 13.7 above):

1. The change requests are released and exported.

2. The import queue of the target system is adjusted.

3. The change requests are imported into the target system.

To perform such an adjustment, from the *Import Queue* screen of
the target system, choose *Extras* ➢ *Other requests* ➢ *In foreign
groups*. Similarly, to adjust an import queue with requests originating in an external group, choose *Extras* ➢ *Other requests* ➢ *In
external groups*. When you confirm the transfer of these change
requests, the TMS will transfer the requests to the import queue
of the target system (QAS). Accordingly, the corresponding data
files and control files are transferred. If an error occurs, you can
still restart the adjustment despite the message that will appear
stating that the import queue is locked. In this situation, you can
confirm the message.

Transport log files that are available in an R/3 System of R/3 Release 4.0 or 4.5 are specific to the transport group of the actual R/3 System being used.

Transporting between Transport Domains

A transport domain is an administrative unit. Generally, all R/3 Systems that are connected by transport routes and that have a regular transport flow belong to the same transport domain. Even if you are forced to use more than one transport directory, by taking advantage of the concept of transport groups, all R/3 Systems can be kept in one domain and administered centrally by the domain controller.

Occasionally, there may be reasons to have more than one transport domain. For example, global companies or groups may configure one domain for the headquarters and one domain for each subsidiary. Possible reasons for multiple transport domains are as follows:

- Organizational or political reasons require that you have separate administrative units.

- The number of R/3 Systems (50 to 100) is too high to be administered within one transport domain.

- There are network limitations or considerations that technically make it advantageous to have separately administered transport domains.

Before configuring several transport domains, determine whether this is really necessary. Transports between R/3 Systems in different transport domains are possible, but increase the administrative workload.

Figure 13.8 shows the simplified representation of two R/3 Systems—GDV and DDV—that belong to different transport domains: DOMAIN_HDQ and DOMAIN_ESP. GDV is the R/3 System for the headquarters of a multinational organization, and DDV is the R/3 System of a subsidiary in Spain belonging to the organization. Only the involved systems are shown in this example. The system administrator wants to transport from the R/3 System GDV into DDV.

FIGURE 13.8:

Logical transport flow between two transport domains

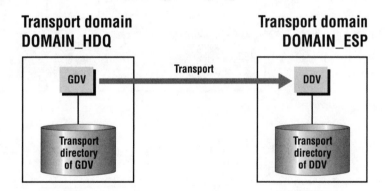

Configuration

To implement the transport route depicted in Figure 13.8, the system administrator has to create an external system DDV in DOMAIN_HDQ and an external system GDV in DOMAIN_ESP. The external systems are placeholders for the real systems. For both external systems, a transport directory, called the *external transport directory,* must be defined, which is accessible from both transport domains. Within each domain, one available R/3 System has to be defined as the *communications system* for the respective external system and must have access to the external transport directory. Figure 13.9 shows that GDV serves as the communications system for the external system DDV in DOMAIN_HDQ, and DDV serves as the communications system for the external system GDV in DOMAIN_ESP.

FIGURE 13.9:

Configuration of the transport domains

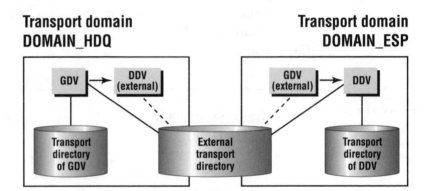

To configure the transports between two domains, follow these steps:

1. Manually create the external transport directory (see Chapters 7 and 8). Ensure that all transport subdirectories exist.

2. To ensure access to the external transport directory, check whether the communications systems in both transport domains have read and write authorizations on all subdirectories. In the example in Figure 13.9, all files that are written by user GDVADM from DOMAIN_HDQ into the external transport directory have to be readable and replaceable by user DDVADM (the reverse also must be possible).

3. Create an external system in both transport domains (see Chapter 8). Ensure that the SID of the external system in one transport domain is identical with the SID of the R/3 System in the other transport domain, and vice versa.

4. To check the access authorizations in both transport domains, from the initial *Systems Overview* screen, choose *R/3 System* ➤ *Check* ➤ *Transport directory* (see Chapter 8). The *Check Transport Directory* screen appears.

5. To check whether there are discrepancies between the transport group configuration of the TMS and the configuration of the transport directories on the operating system level in both transport domains, from the *Check Transport Directory* screen in step 4, choose *Goto* ➤ *Transport groups*.

6. Configure a transport route from the available R/3 System GDV to the external system DDV in DOMAIN_HDQ. The transport route can be a consolidation route or a delivery route.

Transport

Transporting change requests between transport domains—in the previous example, from GDV in DOMAIN_HDQ to DDV in DOMAIN_ESP—uses the external transport directory. In general, two adjustment steps are required (see Figure 13.10):

- On the source transport domain (DOMAIN_HDQ), all transport files, such as data files and control files, that belong to change requests that are waiting for import into the external system (DDV) must be copied into the external transport directory.

- On the target transport domain (DOMAIN_ESP), the files from the external transport directory must be copied into the target transport directory, the transport directory of the target system DDV in DOMAIN_ESP.

FIGURE 13.10:

Adjusting import queues

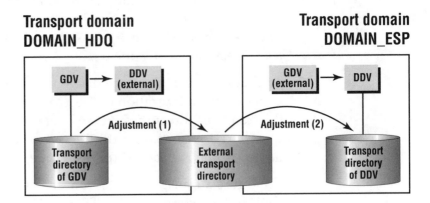

To transport a change request as in the example in Figure 13.10 — that is, from GDV in DOMAIN_HDQ to DDV in DOMAIN_ESP—proceed as follows.

In the transport domain for the headquarters:

1. Release the change request in the "real" system GDV. As a result, the corresponding files are written to the transport directory of GDV. Because of the configured consolidation route in this example, DDV is specified as the target system of the change request. The change request is added to the import queue for DDV in the transport directory of GDV.

2. The change requests sitting in the transport directory of GDV need to be transferred to the external transport directory. For this adjustment step, use the TMS to search for the change request. To do this, from the *Import Queue* screen of the external system DDV, choose *Extras* ➤ *Other requests* ➤ *In foreign groups*.

In the transport domain for Spain:

1. For the second adjustment step, use the TMS to search for the change request. To do this, from the *Import Queue* screen of

the "real" system DDV, choose *Extras* ➢ *Other requests* ➢ *In external groups*.

2. Choose *Enter*. As a result, the change request is copied to the transport directory of the "real" system DDV.

3. The change request is now part of the import queue of DDV in the Spanish domain and can be imported as usual.

NOTE   Because there is no RFC connection between the transport domains, short texts cannot be displayed for change requests originating in a different domain.

TMS Authorization

The TMS uses RFCs for the connections between the R/3 Systems in a transport domain (see Chapter 8). Performing imports is not restricted to the domain controller. With proper authorizations, you can initiate imports into any R/3 System from each R/3 System within the domain. When using the TMS, a user's authorization is checked twice during the import process:

1. To initiate an import in the TMS, the system validates the user's authorization in the current client.

2. The TMS makes a remote function call to the target system. The user must log on to the target system with a username and password. After the user's authorization is validated in the target system, the import process begins in this target system.

To perform imports using the TMS, a user requires authorization in the client from which the import command will be issued as well as in the target system. This authorization concept allows you to assign from which client and into which target R/3 Systems a user may perform imports.

SAP provides the authorization S_CTS_ADMIN for importing change requests using the TMS. This authorization is required to confirm that imports into the target system are allowed.

There is no SAP profile simply allowing import functionality. You can assign the authorization profile S_A.SYSTEM to users who need to perform CTS administrative activities, including the initialization of the Change and Transport Organizer, as well as all TMS functions—for example, setting up the TMS to perform imports. Alternatively, you may wish to assign a user the ability to perform imports without the ability to initialize or set up any parts of the CTS. Rather than assigning the profile S_A.SYSTEM, you can restrict this user to performing imports by creating a new authorization profile for the authorization object S_CTS_ADMI and assigning the user the new profile. This authorization profile then prevents the user from accessing administrative functions.

Review Questions

1. Which of the following statements are correct in regard to import queues?

    A. Import queues are the TMS representation of the import buffer on the operating system level.

    B. You have to manipulate import queues to transport change requests.

    C. Import queues should be closed before starting an import using TMS.

    D. You can import only an entire import queue.

2. Which of the following statements are correct in regard to preliminary imports?

   A. SAP recommends using preliminary imports rather than imports of entire queues.

   B. Preliminary imports should be performed only in exceptional cases.

   C. Change requests imported as preliminary imports remain in the import queue.

   D. Change requests are deleted from the import queue after preliminary imports. This prevents them from being imported again with the next import of the entire import queue.

3. Which of the following statements is correct in regard to imports into an R/3 System?

   A. Imports can be performed only by using the *start import* functionality in the TMS.

   B. Imports can be performed only by using *tp* commands on the operating system level to prepare the import queue and then using the *start import* functionality in the TMS.

   C. Imports can be performed only by using *tp* commands at the operating system level.

   D. Imports can be performed by using either a *tp* command on the operating system level or the TMS import functionality.

4. Which of the following statements is correct in regard to transports between different transport groups?

   A. They are not possible.

   B. They can be performed only by using *tp* on the operating system level with special options.

    C. They can be performed using the TMS with special options provided by the expert mode.

    D. They require you to adjust the corresponding import queues.

5. Which of the following statements are correct in regard to transports between different transport domains?

    A. They are not possible.

    B. They require you to create a virtual system and a virtual transport directory.

    C. They require you to configure identical transport groups within the different transport domains.

    D. They require you to create external systems and an external transport directory.

    E. They require you to adjust the corresponding import queues.

CHAPTER
FOURTEEN

Technical Insight—the Import Process

The previous chapter described how imports are performed using the Transport Management System (TMS). When you use the TMS interface, you are not aware of the activities that take place on the operating system level during imports, such as calls for the transport control program *tp*. This chapter provides an insight into the technical side of the import process on the operating system level. You will learn:

- How to perform imports on the operating system level using *tp*

- About the *tp* processing sequence and the import steps

- How to use log files and return codes for troubleshooting

- How imports affect R/3 buffer synchronization

- How to identify file naming conventions in the transport directory

- About the different transport tools, their activities, and the way they communicate

By covering these issues, the chapter provides the system administrator with the background knowledge needed to use *tp* on the operating system level and to perform successful trouble-shooting. This chapter is also of interest to project leaders, because learning details on what happens beyond the TMS—for example, the *tp* processing sequence and the R/3 buffer synchronization—allows a better understanding of the concepts and strategies that were introduced in Part 1 of this book.

The Transport Control Program

The transport control program *tp* is a tool on the operating system level that uses special programs (such as C programs), operating system commands, and ABAP programs in R/3 to control transports between R/3 Systems. Accordingly, *tp* stands for "transports and programs."

tp controls the exports and imports of objects between R/3 Systems by ensuring that the steps for exporting and importing are performed in the correct order and that the change requests are exported and imported in the same order.

As a rule, it is not necessary to call *tp* directly because you can perform most transport activities using the TMS. Nevertheless, you may occasionally need to use *tp* commands on the operating system level instead of the TMS or in conjunction with the TMS. With each new R/3 Release, SAP offers more advanced transport functionality through the TMS. Although the TMS provides a wide range of functions, to perform certain tasks, such as cleaning up the transport directory, you must still call *tp* directly.

Prerequisites

To use *tp*, the following prerequisites must be fulfilled (for details, see Chapter 7):

- All R/3 Systems in the transport domain must have a unique system name (SID).

- Each R/3 System involved must have access to a correctly installed transport directory.

- The transport profile must be maintained correctly. The transport profile configures the transport control program *tp*.

- Each source system and each target system must have at least two background work processes.

- The transport dispatcher RDDIMPDP must be scheduled as an event-periodic background job in each R/3 System that acts as a source system for exports or a target system for imports.

Authorizations for Using *tp*

Because *tp* is an operating system level command, you require operating system level authorization to access it. To call *tp*, you have to log on to the operating system of the computer that houses the transport directory of the target system as one of the following users:

- <SID>adm on UNIX and Windows NT
- <SID>OPR on AS/400 platforms

Typically, only technical consultants and system administrators have access to the operating system level, and therefore are responsible for issuing *tp* commands. If necessary, you can write scripts to enable users to perform imports without logging on as user <SID>adm or <SID>OPR.

Command Syntax

To call *tp* directly on the operating system level, follow these steps:

1. Log on to the operating system.
2. Change to subdirectory *bin* in the transport directory.
3. Execute a *tp* command with the following syntax:

```
tp <command> [argument(s)] [option(s)]
```

Table 14.1 contains a list of *tp* commands that may be helpful for troubleshooting or everyday operations.

TABLE 14.1: Helpful *tp* Commands

tp Command	Function
`tp help`	Provides general information about *tp* functionality—for example, about syntax and available *tp* commands.
`tp <command>`	Describes the syntax and function of the specified command.
`tp go <SID>`	Checks the database destination by displaying the environmental variables required for accessing the database of a specific R/3 System. To do this, *tp* checks the values in the transport profile. Note that this command does not actually establish a database connection.
`tp connect <SID>`	Checks whether a connection to the database of the specified R/3 System can be established.
`tp showinfo <change request>`	Displays information about a specific change request, including the owner and the type of change request.
`tp count <SID>`	Displays the number of change requests waiting to be imported into the specified R/3 System.
`tp checkimpdp <SID>`	Displays how the transport dispatcher RDDIMPDP is scheduled for the specified R/3 System.
`tp showparams <SID>`	Displays all current transport profile parameter settings for the specified R/3 System.

Import Queues and Import Buffers

In the previous chapter, you learned how to use the import queue in TMS to manage and import change requests. On the operating system level, the same change requests are contained in the import buffer. The subdirectory *buffer* of the transport directory contains an import buffer for each R/3 System in the transport group. The buffer file is named after the corresponding SID and contains transport control information such as the following:

- Which change requests are to be imported

- The order to follow when importing the change request

- The possible import options (explained below in the section "Import Options")

- The import steps (explained below in the section "*tp* Import Steps")

Import queues are TMS representations in R/3 of the buffer files located on the operating system level. Import queues show all change requests that are listed in the corresponding import buffer.

When an end mark is set in the TMS, the change requests that will not be included in the next import are grayed out in the import queue. By definition, these change requests no longer belong to the import queue. Consequently, more change requests may belong to the import buffer than to the import queue. For example, in Figure 14.1, the import queue displays the four change requests before the end mark as included in the next import, whereas the three change requests after the end mark would be grayed out—that is, they are not included in the next import.

FIGURE 14.1:

Import queue and import buffer

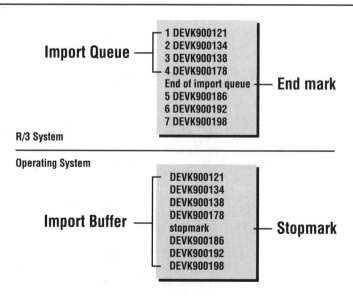

An end mark is indicated in an import queue by the statement *End of import queue*, whereas on the operating system level, the import buffer shows the term *stopmark* (see Figure 14.1). Regardless of where the marker is created, it is always set in both the import buffer and the import queue.

To set an end mark, and therefore simultaneously set the stopmark, close the import queue by choosing *Queue* ➤ *Close* from the TMS import queue screen. The operating system level equivalent is the command `tp setstopmark <SID>`. If you have not set the end mark/stopmark before starting an import, *tp* will automatically execute this command and place a stopmark at the end of the existing import queue right after the import command has been issued.

To manually remove an end mark/stopmark, open the import queue from the TMS import screen by choosing *Queue* ➤ *Open*. The operating system equivalent is the command `tp delstopmark <SID>`. This command is normally not needed because *tp* will automatically remove the marker after an import of all change requests above the stopmark has been successfully completed.

tp Commands for Import Buffers

In addition to the *tp* commands already mentioned, you can use the *tp* commands listed in Table 14.2 to access and maintain the import buffers.

WARNING When you access import buffers, it mostly results in mixing up the correct order of the change requests and thus may cause serious inconsistencies. These *tp* commands should be used only in exceptional cases.

TABLE 14.2: *tp* Commands Affecting Import Buffers

Command	Description
tp showbuffer <SID>	Displays the buffer entries of the specified R/3 System.
tp addtobuffer <change request> <SID>	Adds the specified change request as the last request to be imported, and therefore places it at the end of the import buffer of the specified R/3 System. If the change request has already been added to this buffer, it will be removed from its current position and placed at the end of the import buffer.
tp delfrombuffer <change request> <SID>	Deletes the specified change request from the import buffer of the specified R/3 System.
tp cleanbuffer <SID>	Removes successfully imported change requests from the import buffer of the specified R/3 System. If you perform an import of an entire queue (that is, an *import all*), *tp* automatically executes this command at the end of the import process.

All commands listed in Table 14.2 affect both the import buffer and the related import queue. If you execute any of these *tp* commands on the operating system level, you must refresh the import queue display in the TMS to see the results.

NOTE The import buffer is the basis of all operations, regardless of whether *tp* is called through the TMS or on the operating system level.

Performing Imports Using *tp*

Although SAP recommends that you use the TMS to perform imports, you may need to use *tp* commands for the following reasons:

- To script the import process so that it can be automated and scheduled

- To support the import of change requests into multiple clients (not necessary as of R/3 Release 4.5)

The *tp* commands allow you to perform imports of all change requests (*import all*) as well as imports of single change requests (*preliminary imports*).

Importing All Change Requests

To import all the change requests in the import buffer, execute the *tp* command `tp import all <target SID> [client=<target client number>]`.

If you are using the TMS to import an entire queue, the TMS will automatically trigger the above *tp* command on the operating system level. This command imports all change requests before the end mark/stopmark in their export sequence into the target system and specified target client number. If no target client ID is provided, the change requests are imported into a target client with the same client ID as the source client.

As already mentioned in Chapter 6, if change requests near the start of the import and change requests near the end of the import affect the same object, the version of the object at the end of the import will overwrite the earlier versions with the latest changes. This ensures that incorrect object versions that have been corrected will not affect your production environment (see also the section "*tp* Processing Sequence" later in this chapter).

NOTE If an error occurs during import, after you have eliminated the cause of the error and restarted *tp*, *tp* will automatically restart the import at the point where it was interrupted.

Importing Individual Change Requests

To import a single change request, execute the *tp* command `tp import <change request> <target SID> [client=<target client number>] u0`. This *tp* command is the operating system equivalent of the TMS function *preliminary import*.

NOTE   To ensure object dependencies and consistency, SAP strongly recommends using the *import all* function.

To ensure that the objects that were imported individually are not overwritten by an older version, always use the preliminary import option *u0* (see the section "Import Options") to import individual change requests. If you use this import option, rather than being deleted from the import queue after import, the change request will remain in the import queue. When the entire import queue is later imported, the request will automatically be imported again in its original sequence.

SAP recommends avoiding the import of individual requests without this import option, because the export sequence will not be maintained. Consequently, newer versions of objects may be overwritten by older versions when the entire import queue is imported.

Import Options

When performing imports in the TMS, you can select import options using the expert mode (see Chapter 13). Import options are also referred to as *unconditional modes*. On the operating system level, unconditional modes are options that you can assign to *tp* commands to override specific rules of the Change and Transport System (CTS).

Each unconditional mode is represented by a digit. To use an unconditional mode, add a leading *u* followed by a concatenated list of single digits representing the different unconditional modes that should affect the *tp* command. For example, if you want to import a change request that should be kept in the import queue after the import, add *u0*. If you additionally want to ignore that originals in the target system are overwritten by imported objects, you can simply specify *u02* as follows: `tp import <change request> <SID> u02`.

<table>
<tr><td>**NOTE**</td><td>Use unconditional modes carefully. SAP recommends transporting according to the rules of the Change and Transport System (CTS).</td></tr>
</table>

Table 14.3 lists the unconditional modes that you can use in conjunction with *tp* commands for performing imports.

TABLE 14.3: Unconditional Modes

Unconditional Mode	Description
0	This option is used to preliminarily import a change request. After import, the change request remains in the import buffer and is marked to be imported again.
1	Despite the fact that the change request has already been imported, *tp* will import it again when the entire import queue is imported.
2	Objects in change requests will overwrite the original objects in the target system.
6	Objects in change requests will overwrite objects that are currently being repaired in the target system and that have not yet been confirmed.
8	This option will ignore transport restrictions for table delivery classes.
9	This option will override certain transport profile settings that otherwise would have prevented the change request from being imported. For example, despite the fact that the transport profile parameter *t_import* has been set to FALSE, change requests resulting from a transport of copies (type *T*) will be imported.

In the import buffer in column *Umode* and also in the import queue in column *U modes* in the TMS, you may find a character that indicates certain conditions for the next *import all* caused by a previous import with the preliminary import option (u0). Table 14.4 lists the possible letters and the corresponding conditions for the next import of all change requests waiting for import.

TABLE 14.4: Indicator in the Import Buffer

Indicator	Description
I	The import of the change request will be repeated from the beginning.
J	The import of the change request into the respective client is repeated from the beginning, but client-independent objects are not imported again.
F	The buffer entry is in the wrong position. *tp* will resolve this problem by implicitly executing the command `tp addtobuffer`.

Importing into Multiple Clients

As of R/3 Release 4.5, to perform imports into multiple clients, you can use the TMS and its import options and the extended transport control (see Chapter 13). In releases before R/3 Release 4.5, you have to perform the imports using *tp* on the operating system level with certain import options.

To import change requests into the client with the same client ID as the source client, execute a regular *tp* command without any import options: `tp import all <target SID>`. This can be bypassed by specifying the client name as follows: `tp import all <target SID> [client=<target client ID>]`.

These commands will ensure that a single R/3 client receives all client-dependent changes recorded in the change requests and that the R/3 System will receive all client-independent changes.

However, if there are several target clients, you encounter problems because:

- Only one target client can be specified.

- The change request will be deleted from the import buffer after a successful import and therefore cannot be imported into other R/3 clients.

This will result in problems if other clients are waiting to receive the changes. One solution is to specify the preliminary import option *u0*. This import option will keep the change request in the buffer so that it can be imported again when the entire import queue is imported into another client with the same R/3 System.

Example: Importing into Multiple Clients

A company's quality assurance system has three clients:

- Client 100 for business integration validation

- Client 200 for testing data migration routines

- Client 300 for user training

Because the company is using R/3 Release 4.0B, they do not have the option of using the extended transport control with its client-specific transport routes. Therefore, the import queue of the quality assurance system contains a list of change requests that need to be imported into all three clients. To import into the three clients, the system administrator will execute the following *tp* commands:

```
tp import all QAS client=100 u0
tp import all QAS client=200 u0
tp import all QAS client=300
```

Continued on next page

The last command is the import command for the last remaining client. At this point, all clients have been delivered with the changes—the change requests are no longer needed in the import queue. In the final step, to delete the change requests from the import buffer after the import, the system administrator can leave out the import option *u0*.

Setting a Stopmark   A stopmark prevents all change requests that are positioned after the stopmark in the queue from being imported. This also applies to change requests that are released during a running import, because they are placed after the stopmark in the import queue.

tp automatically sets a stopmark at the beginning of an import and removes it at the end of the import. This removal is a problem when importing into multiple clients, because subsequent imports will include change requests that were after the stopmark in the previous imports.

As a solution, *tp* does not remove the stopmark after import when the preliminary import option (u0) is used. This was first valid in the following versions of *tp*:

- *tp* version 252.08.10 as of R/3 Release 4.0B

- *tp* version 267.03.08 as of R/3 Release 4.5B

If you have an earlier *tp* version, there is still a way to perform imports into multiple clients. In this case, you have to add one stopmark explicitly for each client into which you will import before starting the first import to ensure that all clients receive the same change requests. These additional stopmarks prevent change requests from being added to the import buffer between the import processes. Although this option will technically work, SAP recommends that you implement the latest version of *tp* for your R/3 Release as listed above.

Script   Because many steps are involved in delivering all the clients in your system landscape with the changes made in the development system, you may choose to automate the import process for multiple clients with a script on the operating system level. Such a script has to fulfill two important requirements:

- The script must set a stopmark before starting the first import (see above).

- The script must check whether an import was successful before starting the next imports. For an import to be successful, the number of corresponding return codes written to the SLOG file cannot be greater than eight.

Example: Script for Performing Imports into Multiple Clients on a UNIX Operating System

A company has a UNIX operating system, and its system administrator has written the following script to perform imports into multiple clients (100, 200, and 300). Because the return code from the import is recorded in the SLOG file, the script will scan the SLOG file to determine the success of the last import. If the import was not successful (a return code greater than eight), the script is aborted, and the next import does not take place. (See also the section "Generic Log Files.")

```
#!/usr/bin/ksh
# Shell script to import all requests in the R/3 buffer
# file to multiple clients

# Set script variables
# sid - system ID for the target R/3 System
# clients - a list of clients to receive all change requests

sid=QAS
clients="100 200 300"
```

Continued on next page

```
# Set logfile variable
# The current SLOG for this week
logfile=/usr/sap/trans/log/SLOG$(date +%y%U).$sid

# Count the number of clients in the list
cnt=0
for i in $clients
do
    cnt=$((cnt+1))
done

# Set stopmark to ensure that any newly released change
# requests are not imported until the next import
tp setstopmark $sid

# Loop and perform the imports for each client in this sid
# Unconditional setting 0 is used for all but the last import
inc=0
for i in $clients
do
  inc=$((inc+1))
  if test $inc -eq $cnt

  then
    echo "Importing into client "$i
    tp import all $sid client=$i
  else
    echo "Importing into client "$i
    tp import all $sid u0 client=$i
  fi

# Check the current SLOG file for an error
# Stop if an error exists
  if awk 'BEGIN{statuscode=" "}\
    {if ($1 == "STOP" && $2 == "imp" && $3 == "all")
statuscode=$5}\
    END{if (statuscode == "0012" || statuscode == "0016") exit 0;
  else exit 1}' $logfile
  then
```

Continued on next page

```
      echo "Errors have occurred importing into "$sid
      echo "Review system log "$logfile
      echo "Execution stopped"
      exit
done

# If the script is here, import was successful
echo "Import Successful"
```

tp Processing Sequence

The contents of the import buffer are organized as a table. Each column represents an import phase, except the last one, which specifies the import option (column UMODE). The numbers in the columns indicate whether the import step is necessary or the number of objects in the request that require the step. Figure 14.2 shows an example of an import buffer. The transport control program *tp* does not process all import steps for one request before proceeding to the next change request. Instead, *tp* collectively processes each import step for all change requests in an import queue before proceeding with the next import step.

During an import, a change request passes through nine *import phases.* These phases are shown in Figure 14.2. The import phases are the technical names for the *import steps* in the *tp* processing sequence. Only the import phase ACTIV contains more than one import step (see Table 14.5 in the next subsection).

During an *import all*, *tp* first processes any change requests containing changes to the ABAP Dictionary—that is, *tp* first imports these objects. This occurs during the *ABAP Dictionary import* phase (DDIC). In Figure 14.2, the change requests DEVK900069 and DEVK900092 contain such changes and are therefore processed by *tp* in the first phase. In the second phase (ACTIV), *tp* activates any objects that have been imported in phase DDIC. In Figure 14.2, this again affects change requests DEVK900069 and DEVK900092. In the third phase, *tp* returns to the first request in the list, and performs the main import (MAIN I) for that change request and then all subsequent change requests in the buffer. This continues until each phase has been completed for all requests in the import queue. The required steps for each change request are listed in the import buffer.

FIGURE 14.2:   *tp* processing sequence for imports

	1st	2nd	3rd	4th	5th	6th	7th	8th	9th
TASK	**DDIC I**	**ACTIV**	**MAIN I**	**MC ACT**	**ADO I**	**LOG I**	**VERS F**	**XPRA**	**GENERA**	**UMODE**
DEVK900048			1				1793			
DEVK900057			1				25		23	
DEVK900053			1				5			
DEVK900069	1	1	1				1		1	
DEVK900078			1				197			
DEVK900083			1				25		23	
DEVK900087			1				5			
DEVK900092	1	1	1				1		1	

Processing the import buffer in a particular sequence of phases technically and logically allows the import of multiple change requests for the following reasons:

- Dictionary structures (such as table structures) are imported and activated prior to the main import phase. The current structures are thereby able to "receive" new data (such as table entries) that may be imported in the same or another change request during the main import phase.

- The Repository objects with the fewest dependencies (the ABAP Dictionary objects) are imported and checked for consistency before ABAP programs and screen definitions are imported. This is important because these objects tend to highly depend on proper ABAP Dictionary settings.

- Since ABAP program generation takes place after the main import process, only the last imported version of the programs and screens is activated. Consider this situation: A "bad" version of a program is released and exported, and then corrected in a change request released later. Even though the bad version was imported, it is quickly overwritten during the main import phase with the "good" version of the program that is contained in the latest change. When the generation phase eventually takes place, only the correct version of the program is generated.

- The amount of import time required for importing multiple change requests is less than that needed for individual requests imported one at a time. Time is saved because standard activities and generic import steps (such as post-activation conversions) take place collectively for all change requests in the queue and not for each individual change request.

NOTE   The processing sequence ensures that if you detect an error in a change request that has already been released, you can correct the object in a new change request. After releasing and exporting the change request, the next *import all* command then imports the whole import buffer in the sequence of export, and the faulty object is overwritten and does not affect your production system.

Example: Advantages of the *tp* Processing Sequence

Change requests DEVK900069 and DEVK900092 (see Figure 14.2 earlier in this section) both contain changes to the same table structure. By mistake, DEVK900069 contains a "bad" change that deletes a very important field from a table containing critical data. Through testing in the quality assurance system, the error is detected before DEVK900069 is imported into the production system. Change request DEVK900092 is released from the development system to correct the problem by redefining the field in its original state. Because the change requests are imported in the proper sequence, as is the case with *tp* processing, the bad change does not affect the production system, and the data in the important field is not deleted. While the bad table structure is imported in the first phase during ABAP Dictionary import, the corrected version of the table structure is then imported and overwrites what is faulty. The table structure activated during import is the table structure imported in change request DEVK900092. The table structure in change request DEVK900069 is never activated in the production system.

Import Steps

The import process includes several import steps (see Table 14.5) that are performed by different transport tools. All of these steps are coordinated by *tp*. Phase ACTIV is the only phase that contains more than one import step. In addition to the activation of ABAP Dictionary objects, this phase includes the generic import steps: distribution, structure conversion, and the moving of nametabs. Generic steps are not related to certain change requests, but are performed for all change requests in one step. Another generic step is the enqueue conversion, which is performed in the phase MC CONV. Note that you cannot display the log files related to generic steps using the TMS. However, you can view them on the operating system level.

For each import step, Table 14.5 lists the character (a letter or number) that is used to represent the step in the generic log files and a description that includes the transport tool involved.

TABLE 14.5: Import Steps

Import Phase	Import Step	Char.	Description	Supporting Transport Tool
DDIC I	Import of ABAP Dictionary objects	H	To enable imports into production systems, the transport program *R3trans* imports the ABAP Dictionary structures inactively.	*R3trans*
ACTIV	Activation of ABAP Dictionary objects	A	Runtime descriptions (nametabs) are written inactively, but during this phase, the steps required for activation are initiated.	RDDMASGL
ACTIV	Distribution of ABAP Dictionary objects	S	Logical checks decide what additional actions are required to bring the new ABAP Dictionary objects into the running system.	RDDGENBB (job name: RDDDIS0L)
ACTIV	Structure conversion	N	ABAP Dictionary structural changes are made.	RDDGENBB (job name: RDDGEN0L)
ACTIV	Move nametabs	6	The new ABAP runtime objects are put into the active runtime environment.	pgmvntabs
MAIN I	Main import	I	Import of all data including table entries.	*R3trans*
MC ACT	Activation and conversion of enqueue objects	M	Enqueue objects such as matchcodes that were not previously activated are now activated. These objects are used immediately in the running system.	RDDGENBB
ADO I	Import of application defined objects (ADOs)	D	Import of additional objects including SAPscript forms and styles, and printer definitions.	RDDDIC1L

Continued on next page

TABLE 14.5: Import Steps *(Continued)*

Import Phase	Import Step	Char.	Description	Supporting Transport Tool
LOG I	Logical import	U	This phase is currently not active and is ignored during the import process.	
VERS F	Versioning	V	Versions of Repository objects are created on the R/3 System from which the objects were exported. The import process modifies the object's version counter, which is incremented during this step for all Repository objects imported.	RDDVERSL
XPRA	Execution of post-import methods	R	Post-import methods are required activities (such as the execution of an ABAP program) that rely on transported data.	RDDEXECL
GENERA	Generation of ABAP programs and screens	G	The generation of imported objects.	RDDDIC03L

From the beginning of the step that moves nametabs until the end of the main import, inconsistencies may occur in the R/3 System. After the main import phase, these inconsistencies will be removed because the R/3 System returns to a consistent state. However, it is not until after the generation of ABAP programs and screens at the end of the import process that you can be assured business activities in the R/3 System will be unaffected (see "R/3 Buffer Synchronization" below for more details).

Using Log Files for Troubleshooting

Occasionally, you will encounter problems during import. The information provided in the following areas will help you to solve these problems:

- Log files stored in the transport subdirectory *log*
  - Generic log files
  - Single step log files
- Return codes

In addition to this information, certain troubleshooting techniques will prove beneficial in remedying errors to ensure a successful import.

Generic Log Files

The transport control program *tp* creates and writes three *generic log files:* the SLOG file (more commonly known as the TP System Log), the ALOG file (referred to as the Transport Step Monitor), and the ULOG file.

The TP System Log that reports the contents of the SLOG file is accessed from within TMS (Transaction STMS) using the menu option *Overview* ➢ *Imports* ➢ *Goto* ➢ *TP System Log* (see Chapter 13). The TP System Log contains a general overview of performed imports, including the respective return code, and thus indicates the success of each import. You can use the TP System Log to monitor the transport activities of a specific R/3 System. To set the name of the SLOG file in the transport profile, use the global transport parameter *syslog*. The default naming convention is SLOG($syear)($yweek).($system), where ($syear) represents the calendar year, ($yweek) is the week of the year, and ($system) is the SID for the R/3 System.

The Transport Step Monitor that reports the contents of the ALOG file is accessed from within TMS (Transaction STMS) using the menu option *Overview* ➤ *Imports* ➤ *Goto* ➤ *TP System Log* ➤ *Goto* ➤ *Transport step* (see Chapter 13). The Transport Step Monitor records the return codes for all transport steps handled in the transport directory. To set the name of the ALOG file in the transport profile, use the global transport parameter *alllog*. The default value is ALOG($syear)($yweek), where ($syear) represents the calendar year and ($yweek) is the week of the year. Each entry in the ALOG file is related to a single step log file from within the Transport Step Monitor.

The ULOG file records all *tp* commands that have been executed and are free of syntax errors. This log uses the naming convention ULOG($syear)_<one digit>, where ($syear) represents the current calendar year and the single digit represents the quarter of the year. For example, ULOG99_4 specifies the log for the fourth quarter—October, November, and December—of the year 1999. The file contents are organized as a table consisting of a row for each *tp* command and three columns containing the following information:

- The operating system user who issued the *tp* command

- The time stamp

- The complete *tp* command executed on the operating system level containing all options and paths

---

TIP The ULOG file is not available from within TMS, but can be viewed on the operating system level in the transport directory *log*.

Single Step Log Files

For each import step, the respective transport tool, either *R3trans* or one of the ABAP programs involved (whose names all begin with *RDD*), writes a log file to the transport directory. The log files are written to the subdirectory *tmp*. At the end of an import, *tp* moves all log files contained in subdirectory *tmp* to subdirectory *log* (see Figure 14.3).

FIGURE 14.3:

Single step log files

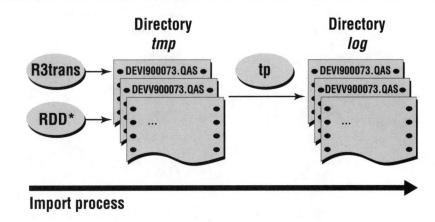

Import process

Each log file contains a list of message texts containing either information, warnings, or errors, which reflect the results of the respective import step. At the end of the log file, the exit or return code of the transport tool is specified. This code indicates the overall success of the import step.

Table 14.6 lists log files for the sample change request DEVK900021 after all import steps have been performed. The naming convention for single step log files is `<source SID> <import step> <6 digits>.<target SID>`. The import step is represented by a single character (see Table 14.5 earlier in this chapter). The six digits following the import step denote the corresponding change request.

The generic import steps—distribution, structure conversion, nametabs movement, and enqueue conversion—are not related to certain change requests like the other steps. These log files cannot be displayed in the TMS. The naming convention for these log files is `<import step><year><month><day>.<target SID>`.

TABLE 14.6: Possible Log Files Generated or Written to during the Import of Change Request DEVK900021

Log File	Import Step	Import Phase
DEVH900021.QAS	Dictionary import	DDIC I
DEVA900021.QAS	Dictionary activation	ACTIV
DS991005.QAS	Distribution	ACTIV
N991005.QAS	Structure conversion	ACTIV
P991005.QAS	Move nametabs	ACTIV
DEVI900021.QAS	Main import	MAIN I
DEVMS900021.QAS	Activation of the enqueue definitions	MC ACT
N991005.QAS	Enqueue conversion	MC CONV
DEVD900021.QAS	Import of ADOs	ADO I
DEVV900021.QAS	Versioning	VERS F
DEVR900021.QAS	Execution of XPRAs	XPRA
DEVG900021.QAS	Generation of ABAP programs and screens	GENERA

Return Codes

Each transport tool involved in the import process exits with a *return code* to *tp* that is also recorded in the respective log file. In addition, *tp* may receive signals and messages from the operating system or the database. *tp* interprets the return codes and calculates its own return code, which indicates the result of the whole import process (see Figure 14.4).

FIGURE 14.4:

Return codes

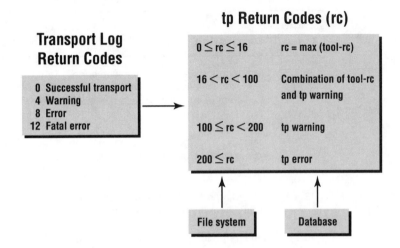

Typically, *tp* only receives return codes from the transport tools that have a value between zero and 16 (see Table 14.7). The overall success of the import then depends on the highest return code that has occurred in an import step. If no other problems occurred, *tp* will display the return code with the highest value received from a transport tool. This is called the *maximum return code*.

By default, if *tp* receives a return code larger than eight during an import phase, *tp* will abort the import process. The transport profile parameter *stoponerror* defines which return code value will cause *tp* to abort.

TABLE 14.7: Examples of *tp* Return Codes

Return Code	Description	Example
0	The transport activities were successful.	
4	Warnings occurred during the transport. All objects were transported successfully, but irregularities occurred.	A change request contains an object deletion.

Continued on next page

TABLE 14.7: Examples of *tp* Return Codes *(Continued)*

Return Code	Description	Example
8	The transport was carried out with errors; however, there is at least one object that could not be transported successfully.	An ABAP program had a syntax error and, while imported, was not able to be generated due to the error.
12	The transport was terminated. A serious error occurred, but was not caused by the contents of a change request.	During the import process, the database of the R/3 System was unavailable for import—for example, because of a lack of tablespace.
13	The transport tool was terminated by a signal from the operating system.	*R3trans* contains a serious error.
16	The transport tool terminated due to an internal error.	There is a possible development error in *tp* or *R3trans* for which you will need to contact SAP's Hotline for assistance.

A return code from 17 to 99 is a combination of the return codes from the different transport tools. This results in a *tp* warning, such as one indicating that the import buffer of the target system has no write permission.

A return code from 100 to 199 displays a *tp* warning. *tp* has calculated the return code by adding 100 to the original return code value. There are two groups of return codes resulting in *tp* warnings:

- Return codes from 100 to 149 indicate "normal" *tp* warnings—that is, *tp* could not perform all tasks. For example,

  RDDIMPDP could not be triggered by the program *sapevt*. To evaluate this kind of return code, refer to its last two digits.

- Return codes from 150 to 199 are rare and indicate incorrect user operation. For example, if *tp* tries to import a change request that is not included in the import buffer, the return code 152 will be displayed. To evaluate the return code, refer to its last two digits.

A return code of 200 or more indicates a *tp* error. For example, if *tp* could not access a file as required by the import process, the return code 212 will be displayed.

TIP   To display the text of a specific *tp* return code, use the command `tp explainrc <value of return code>`.

Troubleshooting Techniques

At the beginning of the implementation phase of an R/3 System landscape or after TMS configuration changes, SAP recommends using the Alert Monitor, which records all TMS transport activities, to eliminate the obvious TMS setup issues. To call the Alert Monitor, use Transaction STMS and choose *Monitor* ➤ *Alert monitor*. The following information is displayed for each TMS function:

- Date and time
- Username
- TMS status message
- Target R/3 System

To display the full text of an error message, double-click the error message. The Alert Monitor reveals mainly TMS configuration errors and TMS connection errors. Once your TMS configuration is stable, you can detect the cause of errors and problems in the related log files.

Always use the import monitor in the TMS to ensure that imports run smoothly. If the import monitor indicates problems and errors, SAP recommends performing the following steps:

1. Use TP System Log in TMS (or the SLOG file on the operating system level) to monitor the transport activities of an R/3 System and determine the results of import activities.

2. If import failures are recorded in the TP System Log, drill down to the Transport Step Monitor in TMS (or the ALOG file at the operating system level) and locate the import step that sent the return code listed in the TP System Log.

3. From the Transport Step Monitor, locate the log file for the specific change request that produced the error and evaluate the cause of the problem. Note that although all transport log files for a specific change request can be viewed from within TMS (see Chapter 12 and Chapter 13), single log files of generic import steps cannot be displayed using the TMS.

These steps can be performed either in R/3 or on the operating system level. The procedure for using the TMS in R/3 is described in the following example.

Example: Troubleshooting an Import Problem

As shown in the following graphic, there are four change requests in the import queue of system QAS.

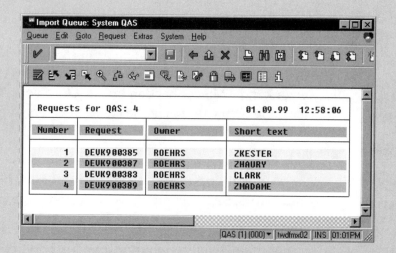

Continued on next page

From the import queue screen of QAS, the import is started using *Queue* ➢ *Start import.*

The import process is monitored by choosing *Goto* ➢ *Import monitor.* The display is refreshed using *Refresh.* The following graphic shows the import monitor as the import is finished (status *tp finished*). It shows that the import process resulted in a maximum return code of 0008. The return code indicates that errors occurred during the import process by *tp*, but no other details are provided, so you must check where and why the error occurred.

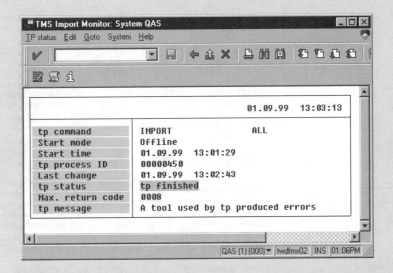

To check whether this error originates from setup errors, from the TMS menu, choose *Monitor* ➢ *Alert monitor.* In this example, the Alert Monitor has not recorded any errors for the time frame of this import (screen not depicted).

In the next step, the TP System Log is checked using *Goto* ➢ *TP system log* from the import monitor screen. As shown in the following graphic, the TP System Log indicates that the import has been completed and that it ended with a return code of eight (0008 in the fifth column of the last row of the screen).

Continued on next page

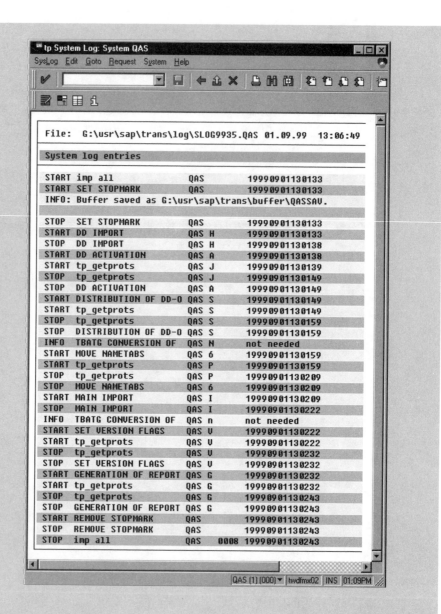

```
tp System Log: System QAS                                    _ □ ×
SysLog  Edit  Goto  Request  System  Help

 ✔  [            ] ▼  🖫  ← 🔒 ✗  🖺 🔍 🗂  🔁 🗂 🗂 🔁   📑

 📝 🖫 🖽 ℹ


 File:  G:\usr\sap\trans\log\SLOG9935.QAS  01.09.99   13:06:49

 System log entries

 START imp all                 QAS        19990901130133
 START SET STOPMARK            QAS        19990901130133
 INFO: Buffer saved as G:\usr\sap\trans\buffer\QASSAV.

 STOP  SET STOPMARK            QAS        19990901130133
 START DD IMPORT               QAS H      19990901130133
 STOP  DD IMPORT               QAS H      19990901130138
 START DD ACTIVATION           QAS A      19990901130138
 START tp_getprots             QAS J      19990901130139
 STOP  tp_getprots             QAS J      19990901130149
 STOP  DD ACTIVATION           QAS A      19990901130149
 START DISTRIBUTION OF DD-O QAS S         19990901130149
 START tp_getprots             QAS S      19990901130149
 STOP  tp_getprots             QAS S      19990901130159
 STOP  DISTRIBUTION OF DD-O QAS S         19990901130159
 INFO  TBATG CONVERSION OF    QAS N       not needed
 START MOVE NAMETABS           QAS 6      19990901130159
 START tp_getprots             QAS P      19990901130159
 STOP  tp_getprots             QAS P      19990901130209
 STOP  MOVE NAMETABS           QAS 6      19990901130209
 START MAIN IMPORT             QAS I      19990901130209
 STOP  MAIN IMPORT             QAS I      19990901130222
 INFO  TBATG CONVERSION OF    QAS n       not needed
 START SET VERSION FLAGS       QAS V      19990901130222
 START tp_getprots             QAS V      19990901130222
 STOP  tp_getprots             QAS V      19990901130232
 STOP  SET VERSION FLAGS       QAS V      19990901130232
 START GENERATION OF REPORT QAS G         19990901130232
 START tp_getprots             QAS G      19990901130232
 STOP  tp_getprots             QAS G      19990901130243
 STOP  GENERATION OF REPORT QAS G         19990901130243
 START REMOVE STOPMARK         QAS        19990901130243
 STOP  REMOVE STOPMARK         QAS        19990901130243
 STOP  imp all                 QAS   0008 19990901130243

                                      QAS (1) (000) ▼  twdfmx02  INS  01:09PM
```

Continued on next page

To display more information about the error, the Transport Step Monitor (the log file ALOG) in the TMS is opened using *Goto* ➤ *Transport steps* from the screen *TP System Log: System QAS*. As shown in the following graphic, the Transport Step Monitor indicates that when the change request DEVK900383 was processed, the return code 0008 (column *RC*) was sent during the import step A (column *S*). This import step is the *ABAP Dictionary activation* in the import phase ACTIV.

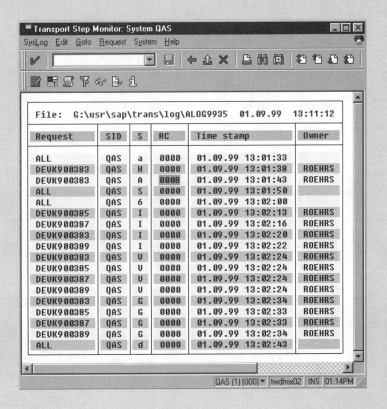

File: G:\usr\sap\trans\log\ALOG9935   01.09.99   13:11:12

Request	SID	S	RC	Time stamp	Owner
ALL	QAS	a	0000	01.09.99 13:01:33	
DEVK900383	QAS	H	0000	01.09.99 13:01:38	ROEHRS
DEVK900383	QAS	A	0008	01.09.99 13:01:43	ROEHRS
ALL	QAS	S	0000	01.09.99 13:01:50	
ALL	QAS	6	0000	01.09.99 13:02:00	
DEVK900385	QAS	I	0000	01.09.99 13:02:13	ROEHRS
DEVK900387	QAS	I	0000	01.09.99 13:02:16	ROEHRS
DEVK900383	QAS	I	0000	01.09.99 13:02:20	ROEHRS
DEVK900389	QAS	I	0000	01.09.99 13:02:22	ROEHRS
DEVK900383	QAS	U	0000	01.09.99 13:02:24	ROEHRS
DEVK900385	QAS	U	0000	01.09.99 13:02:24	ROEHRS
DEVK900387	QAS	U	0000	01.09.99 13:02:24	ROEHRS
DEVK900389	QAS	U	0000	01.09.99 13:02:24	ROEHRS
DEVK900383	QAS	G	0000	01.09.99 13:02:34	ROEHRS
DEVK900385	QAS	G	0000	01.09.99 13:02:33	ROEHRS
DEVK900387	QAS	G	0000	01.09.99 13:02:33	ROEHRS
DEVK900389	QAS	G	0000	01.09.99 13:02:34	ROEHRS
ALL	QAS	d	0000	01.09.99 13:02:43	

Continued on next page

Now that the change request that caused the error has been located, the respective single log file is accessed. To do this, the cursor is positioned on change request DEVK900383. Then, *Request ➤ Logs* is chosen from screen *Transport Step Monitor: System QAS*. As shown in the following graphic, an overview of all transport logs is given.

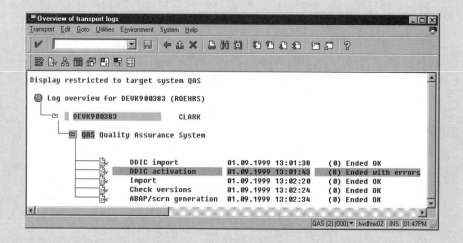

In the screen *Overview of transport logs*, the log file for the import step *ABAP Dictionary activation* (indicated by *DDIC activation*) is highlighted and listed with a return code of eight.

To display the log file for this import step, the highlighted line is double-clicked.

As shown in the following graphic, the single step log file for the import step *ABAP Dictionary activation* is displayed.

Continued on next page

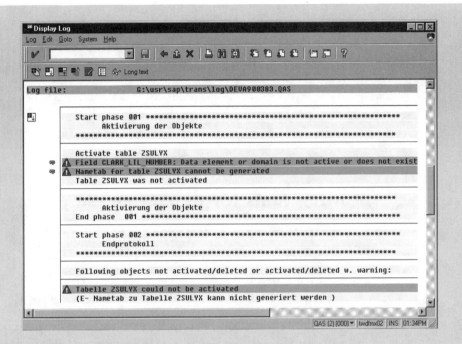

The above extract of log file **DEVA900383.QAS** indicates that the change request DEVK900383 contained the table ZSULYX. The field CLARK_LIL_NUMBER of table ZSULYX could not be activated, because the data element or the domain of this field is not active or does not exist. For this reason, the table was imported, but cannot be activated.

To find out why the data element or domain is not available or activated, Transaction SE11 (Dictionary Browser of the ABAP Workbench) is used. It turns out that the data element does not exist in system QAS. Further examination detects that the data element was created and activated in the development system DEV, but has been recorded in a change request other than DEVK900383, which has not been released yet.

To solve the problem, a new change request is created in the development system that contains all components—the table structure, related data elements, and related domains. The request is released, exported, and then imported into the target system without any errors.

Continued on next page

If the table structure and the data element had been in the same change request, activation of the table structure would have been successful. To prevent such problems, you should encourage developers to transport all related ABAP Dictionary objects in the same change request. This ensures proper activation. Also note that corrections should always be made in the development system.

Further Hints for Troubleshooting

To detect other typical sources of errors, use any of the following methods:

- In R/3, use the job overview (Transaction SM37) to monitor the results of all related background processes (RDD*-jobs).

- On the operating system level, check the import buffer. This provides information about the progress and success of imports. Use the following command: `tp showbuffer <target SID>`.

- In R/3, check the entries in tables TRBAT and TRJOB (see the section "Communication between *tp* and ABAP Programs"). You should also compare them with the log file and import buffer entries on the operating system level.

- In R/3, use the job overview (Transaction SM37) to check whether the import dispatcher RDDIMPDP is scheduled as an event-periodic background job. The related event has to be SAP_TRIGGER_RDDIMPDP. You can also perform this check on the operating system level using the following *tp* command: `tp checkimp <target SID>`.

- Check whether RDDIMPDP is executed when the event SAP_TRIGGER_RDDIMPDP is triggered. In R/3, use Transaction SM64; on the operating system level, use the R/3 executable *sapevt*.

- If necessary, verify the version of the transport tools *tp* and *R3trans*. The version is indicated in the first output line after calling any *tp* command.

- Check whether *tp* is running—for example, on UNIX platforms, use the following command: `ps -ef | grep tp`.

- Check whether there are permission or share problems with the transport directory.

- Check whether there is enough free disk space in the transport directory.

R/3 Buffer Synchronization

To reduce database accesses and network load, as well as improve system performance, frequently used data in an R/3 System is stored in R/3 buffers. These buffers are located in the shared memory of an application server. Every work process in an instance accesses these buffers. Data stored in the R/3 buffers includes ABAP program, screens, ABAP Dictionary data, and company-specific data, which normally remains unchanged during system operation.

If an R/3 System consists of several instances on multiple application servers, changes to data stored in the local buffers of the application servers must be updated at regular intervals. This prevents inconsistencies between the local buffers on each instance. The synchronization process is asynchronous to minimize network load. Imports into an R/3 System may also affect R/3 buffers, because imported objects can be objects that are stored in one of the R/3 buffers. Therefore, central systems with only one instance also have to be synchronized.

Because of the required amount of network and database accesses, updating buffers places a high load on the system. In large systems, it may take two to three hours for performance to stabilize again after a complete buffer reset. You must take this into consideration when importing change requests.

WARNING   Importing data into a production system can significantly impact performance.

Data inconsistencies can occur if an application server reads data from its buffer between two synchronization procedures. If, at the time of access, the data is being processed by another server or is in the process of being imported, it will not be up to date. The following examples illustrate the risk of temporary and permanent inconsistencies when importing changes into production systems.

Example: Temporary Inconsistencies

A change to the structure of a table—that is, a Dictionary change—has been entered by an import into an R/3 System. Before the buffers are synchronized, a dependent program is loaded. The program is generated with the old structure and saved with a time stamp indicating a time after the new structure was imported and activated. After the subsequent buffer synchronization, the program retains the incorrect structure. This is an inconsistency that cannot be easily detected. When this dependent program runs, the work area of the table will no longer match the structure used when the work area was generated. When the program is executed, it will terminate with the runtime error GETWA_CANT_CLEAR. When a transaction is called, you must manually regenerate all the related programs that are listed in the short dump.

Example: Permanent Inconsistencies

Program A is being generated in the production system, so the database sets a lock on the program data. While program A is being generated, *tp* imports an include program, on which both programs A and B depend. During buffer synchronization, the system tries to set a new change time stamp for programs A and B. Although the time stamp is specified, it cannot be set because program A is still being generated and is thus locked by the database.

After program A has been generated, the system sets a generation time stamp for program A, and the database lock is removed. The program then tries to set the change time stamp for programs A and B. Program B is regenerated because its last generation time stamp was set before the change time stamp. Program A, however, will not be regenerated because its most recent generation time stamp was set after the change time stamp was determined. The program retains the old structure. Consequently, this inconsistency will remain in R/3 until program A is changed.

Temporary inconsistencies are less critical than permanent ones because temporary inconsistencies exist only until the transaction is restarted or failed programs are regenerated. Restarting the transaction causes the buffers to be synchronized, which restores the consistency between the object and the buffers. Permanent inconsistencies remain in the R/3 System until corrected either manually or by importing new versions of the inconsistent objects.

WARNING Transporting programs and ABAP Dictionary data can cause both temporary and permanent inconsistencies if they affect running programs and their environment. SAP recommends scheduling imports into production systems to run at night in the background when there is low system load. Alternatively, you could perform a detailed check on the jobs that are running and monitor the effects carefully.

Naming Conventions in the Transport Directory

Chapter 7 introduced the transport directory and its subdirectories. Because the transport control program *tp* runs on many different operating systems, the files of the transport directory use restrictive naming conventions. The naming conventions are applied to the files automatically and can help you with troubleshooting. Once you have identified a change request that caused errors, you can use the naming conventions to access the related log files and find out how to resolve the errors.

Figure 14.5 illustrates the file naming conventions for the subdirectory files that are related to a specific change request. The sample change request DEVK900073 serves as the basis for the subdirectory files. The user SMITH created the change request in the development system, DEV. There is a consolidation route between DEV and the quality assurance system, QAS. QAS is the first system into which the change request will be imported. Therefore, DEV is the source SID of this change request; QAS is the target SID.

As mentioned in Chapter 4, change requests are named following this convention: `<source SID>K9<5 digits>`. K9 indicates that this is a customer change request. The subsequent five digits are a serial number. The naming convention for the subdirectories in the transport directory follows these rules:

actlog: For each change request and also for each task, one file named `<source SID>Z9<5 digits>.<source SID>` is written. The file records each user action on the request or task—for example, creation, release, or change of ownership. In Figure 14.5, the files `DEVZ900073.DEV` for the change request and `DEVZ900074.DEV` for the only related task have been stored. If, for example, the owner of the task is changed, a new entry containing this action will be added to `DEVZ900074.DEV`.

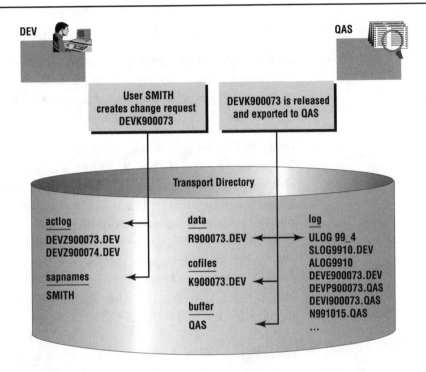

sapnames: A file is automatically created for each R/3 user who performs transport activities on a change request. This file is updated when the user releases and exports a request. The naming convention is the user's logon name. In Figure 14.5, this file is named SMITH.

buffer: When the change request is released, an entry is added to the import buffer for the target system, QAS. The naming convention for the import buffer is the SID of the target system. In Figure 14.5, the change request is added to the import buffer QAS.

data: As the change request is exported, the contained objects are stored to files named according to this naming convention: R9<5 digits >.<source SID>. In Figure 14.5, the corresponding file is named R900073.DEV. If application defined objects (ADOs) are contained in the change request, another file is created, which begins with D9 instead of R9.

cofiles: When exporting, a control file named K9<5 digits> .<source SID> is created. This control file contains, for example, the import steps that have to be performed. The control file in Figure 14.5 is named K900073.DEV.

log: Various log files are contained in this subdirectory. The generic log files ULOG, ALOG, and SLOG either get new entries or are created if they did not previously exist. The change request in Figure 14.5 was transported in October 1999. Thus, the generic log files are ULOG 99_4, SLOG9910 .DEV, and ALOG9910. (For information on the naming convention of these files, see the section "Generic Log Files.") For each executed transport step, a single step log file is stored. Some sample log files related to the change request include DEVE900073.DEV, DEVP900073.DEV, DEVI900073.QAS, and N991015.QAS. (For information on the naming convention of these files, see the section "Single Step Log Files.")

Removing Files from the Transport Directory

In the course of time, many large files may accumulate in your transport directories. These files will become obsolete over time. Depending on your transport activities and your amount of free disk space, you should occasionally clean up the transport directory. This activity can be performed only on the operating system level using the appropriate *tp* commands. To clean up the transport directory, proceed as follows (see also Figure 14.6):

1. Execute the following command:

   ```
   tp check all
   ```

This command reads all import buffers and searches in sub-directories *data*, *cofiles*, and *log* of the transport directory for files that are no longer needed. Such files refer to change requests that are no longer contained in any import buffer. The names of these files are listed in the file ALL_OLD.LIS in the transport subdirectory *tmp*.

2. Execute the following command:

   ```
   tp clearold all
   ```

   tp checks each file listed in ALL_OLD.LIS to determine whether it has exceeded a maximum age. The maximum age is specified in days by the transport profile parameters *datalifetime* (default 200), *olddatalifetime* (default 365), *cofilelifetime* (default 365), and *loglifetime* (default 200). *tp* then processes the files in the following way:

   - Data files in the transport subdirectory *data* that are older than the value specified in the parameter *datalifetime* are moved by *tp* to the transport subdirectory *olddata*.

   - Files in the subdirectories *log* and *cofiles* are immediately deleted by *tp* if they are older than the value specified by the parameter *loglifetime* or *cofilelifetime*.

   - Files in *olddata* are deleted if they are older than the value specified in the parameter *olddatalifetime*.

FIGURE 14.6: Cleaning up the transport directory

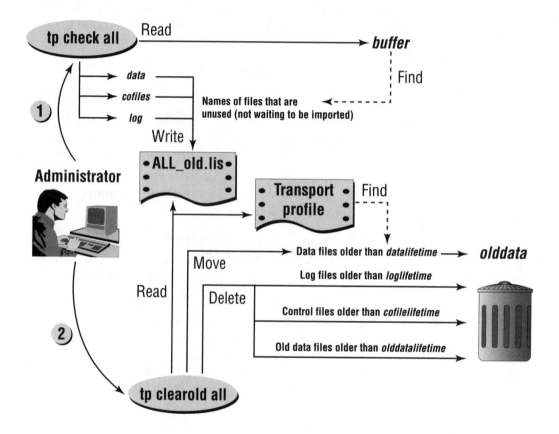

Understanding Transport Tools

The Change and Transport System (CTS) uses several transport tools to transport data to and from an R/3 System. On the operating system level, these tools include the transport control program *tp* (*tp.exe* on Windows NT platforms), the transport program

R3trans (*R3trans.exe* on Windows NT platforms), and the program *sapevt* (*sapevt.exe* on Windows NT platforms).

These tools are automatically installed as executables on the operating system level during the installation process of an R/3 System. Note that they are not stored in the subdirectory *bin* of the transport directory, but in the following directory, which houses most R/3 executables:

- /usr/sap/<SID>/SYS/exe/run on UNIX and AS/400 platforms
- \usr\sap\<SID>\SYS\exe\run on Windows NT platforms

TIP   After an R/3 Release upgrade, check the transport directory *bin*. If you find variants of the programs *tp* and *R3trans* that have been stored by a former R/3 Release, delete the programs to ensure that the correct transport programs are used from the executable directory.

Several R/3 components are involved in performing transports. These include the transport dispatcher RDDIMPDP and several ABAP programs that carry out various steps required in the transport process—for example, generating imported reports. (See Table 14.8 later in this chapter in the column *ABAP Program*.)

The Transport Program *R3trans*

R3trans is the transport tool on the operating system level that actually transports data between R/3 Systems. *R3trans* exports objects from the source database and stores them in data files on the operating system level. During import, *R3trans* reuses the data files and imports the objects into the target database.

The format of the data files written by *R3trans* is also known as *R3trans* format and is independent of the platform. Thus, you can transport data between different databases or operating systems. Additionally, upward compatibility is guaranteed; that is, you can export data with an old *R3trans* version and import the data with a newer version.

Although exports and imports are independent of the *R3trans* version, the database platform, or the operating system, because of logical dependencies within R/3, SAP does not support transports between different R/3 Releases.

R3trans is called by other programs, such as *tp* and the upgrade control program *R3up*. Because *R3trans* is not the only tool needed to perform a complete and correct import of change requests, SAP does not recommend directly calling *R3trans*. Always use *tp* to ensure that all export and import steps, including *R3trans* activities, are completed successfully.

Transport Tool Interaction on the Operating System Level

On the operating system level, *tp* interacts with *R3trans*. In the import process, *tp* tracks the extracted objects, ensuring that they are added to the database of the target system. The interaction between *tp* and *R3trans* is depicted in Figure 14.7.

FIGURE 14.7:

Transport tool interaction on the operating system level

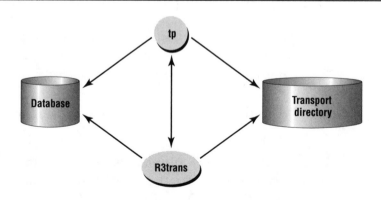

tp always reads the transport profile in the transport directory that determines how *tp* should behave. This transport file specifies the host, database, and path information through certain parameter settings.

When starting an import, *tp* sets a stopmark at the end of the import buffer of the target system and reads the import buffer to determine which change requests have to be imported and which import steps have to be performed for which change request. In addition, *tp* reads the corresponding control file in the subdirectory *cofiles* for details on the steps to be performed.

tp passes a control file to the transport subdirectory *tmp* for use by *R3trans*. *tp* then calls *R3trans* by initiating a new process using the following operating system commands:

- *fork()* on UNIX platforms

- *CreateProcess()* on Windows NT platforms

- *spawn()* on AS/400 platforms

R3trans reads the control file in the subdirectory *tmp*. This control file determines what activities *R3trans* should perform. *R3trans* reuses the data files that it stored to the subdirectory *data* during exports and connects to the database of the target system to import the objects. When importing objects to the target database, *R3trans* updates, inserts, and deletes data in the database.

R3trans is responsible for the import steps *ABAP dictionary import* for the import of ABAP Dictionary definitions and *main import* for the import of table contents (see the section "Import Steps").

R3trans always passes a return code to *tp* when exiting. For each transport action, *R3trans* writes a log file in the transport subdirectory *tmp*. After *R3trans* completes its work, *tp* interprets the return code from *R3trans* and moves its log file to the transport subdirectory *log*.

After the import process, *tp* cleans up the import buffer and removes the stopmark.

R3trans does not interact with the other transport tools. In contrast, *tp* communicates extensively with ABAP programs within R/3 when performing certain steps in the target system (see below in the section "Communication between *tp* and ABAP Programs").

ABAP Programs

Importing change requests involves different ABAP programs within R/3, depending on the import steps that have to be performed—for example, activating the ABAP Dictionary, converting structures, or generating reports and screens. The ABAP programs are executed as background jobs.

NOTE   Because the ABAP programs are executed as background jobs, there must be at least two background work processes running in the target R/3 System.

To execute the necessary transport steps, *tp* uses the control tables TRBAT and TRJOB to communicate with the various ABAP programs. TRBAT and TRJOB are control tables that contain temporary data. After reading the control file (subdirectory *cofiles*) for the import of a change request, *tp* writes entries to the control table TRBAT, specifying the steps to be performed for the respective request. Table 14.8 lists the ABAP programs, the related job name, a description of the function, and the function code specifying the function to be performed in table TRBAT.

TABLE 14.8: Functions of ABAP Programs during Change Request Import

Function Code	Job Name	ABAP Program	Description
X	RDDDIC0L	RDDDIC0L	ADO export
J	RDDMASGL	RDDMASGL	Mass activator
B	RDDTACOL	RDDTACOL	TACOB activator
S	RDDDISOL	RDDGENBB	Distributor
N	RDDGEN0L	RDDGENBB	Import converter
M	RDDMASGL	RDDMASGL	Mass activator (Enqueue)
Y(n)	RDDGEN0L	RDDGENBB	Matchcode converter
O	RDDGEN0L	RDDGENBB	Batch converter
D	RDDDIC1L	RDDDIC1L	ADO import
V	RDDVERSL	RDDVERSL	Create version
R	RDDEXECL	RDDEXECL	XPRA execution
G	RDDDIC3L	RDDDIC3L	Generation

The interaction between *tp* and the ABAP programs is depicted in Figure 14.8. After making the required entries to table TRBAT, *tp* triggers the import dispatcher RDDIMPDP.

As a prerequisite, RDDIMPDP must be scheduled as an event-periodic background job in client 000 of the target system. Additionally, a similar background job must be scheduled in every target client. This background job is called RDDIMPDP_CLIENT_<nnn>, where <nnn> represents the client ID. These jobs are normally scheduled automatically after a client copy. You can also schedule them manually by running the program RDDNEWPP in the respective client (see Chapter 7).

RDDIMPDP reads the information on import steps that *tp* writes to the control table TRBAT and then starts the corresponding programs as background jobs. The names of these programs and jobs all start with *RDD*—for example, RDDMASGL is for mass activation, RDDGENBB is for conversion, and RDDVERSL is for versioning. Each RDD*-job (as they are commonly referred to) collectively receives a job number, which is recorded in table TRJOB. The jobs report their status and final return code back to table TRBAT and delete the corresponding TRJOB entry just before they finish.

They also write log files into the transport directory in the subdirectory *tmp*. At the end of an import, these log files are moved to the subdirectory *log* by *tp*.

FIGURE 14.8:

Interaction between ABAP programs and *tp*

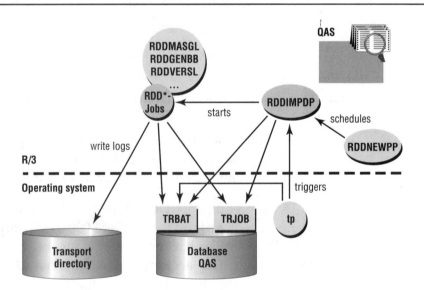

Communication between *tp* and ABAP Programs

The following section focuses on how *tp* communicates with the ABAP programs that are involved in the import process. The main components for performing an import are depicted in Figure 14.9. The figure is divided into three parts: the operating system (OS) level, the database, and the ABAP programs within R/3.

FIGURE 14.9:

tp starts the import process.

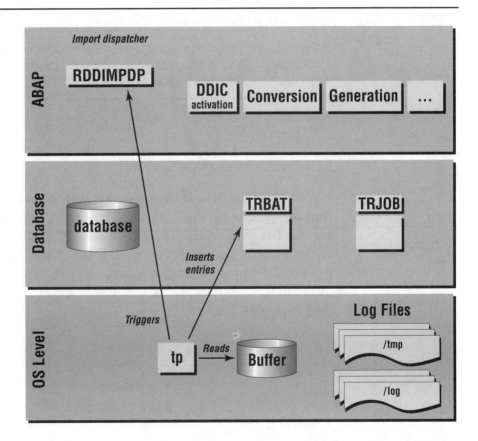

When you perform an import, *tp* reads the import buffer and then writes an entry to the control table TRBAT for every change request in the import buffer. *tp* groups the change requests according to the import step to be performed. The entry in table TRBAT contains the name of the change request, the function performed during the import step, the return code, and the time stamp. The import function is represented by a character. For example, *J* indicates that the *mass activator* is performing the import step *ABAP Dictionary activation*. For a list of TRBAT function codes, refer back to Table 14.8. As a signal to RDDIMPDP to start processing, *tp* writes a *header entry* after every group of change requests that have the same function code.

NOTE   For generic import steps that are independent of certain change requests, such as distribution and structure conversion, *tp* writes only a header entry in table TRBAT.

To trigger the import dispatcher RDDIMPDP, *tp* calls the operating system tool *sapevt*, which sends the event SAP_TRIGGER_RDDIMPDP to the R/3 System.

When RDDIMPDP starts processing, it checks table TRBAT to find out whether there is an import step to be performed, such as mass activation, distribution, or table conversion. It sets the return code of the header entry to R (for "run"), starts the appropriate RDD* program as a background job, enters the job number of the new job into table TRJOB, reschedules itself, and then exits (see Figure 14.10).

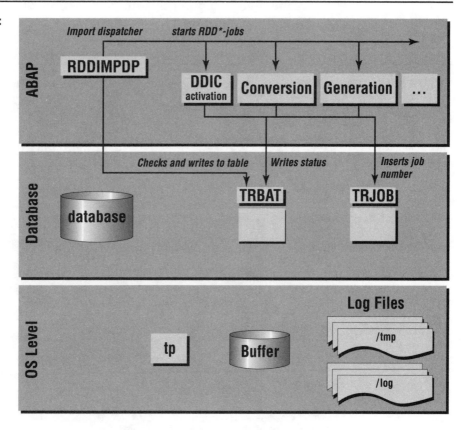

FIGURE 14.10:

The ABAP programs access the database tables.

Each RDD* background job receives a job number generated by R/3 background processing. The job number and the function code are recorded in table TRJOB. The respective RDD*-jobs indicate their status in table TRBAT by logging their current return code.

When the background jobs exit, they write their final status as return codes in table TRBAT and delete the corresponding job number in table TRJOB. Return codes other than 9999 and 8888 indicate that the import step is complete. In table TRBAT, the column *Timestamp* contains the time of completion. When all the necessary actions have been performed for all change requests, the respective RDD* job sets the header entry to F (for "finished"). (See Figure 14.11.)

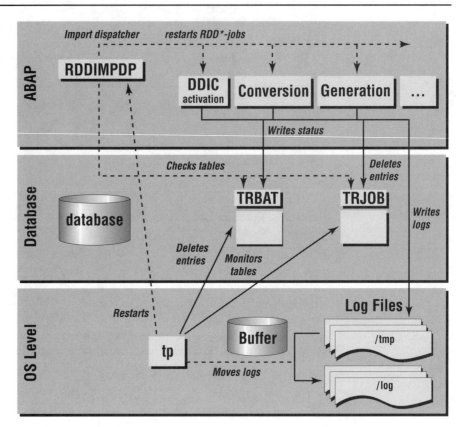

All background jobs log the steps they perform either in the database or in the transport subdirectory *tmp*. *tp* monitors the entries in the tables TRBAT and TRJOB. When an entry that is not a header entry has a return code other than 8888 or 9999, the job is considered finished. Then, *tp* copies the log file from the subdirectory *tmp* to the subdirectory *log* and deletes the corresponding TRBAT entry. When the header entry in TRBAT is set to F and

TRJOB is empty, the ABAP programs have completed their role in the import steps.

If *tp* detects problems when monitoring the tables TRBAT and TRJOB, *tp* retriggers RDDIMPDP using *sapevt*. RDDIMPDP automatically recognizes whether an import step is still active or has been aborted by checking tables TRJOB and TRBAT. If a step was aborted, RDDIMPDP will restart this step.

Example: TRBAT Entries during an Import

When *tp* reads the import buffer of the target system, it notices that three of the change requests require the import step *ABAP Dictionary activation*. Therefore, *tp* writes the three change requests to table TRBAT, and it assigns the function code J to the change requests. This indicates that *ABAP Dictionary activation* has to be performed.

tp then writes a header entry to tell RDDIMPDP to start processing. The return code 9999 indicates that the step is waiting to be performed. For the header entry, *tp* inserts a B (for "begin") as the return code. The contents of table TRBAT are as follows:

Request	Function Code	Return Code	Time Stamp
DEVK904711	J	9999	00000001
DEVK904712	J	9999	00000002
DEVK904713	J	9999	00000003
HEADER	J	B	19983103143701

After RDDIMPDP sets the return code of the header entry to R, it activates the program RDDMASGL. The program RDDMASGL is the *mass activator*, which performs the import step *ABAP Dictionary activation*. While RDDMASGL is running, the status of the first entry in table TRBAT is changed to "active," which is indicated by the return code 8888.

Continued on next page

Request	Function Code	Return Code	Time Stamp
DEVK904711	J	8888	00000001
DEVK904712	J	9999	00000002
DEVK904713	J	9999	00000003
HEADER	J	R	19983103143903

When the program RDDMASGL (the *mass activator*) has completed the import step *ABAP Dictionary activation*, it enters the return codes for each change request in table TRBAT and changes the status of the header entry to F. In this way, RDDIMPDP will recognize that the import step *ABAP Dictionary activation* has been completed.

Request	Function Code	Return Code	Time Stamp
DEVK904711	J	4	19983103144202
DEVK904712	J	0	19983103144357
DEVK904713	J	0	19983103144512
HEADER	J	F	19983103144512

Review Questions

1. Which of the following statements are correct in regard to the transport control program *tp*?

   A. To perform imports, *tp* must always be used directly on the operating system level.

   B. SAP recommends that you use the TMS instead of *tp* to perform imports.

C. *tp* is responsible for exporting and importing objects from and to R/3 Systems.

D. *tp* does not observe the sequence of change requests in the import queue when performing imports.

2. Which of the following statements are correct in regard to import queues and import buffers?

A. Import queues are TMS representations in R/3 of the import buffer files on the operating system level.

B. Import queues and import buffers are completely independent of each other.

C. Import buffers have to be manipulated before imports can be performed on the operating system level.

D. Manipulating import buffers may cause serious inconsistencies and should be performed only in exceptional cases.

3. Which of the following statements are correct in regard to the import options formerly known as *unconditional modes*?

A. Import options cannot be used when imports are performed on the operating system level using *tp*.

B. Import options are used to cause specific rules of the Change and Transport System (CTS) to be ignored.

C. Import options must be used when importing into multiple clients using *tp*.

D. Import options can be selected in the TMS using the expert mode.

4. Which of the following statements are correct in regard to the sequence of processing steps *tp* follows when performing imports?

   A. *tp* collectively processes each import step for all change requests in an import queue before proceeding with the next import step.

   B. *tp* processes all import steps for a single request before proceeding to the next change request.

   C. The processing sequence followed by *tp* ensures that when a change request with a faulty object is followed in the import queue by a change request with the corrected object, the faulty object will not affect the runtime environment of the target system.

   D. *tp* imports and activates ABAP Dictionary structures prior to the main import phase to ensure that the current structures are able to receive new data during the main import phase.

5. Which of the following statements are correct in regard to troubleshooting imports?

   A. In R/3, you cannot display log files that do not depend on a specific request. For example, you cannot display log files related to generic import steps, such as structure conversion.

   B. SAP recommends that you check the SLOG file and the ALOG file before checking the single step log files.

   C. By default, all return codes greater than eight cause *tp* to abort a running import.

   D. *tp* is the only transport tool that uses return codes.

6. Which of the following statements are correct in regard to buffer synchronization?

   A. Transport activities do not affect buffer synchronization.

   B. Imports affect buffer synchronization even in central R/3 Systems.

   C. *R3trans* can invalidate buffer content.

   D. Importing data into a production system can significantly impact performance, because some buffer content may be invalidated and reloaded. This causes high system load.

   E. Importing programs and ABAP Dictionary data cannot cause inconsistencies in the target system, even if the programs or data affect running programs and their environment.

7. Which of the following statements are correct in regard to the interaction between transport tools?

   A. During exports, *tp* calls *R3trans* to access the database of the source system and extract the objects to be transported.

   B. *tp* triggers the transport daemon RDDIMPDP in R/3 using the operating system tool *sapevt*.

   C. Using the tables TRBAT and TRJOB, *tp* communicates with ABAP programs involved in the transport process.

   D. *tp* communicates with only RDDIMPD.

Support Packages and Upgrades

In this chapter, you will learn how to use the Online Correction Support (OCS) to apply Support Packages in your R/3 System. This chapter also outlines the general guidelines to follow when upgrading a system, including the steps necessary for making modification adjustments during upgrade or when applying Support Packages. Although the procedures for applying Support Packages and performing modification adjustments are explained in detail, this overview of the upgrade process cannot replace the SAP-delivered R/3 Upgrade Guides.

The relevant tools for this chapter include:

- The SAP Patch Manager (Transaction SPAM), which is used to apply Support Packages

- Transaction SPDD, which is used to perform modification adjustments for ABAP Dictionary objects

- Transaction SPAU, which is used to perform modification adjustments for R/3 Repository objects

Although the primary target audience for this chapter is the system administrator who needs to support the R/3 System landscape in its evolution, an implementation project manager can also benefit from the information provided here. For example, the sections on upgrades and modification adjustments will help a project manager plan upgrades and estimate the time and staff required.

Evolution of an R/3 Production System

Over time, your R/3 production system will undergo an evolutionary process that allows you to better react to your changing business needs. One part of this evolution is the production support discussed in Chapter 6. After the introduction of a new implementation phase and a period of stabilizing the production environment, production support allows for necessary changes to the production environment—for example, because of the emergence of errors or frequently changed configuration requirements. Ideally, you should restrict these changes to urgently required corrections. You should not create new functions in the production system.

In addition to production support, the evolutionary process (see Figure 15.1) includes the following:

- The application of Support Packages from the Online Correction Support (OCS). Support Packages were formerly known as *patches*.

- Upgrades to newer R/3 Releases.

FIGURE 15.1:

Evolutionary process of the production system

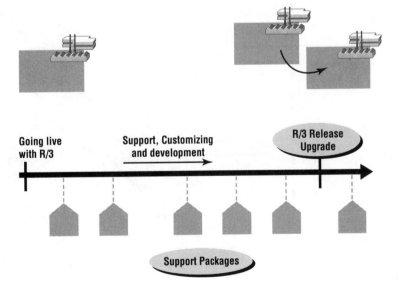

R/3 Release Strategy

To plan and support the evolutionary process of your production environment more efficiently, you need a thorough understanding of SAP's R/3 Release strategy. SAP distinguishes between two types of R/3 Releases (see Figure 15.2):

- R/3 Functional Releases
- R/3 Correction Releases

FIGURE 15.2:

R/3 Release strategy

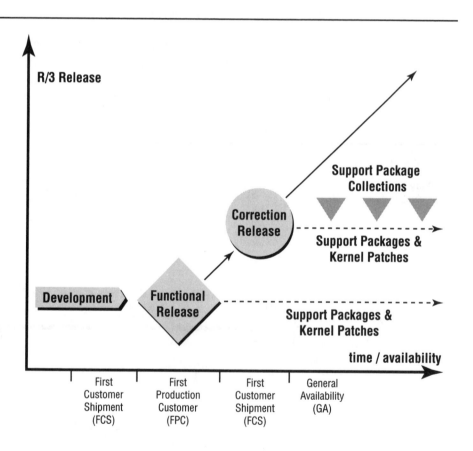

An R/3 Functional Release contains SAP's newest, enhanced business processes and technology. It has only controlled availability (CA); that is, SAP ships a new R/3 Functional Release to only a limited number of customers who request it. To receive an R/3 Functional Release, you must contact your sales representative. For both Functional Releases and Correction Releases, SAP calls the initial delivery of these Releases the *First Customer Shipment (FCS)*. As of the R/3 Functional Release, the FCS phase is followed by the *First Production Customer (FPC)* phase, in which customers are productive with these releases. Customers working with a Functional Release verify the new functions and provide SAP with feedback to help improve the subsequent Correction Release.

> **NOTE** R/3 Functional Releases receive only limited OCS maintenance; that is, only very urgent corrections to priority 1 problems are available as Support Packages for these releases.

Based on the feedback from customers using the R/3 Functional Release, SAP makes the necessary improvements, thereby producing the corresponding R/3 Correction Release. An R/3 Correction Release contains the new functions of the previous R/3 Functional Release and all of the necessary corrections.

In contrast to the controlled availability of R/3 Functional Releases, once an R/3 Correction Release reaches the stage of general availability (GA), SAP automatically delivers it to all R/3 customers. Correction Releases receive a high level of OCS maintenance, including Support Packages for problems with priority 1 and 2. All customers also automatically receive Support Package Collections, which are CD-ROMs containing all Support Packages available at that time for a particular R/3 Correction Release. This support and the stability of Correction Releases make them suitable for production use.

In addition to R/3 Functional and Correction Releases, SAP provides its customers with kernel patches. Since the R/3 kernel software is backwards compatible—that is, it can be upgraded without applying a complete R/3 Release upgrade—customers can correct kernel errors by simply installing a more up-to-date kernel in a kernel patch. A complete R/3 upgrade is not necessary. (For more details, see below under "Other Updates.") Figure 15.3 illustrates the R/3 Release strategy using the R/3 Releases 4.0 and 4.5 as examples.

FIGURE 15.3:

Release strategy for R/3 Releases 4.0 and 4.5

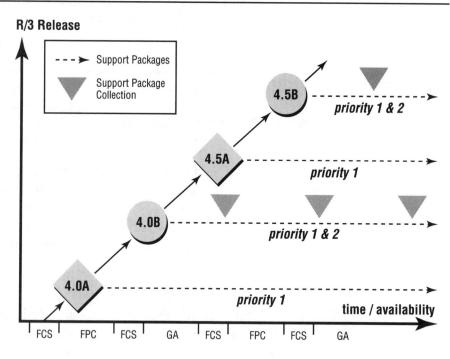

Online Correction Support (OCS)

Online Correction Support comprises several tools that support your production environment between going live and an upgrade, or between two upgrades. OCS is the official service for supplying SAP customers with Support Packages and the tools necessary for applying Support Packages at a particular R/3 level.

Support Packages allow you to eliminate errors in SAP standard objects in your R/3 System prior to the next R/3 Release. Each new R/3 Release includes the corrections in previous Support Packages. Technically, Support Packages are change requests containing corrections for errors in programs residing in the R/3 Repository. When imported, these change requests replace the objects that need to be corrected. Each new R/3 Release includes the corrections supplied in previous Support Packages.

Each Support Package contains corrections mentioned in one or more SAPNet R/3 Notes related to priority 1 or 2 problems. While R/3 Notes require you to manually enter coding, a Support Package eliminates this need, thereby preventing any possible errors or complications. Support Packages are not recognized as modifications during an upgrade—unlike manual corrections. Using Support Packages is one way of avoiding modifications to the SAP standard that may require time-consuming modification adjustments during an upgrade.

Support Packages are available to all customers. The OCS service enables you to download Support Packages using a remote connection. SAP takes full responsibility for changes that have been applied through Support Packages. The OCS enables you to protect your modifications and add-ons from being overwritten during upgrades. After downloading the Support Packages, the SAP Patch Manager (Transaction code SPAM) is used to apply the Support Packages within your R/3 System. The SAP Patch Manager is integrated into the SAP upgrade procedure and is referred to as the customer side of the OCS service.

> **NOTE** SAP recommends that you apply Support Packages as they become available to keep your R/3 Systems up to date and avoid encountering problems that may exist in earlier versions of SAP objects.

Types of Support Packages

Support Packages exist for different R/3 application components as well as for SAP add-ons and other SAP products. Table 15.1 lists the various Support Packages, the types, and the technical naming convention. For example, the filename SAPKH45B03 indicates that the Support Package is the third Hot Package for R/3 Release 4.5B.

TABLE 15.1: Types of Support Packages

Support Package Name	Type	Technical Naming Convention
Hot Package	HOT	SAPKH<Release ID><serial #>
Legal Change Patch	LCP	SAPKE<release ID><serial #>
FCS Final Delta Patch (FFDP)	FFD	SAPKD<release ID>XX
Conflict Resolution Transport	CRT	SAPKI<add-on ID><serial #>; SAPKG<add-on ID><serial #> for SAP add-ons; SAPKJ<add-on ID><serial #> for add-ons from SAP partners; and SAPKP<add-on ID><serial #> for country versions
SPAM Update	PAT	SAPKD<serial #>
SAP Business Warehouse Patch	BWP	SAPK<release ID for BW><serial #>
Software Component Patch (as of R/3 Release 4.5A)	COP	SAPK<X><release ID><serial #>, where X represents the Software Component
Add-On Patch (as of R/3 Release 4.0B)	AOP	SAPKI<add-on ID><serial #> and SAPKG<add-on ID><serial #>

*A serial # is an incremented two-digit number that is used to ensure that Support Packages are applied sequentially.
**A release ID is a three-character unique identifier for an SAP product release.

Each Support Package has a defined number of predecessors since the last R/3 Correction Release. The SAP Patch Manager ensures that Support Packages are applied in the ascending order of the serial numbers. Although each Support Package is valid for only one R/3 Release, it is valid for all platforms—that is, all databases and operating systems.

Before you apply a Support Package, you must ensure that it is the correct type of Support Package for your R/3 implementation. The type of Support Package you need depends on your application components and the R/3 add-ons in your system, as well as whether you have an R/3 Functional Release or Correction Release. This is explained in more detail in the following sections.

Hot Packages

Hot Packages contain a collection of corrections for serious errors in R/3 Repository and Dictionary objects, with the exception of objects in the application component SAP Human Resources (SAP HR). Each correction is associated with a particular R/3 Note describing the correction. All the currently available Hot Packages for a specific R/3 Release are periodically combined in CD-ROMs called *Support Package Collections*. As explained earlier in this chapter, for R/3 Functional Releases, SAP issues only a small number of Hot Packages for urgent corrections.

Legal Change Patches

In releases prior to R/3 Release 4.5B, Legal Change Patches (LCPs) contain the same collections of corrections for serious errors in the R/3 Repository as Hot Packages. LCPs also contain general corrections and other adjustments required by legal changes affecting the Human Resources (HR) component. LCPs are offered as an alternative to Hot Packages to all customers who use the HR application component in their implementation. To use LCPs, you must configure your R/3 System as an LCP system. After a system is configured as an LCP system, Hot Packages cannot be applied in it. The combination of HR corrections and Hot Packages is necessary because of interdependencies between the two areas.

NOTE For more information on configuring an R/3 System for Legal Change Patches, see R/3 Note 89089.

As of R/3 Release 4.5B, LCPs contain only the corrections and other adjustments required by legal changes affecting the Human Resources (HR) component. They no longer contain the general corrections provided by Hot Packages. If you need corrections for both the HR component and the other components, as of R/3 Release 4.5, you need to apply Support Packages of both types, which can be done simultaneously. The SAP Patch Manager has been adjusted so that it enables an independent application of both Support Package types (*LCP* and *HOT*).

In rare cases, there are dependencies between the two types of corrections; that is, a particular Legal Change Patch presumes a particular Hot Package.

NOTE For more information on applying Legal Change Patches in R/3 Release 4.5, see R/3 Note 135568.

FCS Final Delta Patches

FCS Final Delta Patches are for customers who participated in the First Customer Shipment (FCS) program (see above). These Support Packages bring the R/3 System up to date with the Correction Release so that the Support Packages for the Correction Release can subsequently be applied when required. Before the FCS Final Delta Patch is applied, these systems are registered as FCS systems.

Conflict Resolution Transports

Conflict Resolution Transports (CRTs) are exclusively used for R/3 add-ons that are industry solutions, such as SAP Oil & Gas, SAP Utilities, and SAP Healthcare. CRTs are designed to resolve conflicts that can occur between the add-on and Support Packages (of either type, *HOT* or *LCP*).

R/3 add-ons adapt the SAP standard to the needs of a particular branch of industry. The objects modified by the add-on may also be affected by applying Support Packages. CRTs prevent this. When you apply Support Packages, if your system contains an add-on that conflicts with the Hot Package or LCP, you are prompted to download and apply the corresponding CRT. A Support Package that conflicts with an add-on can be applied only once if the corresponding CRT is in the right sequence in the queue of Support Packages to be applied.

SPAM Updates

A SPAM Update contains corrections for the SAP Patch Manager (Transaction SPAM). At any given time, only one SPAM Update is available for a specific R/3 Release. Applying a SPAM Update is different from applying any other type of Support Package (see below, under "Applying SPAM Updates").

> **NOTE**   Before you apply Support Packages, SAP recommends that you check whether you have applied the latest SPAM update.

SAP Business Warehouse Patches

SAP Business Warehouse Patches contain corrections for the SAP Business Information Warehouse (SAP BW) component. They may include SAP Basis corrections. You can apply SAP Business

Warehouse Patches only in systems in which the SAP BW component is installed.

Software Component Patches

The Support Package type Software Component Patch (SCP) is introduced with R/3 Release 4.5. SCPs are valid for only one particular software component and contain corrections for errors in the R/3 Repository and the ABAP Dictionary only in this component. In R/3 Release 4.5, SCPs are available only for the SAP New Dimension Products, Business-to-Business Procurement (B2B) and Advanced Planner & Optimizer (APO).

As of R/3 Release 4.6, SCPs are being made available for all SAP products offered instead of Hot Packages and LCPs. For example, there will be SCPs for the Logistics module, SCPs for the Human Resources module, SCPs for Basis components, etc. SPAM Updates, Add-On Patches, and CRTs, however, will continue to exist. SCPs may then be a prerequisite for applying SCPs for other components.

Add-On Patches

Available as of R/3 Release 4.0B, Add-On Patches are specific to add-ons for a particular R/3 Release and must be used after applying the SPAM Update from June, 1999, or later. They contain corrections for only the specific add-on.

Unlike Conflict Resolution Transports, Add-On Patches do not resolve conflicts with other Support Packages. They are mainly available for add-ons that do not modify the SAP standard.

SAP Patch Manager

The SAP Patch Manager (Transaction SPAM), known in newer R/3 Releases as the SAP Package Manager, enables you to apply

Support Package Collections from a CD-ROM as well as Support Packages that have been downloaded from SAPNet. The Patch Manager is the customer side of the OCS and provides the following features:

- You can apply more than one Support Package at a time (by defining a patch queue).

- You will always apply Support Packages in the correct sequencing. Applying a Support Package assumes you have already applied its predecessor—a Support Package of the same type. Support Packages must be applied sequentially to avoid problems that may result from object interdependencies.

- It is verified that a Support Package is compatible with an R/3 Release and installed add-ons. If you have loaded the wrong Support Package into your system, the Patch Manager will not apply it.

- You can restart Support Package application if there is a processing error.

- You will be warned if any unreleased change requests or tasks contain objects that will be imported with a Support Package.

- You will be prompted for modification adjustment. If you have modified SAP standard objects, and new versions of these objects are to be imported with the Support Package, the Patch Manager will prompt you to perform a modification adjustment for the object. (See below, under "Modification Adjustments.").

- Your add-ons are protected. If your system contains an add-on that conflicts with the Support Package, you will be prompted to download and apply the corresponding Conflict Resolution Transport.

Applying Support Packages

Applying Support Packages involves several components inside and outside R/3. SAP has to deliver Support Packages on CD-ROM or make them available on SAPNet. You require an R/3 authorization profile that enables you to run Transaction SPAM in the R/3 System where you will apply the Support Packages. On the operating system level, the transport directory requires the subdirectory *eps* to store Support Packages.

As summarized in Figure 15.4, applying a Support Package includes the following steps:

1. Request and download Support Packages from SAPNet or obtain a Support Package Collection CD-ROM from SAP.

2. If required, make the Support Packages available in the correct format in subdirectory *eps* of the transport directory.

3. Using the SAP Patch Manager, do the following:

    A. Apply a SPAM Update if necessary.

    B. Define a patch queue.

    C. Apply the patch queue to the R/3 System.

    D. Perform modification adjustments if necessary.

    E. Monitor the generated logs.

    F. Confirm the patch queue.

4. Test and sign off the result.

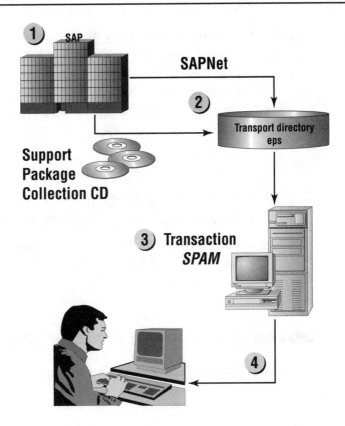

FIGURE 15.4:

Applying Support
Packages

Prerequisites

Before applying Support Packages, ensure that:

- You have correctly configured all R/3 transport tools. To do
  this, from the initial SAP Patch Manager screen (Transaction
  SPAM), choose *Utilities* ➢ *Check transport tool*.

- You have enough disk space available for the transport directory. You usually require between 50MB and 200MB.

- You have the latest SPAM Update available from SAPNet.

- You did not partially apply a Support Package to your R/3 System. To confirm this, from the initial screen of the SAP Patch Manager (Transaction SPAM), select *Aborted patches* and choose *Display*. No Support Package should be displayed, and a green traffic-light icon should be displayed.

- You apply Support Packages to your quality assurance system before applying them to the production system (see below, under "Applying Support Packages to a System Landscape").

- You perform imports into running production environments at times of low system activity (see Chapter 14).

- You have the latest versions of the executables *tp* and *R3trans* from an SAP FTP server (see "Other R/3 Updates" later in this chapter).

Obtaining Support Packages

There are three ways to obtain Support Packages:

- *SAPNet—R/3 Frontend*

- *SAPNet—Web Frontend*

- *Support Package Collection CD-ROMs*

SAPNet—R/3 Frontend

When you access SAPNet from an R/3 frontend using a remote connection, this is called accessing *SAPNet—R/3 Frontend*. In the standard R/3 System, the network administrator configures the remote connection as a post-installation activity. *SAPNet—R/3 Frontend* was formerly known as the Online Service System.

To use *SAPNet—R/3 Frontend* to obtain Support Packages, proceed as follows:

1. Use Transaction code OSS1 to access the initial screen (*Inbox*) of *SAPNet—R/3 Frontend*.

2. Choose *Service* ➢ *SAP Patch Service*. The dialog box *SAP Patch Service* is displayed.

NOTE   If you have an add-on installed, choose *add-on view* and expand the corresponding list of Support Packages.

---

3. Double-click the type of Support Package you want to apply—for example, *SAP Hot Packages*. The screen *List of SAP Hot Packages* is displayed.

4. Expand the list that corresponds to your R/3 Release as depicted in Figure 15.5.

5. Position the cursor on the required Support Package.

   - To display the object list or R/3 Notes for a particular Support Package, choose *Object list* or *Notes for patch*.

   - To list all Support Packages you previously requested, choose *Request overview*.

6. To request a Support Package, choose *Request patch*.

7. Enter the installation number of the R/3 installation you want to apply the Support Package to, and enter the SID beside it.

8. Choose *Continue*.

FIGURE 15.5:

Hot Packages in the
SAPNet—R/3 Frontend

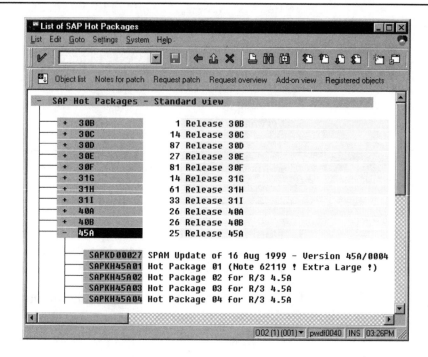

After requesting the Support Packages, you must download them in R/3 using the SAP Patch Manager (see below, under "Making Support Packages Available to R/3").

WARNING You can use *SAPNet—R/3 Frontend* to download Support Packages up to only 30MB in size. For patches between 10MB and 30MB in size, using *SAPNet—R/3 Frontend* is very time-consuming. Alternatively, Support Packages of all sizes can be downloaded from *SAPNet—Web Frontend*. Downloads via *SAPNet—Web Frontend* are less time-consuming, because they use archive files with approximately one-third of the original size.

SAPNet—Web Frontend

The *SAPNet—Web Frontend* is a connection to SAPNet from your Web browser. To obtain Support Packages from *SAPNet—Web Frontend*, proceed as follows:

1. Access SAP's Internet site, SAPNet, at www.sap.com.

2. Once you have reached SAPNet, choose *Online service* ➤ *Online correction support*. Alternatively, use the alias *OCS*. This requires changing the URL in the address bar so that only "OCS" appears to the right of the initial slash after the dot.

3. Choose *Download*.

4. In the tree structure on the left-hand side of the screen, choose a type of Support Package—for example, *SPAM Updates* or *R/3 Support Packages*. Drill down until the right-hand side of the screen displays a list of all available Support Packages. Click the Support Package that you want to download.

5. In the resulting screen, to display the included objects, choose *Object list*. To display related R/3 Notes, choose *Notes*. Then, choose *Download*. The dialog box *File Download* is displayed.

6. Select *Save this file to disk* and choose *OK*. The dialog box *Save as* is displayed.

7. Choose a local directory and choose *Save*. The dialog box *File Download* is displayed, informing you of the download status.

8. After the download is complete, to unpack the archive files and upload the patches into the R/3 System, you must use operating system tools to move the archive files to the subdirectory *tmp* of the transport directory (see below, under "Unpacking Archive Files").

> **NOTE** For information on downloading Support Packages from SAPNet and browser prerequisites, see R/3 Note 83458.

Support Package Collection CD-ROMs

For R/3 Correction Releases such as 4.0B and 4.5B, Hot Packages and Legal Change Patches are grouped into Support Package Collections at regular intervals. These are delivered on CD-ROMs to all customers that require either Hot Packages or LCPs.

The CD-ROM includes all the individual Hot Packages or Legal Change Patches that are available when the collection is created. It may also include a new R/3 kernel, which is downward compatible. Collection CDs come with an installation guide. The intervals at which Support Package Collections are produced range from a few weeks to a few months, depending on the volume of corrections in SAP's repair systems.

NOTE   To learn anticipated delivery dates for Collection CDs, see R/3 Note 63974.

Support Package Collections are also the only way of obtaining large Support Packages that cannot be downloaded from SAP-Net. Support Package Collections have the following naming conventions:

- For Hot Package Collections: HP <Release ID>/<#> (for example, HP4.0B/1)

- For LCP Collections: LCP<Release ID>/L<#> (for example, LCP4.5B/3)

Unpacking Archive Files

Support Packages that were either downloaded from the *SAP-Net—Web Frontend* or installed from a Collection CD-ROM are in the compressed format of archive files. Before applying these

Support Packages using the Patch Manager, you must unpack the archive files. To do this, proceed as follows:

1. Log on to the operating system using one of the following users:

   - <SID>adm (for UNIX and Windows NT)

   - <SID>OFR (for AS/400)

2. Access the transport directory.

3. To unpack the archive files containing the Support Packages, use one of the following commands:

   - For UNIX, use CAR -xvf /<directory>/<path>/ <archive file>.CAR.

   - For AS/400, use CAR -xvf /QOPT/<vol. id>/ <path>/ <archive file>.CAR.

   - For Windows NT, use CAR -xvf <drive>:/ <path>/ <archive file>.CAR.

4. As Support Packages are unpacked, they are automatically deposited in the "inbox" of the *eps* subdirectory of the transport directory—for example, in the UNIX directory /usr/ sap/trans/eps/in.

After obtaining Support Packages either through the *SAPNet—Web Frontend* or from a Collection CD-ROM, you must make the Support Packages available to R/3 using the SAP Patch Manager (see below, under "Making Support Packages Available to R/3"). After applying the Support Packages to all R/3 Systems in your system landscape, you can delete the archive files from the subdirectory *tmp* of the transport directory.

Activities within R/3

All activities in R/3 that are related to Support Packages are performed using the SAP Patch Manager (Transaction SPAM). These activities are explained under the subheadings of this section.

To use the SAP Patch Manager, you require the authorizations S_CTS_TR_ALL and S_CTS_ADMIN. Both of these authorizations are included in the authorization profile S_A.SYSTEM.

To access the initial screen of the SAP Patch Manager (see Figure 15.6), proceed as follows:

1. With the required authorizations, log on to client 000 of the R/3 System where you want to apply the Support Packages.

2. Use Transaction code SPAM or, from the R/3 initial screen, choose *Tools* ➤ *Administration* ➤ *Transports* ➤ *Transport Management System* ➤ *Environment* ➤ *Patch Manager*.

FIGURE 15.6:

The initial screen of the SAP Patch Manager

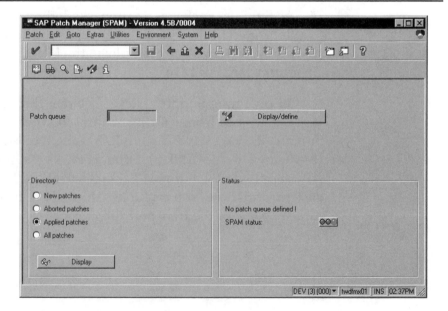

Making Support Packages Available to R/3

If you used the *SAPNet—R/3 Frontend* to request Support Packages, make the Support Packages available to R/3 by using the following steps:

1. From the initial screen of the SAP Patch Manager (Transaction SPAM), choose *Patch* ➢ *Download*.

2. In the list that is displayed, select the required Support Packages. A confirmation dialog box is displayed.

3. Choose *Enter*.

If you used the *SAPNet—Web Frontend* or a Support Package Collection CD-ROM and have unpacked the archive files available in subdirectory *eps/in* of the transport directory, make the Support Packages available to R/3 by using the following steps:

1. From the initial screen of the SAP Patch Manager (Transaction SPAM), choose *Patch* ➢ *Upload*. A confirmation dialog box appears.

2. Choose *Enter*.

3. On the resulting screen, to display the patches, select *New patches* and choose *Display*.

Applying SPAM Updates

Applying a SPAM Update differs slightly from applying other types of Support Packages. At any given time, SAPNet includes only one SPAM Update for each R/3 Release, and this SPAM Update is updated periodically. Before applying Support Packages, ensure that you have the latest SPAM Update.

To check the version of your most recent SPAM Update, from the initial screen of the SAP Patch Manager (Transaction SPAM), select *Applied patches* and choose *Display*. Compare the indicated serial number of your SPAM Update version with the one shown in SAPNet. If a newer version is available in SAPNet, apply it to all R/3 Systems in your system landscape. You should never overwrite a newer SPAM Update version in your R/3 System with an older version that may exist—for example, on a Support Package Collection CD.

NOTE   SAP advises you to apply the latest SPAM Update before you apply any other Support Packages.

SPAM Updates are not displayed in the patch queue. To apply a SPAM update using the Patch Manager, proceed as follows:

1. From the initial screen of the SAP Patch Manager (Transaction SPAM), choose *Patch* ➢ *Apply SPAM update*. If a problem occurs, such as *tp* termination or short dumps, a description of the problem is automatically displayed. Solve the problem and then repeat this step.

2. When the SPAM update has been successfully applied, you automatically exit the SAP Patch Manager. Next, reenter the Patch Manager and choose *Information* to obtain news on this update. Alternatively, choose one of the following:

   • *Goto* ➢ *Log* ➢ *SPAM update*

   • *Goto* ➢ *Status* ➢ *SPAM update*

   • *Goto* ➢ *Object list* ➢ *SPAM update*

Defining a Patch Queue

Before applying Support Packages (other than SPAM Updates), you must define a patch queue. This enables you to apply Support Packages and determines the order in which they are applied.

To define a patch queue, proceed as follows:

1. From the initial screen of the SAP Patch Manager (Transaction SPAM), choose *Display/define*.

- As of R/3 Release 4.5 and R/3 Release 4.0 with an add-on, the dialog box *Component Selection* is displayed. Double-click the application component to which you want to apply Support Packages; for example, select SAP_HR to apply Support Packages to the component Human Resources.

2. A list is displayed of all patches that are valid for your R/3 System. To specify the group of Support Packages that will be applied, double-click the last Support Package that you wish to include in the group. This Support Package is marked with a green check mark in the left column. It and the group of Support Packages preceding it in the queue are marked green. This is the group of Support Packages that will be applied.

3. To confirm the selections, choose *Continue*. The initial screen of the Patch Manager now displays the first and the last Support Packages in the queue.

The order and contents of a patch queue are correct if the following requirements are met:

- If you are a participant in the FCS program, the first Support Package in the patch queue must be an FCS Final Delta Patch (type FFDP). Note also that a Support Package of type FFDP cannot be applied to a non-FCS system.

- The Support Packages in the patch queue are automatically in the order of their creation date. If the predecessor of one Support Package is missing—for example, because it was not downloaded—this Support Package and all subsequent ones are missing from the queue and cannot be applied.

- If a Support Package in the queue requires other Support Packages for successful application, such as a required Conflict Resolution Transport (CRT), you must add these Support Packages to the queue to satisfy all predecessor relations.

Once a patch queue is correctly defined, you can no longer change the selection without first deleting the whole queue. To do this, from the initial Patch Manager screen, choose *Delete* and then define a new patch queue.

To display the objects that will be imported by the patch queue or a single Support Package, from the initial Patch Manager screen, choose *Goto* ➤ *Object list* ➤ *Patch queue* or *Single patch.*

SAP Patch Manager Settings

Various SAP Patch Manager settings influence down-loading and applying different Support Packages. To set these settings, proceed as follows:

1. From the initial screen of the SAP Patch Manager (Transaction SPAM), choose *Extras* ➤ *Settings*. The dialog box *SPAM: Settings* is displayed (see Figure 15.7).

2. Select or deselect settings as required. These settings are described below under the subsequent subheadings.

3. Choose *Enter.*

FIGURE 15.7:

SAP Patch Manager settings

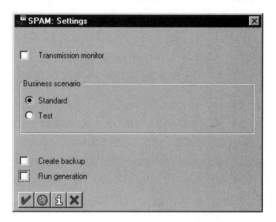

Transmission Monitor Option   The *transmission monitor* is a graphical monitor that displays the status of Support Packages being downloaded using the SAPNet R/3 Frontend. By default, this monitor is deactivated. To activate it, select the transmission monitor in the dialog box *SPAM: Settings*. If this tool is activated, during download, the status bar indicates the progress of the download.

Scenario Options   In the dialog box *SPAM: Settings*, you can select a scenario to determine how the Support Package is applied. The following scenarios are available:

S (Standard):   SPAM will apply the patch queue completely; that is, all steps are performed (see below, under "SPAM Steps during the Import"). This setting is the default setting for Transaction SPAM.

T (Test):   When applying Support Packages using the test scenario, objects that may require modification adjustment and conflicts with installed add-ons are detected. Since this scenario imports no data or objects, you can use it before actually applying the patch queue using the standard scenario. Knowing whether or how many modification adjustments will be necessary will help to plan the time required to apply the patch queue. If the scenario detects objects that may require modification adjustment, a description of these objects and possible solutions are automatically displayed. There is no test scenario available for SPAM Updates.

TIP   SAP recommends applying a patch queue using the test scenario before applying it using the standard scenario. This reveals any modified SAP objects that have to be adjusted and conflicts with installed add-ons that may arise.

Generation Option   Normally, programs and screens imported with Support Packages are generated the first time they are called. To initiate the automatic generation of all programs and screens immediately after the patch queue is applied, in the dialog box

SPAM: Settings, select *Run generation*. By default, *Run generation* is deselected. Since automatic generation is very time-consuming, you should use it only when it is really needed. This option affects only the patch queue application process if permitted by SAP. For example, this option has no effect on SPAM Updates.

Applying a Patch Queue

Before applying a patch queue, ensure that the transport tool *tp* functions correctly. To do this, from the initial screen of the SAP Patch Manager (Transaction SPAM), choose *Utilities* ➢ *Check transport tool* (see Chapter 13). In addition, you should perform a test run by using the Test scenario in the SAP Patch Manager settings as described above. After a test run, the patch queue is deleted. To actually apply the patch queue, you must redefine the patch queue and select the standard scenario for applying it. Then, proceed as follows:

1. From the initial screen of the SAP Patch Manager (Transaction SPAM), choose *Patch* ➢ *Apply patch queue*. A confirmation dialog box is displayed.

2. Choose *Enter*.

3. If the application process terminates, a description of the problem and possible solutions are automatically displayed. After solving the problem, restart the application process beginning with step 1.

4. After the patch queue has been successfully applied, check the status and log files by choosing one of the following:

   • *Goto* ➢ *Log* ➢ *Patch queue* or *Single patch*

   • *Goto* ➢ *Status* ➢ *Patch queue* or *Single patch*

SPAM Steps during Import   Table 15.2 lists the steps that the SAP Patch Manager performs when applying Support Packages.

TABLE 15.2: SPAM Import Steps for Support Packages

SPAM Import Step Name	Description
PROLOGUE	Checks whether you are authorized to apply Support Packages and whether any Support Packages have been applied but not confirmed. (See below, under "Confirming a Patch Queue.")
CHECK_REQUIREMENTS	Checks various prerequisites for applying a Support Package, such as whether *tp* can connect to the database of the R/3 System.
DISASSEMBLE	Extracts data files from the transport subdirectory *eps/in* and stores them in the subdirectory *data*.
DISASSEMBLE_PATCH	Creates control files for the data files in the directory *cofiles*.
ADD_TO_BUFFER	Adds a change request to the import queue of the target R/3 System for each Support Package in the patch queue.
TEST_IMPORT	Imports the patch queue in test mode to check whether objects to be replaced in the target system are in open tasks or change requests—that is, they have not been released.
IMPORT_OBJECT_LIST	Imports a control file for each downloaded Support Package and introduces the corresponding object lists into R/3. The list is used to determine whether any object to be imported conflicts with a customer modification or an add-on prior to Support Package application.
OBJECTS_LOCKED_?	Checks whether an object to be replaced in the target R/3 System is locked by a change request.
SCHEDULE_RDDIMPDP	Checks whether the transport daemon (program RDDIMPDP) is scheduled as event-periodic—that is, it will be started by an event. If RDDIMPDP is not scheduled, it is scheduled correctly in this step.
ADDON_CONFLICTS_?	Checks for conflicts between objects in the patch queue and installed add-ons to determine whether a Conflict Resolution Transport must be applied.
SPDD_SPAU_CHECK	Checks whether a modification adjustment is necessary through Transaction SPDD or Transaction SPAU, and stores all detected modifications in a table.

Continued on next page

TABLE 15.2: SPAM Import Steps for Support Packages *(Continued)*

SPAM Import Step Name	Description
DDIC_IMPORT	Imports all ABAP Dictionary objects contained in the patch queue.
DELETE_FROM_BUFFER	Deletes all entries related to the patch queue from the import queue.
AUTO_MOD_SPDD	Checks whether modifications to ABAP Dictionary objects can be adjusted automatically.
RUN_SPDD_?	Prompts you to adjust your modifications to ABAP Dictionary objects using Transaction SPDD (see below).
IMPORT_PROPER	Imports all R/3 Repository objects and table entries into the target system and performs all required functions, such as distribution, conversion, activation, and generation.
AUTO_MOD_SPAU	Checks whether modifications to R/3 Repository objects can be adjusted automatically.
RUN_SPAU_?	Prompts you to adjust your modifications to the R/3 Repository objects using Transaction SPAU (see below).
EPILOGUE	Checks whether the patch queue has been completely processed and updates administration data in the SAP Patch Manager.

Resetting the Patch Queue   If problems occur during the import of the patch queue and the application process terminates, you may have to reset the patch queue to undo any changes caused by the incomplete application.

To reset the patch queue prior to the DDIC_IMPORT step, in the notification of termination dialog box that appears, choose *Delete*.

To reset the patch queue after the DDIC_IMPORT step (but before confirming the patch queue), choose *Extras* ➤ *Reset status* ➤ *Patch queue*. In the resulting screen, choose *Delete*. (See also below, under "Confirming a Patch Queue.") The reset function is also available for SPAM Updates. (See also below, under "Checking the Log Files.")

WARNING SAP does not recommend resetting a patch queue after the import of Dictionary objects, because serious inconsistencies a may result.

Modification Adjustments for Support Packages   If you have modified SAP standard objects in your R/3 System and these objects are included in a Support Package you wish to apply, during application, you will be prompted to adjust these objects.

The application of a patch queue will terminate in the import step RUN_SPDD_? if you modified ABAP Dictionary objects. If you modified other R/3 Repository objects, it will terminate in the step RUN_SPAU_?. At that point, a dialog box appears—the *SAP Patch Manager SPDD/SPAU Prompter*—allowing you to indicate whether you want to perform modification adjustment—that is, transfer the changes in the modification to the new version of the object imported by the Support Package. To perform modification adjustment, you can do one of the following:

- In the dialog box that appears, choose *Call SPDD* or *Call SPAU*. This accesses the respective transaction.

- From the initial screen of the SAP Patch Manager (Transaction SPAM), choose *Extras* ➤ *Adjust modifications*. This is the option to use if you have already exited from the Support Package application process.

Perform the modification adjustments as described below, under "Modification Adjustments." After the modifications have been adjusted, proceed as follows:

1. Access the SAP Patch Manager by using Transaction code SPAM.

2. Choose *Patch* ➤ *Apply Patch queue*. A confirmation dialog box appears.

3. Choose *Enter*. The dialog box *SAP Patch Manager SPDD Prompter* (or *SAP Patch Manager SPAU Prompter*) is displayed.

4. To complete the import process, choose *Continue*. A final information box is displayed, indicating successful application of the patch queue.

5. Choose *Enter*.

Checking the Log Files

After applying a patch queue, check the log files for warnings and errors as follows:

1. From the initial screen of the SAP Patch Manager (Transaction SPAM), choose *Goto* ➢ *Log* ➢ *Patch Queue*. A list is displayed, showing all Support Packages that have been applied.

2. Expand the list. The names of the respective log files are displayed. Log files that contain return codes higher than four are marked red.

3. Double-click the respective log filename to display the log file.

4. To display any additional information on a message, double-click the corresponding line in the log file.

Table 15.3 displays sample log files that may be generated after applying the Support Package SAPKH45B01 to R/3 System DEV.

TABLE 15.3: Log Files Generated for SAP Support Package SAPKH45B01

SPAM Import Step Name	Activity Described in Log File	Log File
DISASSEMBLE_PATCH	Creation of the control file	SAPLH45B01
TEST_IMPORT	Test import	SAPPH45B01

Continued on next page

TABLE 15.3: Log Files Generated for SAP Support Package SAPKH45B01 *(Continued)*

SPAM Import Step Name	Activity Described in Log File	Log File
IMPORT_OBJECT_LIST	Command file import	SAPLH45B01
DDIC-IMPORT	ABAP Dictionary import	SAPHH45B01
IMPORT_PROPER	ABAP Dictionary activation	SAPAH45B01
IMPORT_PROPER	Main import	SAPIH45B01
IMPORT_PROPER	Matchcode and enqueue activation	SAPMH45B01
IMPORT_PROPER	ADO imports	SAPDH45B01
IMPORT_PROPER	Check versions	SAPVH45B01
IMPORT_PROPER	Method execution	SAPRH45B01
IMPORT_PROPER	Generation of ABAP programs and screens	SAPGH45B01

A return code from zero to four indicates that system information or warnings are available. These warnings are not usually critical for the import process. However, you should ensure that these errors do not impact the target system.

Return codes that are greater than four indicate serious errors that must be corrected for the Support Packages to be applied successfully and also confirmed.

Confirming a Patch Queue

After a patch queue has been applied successfully, you must confirm it, thereby making it possible to apply future Support Packages. To confirm a patch queue, from the initial screen of the SAP Patch Manager (Transaction SPAM), choose *Patch* ➤ *Confirm*.

If you do not confirm an applied patch queue, it is not possible to apply other Support Packages. Although you should confirm a patch queue immediately, it can be confirmed any time between its application and the start of the next R/3 System upgrade or the application of additional Support Packages.

Applying Support Packages to a System Landscape

In contrast to change requests, SAP Support Packages are applied to an R/3 System on demand. In other words, using the SAP Patch Manger, you download and then apply a Support Package to an R/3 System. Support Packages can be applied in conjunction with one another or individually. Because you have many R/3 Systems, the application of Support Packages must be done on each R/3 System.

You can use the procedures described above to apply Support Packages to the development system in your system landscape. However, the procedure is different for the other R/3 Systems in your system landscape, particularly if you must make modification adjustments. An example of distributing Support Packages in a three-system landscape is depicted in Figure 15.8.

FIGURE 15.8:   Distributing Support Packages in a three-system landscape

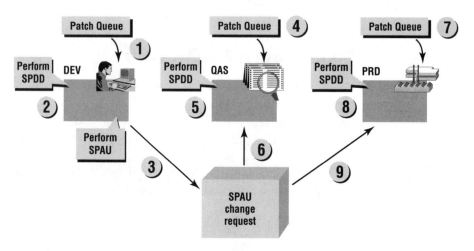

Ideally, all R/3 Systems are at a similar state, because they are after installation or after an R/3 Release upgrade or rollout of an implementation phase. If this is the case, a Support Package (or Support Packages) can be applied in a fashion similar to how you manage the transport of change requests (see Figure 15.8):

1. Apply the Support Packages to the development system (step 1 in Figure 15.8). Objects imported in the Support Package that have also been modified by the customer are adjusted:

   - If required, perform modification adjustments to ABAP Dictionary objects in the development system using Transaction SPDD (step 2 in Figure 15.8). These adjustments are recorded to a change request. However, this change request cannot be used for automatic modification adjustments to ABAP Dictionary objects in the subsequent R/3 Systems. The adjustment procedure must be repeated manually for each R/3 System (steps 5 and 8).

   - If required, perform modification adjustment to other R/3 Repository objects with Transaction SPAU (step 3 in Figure 15.8). These adjustments should be recorded to a change request. This change request can then be used to transport modification adjustments to R/3 Repository objects to other systems.

2. Apply the Support Packages to the quality assurance system (step 4 in Figure 15.8).

3. Import the change request containing the modification adjustments (if one exists) into the quality assurance system (step 6 in Figure 15.8).

4. Verify the Support Package through business validation testing. If changes are necessary due to the application of the Support Package, changes are made in development and tested in the quality assurance system.

5. After testing and verifying the Support Packages, apply them to the production system (step 7 in Figure 15.8) along with any change requests associated with the Support Package (step 9 in Figure 15.8).

6. If you made modification adjustments to ABAP Dictionary objects in the development system, you must manually repeat the modification adjustments using Transaction SPDD in each subsequent R/3 System (steps 5 and 8 in Figure 15.8).

This process is based on the fact that no change requests are waiting for import into the quality assurance or production system. In other words, the R/3 Systems, particularly the quality assurance and production systems, are at similar states. Validation in the quality assurance system assures that the Support Package and any change requests as a result of modification adjustments can be applied to the production system.

Support Packages during an Implementation Phase

It is more difficult to manage Support Packages when you are in the middle of an implementation phase. At this point in time, many changes are being made and transported to the quality assurance system, and are waiting for eventual import into the production system. Therefore, the application of Support Packages requires that you manage:

- When Support Packages are applied to the quality assurance system

- What change requests (if any) are made as a result of modification adjustment

- What change requests contain modifications to SAP standard objects

Implementations generate a variety of change requests that can be classified as either Customizing and customer-development changes, or modifications to SAP standard objects. These modifications are the result of an R/3 Note or a modification adjustment, or the change request is for the support of customer-required functionality. Regardless of what a change request has recorded, the transport of change requests is the same. The change requests all reside in the import queue of a target system waiting for import in the sequence in which they were exported.

The sequence of change requests in an import queue does not take into account Support Packages. There is no indication in the import queue that prior to the release of one change request, a Support Package was applied. There is no indication in the import queue of what Support Packages have been applied to the R/3 System. Therefore, there may be problems with the results of applying a Support Package to the quality assurance system or the production system. Or, there may be a problem when importing a change request containing a modification. The correct version of an object may be overwritten.

To manage the application of Support Packages during an implementation rather than at the beginning or end of different implementation phases, you can use one of the following methods:

- Support Packages are applied to the production system in the same order and at the same chronological time that they were applied to the quality assurance system. This requires that you document when a Support Package was applied to the quality assurance system and the last change request in the import queue at that time. This will drive a process of importing only a certain number of change requests to the production system, applying the required Support Package, importing more change requests, applying the required Support Packages...

- Apply Support Packages to the development and quality assurance systems when needed. Apply all Support Packages to the production system and import all change requests. After the import of all change requests, verify that the correct versions of all modified SAP Repository objects are the resultant. This is possible in environments where there are very few customer-required modifications.

TIP   Allow for the application of all available Support Packages at the beginning of an implementation phase.

Manual Corrections Based on R/3 Notes

Some R/3 Notes provide solutions to problems that require a change to SAP standard objects—that is, a modification. Wherever these problems are also corrected by a Support Package, SAP recommends that you correct the problem using a Support Package rather than manually making the correction from R/3 Notes. However, because of testing requirements and your implementation cycle, you may be required to manually correct the problem according to the R/3 Note.

Also, you occasionally will encounter a problem for which there is an R/3 Note but not yet a Support Package. If the problem is very urgent, you may not be able to wait for the Support Package and will have to make the manual correction based on the R/3 Note. Keep in mind that this will create extra work later, because modification adjustments will be required when you subsequently apply Support Packages or perform R/3 upgrades.

When performing such manual corrections, adopt the following procedure:

1. Verify that the respective R/3 Note is applicable to your R/3 Release and that the symptoms in the R/3 Note are the same as the symptoms apparent in your R/3 System.

2. Perform all modifications of SAP standard objects in the development client of your development system.

3. Document the modifications fully to facilitate subsequent modification adjustments. Include the relevant R/3 Note number and R/3 Release dependencies.

4. Test the corrections thoroughly in the quality assurance system.

5. Before distributing the modifications to your production system, explicitly sign off the testing in the quality assurance system to verify that the corrections have solved the original problem and not created new problems.

R/3 Release Upgrades

R/3 upgrades are part of the evolution of your R/3 System, providing new and improved functionality created by professional SAP developers and inspired by the experiences and development requests of many customers.

Although Support Packages provide a select number of new R/3 Repository objects, an R/3 Release upgrade supplies a completely new R/3 Repository. During the import of the new R/3 Release and post-upgrade Customizing activities, downtime is required for each R/3 System. Thus, the upgrade procedure requires a wider range of activities than those associated with Support Packages. This section will familiarize you with the upgrade process and enable you to plan, schedule, and supervise an R/3 Release upgrade.

| NOTE | For detailed information on how to perform an upgrade, see the Upgrade Guide suitable for your platform and target R/3 Release. This guide is delivered with the R/3 Release upgrade on CD-ROMs. |

Upgrade Processing

An overview of the five phases of upgrade processing is provided in Figure 15.9.

FIGURE 15.9:

Overview of the
upgrade process

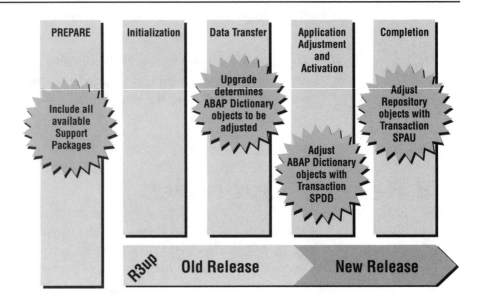

In the preliminary phase of an R/3 Release upgrade, the script PREPARE is executed on the operating system level. This script runs preliminary checks that will save time during the upgrade process. For example, the amount of free disk space or the existence of corrections in unreleased change requests is checked. After the preliminary phase, you can examine the results of the checks and adjust your R/3 System if necessary. For example, you may need to increase the size of tablespaces and provide additional disk space. The next four phases are performed by the *R3up* program.

The *initialization* phase repeats most of the PREPARE checks. If you have resolved any reported problems from the running of PREPARE, the initialization phase should run without interruptions.

The *data transfer* phase transfers new R/3 Repository objects to the system from the shipped CDs. The new objects are compared with objects in the customer's R/3 Repository to identify customer-developed objects and modifications.

In both the *application adjustment and activation* phase and the *completion* phase, all modifications you want to keep and whose corresponding objects in the new Release have also been changed by SAP are merged with the new SAP objects through the process known as modification adjustment. To avoid data loss, modification adjustments to ABAP Dictionary objects must be performed with Transaction SPDD during the *application adjustment and activation* phase—that is, before the Repository switch.

At the end of the *application adjustment and activation* phase, the new R/3 Repository is activated. While the new R/3 Repository is being activated, the system is not available. The activation process may take several hours. After activation, the new R/3 Repository objects and the new R/3 kernel are active.

Before the upgrade is complete, you must adjust R/3 Repository objects with Transaction SPAU.

After upgrade, the R/3 System will be successfully running at the new R/3 Release level with all customer-developed objects and necessary modifications preserved.

R/3 Repository Switch

The switch and activation process of the R/3 Repository is the heart of the R/3 upgrade. Prior to this, a completely new R/3 Repository is set up in your system and remains inactive. The inactive R/3 Repository requires temporary disk space, which is freed after it is activated and the old R/3 Repository is deleted.

To preserve customer developments and modifications, the old R/3 Repository is not simply overwritten during the R/3 Repository switch. Instead, the modification adjustment process transfers customer objects to the new R/3 Repository and replicates customer modifications on the equivalent new SAP objects.

Modification adjustments are necessary only if both of the following conditions apply:

- In the new R/3 Release, SAP changed the object corresponding to the object modified by the customer. (If the object corresponding to the modified object in the new R/3 Release has not been changed by SAP, the upgrade process retains the old object by transferring it to the new Release.)

- The customer wants to discard the modification. (If the new SAP object has similar functionality to that previously achieved by the modification, for example, the customer no longer requires the modification.)

To ensure that customer developments are not lost during the upgrade, the R/3 upgrade process prepares for the R/3 Repository switch by performing the following activities (see Figure 15.10):

- It adds to the new R/3 Repository those modifications whose corresponding objects in the new Release were *not* changed by SAP, as well as all customer-developed objects.

- It backs up to the version database all customer modifications whose corresponding objects in the new Release were changed by SAP. This enables them to be later used to adjust the new R/3 Release.

- It copies to the new R/3 Repository all objects that were automatically generated as a result of some client-independent Customizing activities (see Chapter 11).

- It transfers to the new R/3 System all inactive ABAP Dictionary object versions, documentation on customer developments, and local objects. After upgrade, these objects can be restored to their pre-upgrade state or compared with the current version and adjusted.

As soon as these processes are completed, the R/3 Repository switch can occur.

FIGURE 15.10:

Preparing for an R/3 Repository switch

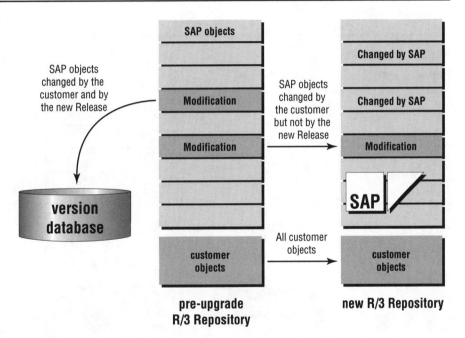

If you have not modified any SAP objects or made your own developments, the R/3 Repository switch upgrade is a simple replacement of the existing R/3 Repository. This kind of upgrade is faster than when modification adjustments are required.

After an R/3 Repository switch involving modifications, R/3 Repository objects that have been changed by both you and SAP require modification adjustment (see Figure 15.11).

NOTE   Customer modifications to specific R/3 Repository objects such as background and spool objects, which are regarded as essential to the normal functioning of R/3, are lost at the time of an R/3 Release upgrade.

FIGURE 15.11:

Performing the R/3 Repository switch

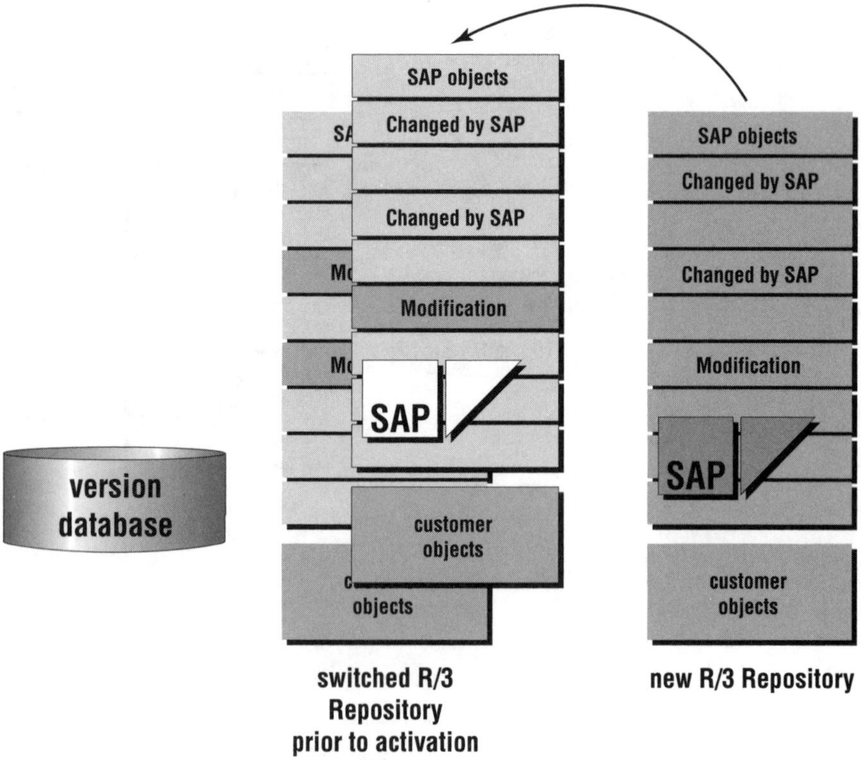

switched R/3
Repository
prior to activation

new R/3 Repository

Modification Adjustments

When new SAP standard objects are imported either by applying Support Packages or by performing an R/3 Release upgrade, the R/3 System detects modifications that you have made to SAP Repository objects (see Figure 15.12). In other words, if you have changed a Repository object delivered by SAP, you have modified this object from the standard default. The customer changes made to the SAP standard need to be compared to the new version of the object delivered by SAP. This process is referred to as a modification adjustment and requires that you determine the differences between the objects and provide a solution for how the objects need to be in the current R/3 System. An adjustment is required for all objects that were modified by you and that form part of the new delivery from SAP. Customer-developed objects are not affected by modification adjustments.

FIGURE 15.12:

Import of new SAP
standard objects

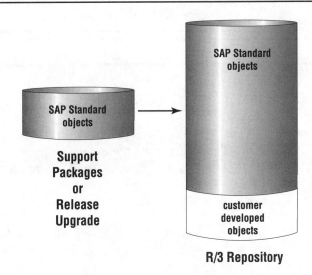

SAP Standard
objects

SAP Standard
objects

**Support
Packages
or
Release
Upgrade**

customer
developed
objects

R/3 Repository

The SAP Patch Manager or the upgrade program *R3up* prompts you to perform a modification adjustment, if necessary. Modification adjustments result in either:

- Rejecting the modification adjustment—that is, replacing the old object with its new SAP standard version. This is known as a "return to the SAP standard."

- Retaining the modification. This replicates the modifications on the equivalent new SAP objects. If you choose this option, the appropriate modification adjustment transaction appears (Transaction SPAU or Transaction SPDD).

WARNING   Under no circumstances should you ignore the prompt. If you do, the modified objects will be automatically overwritten by the new SAP standard. Even if you opt to return to the new SAP standard object, you should use the explicit return procedure in Transaction SPDD and Transaction SPAU. This avoids the same modifications being prompted for modification adjustment during subsequent upgrades and thus saves time during those upgrades.

Example: Modification Adjustment

The following graphic displays the source code from the SAP standard object M07DRAUS. The customer has added additional functionality to the program in source code lines 12–14. The program is delivered in a Support Package with the addition of source code lines 10 and 13 to correct a reported error.

Because the Support Package is delivering the SAP standard object and the customer has also modified that object, a modification adjustment is necessary. The customer is able to:

- Accept the new SAP standard and lose the functionality provided in lines 12–14 of the customer's modified version

Continued on next page

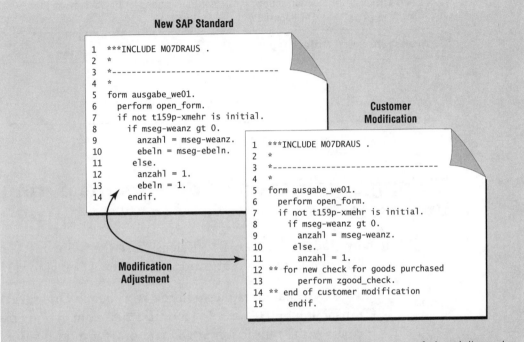

New SAP Standard

```
1   ***INCLUDE M07DRAUS .
2   *
3   *---------------------------------
4   *
5   form ausgabe_we01.
6     perform open_form.
7     if not t159p-xmehr is initial.
8       if mseg-weanz gt 0.
9         anzahl = mseg-weanz.
10        ebeln = mseg-ebeln.
11      else.
12        anzahl = 1.
13        ebeln = 1.
14      endif.
```

Customer Modification

```
1   ***INCLUDE M07DRAUS .
2   *
3   *---------------------------------
4   *
5   form ausgabe_we01.
6     perform open_form.
7     if not t159p-xmehr is initial.
8       if mseg-weanz gt 0.
9         anzahl = mseg-weanz.
10      else.
11        anzahl = 1.
12  ** for new check for goods purchased
13        perform zgood_check.
14  ** end of customer modification
15      endif.
```

Modification Adjustment

- Reject the new SAP standard and not take advantage of the delivered correction found in lines 10 and 13

- Accept the new SAP standard and manually add back lines 12–14 so that the customer's required check takes place.

Depending on the type of object involved, to perform the modification adjustment, you must use either Transaction SPDD or Transaction SPAU (see Table 15.4). Transaction SPDD is for most ABAP Dictionary objects and must be used before new R/3 Dictionary objects are activated. Transaction SPAU is for all other R/3 Repository objects and is used after activating the new R/3 Repository objects.

NOTE   If you omit Transaction SPDD where it is necessary, you may cause data loss. You also should not omit Transaction SPAU where it is necessary, but the omission of Transaction SPAU does not cause data loss.

TABLE 15.4: Modification Adjustment Transactions for Object Types in the R/3 Repository

Transaction	Object Type
SPDD	Domains; data elements; tables
SPAU	Reports; menus; screens; views; lock objects; matchcodes

Making Modification Adjustments during Upgrades

When upgrading to a new R/3 Release, use the following general procedure in regard to modification adjustments (see Figure 15.13):

1. Create two change requests in the Workbench Organizer (Transaction SE09)—one for modification adjustments performed with Transaction SPDD and one for modification adjustments performed with Transaction SPAU.

2. Create a task for each developer who will perform modification adjustments.

3. Using Transaction SPDD or Transaction SPAU, developers should determine whether modifications have to be retained or can be discarded. As developers work through the list of objects, when they are finished with an object, they should mark it as *completed* (marked as processed) after they are finished with it (see below, under "Transaction SPDD" and "Transaction SPAU"). All changes must be recorded to the respective task in the corresponding change request.

4. After completing all desired modification adjustments, the developers must release their tasks.

5. When all modified objects in the list are marked as *completed*, you must select the change requests as being *Marked for transport*. However, you should not yet release the change requests.

R3up will automatically release and export the change requests at the end of the upgrade.

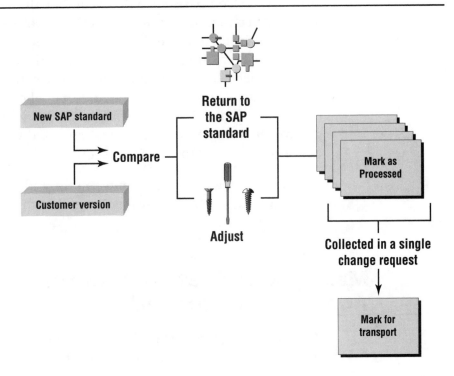

During the subsequent upgrade of other systems in the system landscape, *R3up* notices the existence of the change requests as a result of Transaction SPDD and Transaction SPAU, and will prompt you to import them. By importing the change requests to these systems, you avoid needing to perform the same modification adjustments in each system. The *Mark for transport* step accomplishes this for you.

After you agree to import the change requests when prompted, the modifications in the change requests are automatically compared with the corresponding objects in the target R/3 System. The results of the comparison are displayed. Subsequently, during the upgrade, you must confirm that you want to adopt the changes in these change requests.

Ideally, the comparisons will reveal that all the systems in the landscape contain identical modifications before the upgrade. This is the case, for example, if you followed the recommended procedure of creating all modifications in the development system and then transporting them to all downstream systems before the upgrade. If the comparisons find that all existing modifications are included in a change request, *R3up* will omit prompting you to perform modification adjustment and will proceed directly to the activation of the ABAP Dictionary.

As a prerequisite for performing an upgrade in each successive system of the system landscape, the global change option must be set to *modifiable*.

Making Modification Adjustments when Applying Support Packages

When applying Support Packages, use the following general procedure in regard to modification adjustments:

1. Create two change requests in the Workbench Organizer (Transaction SE09) for the modification adjustments.

2. Create a task for each developer who will perform modification adjustments.

3. Using Transaction SPDD or Transaction SPAU, developers should determine whether modifications should be retained or can be discarded. As developers work through the list of objects, when they are finished with an object, they should mark it as *completed* (marked as processed) after they are finished with it (see below, under "Transaction SPDD" and "Transaction SPAU"). All changes to R/3 Repository objects

must be recorded to the respective task in the change requests (see Figure 15.13 in the previous section).

4. After completing all desired modification adjustments, the developers must release their tasks.

5. Access the SAP Patch Manager using Transaction SPAM.

6. Choose *Patch* ➤ *Apply Patch queue*. A confirmation dialog box appears.

7. Choose *Enter*. This completes the process of applying the Support Package.

8. Release the change requests that result from the modification adjustments using Transaction SPAU and Transaction SPDD. The change request for Transaction SPAU is subsequently used to import the modification adjustments after applying the same patch queue to other R/3 Systems in the system landscape. The change request for Transaction SPDD cannot be used to eliminate the need to perform SPDD adjustments during the application of other R/3 Systems.

TIP   The change request that results from modification adjustments with Transaction SPAU and Transaction SPDD during the application of a patch queue should not be imported into subsequent R/3 Systems in the system landscape until the patch queue itself has been applied.

Transaction SPDD

Transaction SPDD lets you perform modification adjustments for ABAP Dictionary objects that you have modified in your R/3 System. Modification adjustments for ABAP Dictionary objects must be performed before the activation of the new R/3 Repository during an R/3 upgrade or before importing the objects in a Support Package. This timing is important to avoid the risk of data loss.

To perform a modification adjustment using Transaction SPDD, proceed as follows:

1. Use Transaction SPDD. On the resulting screen, choose *Execute*. The screen *Modification Adjustment: Dictionary* is displayed.

2. To list all modifications that conflict with new objects, expand the tree structure. Figure 15.14 shows a sample of modified objects obtained using Transaction SPDD.

FIGURE 15.14:

Modification adjustment using Transaction SPDD

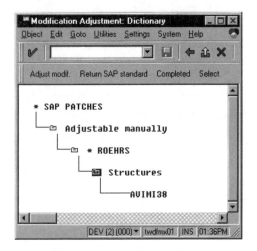

The text indicating the modified objects appears in different colors. To display a legend for these colors, choose *Utilities* ➤ *Color legend*.

For each of the objects in the list, you can view all existing versions of an object that are stored in the version database (see Chapter 12). To view these versions, position the cursor on the respective object and choose *Utilities* ➤ *Version management*. The version displayed at the beginning of the list is the new SAP standard version. All the other versions listed are previous versions, providing you with the history of the object. By comparing the most important attributes of previous and current versions for domains and data elements, for example, you can determine whether to retain a modification adjustment.

If you decide that a modification adjustment for an ABAP Dictionary object is necessary, make the adjustment using the ABAP Dictionary Maintenance (Transaction SE11) in a separate user session. When SPDD recommends the sequence of the fields that need to be maintained, you can automatically accept the recommendations.

Consider this example: A modification is a correction that was made based on an R/3 Note. In the Support Package, the new SAP standard object incorporates this change. In this case, you would opt to return to the SAP standard object. To do this, on the screen *Modification Adjustment: Dictionary*, you would choose *Return to SAP standard* and then *Yes* in the confirmation dialog box. The return to the SAP standard causes the modified objects to be treated like normal SAP objects that were not modified; that is, they are overwritten by the new SAP objects, and no version is stored.

After either adjusting the modification or restoring the SAP standard object, assign the status *completed* to each object. To do this, from the initial screen of Transaction SPDD, position the cursor on the object and choose *Completed*. This new status simply notifies you that the object has been dealt with, thereby simplifying the task of processing the list of modified objects.

When performing an R/3 Release upgrade, the function *Select for transport* is automatically active in the screen *Modification Adjustment: Dictionary*. This function assigns the objects to the Transaction SPDD–specific change requests that you should create to help upgrade other systems of the system landscape. The *Select for transport* function is not available for Support Packages and is automatically deactivated.

Transaction SPAU

To perform modification adjustments for R/3 Repository objects that you have modified in your R/3 System, use Transaction SPAU. Modification adjustments for R/3 Repository objects must be performed after the activation of the new R/3 Repository during an R/3 upgrade, or after importing the objects in a Support Package. The old modified version is saved in the version database.

To perform a modification adjustment to an R/3 Repository object, proceed as follows:

1. Use Transaction SPAU. In the resulting screen, choose *Execute*. The screen *Modification adjustment* is displayed.

2. To list all modifications affecting new objects, expand the tree structure. Figure 15.15 shows a sample tree listing all modifications that conflict with new objects.

FIGURE 15.15:

Modification adjustment using Transaction SPAU

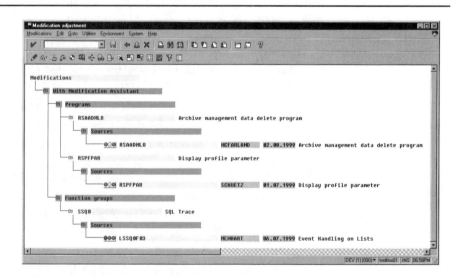

The objects listed under *Without Modification Assistant* are either objects that were modified in the current R/3 System before the

Modification Assistant was installed or objects for which modifications are not supported by the Modification Assistant (see Chapter 10).

Different icons are shown for each modification listed. Table 15.5 indicates the meaning of the different symbols. To display a legend for the traffic lights and other icons, choose *Utilities* ➢ *Legend*.

TABLE 15.5: Icons in the SPAU List of Modified R/3 Repository Objects

Icon	Meaning
	Automatic adjustment is possible. "Automatic" means that you do not require a tool such as the ABAP Editor in addition to Transaction SPAU. This icon can appear only if the Modification Assistant is available for the current R/3 Release. To start the modification adjustment process, click the green traffic light.
	Semi-automatic adjustment is possible. "Semi-automatic" means that you require a tool such as the ABAP Editor in addition to Transaction SPAU for parts of the object to be adjusted. This icon can appear only if the Modification Assistant is available for the current R/3 Release. You need to use a different tool to adjust different types of objects.
	Manual adjustment is required. This means that you require a tool such as the ABAP Editor in addition to Transaction SPAU for all parts of the object to be adjusted. For objects with a red traffic light, you can use Transaction SPAU only to obtain the version comparison. If the Modification Assistant is not available for the current R/3 Release, red traffic lights appear for all objects.
	The new object has been adjusted to include the modification.
	The object has been replaced by the corresponding SAP standard object.

To adjust a modification listed in Transaction SPAU, proceed as follows:

1. From the initial screen of Transaction SPAU, position the cursor on the object and choose *Modifications* ➢ *Adjust modifications*. The dialog box *Set Repair Flag* appears.

2. Choose *Enter*.

3. In the resulting screen, select the change request that has been created for Transaction SPAU and choose *Enter*.

4. Depending on the classification of the modification (automatic, semi-automatic, or manual), you may have to perform the adjustment manually using the appropriate tools. For automatic and semi-automatic modifications, the adjustment is guided—for example, by a split-screen editor displaying the new SAP standard object on the left-hand side and the modified object on the right-hand side.

If you wish to return to the SAP standard and discard the modification, from the screen *Modification adjustment*, position the cursor on the respective object and choose *Modifications* ➤ *Reset to original*. Note that this results in the loss of the modification.

Upgrading the System Landscape

In a system landscape, upgrades are performed strictly in the order dictated by the transport path. Modification adjustments are performed during development system upgrade and transported to downstream systems along the transport path.

The sequence of tasks in upgrading a three-system landscape is as follows (see Figure 15.16):

1. Upgrade the development system DEV and perform modification adjustments in DEV.

2. Upgrade the quality assurance system QAS or, for even better results, upgrade a copy of the production system PRD. Then, import change requests containing the modification adjustments into QAS, and test and validate system functionality.

3. Upgrade the production system PRD. Import the change requests containing the modification adjustments into PRD.

> **WARNING** Numerous, complex modifications significantly increase the time required for a development system upgrade.

Modification adjustments should be performed by developers (not by R/3 System administrators). The people responsible for the modifications must be involved in and present during the upgrade process, and should examine the complete documentation for each modified object.

FIGURE 15.16:

Upgrade sequence in a three-system landscape

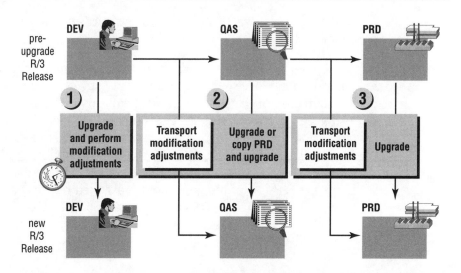

If you plan to perform an R/3 Release upgrade for additional functionality or stability, or to implement a new SAP module (such as PP, MM, or HR), you will need to set up a phased implementation While configuring this new Release, there is still the need to perform development and Customizing work for the current production release. Development and Customizing work for the different release levels must be performed in separate R/3 environments as described in Chapters 4 and 6. (Also see the example below.)

Example: Upgrading a System Landscape as a Phased Implementation

A company is in production operation with the R/3 business application modules Financials, Logistics, and Human Resources. The current R/3 implementation consists of a standard three-system landscape with a development system DEV, a quality assurance system QAS, and a production system PRD.

The company plans to upgrade from R/3 Release 3.1H to R/3 Release 4.5B. Because of the length of time required to test and verify the new R/3 Release and a need to supply production with production-support corrections on a bimonthly basis, two additional R/3 Systems are installed to support the upgrade plan.

To be able to support production with bimonthly changes, the production support system PPS is created as a system copy of the development system. A system copy of the existing QAS system is used to create a second quality assurance system called PQA. The systems PPS and PQA now become the production support systems for the production system PRD. All Customizers and developers that need to make changes to support production are told to make those changes in the PPS system. Testing and validation are performed in PQA. After the corrections are signed off, they are imported into the production system PRD. All changes are documented so that they can be realized in DEV after it has been upgraded. This synchronization is required to ensure consistency between all R/3 Systems.

The PPS system enables the technical team to upgrade DEV and QAS to R/3 Release 4.5B. After the upgrades are complete and all available Support Packages have been applied, the Customizing and development team for the new implementation phase begins Release Customizing in DEV. All Customizing and development changes made in PPS are also then realized in DEV. As changes are unit tested, they are released and exported to QAS for verification.

Continued on next page

The three-system landscape is now a five-system landscape (depicted below).

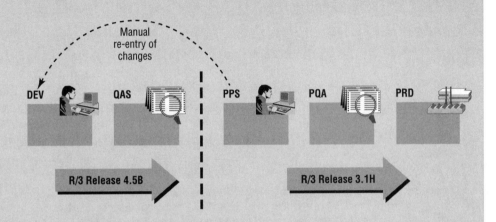

Initially, the proposal for setting up the TMS to enable the implementation of the upgrade and provide production support was depicted as shown in the following diagram.

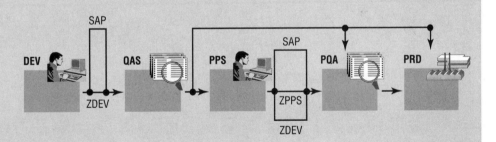

This initial proposal is technically feasible, but system administrators were worried by the fact that the import queues for PQA and PRD would be receiving changes from both development systems DEV and PPS. However, by using the transport profile parameter *sourcesystems*, change requests from DEV can be prevented from being imported into PPS, PQA, and PRD

Continued on next page

before these systems are upgraded. This solution is not entirely satisfactory because having both Release 3.1H and Release 4.5B change requests in the import queues for PPS, PQA, and PRD could still be confusing.

A second proposal was to establish a second transport directory for DEV and QAS. This transport directory would be used to maintain import queues for PPS, PQA, and PRD, and will receive only production support change requests. This solution is viable, but requires that no one use the TMS to adjust and copy change requests between different transport groups, because this would automatically add change requests from R/3 Release 4.5B to the import queues of PPS, PQA, and PRD. Using authorizations to limit TMS access will reduce—but may not entirely remove—this risk.

Therefore, the proposal finally adopted for setting up the TMS is that depicted in the diagram below, which involves the creation of a virtual system R45. The import queue of this virtual system receives a sequenced list of change requests from R/3 Release 4.5B that will need to be applied to the systems PPS, PQA, and PRD after these systems have been upgraded to R/3 Release 4.5B.

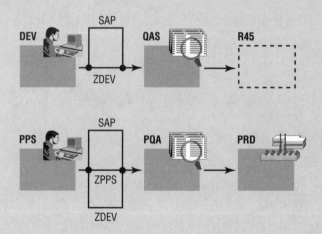

Continued on next page

During the preparation for the R/3 Release upgrade of PRD, change requests are imported from DEV into QAS for verification and subsequently delivered to R45. The import buffer for R45 is then copied to create an import buffer for PQA. PQA is upgraded, and change requests are applied to ensure that the upgrade from R/3 Release 3.1H to Release 4.5B can be completed smoothly. If testing produces positive results, the PRD system is upgraded, the R45 import buffer is copied to create an import buffer for PRD, and the Release 4.5B change requests are imported into the production system PRD. Finally, the upgrade, import buffer copy, and change request import are performed for PPS.

Other R/3 Updates

Other updates that affect your R/3 System include updates to certain R/3 executables on the operating system level as well as updates to the R/3 kernel. These updates often accompany an R/3 upgrade, but can also be performed separately.

Patches for certain R/3 executables or the R/3 kernel are available on SAP's FTP servers, which use the naming convention *sapservx*, where *x* is a single digit. The patches are stored in the directory `/general/R3server/patches` on the appropriate *sapserv* FTP server. The following bulleted list provides information on useful subdirectories on the *sapserv* file server:

- Updates for programs that are independent of the kernel release are stored in the directory `COMMON/<operating system>/<hardware platform>`.

- Updates for programs that depend on the kernel release are stored in the directory `<kernel release>/<operating system>/<hardware platform>`.

- Updates for programs that depend on the kernel release and the database, such as *tp* and the R/3 kernel, are stored in the directory `<kernel release>/<operating system>/ <hardware platform>/<database>`.

NOTE For more information on downloading patches from *sapserv* for UNIX and Windows NT, see R/3 Note 19466. For more information on downloading AS/400 patches, see R/3 Note 49365.

The technical bases of the R/3 System are the R/3 kernel and the operating system services and database services. A particular kernel version can be used only in conjunction with a particular operating system version and a particular database version. Installing a new kernel may enable you to use a database or operating system release that has not yet been approved for your current R/3 kernel. To determine your current kernel version, use Transaction SM51 and then choose *Release info*. The R/3 kernel software is described as "backwards compatible," which means that you can install a more up-to-date kernel without requiring a complete R/3 upgrade.

A kernel update will not correct errors in R/3 application components. To correct application component errors, upgrade to the latest R/3 Correction Release or apply the relevant Support Packages. As a prerequisite of some SAP Support Packages, your R/3 System must have a certain kernel patch level.

Review Questions

1. Which of the following statements are correct in regard to the R/3 Release strategy?

   A. Functional Releases are automatically shipped to all customers.

   B. Correction Releases provide only corrections and no new functionality with respect to the previous R/3 Functional Release.

   C. Functional Releases receive only limited OCS maintenance; that is, only very urgent corrections are available as Support Packages.

   D. R/3 Release upgrades are possible only for Correction Releases.

2. Which of the following statements are correct in regard to Support Packages?

   A. Support Packages change the SAP standard of your R/3 System in advance of the next R/3 Release upgrade.

   B. You can apply all types of Support Packages to all R/3 installations, regardless of the components used in the installation.

   C. Support Packages are available only to customers who are participants in the First Customer Shipment (FCS) program.

   D. Different types of Support Packages may be required for R/3 installations with different components.

3. Which of the following statements are correct in regard to the SAP Patch Manager?

   A. The SAP Patch Manager ensures that Support Packages are applied in the correct sequence.

   B. The SAP Patch Manager does not check whether the type of Support Package you wish to apply is appropriate for your R/3 installation. It is up to you to decide whether, for example, you require a Conflict Resolution Transport.

   C. The SAP Patch Manager does not offer you the chance to protect SAP objects that you have modified. These objects are automatically overwritten.

   D. The SAP Patch Manager automatically prompts you to call the modification adjustment Transactions SPDD or SPAU if necessary.

4. Which of the following statements are correct in regard to R/3 Release upgrades?

   A. Objects in the customer namespace are not overwritten.

   B. A Repository switch is the replacement of your current R/3 Repository by the R/3 Repository in the new R/3 Release.

   C. All customer modifications to ABAP Dictionary objects are lost.

   D. Customer modifications to SAP objects that you want to preserve must be transferred to the new Release through the modification adjustment process.

5. Which of the following statements are correct in regard to the modification adjustment process?

    A. Transaction SPAU is used for most ABAP Dictionary objects.

    B. Transaction SPDD is used for most ABAP Dictionary objects.

    C. Not using Transaction SPDD where applicable may cause data loss.

    D. During modification adjustment, you must choose to return to the SAP standard.

APPENDIX

A

Creating RFC Destinations

In an SAP environment, you can use the Remote Function Call (RFC) interface system to call function modules in the same or different computer systems. RFCs allow communication between two SAP Systems—R/3, R/2, Business Information Warehouse (BW), or Advanced Planner and Optimizer (APO)—or between an SAP System and a non-SAP system.

RFCs are mentioned in this book in the following contexts:

- Remote client copies between two different clients

- Client comparisons using the Cross-System Viewer

- Communication between the Transport Management System (TMS) and the transport control program *tp*

Since the TMS is designed to communicate with the operating system level through a predefined TCP/IP connection, you do not have to manually define the RFC destination. However, to perform a remote client copy or compare two different clients, you must create the required RFC destinations. These procedures require an RFC destination originating from the target client (where you initiate the remote client copy and client comparison) and connecting to a source client.

To create an RFC destination for a remote client copy or a client comparison:

1. Log on to the target R/3 client.

2. Display existing RFC destinations by calling Transaction SM59 or, from the R/3 initial screen, by choosing *Tools ➢ Administration ➢ Administration ➢ Network ➢ RFC destinations*. A tree structure shows the different connection types, such as R/3 connections or TCP/IP connections, and all existing destinations.

3. Create a new RFC destination by choosing *Create*.

4. Provide the following information:

- In the field *RFC destination*, enter a unique name, which should include the system ID and client number of the source R/3 client.

- In the field *Connection type*, enter **3** to indicate a connection with an R/3 System. This type of RFC destination is called an *R/3 Connection.*

- In the field *Description*, enter a short text that describes the RFC destination.

5. To complete the creation of the R/3 Connection, enter the following information:

- In the field *Target host*, enter the host name of the source R/3 System.

- In the field *System number*, enter the system number of the source R/3 System.

6. Choose *Save*.

7. Test the RFC destination:

- From the *RFC Destination* screen, choose *Test connection*. If the connection is successful, the table on the next screen displays the required connection times for logon. If the connection is not successful, an error message will be displayed on this screen. Errors result if the source system is down or if you have entered an invalid combination of host name and system number.

- To test your ability to log on to the source client, from the *RFC Destination* screen, choose *Remote logon*. Since you have not provided logon information for the source system, you will not access that system directly. A logon screen will be displayed—you must log on to a client in this system in the usual way.

Automatic Logon

You can set up RFC destinations with default logon information. For example, you can provide a default language and a default client number. Additionally, you can set up an automatic logon to the source client with a default username and password. This eliminates the need for the user to log on to the source client during a remote client copy or a client comparison. Such a default user requires the correct user authorizations to perform a remote client copy. (See Chapter 9 for more information on client copy user authorizations and Chapter 11 for information on Cross-System Viewer user authorizations.)

TIP

To execute a remote client copy or a client comparison in the background, the logon data defined in the RFC destination must include the username and password.

When you create an RFC destination that provides access to a client in an R/3 System without requiring logon, limit the user authorization of the username for the RFC destination. This prevents inappropriate activities, such as viewing or copying sensitive data.

NOTE

For more information on maintaining RFC destinations, see R/3 online documentation.

APPENDIX
B

Transport Profile Parameters

This section provides information on the different transport profile parameters used to support the delivery of change requests to import buffers and the import of change requests into R/3 Systems. Chapter 7 describes the configuration of the transport profile for R/3 Release 4.5 and prior releases. This section lists useful transport parameters and provides the following information for each:

- Name of the parameter
- Possible values
- The default value
- For which R/3 Releases the parameter is valid
- A description of the parameter

abapntfmode

Values: t or b

Default Value: t

R/3 Release Information: As of R/3 Release 4.5

Description: This parameter is meaningful only if the transport control program *tp* is running on Windows NT platforms. The value of the parameter determines whether text files are opened in UNIX compatibility mode. The UNIX compatibility mode is necessary if a transport directory is shared between UNIX and Windows NT application servers. When *abapntfmode* is set to "t", all text files are opened in normal Windows NT text mode. When *abapntfmode* is set to "b", all text files are opened in binary mode, which is compatible with UNIX file formats.

alllog

Value: Text

Default Value: ALOG$(syear)$(yweek)

R/3 Release Information: All

Description: The name of the log file in the transport directory *log* that lists all the *tp* single steps.

buffreset

Value: Boolean

Default Value: TRUE

R/3 Release Information: All

Description: The transport control program *tp* and *R3trans* reset all the buffers of the R/3 System so that all the application servers can react to changes in the database. Buffer synchronization takes several seconds until all the application servers have read the request to reset all buffers. You can set the repetition period for reading the synchronization requests with profile parameters for the R/3 System (*rdisp/bufreftime*). Although this buffer reset is by default turned on, you disable the buffer reset by *tp* when setting *buffreset* to FALSE.

bufreftime

Value: Integer

Default Value: 180

R/3 Release Information: All

Description: The value of this parameter specifies how long the transport control program *tp* should wait in seconds until it can assume that all the buffers of the R/3 System have been synchronized. The value of this parameter should correspond to the *rdisp/bufreftime* profile parameter of the R/3 System in question.

c_import

Value: Boolean

Default Value: TRUE

R/3 Release Information: All

Description: Allows or disallows the import of change requests that are the result of a relocation transport (change requests of type "c"). By default, all types of change requests can be imported. However, you can disallow the import of relocation transports (created using Transaction SE01) by setting the parameter *c_import* to FALSE.

cofilelifetime

Value: Integer

Default Value: 365

R/3 Release Information: All

Description: The number of days since a control file has been touched. A file in the transport directory *cofiles* is considered to be not needed if the corresponding change request is not in the import buffer for any R/3 System and has a time stamp that is older than the value set by the parameter *cofilelifetime*. If the file is no longer needed based on the criteria, a combination of the commands *tp check* and *tp clearold* will delete the file. You can set the minimum age of a control file in days using this parameter. Because a data file requires a control file for import, the value set by *cofilelifetime* should correspond to the value for *olddatalifetime*.

ctc

Value: Boolean

Default Value: FALSE

R/3 Release Information: As of R/3 Release 4.5

Description: ctc stands for Client Transport Control, and when set to TRUE, it activates extended transport control, allowing you to specify client and system combinations in transport routes. Extended transport control requires a new import buffer format (the transport parameter *nbufform* is set to TRUE implicitly). This new buffer format is only supported beginning with *tp* version 264. As a result, you can set the new parameter *ctc* only if all the transport control programs that work with a specific R/3 System have at least version 264. Older *tp* versions destroy this new import buffer. To protect the new import buffer from being destroyed by older *tp* versions, set the value for transport parameter *tp_version* to at least 264.

datalifetime

Value: Integer

Default Value: 200

R/3 Release Information: All

Description: The number of days since a data file has been touched. A file in the transport directory *data* is considered to be not needed if the corresponding change request is not in the import buffer for any R/3 System and has a time stamp that is older than the value set by the parameter *datalifetime*. The file is then moved to the transport directory *olddata* during a combination of the commands *tp check* and *tp clearold*. You can set the minimum age of a data file in days using this parameter.

dbcodepage

Values: american_america.us7ascii or american_america.we8dec

Default Value: american_america.us7ascii

R/3 Release Information: As of R/3 Release 4.0

Description: The code page of the Oracle database instance. The Oracle databases are installed with the code page american_america. we8dec. In this case, you must enter the value american_america.we8dec in the transport profile. When upgrading a Release from 3.*x* or later to 4.*x*, the code page american_america.us7ascii is retained.

dbconfpath

Value: Text

Default Value: $transdir

R/3 Release Information: All

Description: You can use this parameter to inform the transport control program *tp* where the configuration files for Oracle SQL*NET V2 are located. The default value $transdir mirrors the fact that SAP has already stored these files centrally in the transport directory. From this parameter, *tp* derives the value of the environment variables TNS_ADMIN. However, if the transport parameter *dbswpath* is set, the parameter *dbconfpath* is ignored.

dbhost

Value: Text

Default Value: None

R/3 Release Information: All (no longer required as of R/3 Release 4.0)

Description: This parameter specifies the host name—the computer on which the database runs or (valid for Oracle and DB2 on AIX) on which the database processes run. For an Informix database, the host name is case sensitive. For MS SQL, the TCP/IP host name on which the database runs is used.

dblibpath

Value: Text

Default Value: /usr/sap/$(system)/SYS/exe/run/ for UNIX

R/3 Release Information: As of R/3 Release 4.5

Description: The directory in which the dynamic R/3 database interface is located. In the standard system, these files are always in the executable directory of the application server. Therefore, you do not have to change the default value.

Under Windows NT, you have to enter the path to the dynamic R/3 interface only if it is not located in the environment variable path set under Windows NT. Otherwise, the DLL in the default path is searched for.

As of R/3 Release 4.5, *tp* sets this variable according to the value of the transport profile parameter *dbtype*.

dblogicalname

Value: Text

Default Value: $dbname

R/3 Release Information: All

Description: Sets the logical name that identifies the database instance in an Oracle network.

dbname

Value: Text

Default Value: $(system)

R/3 Release Information: All

Description: The name of the database instance. The standard installation uses the name of the R/3 System for the name of the database instance or the logical name of the database.

dbswpath

Value: Text

Default Value: None

R/3 Release Information: As of R/3 Release 4.0

Description: The value of the directory in which the Oracle client software is installed. If the parameter is set, the transport control program *tp* derives the following environment variables in a UNIX environment:

Oracle_HOME = $(dbswpath)

TNS_ADMIN = $(dbswpath)/network/admin (on UNIX)

ORA_NLS = $(dbswpath)/ocommon/nls/admin/data (on UNIX)

ORA_NLS32 = $(dbswpath)/ocommon/nls32/admin/data (on UNIX)

ORA_NLS33 = $(dbswpath)/ocommon/nls33/admin/data (on UNIX)

Note that the environment variables ORA_NLS, ORA_NLS32, and ORA_NLS33 are no longer set with R/3 Release 4.6.

dbtype

Values: ora, ada, db2, db4, db6, inf, or mss

Default Value: The R/3 System's database type

R/3 Release Information: All (described here as of R/3 Release 4.5)

Description: Used to set the environment variable *dbms_type*. This variable has to be set correctly to be able to load the correct shared dbsl-library.

dummy

Value: Boolean

Default Value: FALSE

R/3 Release Information: All

Description: You can use this parameter to make a dummy system, such as a virtual system, known in the transport profile. Imports are not performed for an R/3 System with the parameter *dummy* set to TRUE, but an import buffer for the system will be maintained. With R/3 Release 4.5, for example, the entry that sets the *dummy* value to TRUE is automatically added to the transport profile for all virtual systems. In releases prior to R/3 Release 4.5, if you create a virtual system—for example, the system TST—you will need to make the entry TST/dummy=TRUE in the file TPPARAM.

informix_server

Value: Text

Default Value: $(dbhost)$(dbname)shm

R/3 Release Information: All

Description: The Informix database server name for a local connection.

informix_serveralias

Value: Text

Default Value: $(dbhost)$(dbname)tcp

R/3 Release Information: All

Description: The Informix database server name for a remote connection.

informixdir

Value: Text

Default Value: /informix/<SID>

R/3 Release Information: All

Description: The directory name where the Informix database software is located.

informixsqlhost

Value: Text

Default Value: $(informixdir)/etc/sqlhosts[.tli|.soc]

R/3 Release Information: All

Description: This parameter is used to specify the complete path and name of the SQL host's file for an Informix database.

k_import

Value: Boolean

Default Value: TRUE

R/3 Release Information: All

Description: Allows or disallows the import of Workbench change requests (change requests of type "k"). By default, all types of change requests can be imported. However, you can disallow the import of Workbench change requests by setting the parameter *k_import* to FALSE.

language

Value: Text

Default Value: None

R/3 Release Information: All

Description: The value passed to *R3trans* to indicate what languages are to be exported. By default, this parameter is empty; therefore, *R3trans* exports language-dependent data from all the languages that it can find—in other words, all languages installed in the R/3 System. If the parameter *language* is transferred, *R3trans* tries to export the languages specified in this text. A single letter identifies each language. You can specify several languages by entering a sequence of letters. Note that the transport parameter *lsm* is used with the parameter *language* beginning with R/3 Release 3.1G.

loglifetime

Value: Integer

Default Value: 200

R/3 Release Information: All

Description: The number of days since a log file has been touched. A file in the transport directory *log* is considered to be not needed if the corresponding change request is not in the import buffer for any R/3 System and has a time stamp that is older than the value set by the parameter *loglifetime*. If the file is no longer needed based on the criteria, a combination of the commands *tp check* and *tp clearold* will delete the log file. You can set the minimum age of a log file in days using this parameter.

lsm

Values: MASTER, VECTOR, TRANSLATION, NOMASTER, or VECTORANDMASTER

Default Value: VECTOR

R/3 Release Information: As of R/3 Release 3.1G

Description: The language selection mode parameter. If this parameter is not set and the default value VECTOR is used, *R3trans* will export language-dependent data from the languages defined by the transport parameter *language*. If the language parameter is empty, all language-dependent data is exported. The other parameters for *lsm* behave as follows:

MASTER: The "master" language for a Repository object is also known as its original language—that is, the language in which the object was created or maintained. In this mode, the language-dependent data for the master language only is exported, and all other translated texts are ignored.

NOMASTER: In this mode, only translated text is exported—that is, all text maintained in languages other than the object's original language.

TRANSLATION: In this mode, only translated text is exported for the languages defined by the parameter *language*.

VECTORANDMASTER: In this mode, all text maintained for an object's original language and all text for the languages defined by the parameter *language* are exported.

mssql_passwd

Value: Text

Default Value: None

R/3 Release Information: All

Description: The password for a user in the MS SQL database. This is used in conjunction with the parameter *mssql_user*.

mssql_user

Value: Text

Default Value: None

R/3 Release Information: All

Description: The username for a connection to the MS SQL database. This information, in combination with *mssql_passwd*, allows for access to an MS SQL database using a unique user and password rather than the default user and password.

nbufform

Value: Boolean

Default Value: FALSE

R/3 Release Information: As of R/3 Release 4.5

Description: Change request names in newer R/3 Releases may have a length of 20 characters. However, these change requests cannot be processed in the previous format of the import buffer. The parameter *nbufform* is set to TRUE implicitly when you set the parameter *ctc* to TRUE. As with parameter *ctc*, you have to protect this change to the import buffer format from transport control programs that use the old import buffer format. The new format of the import buffer requires at least a *tp* version of 264. Older *tp* versions destroy this new import buffer. Therefore, when parameter *nbufform* is activated, set the value for the transport profile parameter *tp_version* to at least 264.

new_sapnames

Value: Boolean

Default Value: FALSE

R/3 Release Information: All

Description: A file is created in the transport directory *sapnames* for each user of an R/3 System in the transport group. By default, the file corresponds to the user's name. However, usernames in the R/3 System may not be valid filenames at the operating system level. For example, a certain length of username or the use of special characters such as a space or a period may not be permissible as filenames and could cause problems. As a solution, the usernames can be modified to create filenames that are valid in all operating systems. The real username is stored in the corresponding file. Setting the parameter *new_sapnames* to TRUE activates this. Once this parameter is set to TRUE, you should not set it to FALSE (unless you also delete all the files in the transport directory *sapnames*).

olddatalifetime

Value: Integer

Default Value: 365

R/3 Release Information: All

Description: A combination of the commands *tp check* and *tp clearold* move data files from the transport directory *data* to the transport directory *olddata* based on the parameter *datalifetime*.

These commands also delete any data files in the *olddata* transport directory whose time stamp is older than the value set by *olddatalifetime*. You can set the minimum age of a data file in days using this parameter. Note that the minimum age refers to the date the file was created and not to the date on which the file was copied to the directory *olddata*. Therefore, the value for *olddatalifetime* should be greater than the value for *datalifetime*.

opticonnect

Value: Boolean

Default Value: FALSE

R/3 Release Information: All

Description: Required to be TRUE for a DB2 database environment when Opticonnect is installed.

r3transpath

Value: Text

Default Value: R3trans for UNIX and AS/400 and R3trans.exe for Windows NT

R/3 Release Information: All

Description: This parameter is used to pass the complete name of the program *R3trans* to the transport control program *tp*. The default value is not a complete path specification. The operating system and the settings of the operating system are used to find the correct value. If this is not case, you can provide the complete path to *R3trans*.

recclient

Values: ALL, OFF, or list of client values separated by a comma

Default Value: OFF

R/3 Release Information: All

Description: Activates the recording of changes to Customizing settings during import for either ALL clients or the clients listed. By default, recording of imported Customizing settings does not take place. The value of this parameter should correspond to the value of the R/3 System's profile parameter *rec/client*.

repeatonerror

Values: 0, 8, or 9

Default Value: 9

R/3 Release Information: All

Description: After successful import, a change request is typically removed from the import buffer (unless a special import option is used to keep the change request in the buffer after import). The parameter *repeatonerror* defines the criteria for a successful import. It specifies the return code up to which a change request is considered successfully processed. Return codes less than the value defined for *repeatonerror* are accepted as successful. Change requests that result in a return code greater than or equal to the value of *repeatonerror* are not removed from the import buffer because they have not been successfully processed.

sourcesystems

Value: Text

Default Value: None

R/3 Release Information: All

Description: A list of R/3 System names separated by a comma. This list defines the R/3 System from which change requests have originated that can then be imported. By default, this value is empty; therefore, change requests from any R/3 System can be imported. However, if the transport parameter has been defined, only those change requests whose source system is listed can be imported. This parameter is useful for protecting an R/3 System's import process.

stopimmediately

Value: Boolean

Default Value: FALSE (as of R/3 Release 4.6, the default value will be TRUE)

R/3 Release Information: As of R/3 Release 4.5

Description: By default, the transport control program *tp* stops at the end of an import step if an error occurred during that import step. When this parameter is set to TRUE, *tp* reacts to errors immediately following the error rather than at the end of the import step. For example, if *stoponerror* is set to 9 and one change request gets an error 12, with *stopimmediately* set to TRUE, the import process stops immediately after the errant change request. If *stopimmediately* is set to FALSE, the main import step is completed for all change requests before *tp* reports an error from the one change request.

stoponerror

Values: 0, 8, and 9

Default Value: 9

R/3 Release Information: All

Description: The maximum return code *tp* checks for at the completion of every transport step. If the return code is equal to or greater than the value set, the import process is stopped. For example, if the DDIC transport step results in return code 8 (indicating an error), the default value of *stoponerror* will not cause *tp* to end the import process. However, if *stoponerror* is set to the value 8, a return code of 8 will cause the import process to stop. If *stoponerror* is set to zero, *tp* is never stopped.

syslog

Value: Text

Default Value: SLOG$(syear)$(yweek).$(system)

R/3 Release Information: All

Description: The name of the log file in the transport directory *log* that lists all the *tp* import activities for a specific R/3 System.

t_import

Value: Boolean

Default Value: TRUE

R/3 Release Information: All

Description: Allows or disallows the import of change requests that result from a transport of copies (change requests of type "t"). By default, all types of change requests can be imported. However, you can disallow the import of the transport of copies (created using Transaction SE01) by setting the parameter *t_import* to FALSE.

testimport

Value: Boolean

Default Value: TRUE (as of R/3 Release 4.6, the default value will be FALSE)

R/3 Release Information: All

Description: By default, after export of a change request, the transport control program *tp* performs a test import, testing whether the Repository objects in the change request may generate errors upon import into the target system. From time to time, the test import into the target system is not possible—for example, when the target system is not running R/3 or is nonexistent, as in the case of a virtual system. Setting *testimport* to FALSE for the source system can turn off the test import. For example, to turn off test imports for all change requests exported from the development system, you must set *testimport* to FALSE for the development system.

testsystems

Value: Text

Default Value: None

R/3 Release Information: All

Description: You can define a list of R/3 System names (up to 50). Commas must separate the names. If the export of a change request is successful, the transport control program *tp* adds the change request to the import buffer for the change request's defined target system as well as any R/3 Systems defined by *testsystems* for that target system. For example, typically, all change requests released from the development system have a target system defined as the quality assurance system. Release and export of such a change request causes the change request to be added to the import buffer of QAS. If the parameter *testsystems* is set to TST, the change request is also added to the import buffer for the R/3 System TST.

tp_version

Value: Integer

Default Value: None

R/3 Release Information: All

Description: This parameter sets the oldest version of *tp* that can be used to perform *tp* commands on an import buffer. Any *tp* version equal to or greater than this version can be used. This parameter does not usually need to be set—except when the parameter for *ctc* or *nbufform* is TRUE. In such a situation, the *tp_version* needs to be set to at least 264. This ensures that older *tp* versions do not destroy import buffers using a new import buffer format.

transdir

Value: Text

Default Value: None

R/3 Release Information: All

Description: The path to the root of the transport directory. This parameter is required and therefore must be set. For example, *transdir* is often set to */usr/sap/trans/* for a UNIX environment.

vers_at_imp

Values: NEVER, C_ONLY, or ALWAYS

Default Value: NEVER

R/3 Release Information: As of R/3 Release 4.5

Description: Normally, versions for Repository objects exist only on the source system—that is, where the object is changed. During the transport of a new source, no version is created in the import system. However, customers often need to have a detailed storage of all versions in either their quality assurance or their production systems so that if these systems are copied or upgraded, version history can be maintained. If you set the parameter to either C_ONLY or ALWAYS, additional steps are started during the import that generate versions of the imported objects in the target system. Prior to the import of the ABAP Dictionary objects, the change request's command file is imported, and a version of all objects listed in the command file is added to the target system's version database.

Versions are created only if the current version of the object is not the same as the latest version in the database, or if a version does not yet exist for the object in the version database. Although the value ALWAYS activates versions at import for all objects, the value C_ONLY creates versions of objects only when the change request to be imported is a relocation transport (with or without development class and transport layer change). Relocation transports are created and released using the Transport Organizer (Transaction SE01).

w_import

Value: Boolean

Default Value: TRUE

R/3 Release Information: All

Description: Allows or disallows the import of Customizing change requests (change requests of type "w"). By default, all types of change requests can be imported. However, you can disallow the import of Customizing change requests by setting the parameter *w_import* to FALSE.

APPENDIX

C

Selected Transaction Codes

Table C.1 lists the most important R/3 Transaction codes for the support of change and transport management in the R/3 System. You can enter R/3 Transaction codes in the command field of an R/3 screen in the following ways:

- /n<Transaction code>

  - Entering the Transaction code in this way exits the current R/3 screen and displays the initial screen of the transaction.

- /o<Transaction code>

  - Entering the Transaction code in this way sends the current user session to the background and creates a new user session to display the initial screen of the transaction.

TABLE C.1: Transaction Codes Used for Change and Transport Management

Code	Description
AL11	Display SAP directories
AL12	Buffer Synchronization
BALE	ALE Administration and Monitoring
DB02	Analyze tables and indexes (missing database objects and space requirements)
OSS1	Log on to SAPNet—R/3 Frontend Services (formerly known as SAP's Online Service System)
PFCG	Profile Generator: Maintain Activity Groups
RZ01	Job Scheduling Monitor
RZ10	Maintain Profile Parameters
RZ20	Alert Monitor
RZ21	Customizing the Alert Monitor
S001	ABAP Workbench
SADJ	Transfer Assistant

Continued on next page

TABLE C.1: Transaction Codes Used for Change and Transport Management *(Continued)*

Code	Description
SALE	ALE IMG activities
SARA	Archive Administration
SB09	Business Navigator
SCAT	CATT
SCC1	Client Copy According to a Transport Request
SCC3	Client Copy Logs
SCC4	Client Administration
SCC5	Client Delete
SCC7	Client Import—post-processing
SCC8	Client Export
SCC9	Remote Client Copy
SCCL	Local Client Copy
SCMP	Individual View/Table Comparison
SCPR2	Business Configuration Sets (R/3 Release 4.5)
SCU0	Customizing Cross-System Viewer and Client Comparison
SCU3	Table History
SCUM	Central User Administration
SE01	Transport Organizer
SE03	Workbench Organizer: Tools
SE06	Processing after Installation for CTO
SE09	Workbench Organizer
SE10	Customizing Organizer
SE11	ABAP Data Dictionary Maintenance
SE12	ABAP Data Dictionary Display

Continued on next page

TABLE C.1: Transaction Codes Used for Change and Transport Management *(Continued)*

Code	Description
SE13	Maintain Technical Settings for Tables
SE14	Utilities for Dictionary Tables
SE15	Repository Information System
SE16	Display Table Content
SE17	General Table Display
SE37	Function Builder
SE38	ABAP Editor
SE41	Menu Painter
SE51	Screen Painter
SE71	SAPscript forms
SE72	SAPscript styles
SE80	Repository Browser
SE93	Maintain Transaction Codes
SE95	Modification Browser
SLIN	ABAP Extended Program Check
SM02	System Messages
SM04	User Overview
SM12	Display and delete R/3 enqueues
SM13	Display update requests and resolve errors
SM21	System Log
SM28	Installation Check
SM30	Table/View Maintenance
SM31	Table Maintenance
SM35	Batch Input Monitoring

Continued on next page

TABLE C.1: Transaction Codes Used for Change and Transport Management *(Continued)*

Code	Description
SM36	Schedule Background Jobs
SM37	Background Job Overview
SM39	Job Analysis
SM50	Work Process Overview
SM51	Instance Overview
SM56	Reset or check the number range buffer
SM58	Error Log for Asynchronous RFC
SM59	Display or Maintain RFC Destinations
SM63	Display and Maintain Operation Modes
SM64	Trigger an Event
SM65	Analysis Tool for Background Processing
SM66	Global Work Process Overview
SMLG	Maintain Assignments of Logon Groups to Instances
SMLI	Language Import Utility
SMLT	Language Transport Utility
SMOD	SAP Enhancement Management
SNRO	Maintain number range objects
SO99	Upgrade Information System
SOBJ	Attribute Maintenance Objects
SPAM	SAP Package Manager (SPAM)
SPAU	Display Modified Objects in the Runtime Environment
SPDD	Display Modified DDIC Objects
SPRO	Customizing from within the IMG
SPRP	Start IMG Project Administration

Continued on next page

TABLE C.1: Transaction Codes Used for Change and Transport Management *(Continued)*

Code	Description
ST02	Statistics of the R/3 Buffer
ST03	Workload Monitor
ST04	Database Performance Monitor
ST06	Operating System Monitor
ST08	Network Monitor
ST09	Network Alert Monitor
STEM	CATT Utilities
STMS	Transport Management System
SU01	Maintain Users
SU01D	Display Users
SU02	Maintain Authorization Profiles
SU03	Maintain Authorizations
SU05	Maintain Internet Users
SU10	Mass Changes to User Master Records
SU12	Mass Delete of User Master Records
SU20	Maintain Authorization Fields
SU21	Maintain Authorization Objects
SU22	Authorization Object Usage in Transactions
SU3	Maintain Own User Data
SU30	Full Authorization Check
SU56	Analyze User Buffer
SUPC	Profiles for Activity Groups
SUPF	Integrated User Maintenance
SUPO	Maintain Organization Levels

APPENDIX

D

Glossary

ABAP

Advanced Business Application Programming. Programming language of the R/3 System.

ABAP Dictionary

Central storage facility containing metadata (data about data) for all objects in the R/3 System. The ABAP Dictionary describes the logical structure of application development objects and their representation in the structures of the underlying relational database. All runtime environment components such as application programs or the database interface get information about these objects from the ABAP Dictionary. The ABAP Dictionary is an active data dictionary and is fully integrated into the ABAP Workbench.

ABAP Editor

ABAP Workbench tool for developing and maintaining ABAP programs, function modules, screen flow logic, type groups, and logical databases. Besides normal text operations (such as insert, search, and replace), the ABAP Editor offers several special functions to support program development.

ABAP Workbench

SAP's integrated graphical programming environment. The ABAP Workbench supports the development of and changes to R/3 client/server applications written in ABAP. You can use the tools of the ABAP Workbench to write ABAP code, design screens, create user interfaces, use predefined functions, get access to database information, control access to development objects, test applications for efficiency, and debug applications.

activation

Process that makes a runtime object available. The effect of activation is to generate runtime objects, which are accessed by application programs and screen templates.

activity group

Subset of actions from the set of actions that were defined in the Enterprise IMG. From the activity group, you can use the Profile Generator to generate the authorizations needed by R/3 users for these actions.

Add-On Patch

Support Packages that are component patches for add-on software. They are specific to an add-on of a particular R/3 Release. They contain corrections for only the specific add-on.

ADO

Application defined object.

ALE

Application Link Enabling. ALE is a technology for building and operating distributed applications. The basic purpose of ALE is to ensure a distributed, but integrated, R/3 installation. It comprises a controlled business message exchange with consistent data storage in nonpermanently connected SAP applications. Applications are integrated not through a central database, but through synchronous and asynchronous communication.

ALE consists of three layers:

- Application services

- Distribution services

- Communication services

ALE Customizing Distribution

Process that enables you to ensure that the Customizing settings related to ALE scenarios are identical on the different R/3 Systems in the system landscape.

Alert Monitor

A tool that enables you to monitor all actions that have been performed with TMS and that draws your attention to critical information.

API

Application Programming Interface. Software package used by an application program to call a service provided by the operating system—for example, to open a file.

application data

Client-specific data that comprises master data and business transactional data.

application server

A computer on which at least one R/3 instance runs.

ArchiveLink

Integrated into the Basis component of the R/3 System, a communications interface between the R/3 applications and external components. ArchiveLink has the following interfaces: user interface,

interface to the R/3 applications, and interface to external components (archive systems, viewer systems, and scan systems).

archiving object

A logical object comprising related business data in the database that is read from the database using an archiving program. After it has been successfully archived, a logical object can be deleted by a specially generated deleting program.

ASAP

AcceleratedSAP. Standardized procedural model to implement R/3.

automatic recording of changes

Client change option that permits changes to the Customizing settings of the client and requires these changes to be automatically recorded to change requests.

background processing

Processing that does not take place on the screen. Data is processed in the background, while other functions can be executed in parallel on the screen. Although the background processes are not visible for a user and are run without user intervention (there is no dialog), they have the same priority as online processes.

backup domain controller

R/3 System that can assume the functions of the transport domain controller if it fails.

BAPI

Business Application Programming Interface. Standardized programming interface that provides external access to business processes and data in the R/3 System.

batch input

Method and tools for rapid import of data from sequential files into the R/3 database.

Business Configuration Sets

A preserved snapshot of Customizing settings that can be used for comparison with the Customizing Cross-System Viewer. Business Configuration Sets can be created as of R/3 Release 4.5.

business integration testing

Testing of a chain of business processes that form part of the same workflow and the relevant cross-functional boundaries. Integration testing also involves outputs, interfaces, procedures, organizational design, and security profiles, and focuses on likely business events and high-impact exceptions.

button

Element of the graphical user interface. Click a button to execute the button's function. You can select buttons using the keyboard as well as the mouse. Place the button cursor on the button and select Enter or choose the Enter button. Buttons can contain text or graphical symbols.

CATT

Computer Aided Test Tool. You can use this tool to generate test data and to automate and test business processes.

CCMS

Computing Center Management System. Tools for monitoring, controlling, and configuring the R/3 System. The CCMS supports 24-hour system administration functions from within the R/3 System. You can analyze the system load and monitor the distributed resource usage of the system components.

Change and Transport Organizers (CTO)

The Organizers in the R/3 System for managing change requests as a result of development efforts in the ABAP Workbench and Customizing activities in the IMG. It comprises the Workbench Organizer, the Customizing Organizer, and the Transport Organizer.

Change and Transport System (CTS)

Tools used to manage changes and development in the R/3 System and their transport to other R/3 Systems. It comprises the Change and Transport Organizers, the Transport Management System, and the operating system level programs *tp* and *R3trans*.

change management

The handling of changes to software and their distribution to various environments. These changes may be required by changes in the way an enterprise does business. From a technical perspective, change management is the process by which changes made to one R/3 System are distributed to one or more R/3 Systems in a consistent and timely manner after appropriate testing and verification to ensure a stable and predictable production environment.

change request

Information source in the Workbench Organizer and Customizing Organizer that records and manages all changes made to R/3 Repository objects and Customizing settings during an R/3 implementation project.

client

From a commercial law, organizational, and technical viewpoint, a closed unit within an R/3 System with separate master records within a table.

client compare

Determining the differences in Customizing settings between two R/3 clients.

client copy

Function that allows you to copy a client in the same R/3 System (a local client copy) or to another R/3 System (a remote client copy). Client copy profiles determine what will be copied: Customizing data, business application data, and/or user master records.

client copy according to a transp. request

Functionality with which you can transport client-dependent objects of either a change request or a task between clients in the same R/3 System.

client copy profile

A profile that enables you to copy certain data (e.g., Customizing data, application data, or user master records) from a client into another client. SAP provides all possible profiles and requires that you select the appropriate one for what you need to copy from one client to another.

client settings

During client maintenance, options exist to determine whether client-dependent and client-independent changes can occur, and whether recording of those changes is automatic. You can also define the client's role, and set additional restrictions and protection for the client. The system administrator should consciously decide the appropriate client settings for all clients in the system landscape.

client transport

Functionality with which you can copy the contents of one client to another client in a different R/3 System by performing first a client export and then a client import.

client-dependent

Specific only to one client. Settings in client-dependent tables relate only to the client that was accessed during the logon process. Such tables contain the client number in the table's primary key.

client-independent

Relevant for all clients in an R/3 System. Client-independent is synonymous with cross-client.

client-specific transport route

A transport route that consolidates or delivers to an R/3 System and client combination rather than simply an R/3 System. Client-specific transport routes are available with extended transport control in R/3 Release 4.5.

Conflict Resolution Transport (CRT)

A type of Support Package exclusively used for R/3 add-ons such as industry solutions—for example, IS-OIL. They are designed to resolve conflicts that can occur between either a Hot Package or a Legal Change Patch and the add-on.

consolidation route

Regular transport route of an R/3 Repository object from the integration system to the consolidation system. The consolidation route is specified for each R/3 Repository object by the transport layer for the object's development class.

consolidation system

System in the system landscape to which change requests are exported as defined by a consolidation route. The consolidation system in a three-system landscape is the quality assurance system and, in the case of a two-system landscape, the production system.

control file

List of required import steps for each released and exported change request. All control files are saved to the transport directory *cofiles*.

Control Panel

Central tool for monitoring the R/3 System and its instances.

Controlled Availability (CA)

Related to phase FCP in the R/3 Release Strategy. In this phase, a new R/3 Functional Release is available. R/3 Functional Releases are available only for a limited number of customers.

Correction R/3 Release

Corrections used primarily to support the continuous improvement of software quality rather than introduce new functionality are collected together in Correction Releases. SAP provides Support Packages for Correction Releases that correct several types of software errors. SAP recommends a Correction R/3 Release for production activities.

cross-client

Relevant for all clients in an R/3 System. Cross-client is synonymous with client-independent.

Current Settings

Allows for certain kinds of Customizing changes, known as data-only Customizing changes, to be carried out in a production client without being saved as change requests.

customer development

Additions to the standard, delivered SAP software using the ABAP Workbench. Customer developments involve creating customer-specific objects using the customer's name range and namespace.

Customizing

Adjusting the R/3 System to specific customer requirements by selecting variants, parameter settings, etc.

Customizing Activity Log

The ability in R/3 Release 4.5 to analyze table logs for Customizing activities. Table logs are generated only when table logging has been activated for the client.

Customizing change request

Change request for recording and transporting changed system settings from client-specific tables.

Customizing Cross-System Viewer

The client comparison tool with R/3 Release 4.5. In addition to determining the differences in Customizing settings, the Customizing Cross-System Viewer provides for the correction/adjustment of differences. It is often simply referred to as the Cross-System Viewer.

Customizing Organizer (CO)

Tool to manage change requests of all types in an R/3 System. The Customizing Organizer is part of the Change and Transport Organizer.

Customizing Transfer Assistant

A tool in R/3 Release 4.5 for the comparison and adjustment of client-dependent changes imported into an R/3 System.

data archiving

Removing data that is currently not needed from the R/3 database and storing it in archives (see "archiving object").

data file

Exported R/3 Repository objects and/or table data that resides at the operating system level in the transport directory *data* for each released and exported change request.

database

Set of data (organized, for example, in files) for permanent storage on the hard disk. Each R/3 System has only one database.

database copy

Also known as system copy. If you create an R/3 System using a database copy, the R/3 installation is not set up with the SAP standard database, but with a database whose content is supplied by an existing R/3 System using R/3 migration tools specific to your platform and R/3 Release.

database instance

An administrative unit that allows access to a database. A database instance consists of database processes with a common set of database buffers in shared memory. There is normally only one database instance for each database. DB2/390 and Oracle Parallel Server are database systems for which a database can be made up of multiple database instances. In an R/3 System, a database instance can either be alone on a single computer or together with one or possibly more R/3 instances.

database server

A computer with at least one database instance.

DBA

Database administrator.

delivery class

Classification attribute for ABAP Dictionary tables. The delivery class determines who (SAP or the customer) is responsible for maintaining the contents of a table. It also controls how a table behaves during a client copy, a client transport, and an R/3 Release upgrade.

delivery route

Continuation of the transport route, after the consolidation route, for developments in the ABAP Workbench and Customizing. After being imported into the consolidation system, change requests are also flagged for import into the target systems of all delivery routes.

delivery system

R/3 System type in a system landscape. A delivery system is linked to a consolidation system. By means of this link, the delivery system continually receives copies of change requests imported into the consolidation system. A production system is an example of a delivery system in a standard three-system landscape.

Delta Customizing

Customizing activities that the customer needs to do to be able to use new functionality in the business application components after an R/3 Release upgrade. While Upgrade Customizing is mandatory for existing functionality, Delta Customizing is only necessary to make use of new functionality.

development class

A grouping of R/3 Repository objects belonging to a common area. Unlike the objects in a change request, the grouping is logical rather than temporal. The development class is assigned a transport layer to ensure that all objects have the same consolidation route.

development system

System in a system landscape where development and Customizing work is performed.

dialog box

Window that is called from a primary window and displayed in front of that window.

dialog work process

R/3 work process to process requests from users working online.

dispatcher

The process that coordinates the work processes of an R/3 instance.

EDI

Electronic Data Interchange. Electronic interchange of structured data (for example, business documents) between business partners in the home country and abroad who may be using different hardware, software, and communication services.

end mark

An end mark is a marker placed in import queues to indicate that only the requests before the marker should be imported. If you look at an import queue, an end mark is indicated with the statement "End of import queue." Only one end mark is possible per import queue. The terms *end mark* and *stopmark* are often used interchangeably.

enhancement

Enhancements generally consist of user exits provided by SAP in the program code to call up external customer-developed programs. The source code of the SAP standard R/3 Release does not need to be changed, as the connected customer objects also lie in the customer name range. The advantage of using enhancements is that during a subsequent upgrade, you do not need to perform a modification adjustment. Enhancements are not affected by upgrading to a new R/3 Release.

enqueue

R/3 enqueues help to ensure data consistency by prohibiting the changing of data by more than one user at a time. An R/3 enqueue is set explicitly within an ABAP program by an enqueue function module and explicitly released by a dequeue function module. R/3 enqueues can continue to be in effect over several steps within an R/3 transaction. Remaining R/3 enqueues are released at the end of the R/3 transaction.

Enterprise IMG

Company-specific Implementation Guide.

export

The processes by which all objects of a change request are extracted from the database of the source R/3 System. The extracted data is saved to a data file at the operating system level. In addition, a control file is created that indicates how the data should be imported into an R/3 System.

extended transport control

Enhanced transport configuration options as of R/3 Release 4.5. With extended transport control, transport routes can include client specifications or groups of client and system combinations.

external system

An R/3 System defined from within TMS for which no physical system exists. As with virtual systems, an import queue is maintained for them if defined as part of a transport layer. Unlike virtual systems, external systems have their own transport directory that may be explicitly defined.

FCS Final Delta Patch

Support Package that brings FCS R/3 Systems into the final state before other types of Support Packages can be applied.

firewall

Software to protect a local network from unauthorized access from outside.

First Customer Shipment (FCS)

The phase between the first shipment of a new R/3 Release and going live. The customer must apply for participation in this program.

First Production Customer (FPC)

Phase following the FCS in the R/3 Release Strategy. In this phase, the first customers are productive with a new R/3 Functional Release. This phase is also referred to as CA (Controlled Availability).

forward

To deliver change requests to other R/3 Systems outside the predefined transport routes.

Functional R/3 Release

An R/3 Release that introduces improved business processes and/or new technology into the R/3 System. Functional Releases are delivered upon request to those customers who want to test the new functionality. For Functional Releases, SAP provides Support Packages that correct major software errors. SAP recommends not using a Functional R/3 Release for production activities.

General Availability (GA)

A phase in the R/3 Release Strategy in which a new R/3 Correction Release is available to all customers.

GUI

Graphical User Interface. The medium through which a user can exchange information with the computer. You use the GUI to select commands, start programs, display files, and perform other operations by selecting function keys or buttons, menu options, and icons with the mouse.

high availability

Property of a service or a system that remains in production operation for most of the time. High availability for an R/3 System means that unplanned and planned downtimes are reduced to a minimum. Good system administration is decisive here. You can reduce unplanned downtime by using preventive hardware and software solutions that are designed to reduce single points of failure in the services that support the R/3 System. You can reduce the planned downtime by optimizing the scheduling of necessary maintenance activities.

Hot Package

A type of Support Package that corrects errors or provides enhancements to the R/3 Repository and ABAP Dictionary for core R/3 services.

IDoc type

Internal document in SAP format, into which the data of a business process is transferred. An IDoc is a real business process formatted in the IDoc type. An IDoc type is described by the following components:

A control record: Its format is identical for all IDoc types.

One or more records: A record consists of a fixed administration segment and the data segment. The number and format of the segments differ for different IDoc types.

Status records: These records describe stages of processing that an IDoc can go through. The status records have the same format for all IDoc types.

Implementation Guide (IMG)

A tool for making customer-specific adjustments to the R/3 System. For each application component, the Implementation Guide contains:

- All steps to implement the R/3 System

- All default settings and all activities to configure the R/3 System

- A hierarchical structure that maps the structure of the R/3 application components

- Lists of all the documentation relevant to the implementation of the R/3 System

import

The process by which all objects of previously released and exported change requests are transported into a target R/3 System using either the TMS or the transport control program *tp*.

import all

The import of all change requests in the import queue or import buffer that are waiting to be imported.

import buffer

A file at the operating system level containing the list of change requests to be imported into a specific R/3 System. This file resides in the transport directory *buffer*. The terms *import buffer* and *import queues* are often used interchangeably.

import options

Import options that can be assigned either from within TMS import functionality or when using the *tp* command. They are used to cause specific rules of the Change and Transport System (CTS) to be ignored. Traditionally, transport options are known as unconditional modes.

import queue

The import queue in R/3 reflects the operating system level import buffer and contains the list of requests that will be imported during the next *import all* process. Because of end marks and nonstandard change requests, there may be more requests in the import buffer than are highlighted in the import queue. The terms *import buffer* and *import queues* are often used interchangeably.

Industry Solution (IS)

Industry-specific applications for R/3. For example, IS-H (IS Hospital), IS-RE (IS Real Estate), or IS-PS (IS Public Sector).

integration system

System in the system landscape where developments and Customizing are carried out and then transported to the consolidation system. Each R/3 Repository object is assigned to an integration system through its development class and transport layer.

Internet Transaction Server (ITS)

Gateway between the R/3 System and the World Wide Web.

LAN

Local area network.

legacy system

Typically refers to a customer's previous system (for example, a mainframe system). The data in this system has to be reformatted before it is imported into a new system (for example, into a client/server system such as R/3).

Legal Change Patch (LCP)

A type of Support Package that provides corrections and other adjustments required due to legal changes for the Human Resources (HR) component.

local change request

Change request that cannot be transported to other R/3 Systems.

local object

A Repository object assigned to a local development class such as the development class $TMP. Local objects are local to the R/3 System on which they are created and cannot be transported.

locks

The locking of data during transaction processing and R/3 Repository objects during development work.

- If a user changes a data record with a transaction or changes a Repository object, the same record or object cannot be accessed simultaneously by a second user. The record or object is locked for the duration of processing (ENQUEUE), and only afterwards is it released or unlocked (DEQUEUE).

- Repository objects are locked in Workbench change requests until the change request is released.

logical system

A way of representing a client in an R/3 System without having to define the R/3 System. Logical systems allow applications to run with a common data basis. In SAP terms, a logical system is a client defined in a database. Logical systems can exchange messages and can be used, for example, by ALE.

manual transport

The recording of Customizing changes to a change request using a manual rather than an automatic method. Some IMG activities can only be transported using a manual transport option.

master data

Master data is a type of application data that changes infrequently, but is required for the completion of most business transactions. Examples of master data include lists of customers, vendors, and materials, and even the company's chart of accounts.

modification

Change made by a customer to SAP-owned R/3 Repository objects. During an R/3 Release upgrade, modifications may require the new SAP standard to be adjusted.

modification adjustment

Editing of R/3 Repository objects during an R/3 Release upgrade or when applying Support Packages, based on a comparison of SAP-owned Repository objects as they were before the upgrade (old state) and the same objects as they will be after the upgrade (new state).

Modification Assistant

Functionality designed to help manage the repair of a Repository object using the ABAP Workbench tools. The Modification Assistant guides the change process to ensure that changes are well documented, original forms of the objects are preserved, and the change request to which the changes are recorded is indicated.

Modification Browser

Detailed documentation of all repairs made in an R/3 System.

name range

A name range is an interval in a namespace. The name range for customer programs is the set of program names beginning with Y or Z. Customer name ranges can be reserved in view V_TRESN.

namespace

Set of all names that satisfy the specific properties of the namespace. A namespace is defined by a prefix SAP provides to the customer or complementary software partner.

nametab

A nametab is the runtime object of a table. The runtime object contains all the information stored in the ABAP Dictionary in a format that is optimized for the application programs.

object checks

When activated, object checks subject Repository objects in a change request to checks, such as a syntax check for ABAP programs, prior to the release of the change request.

Object Directory

Catalog of R/3 Repository objects that contains the following information: object type, object name, original system, person responsible, and development class.

object list

List of R/3 Repository objects and/or Customizing objects in change requests or tasks. Whenever changes are made, objects are added to the object list of a task. When a task is released, its object list is placed in the object list of the request to which it is assigned.

OCS

Online Correction Support. OCS is a global term comprising various tools designed to help you support your production environment by supplying Support Packages.

original object

The original of an object is normally the version maintained in the development system. Because all changes and developments are made using the original, it may never be overwritten by a transport.

OS

Operating system.

performance

Measurement of the efficiency of a computer system.

preliminary import

Import of a single change request. Preliminary imports allow you to expedite an individual request through the defined transport routes. A preliminary import imports the request and adds it to the next import queue defined by the transport route. To minimize the risks associated with preliminary imports, the request remains in the original import queue after the import and is re-imported the next time the entire import queue is imported. This guarantees that the order in which groups of objects are imported is always the same as the order in which they were exported.

presentation server

A computer providing GUI services.

production system

System that contains an enterprise's active business processes. This is where "live" production data is entered.

Profile Generator

Automatically generates an authorization profile based on the activities in an activity group.

Project IMG

Subset of the Enterprise IMG, containing only the documentation for the Enterprise IMG components required in a particular Customizing project.

Project IMG views

Subset of a Project IMG, containing, for example, all mandatory activities for the project.

quality assurance system

System in which final testing is carried out. Tested, stable development objects and Customizing settings are transported into the quality assurance system from the development system at times defined for final testing. After verification and sign-off, development objects and Customizing settings are delivered to the production system.

R/3

Runtime System 3.

R/3 instance

Group of resources such as memory and work processes, usually in support of a single application server or database server in an R/3 client/server environment. Instance processes share a common set of buffers and are controlled by the same dispatcher process. An R/3 System can consist of one or more instances.

R/3 Notes

SAP's announcements of corrections or enhancements to R/3. Often, an R/3 Note provides solutions, or a solution will be provided in a Support Package.

R/3 Repository

Central storage facility for all development objects in the ABAP Workbench. These development objects include ABAP programs, screens, and documentation.

R/3 runtime environment

Set of programs that must be available for execution at runtime. The ABAP interpreters in the runtime environment do not use the original of an ABAP program. Rather, they use a copy generated once only during runtime (early binding). Runtime objects, such as programs and screens, are automatically regenerated (late binding) when a time stamp comparison between the object and the ABAP Dictionary detects a difference.

R/3 System

Consists of a central instance offering the services DUEBMGS (dialog, update, enqueue, background processing, message, gateway, spool), a database instance, optional dialog instances offering the service D (dialog), and optional PC frontends.

R/3 System service

Logical function required to support the R/3 System, such as the database service and the application services, which may include the services dialog, update, enqueue, batch, message, gateway, and spool.

R/3 Upgrade Assistant

Support tool for R/3 upgrades. The R/3 Upgrade Assistant provides one or more graphical user interfaces for the upgrade control program. It also permits you to execute an R/3 upgrade remotely and monitor its status.

R3trans

A transport utility at the operating system level for the transport of data between R/3 Systems. *R3trans* is also used for the installation of new R/3 Systems, for migration to different R/3 Releases, and for logical backups. Other programs usually call *R3trans*, in particular the transport control program *tp* and the upgrade control program *R3up*.

RDBMS

Relational Database Management System.

RDDIMPDP

Background job that is scheduled event-periodic. It starts the background jobs that are required for transports. RDDIMPDP is triggered by *tp*, which uses the executable *sapevt* on the operating system level to send event SAP_TRIGGER_RDDIMPDP. RDDIMPDP is also known as "transport daemon" and "transport dispatcher".

release

The process by which the owner of a change request or task indicates that the contents of the change request or task have been unit tested. Release of a change request of either type Transportable or Customizing initiates the export process.

Release Customizing

Only those IMG activities affected by a given R/3 Release upgrade in the business application components concerned are presented for processing. SAP distinguishes between Upgrade Customizing (corrected or amended functionality) and Delta Customizing (new functionality) for R/3 Release upgrades.

relocation transports

The transport of Repository objects for the purpose of changing the ownership, development class, and/or transport layer for those objects. Relocation transports are possible using the Transport Organizer.

repair

An R/3 Repository object that is changed in a system other than its original system is entered in a repair. All modifications of SAP standard objects are repairs, because the customer's system is not the original system for SAP objects.

repair flag

A flag that protects an object changed in a system other than its original system from being overwritten by an import.

Repository Browser

ABAP Workbench navigation tool for managing development objects. The user interface of the Repository Browser resembles a file manager where development objects are grouped together in object lists in a hierarchical structure.

Repository object

Object in the R/3 Repository. Repository objects are development objects of the ABAP Workbench.

Repository switch

A procedure during an R/3 upgrade that replaces an existing R/3 Repository with a new R/3 Repository.

return code

Value that indicates whether a tool (either within R/3 or on the operating system level) ran successfully, with warnings, or with errors.

RFC

Remote Function Call. RFC is an SAP interface protocol, based on CPI-C. It allows the programming of communication processes between systems to be simplified considerably. Using RFCs, predefined functions can be called and executed in a remote system or within the same system. RFCs are used for communication control, parameter passing, and error handling.

SAP Business Warehouse Patch

Support Packages that contain a collection of corrections for the SAP Business Information Warehouse (SAP BW) component.

SAP Patch Manager (SPAM)

SPAM is the R/3 System interface to SAPNet, SAP's support services, for the purpose of downloading Support Packages. It is also known as SAP Package Manager.

SAP Reference IMG

Complete Implementation Guide containing all Customizing activities supplied by SAP. It is organized according to business application component.

SAP Software Change Registration (SSCR)

A procedure for registering those users who change or create Repository objects using the tools of the ABAP Workbench and for registering changes to SAP Repository objects.

SAPGUI

SAP Graphical User Interface.

SAPNet

SAP's support and information services from which you access R/3 Notes and Support Packages. It was formerly known as SAP's Online Service System (OSS).

SAPNet—R/3 Frontend

Access to SAP support services directly from your R/3 System using a remote connection and going through the SAProuter.

SAPNet—Web Frontend

The communication channel with SAP support services available through the Internet.

SAProuter

A software module that functions as part of a firewall system.

session

A user session in an SAPGUI window.

Session Manager

The tool used for central control of R/3 applications. The Session Manager is a graphical navigation interface used to manage sessions and start application transactions. It can generate both company-specific and user-specific menus. The Session Manager is available from R/3 Release 3.0C under Windows 95 and Windows NT.

shared memory

Main memory area that can be accessed by all work processes in an instance. The term *shared memory* is also used to mean the main memory area shared by the RDBMS processes.

SID

SAP System Identifier. Placeholder for the three-character name of an R/3 System.

Software Component Patches

A type of Support Package available in R/3 Release 4.5. Patches of this type are generic patches for one software component—for example, Basis or Human Resources—and contain corrections for errors in the Repository and the Dictionary only in this component.

software logistics

Procedures and tools required for the creation, documentation, and distribution of development and Customizing changes throughout the system landscape.

SPAM Update

Support Package that contains improvements and extensions to the SAP Patch Manager.

SQL

Structured Query Language. A database language for accessing relational databases.

standard request

A default change request automatically used to record changes without prompting for a request number. A standard request must be manually set and is valid for a specified period of time.

standard transport layer

The default transport layer for an R/3 System and the transport layer used by all Customizing change requests released from that system.

stopmark

A stopmark is a marker placed in the import buffer to indicate that only the requests before the marker should be imported. The terms *end mark* and *stopmark* are often used interchangeably.

Support Package

A generic term for the different collections of general improvements and changes to the SAP standard software that SAP provides through SAPNet.

Support Package Collection

Support Packages are grouped into Support Package Collections at regular intervals. These are stored on CD-ROMs and delivered automatically to all customers. Support Package Collections are available for Support Packages of type Hot Package and Legal Change Patches.

system change option

Global setting to permit changes to R/3 Repository objects based on the object's namespace and type.

system copy

Also known as database copy. If you create an R/3 System using a system copy, the R/3 installation is not set up with the SAP standard database, but with a database whose content is supplied by an existing R/3 System using R/3 migration tools specific to your platform and R/3 Release.

system landscape

The R/3 Systems and clients required for a company's implementation and maintenance of R/3. For example, a common system landscape consists of a development system, a quality assurance system, and a production system.

table logging

Activating the logging of all changes to SAP-selected Customizing tables for the purpose of providing an audit history as to who made what changes to the data.

target group

A group of R/3 System and client combinations to which transport routes can consolidate or deliver. Target groups are available with extended transport control in R/3 Release 4.5.

task

User-specific information carrier in the Change and Transport Organizers for entering and managing all changes to R/3 Repository objects and Customizing settings. When an object is changed, the changed objects are recorded to a task. Tasks are assigned to a change request.

TCP/IP

Transmission Control Protocol/Internet Protocol.

transaction code

Succession of alphanumeric characters used to name a transaction—that is, a particular ABAP program in the R/3 System. For example, Transaction VA01 (*create customer order*).

transaction data

Data collected during standard business activities/transactions and typically related to specific master data. For example, data relating to a specific sale is regarded as transaction data and can be assigned to the master data of the purchaser.

transport

The movement (export and import) of change requests between different R/3 Systems.

transport control program (*tp*)

An operation system level utility for controlling the transport of change requests between R/3 Systems.

transport directory

Operating system disk space that provides the management facility for all data to be transported between R/3 Systems.

transport domain

All R/3 Systems to be administered using the Transport Management System (TMS) belong to a transport domain. In this transport domain, system settings such as the transport route settings are identical for all R/3 Systems. To have consistent settings in the transport domain, one R/3 System (the domain controller) has the reference configuration, and all the other R/3 Systems in the transport domain receive copies of this reference configuration.

transport domain controller

An R/3 System in the transport domain, from which transport configuration activities for the entire transport domain are controlled. These activities include accepting R/3 Systems into the transport domain, creating virtual R/3 Systems, and establishing transport routes between the different R/3 Systems.

transport group

All R/3 Systems in a transport domain that share the same transport directory.

transport layer

Means by which the integration and consolidation system for R/3 Repository objects are determined. A transport layer is assigned to each development class and thus to all R/3 Repository objects in that development class. It determines the R/3 System in which developments or changes to R/3 Repository objects are performed, and whether objects will be transported to other systems when development work has been completed.

transport log

Record of the transfer of the objects in a particular change request from a source system to a target system. A transport log contains:

- A summary of transport activities

- A log detailing the export of objects from a source system
- The results of the import check
- A log detailing the import of objects into a target system

Transport Management System (TMS)

The tool in the R/3 System that enables centralized transport configuration, and the execution and monitoring of exports and imports between R/3 Systems in a single transport domain.

Transport Organizer (TO)

Tool for preparing and managing transports that supplements the more commonly used Workbench Organizer and Customizing Organizer. The Transport Organizer is part of the Change and Transport Organizer.

transport profile

The parameter settings for the operating system transport command program *tp*. This file resides at the operating system level in the transport directory *bin*.

transport request

A released and exported change request. This term is often used synonymously with the term *change request*.

transport route

Transport routes are used to define both the target system in which you want to consolidate change requests and the R/3 Systems to which change requests are delivered after verification and testing. Transport routes are of either type *consolidation* or type *delivery*.

transportable change request

Change request that will be exported to a defined consolidation system when released.

unit testing

Lowest level of testing where the program or transaction is tested and evaluated for faults (contrasted with business integration testing). Unit testing is the first test that is completed, normally during the Customizing and development effort, while business integration testing usually occurs in the quality assurance system. With unit testing, the focus is on the program's inner functions rather than on system integration.

Upgrade Customizing

Customizing activities that are required if you want to continue to use the same functions as before in your business application components after a system or R/3 Release upgrade. Upgrade Customizing covers changes to functions already used in live systems.

user master data

Logon and authorization information for R/3 users. Only users who have a user master record can log on to a client in an R/3 System and use specific transactions.

version database

Storage location for versions of R/3 Repository objects when a change request is released.

view

"Virtual table" simultaneously displaying data from several real tables in the ABAP Dictionary. When you create a table, you assign a key to it. However, the fields in the key may be inadequate for solving some problems, so you can generate a view from several tables or parts of tables.

virtual system

R/3 System configured as a placeholder for an R/3 System that has not yet been set up. Transport routes can be defined for virtual systems, and the import queue can be set up and displayed.

WAN

Wide area network.

work process (WP)

The application services of the R/3 System have special processes—for example, for:

- Dialog administration
- Updating change documents
- Background processing
- Spool processing
- Lock management

Work processes can be assigned to dedicated application servers.

Workbench change request

Change request for recording and transporting R/3 Repository objects and changed system settings from cross-client tables (client-independent Customizing).

Workbench Organizer (WBO)

Tools for managing Workbench change requests required to record changes as a result of development efforts using the tools of the ABAP Workbench. The Workbench Organizer is part of the Change and Transport Organizer.

APPENDIX
E

Review Questions and Answers

Chapter 1

1. Which of the following components indicate that R/3 is a client/server system?

   A. Multiple databases

   B. A database server

   C. Three separate hardware servers—a database server, an application server, and a presentation server

   D. A database service, an application service, and a presentation service

   Answer: D

2. Which of the following is *not* contained in the R/3 database?

   A. The R/3 Repository

   B. The R/3 kernel

   C. Customer data

   D. Transaction data

   E. Customizing data

   F. The ABAP Dictionary

   Answer: B

3. Which of the following statements is correct in regard to R/3 clients?

   A. An R/3 client has its own customer data and programs, which are not accessible to other clients within the same R/3 System.

   B. An R/3 client shares all R/3 Repository objects and client-independent Customizing with all other clients in the same R/3 System.

    C. An R/3 client shares Customizing and application data with other clients in the same R/3 System.

    D. An R/3 client enables you to separate application data from Customizing data.

Answer: B

4. Which of the following statements is correct in regard to SAP's client concept?

    A. All Customizing settings are client-independent.

    B. A client has a unique set of application data.

    C. A client has its own Repository objects.

    D. All Customizing settings are client-dependent.

Answer: B

Chapter 2

1. Which of the following strategies enables R/3 customers to avoid making modifications to SAP-standard objects?

    A. Using enhancement technologies such as program exits and menu exits

    B. Modifying SAP-delivered programs

    C. Changing SAP-standard functionality using the Implementation Guide (IMG)

    D. Performing Customizing to provide the required functionality

Answer: A, D

2. Which of the following statements are correct in regard to the Implementation Guide (IMG)?

   A. The IMG consists of a series of Customizing activities for defining a company's business processes.

   B. The IMG is an online resource providing the necessary information and steps to help you implement R/3 application modules.

   C. The IMG is client-independent.

   D. All of the above.

   Answer: D

3. Which of the following strategies enables an enterprise to meet its business needs by changing or enhancing R/3 functionality?

   A. Maintaining application data using the various R/3 business transactions in the SAP standard

   B. Using the ABAP Workbench to create the required R/3 Repository objects

   C. Using Customizing to modify R/3 programs after obtaining an access key from SAP's Online Support Services (OSS)

   D. Using customer exits to enhance the functionality of existing SAP-standard objects

   Answer: B, D

4. Which of the following statements are correct in regard to modifications?

   A. A modification is a change to an SAP-standard object.

   B. A modification must be registered through SAP Software Change Registration (SSCR).

C. SAP recommends modifications only if the customer's business needs cannot be met by Customizing, enhancement technologies, or customer development.

D. All of the above.

Answer: D

5. Which of the following statements is correct in regard to Customizing?

A. Customizing enables R/3 application processes to be set to reflect a company's business needs.

B. Customizing can be performed only from within a Project IMG.

C. Customizing is necessary because R/3 is delivered without business processes.

D. None of the above.

Answer: A

6. Which of the following statements are correct in regard to R/3 Repository objects?

A. Customers can develop new Repository objects using the tools in the ABAP Workbench.

B. Customer-developed Repository objects reside in the R/3 Repository alongside SAP-standard objects.

C. Customers can create and assign new Repository objects to a development class.

D. All of the above.

Answer: D

Chapter 3

1. Which of the following statements is correct in regard to critical client roles as recommended by SAP?

    A. Customizing changes can be made in any client.

    B. All Customizing and development changes should be made in a single R/3 client.

    C. Repository objects should be created and changed in the quality assurance client.

    D. Unit testing should take place in the Customizing-and-development client.

    Answer: B

2. Which of the following activities should *not* be performed within a system landscape?

    A. Customizing and development changes are promoted to a quality assurance client before being delivered to production.

    B. The R/3 System is upgraded to new R/3 Releases.

    C. Development changes are made directly in the production client.

    D. Clients are assigned a specific role.

    Answer: C

3. Which of the following benefits does the three-system landscape recommended by SAP have?

    A. Customizing and development, testing, and production activities take place in separate database environments and do not affect one another.

    B. Changes are tested in the quality assurance system and imported into the production system only after verification.

C. Client-independent changes can be made in the development system without immediately affecting the production client.

D. All of the above.

Answer: D

4. Which of the following statements is correct in regard to multiple R/3 clients?

A. All clients in the same R/3 System share the same R/3 Repository and client-independent Customizing settings.

B. No more than one client in the same R/3 System should allow changes to client-independent Customizing objects.

C. If a client allows for changes to client-dependent Customizing, the client should also allow for changes to client-independent Customizing objects.

D. All of the above.

Answer: D

5. Which of the following statements is correct in regard to the setup of a three-system landscape?

A. There is only one R/3 database for the system landscape.

B. One client should allow for the automatic recording of client-dependent Customizing and client-independent changes.

C. All R/3 Systems have the same system ID.

D. All clients must have unique client numbers.

Answer: B

6. Which of the following statements is correct in regard to the CUST client?

   A. It should allow changes to client-independent Customizing, but not Repository objects.

   B. It should automatically record all changes to Customizing settings.

   C. It should not allow changes to client-dependent and client-independent Customizing settings.

   D. It should allow for all changes, but not require recording of changes to change requests.

Answer: B

7. Which of the following statements is correct in regard to a two-system landscape?

   A. It is not optimal because there is limited opportunity to test the transport of changes from the development system to the production system.

   B. It allows for changes to Customizing in the production system.

   C. It is recommended by SAP because Customizing and development do not impact quality assurance testing.

   D. All of the above.

Answer: A

8. Which of the following statements are correct in regard to a phased implementation?

   A. All Customizing changes made in the production support system must also be made in the development system.

   B. The system landscape requires five R/3 Systems.

    C. Changes in the production support system do not have to be made in the development environment.

    D. The system landscape needs an environment that supports the production system with any required changes.

Answer: A, D

9. Which of the following statements is *not* valid in regard to a global system landscape?

    A. A global template can be used for the rollout of corporate Customizing settings and development efforts.

    B. Management of different Repository objects (those developed by the corporate office versus those developed locally) can be managed using namespaces and name ranges for the Repository objects.

    C. Merging the Customizing settings delivered by the corporate office with local Customizing efforts can easily be done using change requests.

    D. SAP provides different tools to aid in the rollout of a global template.

Answer: C

Chapter 4

1. Which of the following statements is correct in regard to Customizing and development changes?

    A. All changes are recorded to tasks in Customizing change requests.

    B. The changes should be recorded to tasks in change requests for transport to other clients and systems.

    C. The changes must be manually performed in every R/3 System.

    D. The changes can easily be made simultaneously in multiple clients.

Answer: B

2. Which of the following statements in regard to change requests is FALSE?

    A. The Customizing Organizer and the Workbench Organizer are tools used to view, create, and manage change requests.

    B. A change request is a collection of tasks where developers and people performing Customizing record the changes they make.

    C. All changes made as a result of IMG activities are recorded to Customizing change requests.

    D. SAP recommends setting your R/3 System so that Customizing changes made in the Customizing-and-development client are automatically recorded to change requests.

Answer: C

3. For which of the following activities is the TMS (Transaction STMS) *not* designed?

    A. Releasing change requests

    B. Viewing import queues

    C. Viewing log files generated by both the export process and the import process

    D. Initiating the import process

Answer: A

4. Which of the following statements is correct after you have successfully imported change requests into the quality assurance system?

   A. The change requests must be released again to be exported to the production system.

   B. The data files containing the changed objects are deleted from the transport directory.

   C. The change requests need to be manually added to the import queue of the production system.

   D. The change requests are automatically added to the import queue of the production system.

Answer: D

5. Which of the following statements is correct in regard to the change requests in an import queue?

   A. They are sequenced according to their change request number.

   B. They are sequenced in the order in which they were exported from the development system.

   C. They are sequenced according to the name of the user who released the requests.

   D. They are not sequenced by default, but arranged in a variety of ways using the TMS.

Answer: B

6. Which of the following techniques can be used to transfer application data between two production systems?

   A. Recording transaction data to change requests

   B. Using ALE to transfer application data

C. Using the client copy tool

D. All of the above

Answer: B

7. Which of the following types of data transfer are possible with an appropriate use of interface technologies?

A. Transferring legacy data to an R/3 System

B. Transferring data between R/3 clients

C. Transferring data to non-SAP systems

D. Transporting change requests to multiple R/3 Systems

Answer: A, B, C

8. Which of the following statements is correct in regard to user master data?

A. User master data can be transported in a change request.

B. User master data is unique to each R/3 System, but is shared across clients in the same R/3 System.

C. A specific client copy option enables you to distribute user master data together with authorization profile data.

D. User master data includes all user logon information, including the definition of authorizations and profiles.

Answer: C

Chapter 5

1. Which of the following clients should you copy to create new clients and ensure that all data from post-installation processing is also copied?

    A. Client 001

    B. Client 000

    C. Client 066

    Answer: B

2. Which of the following is *not* an SAP-recommended strategy for setting up a system landscape?

    A. Using a client copy from the development system to set up your quality assurance and production systems when the change request strategy is not an option

    B. Creating the production system as a combination of a client copy from the quality assurance system and change requests from the development system

    C. Using the same setup strategy to establish both the quality assurance and production systems

    D. Setting up the quality assurance and production systems by importing change requests promoted from the development system

    Answer: B

3. Which of the following are correct in regard to the setup of the TMS?

    A. The TMS should be set up when the development system is installed.

    B. The TMS should include all R/3 Systems in the system landscape even if the R/3 Systems do not physically exist.

    C. The TMS is critical in establishing the transport route between the development and quality assurance systems.

    D. The TMS should be set up before change requests are created in the Customizing-and-development client.

Answer: A, B, C, D

4. Which of the following is correct in regard to the system copy strategy?

    A. SAP recommends the system copy strategy, because all Customizing and development objects are transferred.

    B. SAP does not recommend the system copy strategy, because there is no easy way to eliminate unwanted application data.

    C. A system copy is the easiest setup strategy recommended by SAP.

    D. A system copy eliminates the need for change requests for your entire R/3 implementation.

Answer: B

Chapter 6

1. Which of the following activities is *not* necessary for releasing and exporting a change request?

    A. Documenting every task in the change request

    B. Releasing every task in the change request

    C. Verification of the contents of the change request by the system administrator

    D. Unit testing the change request

Answer: C

2. Which of the following statements is correct in regard to the tasks used in change requests that record Customizing and development changes?

   A. Tasks belong to a change request.

   B. Tasks can be used by several R/3 users.

   C. Tasks are the direct responsibility of a project leader.

   D. Tasks record only client-specific changes.

   Answer: A

3. Which of the following indicates that a change request has been signed off after quality assurance testing?

   A. The change request is released after unit testing.

   B. The change request is successfully imported into the quality assurance system.

   C. The change request is added to the import queue of all other R/3 Systems in the system landscape.

   D. The project leader communicates their approval of the change request.

   Answer: D

4. Which of the following is *not* an SAP recommendation?

   A. Imports into the quality assurance and production systems should occur in the same sequence.

   B. Even if the import process is automatically scripted, a technical consultant or system administrator should review the results of the import.

   C. Project leaders should manually add change requests to the import queue of the quality assurance system.

   D. Change requests are imported in the same sequence that they were exported from the development system.

   Answer: C

5. Which of the following is SAP's recommendation on how to rush an emergency correction into the production system?

   A. Make the change directly in the production system.

   B. Transport the change from the development system to the quality assurance system and production system using a *preliminary import*.

   C. Make the change and use a client copy with a change request to distribute the change to production.

   D. Make the change in the quality assurance system and transport the change using a *preliminary import*.

   Answer: B

6. Which of the following transport activities is *not* typically the responsibility of the system administrator?

   A. Importing change requests into all clients within the system landscape

   B. Verifying the success of the import process

   C. Releasing change requests

   D. Assisting in solving either export or import errors

   Answer: C

7. Which of the following does SAP provide as customer support?

   A. R/3 Release upgrades to provide new functionality

   B. Support Packages to correct identified problems in a specific R/3 Release

   C. R/3 Notes to announce errors and corrections for the reported problems

   D. All of the above

   Answer: D

Chapter 7

1. The R/3 System ID (SID):

    A. Must be unique for each system sharing the same transport directory

    B. Must be unique for each system in the system landscape

    C. Can start with a number

    D. Can consist of any three-character combination

    Answer: A, B

2. Which of the following statements is correct in regard to the transport directory?

    A. There can be only one transport directory in a system landscape.

    B. All R/3 Systems within a transport group share a common transport directory.

    C. In system landscapes using heterogeneous platforms, it is not possible to have a common transport directory.

    D. Only the production system can contain the transport directory.

    Answer: B

3. The transport control program *tp*:

    A. Is stored in subdirectory *bin* of the transport directory

    B. Uses program *R3trans* to access the databases when transporting changes

    C. Cannot be used directly on the operating system level

    D. Depends on the settings of the transport profile

    Answer: B, D

4. The transport profile:

   A. Is stored in subdirectory *bin* of the transport directory

   B. Contains comments and parameter settings that configure the transport control program *tp*

   C. Is managed from within TMS as of R/3 Release 4.5, but is modified with operating system text editors in earlier releases

   D. Contains only settings that are valid for all R/3 Systems in the system landscape

   Answer: A, B, C

5. The initialization procedure of the CTO:

   A. Is especially required after a system copy

   B. Establishes the initial value for change request IDs

   C. Is not mandatory for the purpose of enabling transports

   D. Is performed automatically during R/3 installation by program *R3setup*

   Answer: A, B

6. Which of the following statements is correct in regard to the settings governing changes to Repository objects?

   A. Only the customer name range should be modifiable in production systems.

   B. Developments are possible in an R/3 System only if you have applied for a development namespace from SAP.

   C. If the global change option is set to *Not modifiable*, it is nevertheless possible to make changes in certain name spaces or clients that have their change option set to *Modifiable*.

D. The global change option should always be set to *Not modifiable* for the quality assurance system and the production system.

Answer: D

Chapter 8

1. Which of the following statements is correct in regard to the R/3 Systems belonging to a transport domain?

   A. They all share the same transport directory.

   B. They are managed centrally using TMS.

   C. They belong to the same transport group.

   D. They must run on the same operating system and database platform.

   Answer: B

2. Which of the following statements is correct in regard to the domain controller?

   A. It must be the production system.

   B. It occurs once in a transport domain.

   C. It occurs in each transport group.

   D. It can only be the R/3 System that was originally designated as the transport domain controller.

   E. It should never be the production system due to the high system load that the domain controller causes.

   Answer: B

3. Which of the following statements are correct in regard to the TMS?

    A. It needs to be initialized only on the transport domain controller.

    B. It needs to be initialized only on the transport domain controller and the backup domain controller.

    C. It must be initialized on every R/3 System.

    D. It must be set up before you can set up transport routes.

Answer: C, D

4. Which of the following statements are correct in regard to the RFC destinations for TMS connections?

    A. They are generated automatically when a transport route is created.

    B. They are generated between the domain controller and each R/3 System in the transport domain.

    C. They must be established manually before you can use the TMS.

    D. They are generated during the TMS initialization process.

    E. They are only needed for importing change requests.

Answer: B, D

5. How is the actual system landscape, including R/3 System roles and relationships, defined using the TMS?

    A. By including all R/3 Systems in the transport domain

    B. By configuring transport routes

    C. By assigning a role to each R/3 System during the TMS initialization process

    D. By designating real, virtual, and external R/3 Systems

Answer: B

6. Which of the following statements is correct in regard to a consolidation route?

    A. It is defined by an integration system and a consolidation system, and is associated with a transport layer.

    B. It is created in the TMS by defining only an integration system and a consolidation system.

    C. It is not necessarily required in a two-system landscape.

    D. It can be defined only once in a transport group.

    Answer: A

7. Which of the following statements are correct in regard to client-specific transport routes?

    A. They are possible as of R/3 Release 4.0.

    B. They are possible only as of R/3 Release 4.5, and only if extended transport control is activated.

    C. They are only allowed for target groups.

    D. They may not be used in conjunction with client-independent transport routes.

    Answer: B, D

Chapter 9

1. After you create a new client entry in table T000, which of the following activities enables you to provide the client with data?

    A. A remote client copy to populate the client with data from a client in another R/3 System

    B. A client transport to import data from a client in another R/3 System

C. A local client copy to import data from a client within the same R/3 System

D. All of the above

Answer: D

2. Which of the following *cannot* be used to restrict a client from certain activities?

A. The client role

B. The client-dependent change option

C. The client ID-number

D. A client restriction

E. The client-independent change option

Answer: C

3. Which of the following tasks can be performed using the client copy tools?

A. Merging application data from one client into another client

B. Copying only application data from one client to another client

C. Copying only Customizing data from one client to another client

D. All of the above

Answer: C

4. Which of the following tasks can be performed using the client copy profiles?

A. Scheduling a client copy to occur at a time when system use is low

B. Selecting the subset of application data that will be copied when a client copy is executed

    C. Providing required user authorization for the use of client tools

    D. Determining the data that will be copied when a client copy is executed

Answer: D

5. Which of the following statements is correct in regard to table logging?

    A. Table logging should be used instead of change requests whenever possible.

    B. Table logging provides an audit history of who made what changes and when.

    C. Table logging does not negatively impact system resources.

    D. All of the above.

Answer: B

Chapter 10

1. Which of the following statements is *false* in regard to development classes?

    A. Development classes facilitate project management by grouping similar Repository objects.

    B. All Repository objects are assigned to a development class.

    C. A development class determines the transport route that a changed Repository object will follow.

    D. A local object does not need a development class.

Answer: D

2. Which of the following kinds of changes are transported using Workbench change requests?

    A. Client-independent changes

    B. Modifications to SAP-delivered objects

    C. Changes made using the ABAP Editor and ABAP Dictionary

    D. Repairs to R/3 Repository objects that originated in another R/3 System

    E. All of the above

Answer: E

3. Which of the following data is *not* contained in the object list of a task?

    A. The actual change made to the objects listed in the task

    B. The list of changed objects recorded to the task

    C. Whether the objects recorded to the task are locked

    D. The complete Object Directory entry for the object

Answer: A, D

4. Which of the following statements are correct regarding repairs and modifications?

    A. Repairs are changes to SAP-delivered objects; modifications are changes to any object that originated on an R/3 System other than the current R/3 System.

    B. A repair flag protects an R/3 Repository object against being overwritten by an import.

    C. All repairs are saved to Workbench change requests.

    D. A modification is a change to an SAP-delivered object.

    E. All of the above.

Answer: B, C, D

Chapter 11

1. Which of the following requirements must be met before you can change both client-dependent and client-independent Customizing settings in a client?

    A. The client settings must allow for changes to client-independent Customizing objects.

    B. The client role must be *Production.*

    C. The system change option must be set to *Modifiable.*

    D. The client settings must allow for changes to client-dependent Customizing.

    Answer: A, C, D

2. Which of the following statements are correct when project leaders and project team members receive only the recommended authorizations?

    A. Only developers can create change requests.

    B. Only project leaders can create change requests, and are therefore responsible for assigning project team members to change requests.

    C. Project team members can create and release change requests.

    D. Project leaders can release change requests.

    Answer: B, D

3. Which of the following statements are correct with regard to Project IMGs?

    A. The Project IMG provides access to the Customizing activities defined for a particular project.

    B. Customizing is performed in the Project IMG tree structure.

C. The Project IMG enables you to display project status information and document Customizing activities.

D. All of the above.

Answer: D

4. Which of the following activities are performed using the Customizing Organizer?

A. Viewing all Customizing change requests related to a particular user

B. Viewing all Workbench change requests related to a particular user

C. Viewing all change requests related to a particular user

D. Managing change requests you own or reviewing change requests in which you have assigned tasks

Answer: A, B, C, D

5. Which of the following statements is correct in regard to Customizing?

A. All Customizing activities in the IMG are client-dependent.

B. All changes resulting from IMG activities can be transported.

C. All Customizing changes are automatically recorded to a change request if the client change option is set to *Automatic recording of changes.*

D. A Customizing activity may involve the creation of client-independent objects and therefore requires a Workbench change request.

Answer: D

6. Which of the following activities are performed using client comparison tools?

   A. Comparing the Customizing settings of two R/3 clients in the same R/3 System or in a different R/3 System

   B. Adjusting the Customizing differences between two different R/3 clients

   C. Transporting Customizing settings into the production client

   D. Comparing the objects listed in the object list of a change request with an R/3 client

   Answer: A, B, D

Chapter 12

1. Which of the following is a prerequisite for copying client-dependent changes to a unit test client using a *client copy according to a transp. request* (Transaction SCC1)?

   A. The change request has been released.

   B. The tasks have been released, but the change request has not.

   C. The tasks have been released after successful unit testing by the owner of the task.

   D. The change request has not been released.

   Answer: D

2. Which of the following are the result of releasing a task?

   A. A data file is created in the transport directory and contains the objects recorded in the change request.

   B. The object list and documentation for the task are copied to the change request.

C. All objects recorded in the task are locked.

D. You can no longer save changes to that task.

Answer: B, D

3. Which of the following are the result of releasing and exporting a change request?

A. A data file is created in the transport directory to contain copies of the objects recorded in the change request.

B. Versions are created in the version database for all R/3 Repository objects in the object list of the change request.

C. All repairs recorded in the change request are confirmed.

D. You can no longer save changes to that change request.

Answer: A, B, D

4. When you release a Customizing change request, you have the option to do which of the following?

A. Release the change request to another Customizing change request.

B. Schedule the release of the change request for a later time.

C. Release the change request to a transportable change request.

D. Initiate immediate release and export.

Answer: C, D

5. Which of the following is a prerequisite for releasing a transportable change request?

A. There are no syntax errors in the ABAP programs recorded to the change request.

B. You must own the tasks in the change request.

    C. All Repository objects in the change request are locked by the change request.

    D. The change request has documentation.

Answer: C

6. The export process initiates which of the following activities?

    A. The creation of files in the transport directory

    B. The automatic import of change requests into the target system—for example, the quality assurance system

    C. The addition of the exported change request to the import buffer of the target system

    D. The deletion of the change request within the R/3 System

Answer: A, C

7. Which of the following activities result in a version history for all Repository objects?

    A. A Repository object is recorded to a change request.

    B. Change requests are imported into an R/3 System, and the transport parameter *vers_at_imp* is activated.

    C. A task containing a Repository object is released.

    D. A change request containing a Repository object is released.

Answer: B, D

Chapter 13

1. Which of the following statements are correct in regard to import queues?

   A. Import queues are the TMS representation of the import buffer on the operating system level.

   B. You have to manipulate import queues to transport change requests.

   C. Import queues should be closed before starting an import using TMS.

   D. You can import only an entire import queue.

   Answer: A, C

2. Which of the following statements are correct in regard to preliminary imports?

   A. SAP recommends using preliminary imports rather than imports of entire queues.

   B. Preliminary imports should be performed only in exceptional cases.

   C. Change requests imported as preliminary imports remain in the import queue.

   D. Change requests are deleted from the import queue after preliminary imports. This prevents them from being imported again with the next import of the entire import queue.

   Answer: B, C

3. Which of the following statements is correct in regard to imports into an R/3 System?

   A. Imports can be performed only by using the *start import* functionality in the TMS.

B. Imports can be performed only by using *tp* commands on the operating system level to prepare the import queue and then using the *start import* functionality in the TMS.

C. Imports can be performed only by using *tp* commands at the operating system level.

D. Imports can be performed by using either a *tp* command on the operating system level or the TMS import functionality.

Answer: D

4. Which of the following statements is correct in regard to transports between different transport groups?

    A. They are not possible.

    B. They can be performed only by using *tp* on the operating system level with special options.

    C. They can be performed using the TMS with special options provided by the expert mode.

    D. They require you to adjust the corresponding import queues.

Answer: D

5. Which of the following statements are correct in regard to transports between different transport domains?

    A. They are not possible.

    B. They require you to create a virtual system and a virtual transport directory.

    C. They require you to configure identical transport groups within the different transport domains.

    D. They require you to create external systems and an external transport directory.

    E. They require you to adjust the corresponding import
    queues.

Answer: D, E

Chapter 14

1. Which of the following statements are correct in regard to the
   transport control program *tp*?

   A. To perform imports, *tp* must always be used directly on
   the operating system level.

   B. SAP recommends that you use the TMS instead of *tp* to
   perform imports.

   C. *tp* is responsible for exporting and importing objects
   from and to R/3 Systems.

   D. *tp* does not observe the sequence of change requests in
   the import queue when performing imports.

   Answer: B, C

2. Which of the following statements are correct in regard to
   import queues and import buffers?

   A. Import queues are TMS representations in R/3 of the
   import buffer files on the operating system level.

   B. Import queues and import buffers are completely independent of each other.

   C. Import buffers have to be manipulated before imports
   can be performed on the operating system level.

   D. Manipulating import buffers may cause serious inconsistencies and should be performed only in exceptional
   cases.

   Answer: A, D

3. Which of the following statements are correct in regard to the import options formerly known as *unconditional modes*?

   A. Import options cannot be used when imports are performed on the operating system level using *tp*.

   B. Import options are used to cause specific rules of the Change and Transport System (CTS) to be ignored.

   C. Import options must be used when importing into multiple clients using *tp*.

   D. Import options can be selected in the TMS using the expert mode.

   Answer: B, C, D

4. Which of the following statements are correct in regard to the sequence of processing steps *tp* follows when performing imports?

   A. *tp* collectively processes each import step for all change requests in an import queue before proceeding with the next import step.

   B. *tp* processes all import steps for a single request before proceeding to the next change request.

   C. The processing sequence followed by *tp* ensures that when a change request with a faulty object is followed in the import queue by a change request with the corrected object, the faulty object will not affect the runtime environment of the target system.

   D. *tp* imports and activates ABAP Dictionary structures prior to the main import phase to ensure that the current structures are able to receive new data during the main import phase.

   Answer: A, C, D

5. Which of the following statements are correct in regard to troubleshooting imports?

   A. In R/3, you cannot display log files that do not depend on a specific request. For example, you cannot display log files related to generic import steps, such as structure conversion.

   B. SAP recommends that you check the SLOG file and the ALOG file before checking the single step log files.

   C. By default, all return codes greater than eight cause *tp* to abort a running import.

   D. *tp* is the only transport tool that uses return codes.

   Answer: A, B, C

6. Which of the following statements are correct in regard to buffer synchronization?

   A. Transport activities do not affect buffer synchronization.

   B. Imports affect buffer synchronization even in central R/3 Systems.

   C. *R3trans* can invalidate buffer content.

   D. Importing data into a production system can significantly impact performance, because some buffer content may be invalidated and reloaded. This causes high system load.

   E. Importing programs and ABAP Dictionary data cannot cause inconsistencies in the target system, even if the programs or data affect running programs and their environment.

   Answer: B, C, D

7. Which of the following statements are correct in regard to the interaction between transport tools?

   A. During exports, *tp* calls *R3trans* to access the database of the source system and extract the objects to be transported.

   B. *tp* triggers the transport daemon RDDIMPDP in R/3 using the operating system tool *sapevt*.

   C. Using the tables TRBAT and TRJOB, *tp* communicates with ABAP programs involved in the transport process.

   D. *tp* communicates with only RDDIMPD.

   Answer: A, B, C

Chapter 15

1. Which of the following statements are correct in regard to the R/3 Release strategy?

   A. Functional Releases are automatically shipped to all customers.

   B. Correction Releases provide only corrections and no new functionality with respect to the previous R/3 Functional Release.

   C. Functional Releases receive only limited OCS maintenance; that is, only very urgent corrections are available as Support Packages.

   D. R/3 Release upgrades are possible only for Correction Releases.

   Answer: B, C

2. Which of the following statements are correct in regard to Support Packages?

   A. Support Packages change the SAP standard of your R/3 System in advance of the next R/3 Release upgrade.

   B. You can apply all types of Support Packages to all R/3 installations, regardless of the components used in the installation.

   C. Support Packages are available only to customers who are participants in the First Customer Shipment (FCS) program.

   D. Different types of Support Packages may be required for R/3 installations with different components.

   Answer: A, D

3. Which of the following statements are correct in regard to the SAP Patch Manager?

   A. The SAP Patch Manager ensures that Support Packages are applied in the correct sequence.

   B. The SAP Patch Manager does not check whether the type of Support Package you wish to apply is appropriate for your R/3 installation. It is up to you to decide whether, for example, you require a Conflict Resolution Transport.

   C. The SAP Patch Manager does not offer you the chance to protect SAP objects that you have modified. These objects are automatically overwritten.

   D. The SAP Patch Manager automatically prompts you to call the modification adjustment Transactions SPDD or SPAU if necessary.

   Answer: A, D

4. Which of the following statements are correct in regard to R/3 Release upgrades?

   A. Objects in the customer namespace are not overwritten.

   B. A Repository switch is the replacement of your current R/3 Repository by the R/3 Repository in the new R/3 Release.

   C. All customer modifications to ABAP Dictionary objects are lost.

   D. Customer modifications to SAP objects that you want to preserve must be transferred to the new Release through the modification adjustment process.

   Answer: A, B, D

5. Which of the following statements are correct in regard to the modification adjustment process?

   A. Transaction SPAU is used for most ABAP Dictionary objects.

   B. Transaction SPDD is used for most ABAP Dictionary objects.

   C. Not using Transaction SPDD where applicable may cause data loss.

   D. During modification adjustment, you must choose to return to the SAP standard.

   Answer: B, C

APPENDIX
F

Literature

This section provides information on the R/3 online help, R/3 training courses, and Internet links, and a bibliography related to R/3 change and transport management.

R/3 Online Help

To access R/3 online documentation, from the R/3 initial screen, choose *Help* ➤ *R/3 Library*. Then, choose any of the following paths:

- For help on all tools that make up the Change and Transport System (CTS), choose *BC-Basis Components* ➤ *Change and Transport Management* ➤ *Change and Transport System*.

  - For the making and recording of changes to change requests, then choose *Change and Transport Organizers*.

  - For the setup, configuration, and use of TMS, then choose *Transport Management System*.

  - For copying of R/3 clients, then choose *Client Copy and Transport*.

  - For more information on development classes and naming Repository objects, then choose *Namespaces and Naming Conventions*.

  - For details on the transport control program, then choose *Transport Tools*.

- For help on Customizing, choose *BC-Basis Components* ➤ *Business Engineer* ➤ *Configuration Tools*.

R/3 Training Courses

SAP currently offers the following R/3 training courses for change and transport management issues:

- BC325 *Software Logistics*
- CA960 *Customizing and Transport Management*
- MBC030 *R/3 Technical Implementation and Operation Management*

SAP on the Internet

SAPNet is separate from SAP's public Internet site (`http//:www.sap.com`). With appropriate authorization, customers, partners, SAP employees, and others can access SAPNet at `http://sapnet.sap.com`. To access the home page of the Technical Core Competence (TCC) group, use the URL `http://sapnet.sap.com/tcc`.

SAP TechNet

SAP TechNet is a part of SAPNet and contains up-to-date articles explaining technical components of the product, including the area of Software Logistics—the management of changes and transport in an R/3 system landscape.

To enter SAP TechNet, choose from the SAPNet table of contents, *Services* ➤ *Education Services* ➤ *TechNet*. Alternatively, in the Web browser address field, enter the address `http://sapnet.cap.com./technet`.

Select Bibliography

This bibliography lists articles, books, and manuals that are relevant to the topics covered in this book or that explore related issues in greater detail.

Brand, Hartwig. *SAP R/3 Implementation with ASAP: The Official Guide*. San Francisco: Sybex, 1998.

Buck-Emden, Rüdiger, and Galimov, Jürgen. *SAP Systems R/3: A Client/Server Technology*. Bonn: Addison-Wesley, 1997.

Data Transfer Made Easy 4.0B/4.5x. Palo Alto, CA: R/3 Simplification Group, SAP Labs, 1999.

McFarland, Sue. "An Insider's Guide to the SAP Change and Transport System (CTS)" in *SAP Professional Journal*. Issue 1, 1999.

Melich, Matthias. "Enhancements in Customizing: Business Configuration Sets, the Customizing Cross-System Viewer, and the Activity Log" in *SAP Professional Journal*. Issue 2, 1999.

R/3 Installation Guide. Walldorf: SAP AG, 1998.

R/3 System Manuals. Walldorf: SAP AG, 1998.

SAPscript Made Easy 4.0B. Palo Alto, CA: R/3 Simplification Group, SAP Labs, 1999.

Schneider, Thomas. *SAP R/3 Performance Optimization: The Official Guide*. San Francisco: Sybex, 1999.

Schwerin-Wenzel, Sven. *Authorizations Made Easy*. Walldorf: SAP AG, 1998.

System Administration Made Easy Guidebook, Release 4.0B. Palo Alto, CA: R/3 Simplification Group, SAP Labs, 1999.

Will, Liane. *SAP R/3 System Administration: The Official Guide.* San Francisco: Sybex, 1998.

INDEX

Note to the Reader: Throughout this index **boldface** page numbers indicate primary discussions of a topic. *Italic* page numbers indicate illustrations.

A

ABAP programs, **636–644**, **752**
  ABAP Dictionary
    ABAP Dictionary activation import step, 621–622
    ABAP Dictionary Maintenance, **9**, **32**
    ABAP Dictionary objects, 35
    defined, **752**
    Log Data Changes option and, 374
    modification adjustments for ABAP Dictionary objects, 695–696, 698–701, *700*
    RFC system checks and, 350
    tp program import steps and, 608–609
  ABAP Editor
    defined, **752**
    Modification Assistant, 39–40, 420, 422–424, *423*, 774
  ABAP Workbench. *See also* Workbench change requests; Workbench Organizer
    Customizing-and-development clients and, 48
    defined, **9**, **752**
    development activities and, 22, 32–33
    Modification Browser, 424–425, 774
    Test Workbench, 206–207
  log files, 612–614, *614*
  and tp program, **608–609**, **636–643**
    ABAP Dictionary activation import step, 621–622
    RDDIMPDP import dispatcher and, 637–638, *638*, 640–643, *641*, *642*, 779
    tp and ABAP program communication in import process, 639–643, *639*, *641*, *642*
    tp import steps and ABAP Dictionary, 608–609
    TRBAT table and, 636–637, *638*, *638*, 639–644, *639*, *641*, *642*
    TRJOB table and, 636, *638*, 640–643, *641*, *642*
abapntfmode transport profile parameter, 722
accepting R/3 Systems into transport domain controllers, 284–285, *285*
action logs for change requests, 500–501, 574
activating
  backup domain controllers, 292

Current Settings function in production clients, 472–473, 761
extended transport control, 315
object checks, 516–519, *517*, *519*
table logging, 373–375
transport route configurations, 304
activity logging, 377–379, *378*
actlog subdirectory, 229, 628
adding
  change requests to import queues, 109–110, 562
  objects to object lists, 418–419
  objects to object lists manually, 415–416
  R/3 Systems to transport domains, **281–285**, **288–289**
    accepting R/3 Systems into transport domain controllers, 284–285, *285*
    from a different transport group, 281, 283
    external R/3 Systems to transport domains, 288–289, *289*
    from same transport group, 281–282, *282*
  transport routes, 307, *308*, 309–310
  users to Customizing change requests, 451–452
  users to Workbench change requests, 409
Add-On Patches, 656–657, 660, 753
adjustments. *See* modification adjustments
Advanced Business Application Programming. *See* ABAP
ALE (Application Link Enabling)
  configuring multiple production systems, 120–121
  defined, **753–754**
  logical system names and, 337
  and transferring master data, 116–117, *117*
Alert Monitor, 325, 754
alllog transport profile parameter, 722–723
ALOG file, 612
alternative system landscapes, **68–72**, **83–84**. *See also* system landscapes
  alternative phased system landscapes, 83–84, *84*
  defined, **68–69**
  four-system landscapes, 72, *72*
  one-system landscapes, 69–70
  two-system landscapes, 70–72, *71*
analyzing Customizing differences between clients, 482

B

D

F

G

H

I

O

P

Q

R

S

U

W